Burma
a country study

Foreign Area Studies
The American University
Edited by
Frederica M. Bunge
Research completed
March 1983

On the cover: The massive gold- and jewel-crowned stupa of the
great Shwedagon Pagoda in Rangoon

Third Edition, 1983; First Printing 1983

Library of Congress Cataloging in Publication Data
Main entry under title:

Burma, a country study.

(Area handbook series) (DA pam ; 550-61)
Rev. ed. of: Area handbook for Burma. 1971.
"Research completed March 1983."
Bibliography: p.
Includes index.
1. Burma. I. Bunge, Frederica M. II. American
University (Washington, D.C.). Foreign Area Studies.
III. Area handbook for Burma. IV. Series. V. Series:
DA pam ; 550-61.
DS527.4.B88 1983   959.1'05   83-25871

Headquarters, Department of the Army
DA Pam 550-61

For sale by the Superintendent of Documents, U.S. Government Printing Office
Washington, D.C. 20402

Foreword

This volume is one of a continuing series of books prepared by Foreign Area Studies, The American University, under the Country Studies/Area Handbook Program. The last page of this book provides a listing of other published studies. Each book in the series deals with a particular foreign country, describing and analyzing its economic, national security, political, and social systems and institutions and examining the interrelationships of those systems and institutions and the ways that they are shaped by cultural factors. Each study is written by a multidisciplinary team of social scientists. The authors seek to provide a basic insight and understanding of the society under observation, striving for a dynamic rather than a static portrayal of it. The study focuses on historical antecedents and on the cultural, political, and socioeconomic characteristics that contribute to cohesion and cleavage within the society. Particular attention is given to the origins and traditions of the people who make up the society, their dominant beliefs and values, their community of interests and the issues on which they are divided, the nature and extent of their involvement with the national institutions, and their attitudes toward each other and toward the social system and political order within which they live.

The contents of the book represent the views, opinions, and findings of Foreign Area Studies and should not be construed as an official Department of the Army position, policy, or decision, unless so designated by other official documentation. The authors have sought to adhere to accepted standards of scholarly objectivity. Such corrections, additions, and suggestions for factual or other changes that readers may have will be welcomed for use in future new editions.

William Evans-Smith
Director, Foreign Area Studies
The American University
Washington, D.C. 20016

iii

Acknowledgments

The authors are grateful to a number of Burma specialists in the academic world, in the international community, and in various agencies of the United States government who gave of their special knowledge to provide data and perspective for this study. In particular they are grateful to David I. Steinberg, who shared generously not only valuable personal insights but also the resources of his specialized library. The contributions of Jon A. Wiant and Charles B. Smith, Jr., to this book are also gratefully acknowledged.

The authors also thank members of the Foreign Area Studies staff who contributed directly to the preparation of the manuscript. These include Dorothy M. Lohmann, Kathryn R. Stafford, and Andrea T. Merrill, who edited the manuscript and the accompanying figures and tables; Harriett R. Blood and Farah Ahannavard, who prepared the graphics; and Gilda V. Nimer, librarian. The team appreciates as well the assistance provided by Ernest A. Will, publications manager, and Eloise W. Brandt, administrative assistant. Margaret Quinn typed the manuscript and gave valuable help in various phases of production. Special thanks are owed to Gustavo Arce, who designed the illustrations for the cover of this volume and for the title pages of the chapters, and to those persons who provided photographs, some never previously published.

Contents

Donald M. Seekins

EARLY BURMESE KINGDOMS—The Pagan Dynasty, 1044–1287—The Toungoo Dynasty, 1486–1752—THE KONBAUNG DYNASTY AND THE ANGLO-BURMESE WARS—The Reigns of Alaungpaya and His Sons—State and Society under the Konbaung Kings—Expansion and Confrontation, 1784–1826—Dynastic Decline and the Second Anglo-Burmese War, 1826–53—Diplomacy and Reform under King Mindon, 1853–78—Commercial and Diplomatic Relations—Thibaw and the Fall of the Burmese Kingdom, 1878–86—COLONIAL BURMA, 1886–1942—Colonial Economy and Society—The Emergence of Political Movements—WAR AND THE STRUGGLE FOR INDEPENDENCE—The Japanese Occupation—Steps Toward Independence—The Nationalities Issue—Aung San's Assassination—PARLIAMENTARY GOVERNMENT, 1948–62—AFPFL Politics and Issues—1956 General Elections—Caretaker Government, 1958–60—U Nu Returns to Power—MILITARY RULE UNDER GENERAL NE WIN—Student and Sangha Reactions—A Nationalized Economy—The Nationalities Issue and Insurgency—Neutralism and Seclusion—The Socialist Republic of the Union of Burma

John P. Ferguson

PHYSICAL ENVIRONMENT—ELUSIVE SOCIAL UNITY: THE POPULATION MIXTURE—The Seven Divisions—The Seven States—Chinese, Indians, and Other Minorities—Overseas Burmese—THE BURMAN WORLD VIEW—The Buddhism of Burma—Social Status—Anade—The Sense of Uniqueness—The Social Transformation—THE NON-BURMAN WORLD VIEW—COMMUNISM IN BURMA—THE FUTURE OF BURMESE SOCIETY

List of Figures

Preface

This study replaces the *Area Handbook for Burma*, originally published in 1968 and updated in 1971, and reprinted in 1982 as *Burma: A Country Study*. Sufficient reason in itself for the preparation of a new edition is the passage of more than 15 years since completion of the research for the 1968 volume. Beyond this, however, there has been a significant liberalization of the constraints previously imposed on foreign journalists, research scholars, and others working in the country. This has made source materials more readily available, although given the long period in which little research was done on Burma, and some continuing constraints, significant gaps in the data still remain, especially relating to developments since the military takeover in 1962.

The purpose of this study is to provide in a compact, convenient, balanced, and objective form an integrated exposition and analysis of the dominant social, political, and economic aspects of Burmese society. The authors have tried to give readers an understanding of the interrelationships of institutional structures as well as some insight into the attitudes and problems of the country and of its role in the world around it.

Spelling of most place-names has followed official United States government maps and *Burma Official Standard Names Gazetteer, No. 96* of the United States Board on Geographic Names, published in March 1966.

Burmese practice in the use of personal names has been followed in the Bibliography and Index of this volume. Those who are unfamiliar with Burmese practice should note that there are no Burmese surnames, family names, or married names. Burmese have names of one, two, or three syllables, and these do not necessarily bear any relation to the name of the father, husband, sibling, or any other relative. The names are preceded by titles that indicate sex and that also take account of age and social position relative to the speaker. The most common adult title used to address or refer to men of superior age or social status is "U." More modest titles are "Ko" (elder brother) and "Maung" (younger brother). The female equivalent to "U" is "Daw," and that to "Maung" is "Ma." "Thakin," once a title of respect used for Europeans, was adopted by Burmese nationalist leaders in the pre-World War II period.

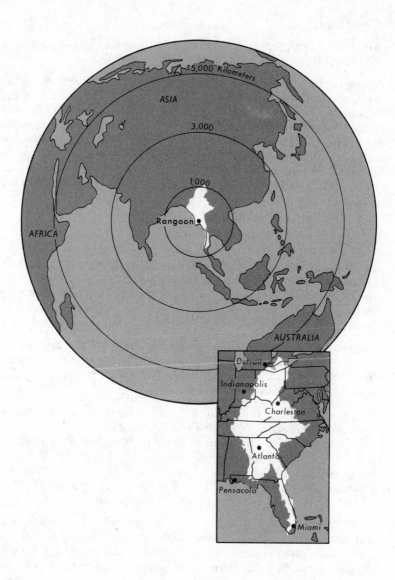

Country

Formal Name: Socialist Republic of the Union of Burma.

Term for Citizens: Burmese.

Capital: Rangoon.

Geography

Size: 678,000 square kilometers; shares boundaries with Bangladesh, India, China, Laos, and Thailand.

Topography and Drainage: Tropical environment composed basically of rich alluvial valleys and drier surrounding hills and high mountains, which separate country into strips of north-south ridges. Monsoon rainfall heaviest in lower part of country where wet-rice agriculture common. In upper part and in mountains, dry rice and other appropriate crops reflect lighter rainfall. Water also supplied by Irrawaddy, Sittang, and Salween rivers, flowing south from high heartlands of Asia to rich delta areas. Borders mainly mountainous, access difficult. Population concentrated near rivers or in coastline communities.

Society

Population: Unofficially estimated at 36 million in 1983. Average annual growth rate 1976–82 estimated at 2.4 percent. Ethnic Burmans about two-thirds of population. Significant minorities include Shans, Karens, Kachins, Chins, and Kayahs. Chinese and Indians also numerous.

Languages: Burmese official language, spoken by nearly all segments of population. Non-Burmans usually speak own tongue as first language. English used frequently by older persons and those with higher education.

Religion: Theravada Buddhism preeminent faith. Nine officially recognized orders within the First Congregation of the Sangha of All Orders for the Purification, Perpetuation, and Propagation of the Sasana, with some 113,000 monks. Hinduism and Islam also have substantial numbers of adherents, latter particularly in Rakhine State. Many Chins, Kachins, Karens, and others Christian. Animist beliefs persist in some areas.

Health: Health care delivery systems improving but still limited. Estimated 0.2 physicians per 1,000 and 0.7 hospital beds per 1,000 inhabitants; sanitation poor and pharmaceuticals in short supply. Less that 20 percent of population has access to safe water.

Education: Education free in three-tiered government system through university level. Traditional Buddhist monastic school now largely overshadowed by secular system. Competitive examinations determine entrance to postsecondary facilities. Emphasis placed on technical and scientific knowledge, regional two-year colleges, and correspondence courses, but prestigious degree from universities at Rangoon and Mandalay still widely sought by country's 65,000 college students.

Economy

Gross Domestic Product (GDP): Equivalent of US$5.9 billion in fiscal year (FY—see Glossary) 1981, or US$180 per capita. Real GDP grew by over 6 percent per year during FY 1978–81 period—over twice average for 1960s and early 1970s. Improved performance caused by increased foreign aid and credit, leading to heightened investment equivalent to some 20 percent of GDP in FY 1978–81 period.

Resources: Tin, antimony, lead, zinc, silver, and other metals; jade and other precious stones; and petroleum and natural gas. Exploration of mineral resources far from complete. Fossil fuels mostly for domestic consumption. Excellent land resources, including some 10 million hectares of cultivated and fallow agricultural land, almost 9 million hectares of potentially cultivable land, and nearly 10 million hectares of reserved teak and hardwood forests. Potentially large offshore fisheries.

Agriculture, Fishing, and Forestry: Produced over 47 percent of GDP in FY 1981 and employed 9.2 million of 13.8 million people in labor force. Almost all farm production on private farms. Public and cooperative enterprises important in fishing and forestry. Principal products include rice—by far most important crop—sesame, pulses, and beans, groundnuts, cotton, maize, sugarcane, wheat, sunflower, rubber, tobacco, jute, teakwood, and prawns.

Industry and Services: Mining and manufacturing produced about 11 percent of GDP in FY 1981 and employed 1.2 million people. Processed agricultural commodities, textiles, light manufactures, petroleum, and natural gas most important. Transportation, power, communications, and construction activities produced 8 percent of GDP and engaged 700,000 people. Remainder of production and employment in services sector. About 62 percent of mining and manufacturing, 68 percent of infrastructure services, and 32 percent of remaining services produced by public enterprises.

Exports: Merchandise exports US$514 in FY 1981. Major categories based on FY 1980 ranking: rice and rice products (42 percent), teak and hardwood (25 percent), base metals (15 percent), pulses and beans (5 percent), jute (3 percent), rubber (3 percent), fish and prawns (3 percent), and other agricultural products (remainder).

Imports: Merchandise imports US$858 million in FY 1981. Major categories based on FY 1980 ranking: capital goods (46 percent), raw materials (28 percent), tools and spare parts (16 percent), and consumer goods (remainder).

Balance of Payments: Current account deficit US$328 million in FY 1981, about 5.6 percent of GDP. Repayments of interest and principal on foreign debt equivalent to over 28 percent of all export earnings.

Exchange Rate: K7.81 per US$1 (November 1982; for value of the kyat—see Glossary). Pegged to value of special drawing right, an international reserve currency.

Transportation: Some 4,385 kilometers of chiefly meter-gauge railroads, about 22,732 kilometers of roads, and over 2,000 kilometers of navigable rivers facilitate travel primarily in north-south direction through center of country. Railroad rolling stock often in poor repair, two-thirds of roads unpaved, motor vehicles and watercraft antiquated. Main ports: Rangoon and Bassein. Main airports for small turboprop and propeller fleet: Rangoon, Mandalay, Sittwe (Akyab), and Meiktila. International airport: Rangoon.

Communications: Poor telecommunications system but developing rapidly in early 1980s. In FY 1981 some 14 telephones per 10,000 people, mostly in urban centers. Overseas satellite linkage. Some 43 radio receivers per 1,000 inhabitants in 1982, but only 400 television receivers in entire country. Radio transmission from one government-owned station only to populous areas. Government-owned color television station transmits in evenings and on weekends.

Government and Politics

Government: Based on 1974 Constitution. Under President U San Yu since November 1981, government divided into legislative, executive, and judicial functions. People's Assembly is top organ, but power actually exercised by State Council, top decisionmaking body. Governmental mandate renewed every four years through parliamentary and local elections.

Politics: One-party political system under Burma Socialist Programme Party (BSPP—see Glossary). Party Chairman U Ne Win most powerful national leader, until 1981 also president and head of state. Party provides leadership at all levels of government; leaders hold overlapping positions in State Council, BSPP Central Executive Committee, and key units of armed forces. Ruling elite narrowly based in military. No organized opposition to BSPP owing to restrictive laws, tight government control of all mass media, and influence of security and party operatives in all sectors of society. Main threat to political stability posed by widespread insurgency and ethnic separatism.

Administrative Divisions: Seven states and seven divisions at top of three-tier structure; townships in middle; at bottom, wards for urban areas and village-tracts for rural areas. Government authority tenuous in outlying border regions controlled by insurgents.

Judicial System: Courts under Council of People's Justices, highest judicial authority. Under sweeping reform since 1972, justice administered under principle of popular participation, and judges from top to bottom of court hierarchy are elected laymen. In rendering decisions on criminal and civil cases, judges rely on professional trained lawyers and law officers attached to court.

International Affairs: Withdrew from Nonaligned Movement in 1979, asserting that movement had lost sight of its original purposes. Burma still nonaligned and neutral, however. Maintains cordial relations with neighbors and major powers. Receives foreign assistance from international lending institutions; Japan, China, and Czechoslovakia; Federal Republic of Germany (West Germany), United States, and other major Western nations; and other nations.

National Security

Armed Forces: In 1983 People's Armed Forces totaled about 179,000. Components: army (163,000), navy (7,000), and air force (9,000). Conscription provided for under law, but in practice services maintained by voluntary enlistment.

Major Tactical Military Units: Army had six light infantry divisions, two armored battalions, 85 independent infantry battalions, four artillery battalions, one antitank and artillery battalion, and one antiaircraft battery. Air force had two attack squadrons, two training squadrons, and various transport aircraft. Navy functioned as fisheries protection and coastal and riverine patrol fleet.

Major Military Equipment: Domestic defense production largely limited to uniforms, small arms, and ammunition. Imported military equipment from variety of sources. Bulk of equipment aging, short of spare parts, or in need of repair.

Defense Expenditures: Over K1.4 billion in FY 1981, representing 19.5 percent of total government expenditures, down from 1950s and 1960s levels of over 30 percent.

Police and Paramilitary Forces: People's Police Force organized under Ministry of Home and Religious Affairs totaled some 58,000. People's Militia units under control of Ministry of Defense numbered some 35,000. Both forces assisted armed forces in suppressing persistent armed insurgency by communist and ethnically based groups.

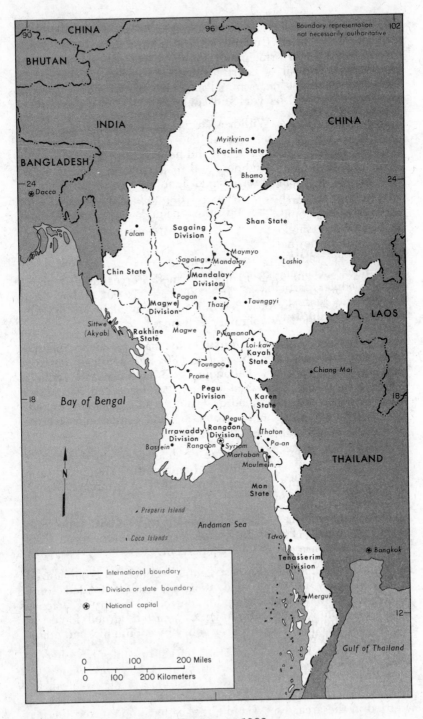

Figure 1. Administrative Divisions, 1983

Introduction

UNION DAY CELEBRATIONS in Rangoon in early 1983 drew delegates from Burma's more than 60 disparate "national groups" to the nation's capital to participate in government-led ceremonies. Posters marking the occasion emphasized the spirit of unity among the varied groups, despite their evident cultural distinctiveness. To many observers, however, there could be no more vivid reminder that national solidarity in Burma was neither easily come by nor easily retained. Since independence in 1948, the country had been plagued by persistent dissension and rebellion arising, in part, from the separatist aspirations of a number of the minority peoples represented at the gathering.

In Burma's single-party state, government and party rhetoric proclaimed the harmonious unity and equality of disparate peoples, yet the preeminence of the Burman ethnic majority in economic, social, and political affairs was clear. To the degree that other peoples participated in the mainstream of national life, it was in the context of Burman dominance. Burmans constituted perhaps two-thirds of the country's estimated 36 million people in 1983.

Circumstances of history have contributed to the difficulty of party and government efforts to unify the nation. Over the past millennium, three dynasties dominated by ethnic Burmans succeeded for relatively brief periods in imposing their political authority over the area within the boundaries of the modern political state, and at times these dynasties expanded to the east and west considerably beyond those perimeters. Not until the Union of Burma was formed in 1948, however, had all the diverse peoples within its ill-defined borders formally been brought together in a single, if somewhat tenuous, federation. Moreover, among Burma's major ethnic groups, apart from the Arakanese, only the Burmans themselves are concentrated wholly within Burma. Shans, Mons, Chins, Karens, and Kachins are also found in various numbers in neighboring countries. Some ethnic minorities in Burma are also represented all over southeast Asia.

The effect of geography in promoting diversity among people within Burma itself makes nationbuilding difficult, both socially and politically. Encompassing some 678,000 square kilometers—about the size of Texas—Burma in the simplest terms consists of two very different kinds of ecological settings. One is the more or less compact lowland area cut by the Irrawaddy and Sittang rivers, with which the Burmans and other lowland peoples have lived in symbiotic alliance as rice-growing farmers for more than 1,000 years. The other is an elongated horseshoe of high plateau and rugged mountain country inhabited by various "hill" peoples long settled in the area. For example, Shans have dominated the high plateau of eastern Burma since the thirteenth century, living in the alluvial valleys and hills of this upland region.

Contact between Burmans and other lowland peoples and between Burmans and certain of the hill peoples has resulted in varying degrees of acculturation. Especially with respect to the hill peoples, however, contact has resulted less often in acculturation than in conflict and the perpetuation and reinforcement of ethnic differences. To a remarkable degree in 1983 ethnic minorities retained their own customs, languages, and historical and political consciousness. Many groups differed from the ethnic Burmans in religion as well. Some have adopted Christianity, introduced to Burma by Western missionaries in the nineteenth century, while others adhered to indigenous beliefs and practices. Among minorities sharing adherence to the uniquely Burmese form of Theravada Buddhism (see Glossary) practiced in Burma—a form that exhibits the influence of indigenous beliefs as well as of Hindu-Brahman doctrine—are the Shans and the Mons. The Mons, whose ancient kingdoms in the central lowlands may substantially predate those of the Burmans, are believed by some to have brought Theravada Buddhism to Burma from Ceylon (present-day Sri Lanka).

Buddhism has been a pervasive force in Burmese society for millennia, although popular tradition stresses the eleventh century when it was established as the state religion by King Anawrahta of Pagan, monarch of the first and greatest of the Burman dynasties on the Irrawaddy riverine plains. Although in mid-1983 Buddhism was no longer the state religion, members of the *sangha* (monkhood) were deeply revered by laypeople as the ultimate living expression of the Buddha's teachings, and they continued to provide spiritual leadership. As the primary source of social values, Buddhism has been an enduring influence on life and thought and has strongly affected social, economic, and political institutions and arrangements. Independent Burma's civilian leaders described their new country broadly as a Buddhist welfare state; their military successors in the Burma Socialist Programme Party (BSPP) leadership have recognized Buddhism and socialism, with an admixture of Burmese nationalism, as the sources of their ideology.

Nationalist spirit runs deep in the society. Burmese are intensely proud of their history and cultural tradition. Their name for the country bespeaks that pride: Myanma (literally, fast, strong) refers to the attributes of early forebears on the central lowland plains. Burmese cherish the recalled splendors of Pagan, with its myriad pagodas, monasteries, and shrines; and although the British deposed the last monarch at Mandalay in the late nineteenth century, Burmese still regard that city as the nation's religious and spiritual fountainhead. Burmese Buddhists see themselves as spiritually blessed and, in that sense, regard themselves as incomparably wealthier than Western societies. Comfortable in the country's nonmodern, non-Western identity, they are grateful to have escaped what they perceive as the decadence of modernity evident in some Westernized Asian nations. A corollary of this intense national pride is a preference for indigenous solutions to the task of nationbuilding.

Another persistent theme of the independence period has been the intermittent insurgency by minority ethnic groups resentful of control by a Burman-dominated central government. The continuation of insurgency in many parts of the country—especially in border regions adjoining China, Laos, and Thailand—by ethnic minorities and members of the outlawed Burmese Communist Party (BCP), continued to present a serious problem to the regime in 1983. Many of these groups engaged in drug trafficking, smuggling, and other illicit activities as a means of support, as did other groups under local warlords, supplying a thriving black market.

Apart from ending insurgency and thereby nurturing national solidarity, the chief priority of the national leadership in 1983 was promoting economic development on a basis of equity for all elements in the population. Burma's natural resources are extensive. The central lowlands are a rich and fertile area, given over in great part to rice cultivation. Raising enough food for the population has never been difficult except in wartime, leaving sizable surpluses for export. Teak, precious stones, oil, and minerals are found elsewhere in the country. Yet Burma numbers among the world's low-income economies, having a per capita gross domestic product equivalent to only US$180 in fiscal year 1981.

The plentiful resources and produce of the country attracted the interest of British and French trading companies as early as the seventeenth century. British power in the subcontinent expanded during the seventeenth and through much of the eighteenth century with only limited interest in Burma. Meanwhile, however, Burmese royal forces invaded and subjugated Arakan (now Rakhine State) and made incursions into the Indian border states of Assam and Manipur. In 1824, after 25 years of border incidents, the British in India sent forces to resolve the problem militarily. The terms of the treaty settling the First Anglo-Burmese War forced the Burmese to give up claims to Assam and Manipur and to cede Arakan and Tenasserim to Britain, giving it a foothold on Burma's southern rim. Over the next 60 years, British hegemony over Burma increased by stages, culminating in the takeover of Upper Burma (see Glossary) and the deposition of the last Burman monarch at Mandalay in 1885.

Under colonial rule the Burmese experienced social dislocation and widespread agrarian distress as foreign interests developed the country's oil, timber, and mineral resources. The Irrawaddy delta region of Lower Burma (see Glossary) was opened for rice cultivation, using Burmese agriculturists to accomplish the difficult and dangerous task of taming the jungle-covered area. Pioneering farmers soon fell victim to Indian moneylenders and absentee landlords, however, while Indians and Chinese monopolized the mid-level posts in the colonial administrative machinery under senior British officials, leaving only minor posts for Burmese occupancy. The inevitable result was the development among Burmese of a deep-seated resentment against these groups. So long lasting was its impact that in 1982 the Burmese legislature enacted a law denying Indians and Chinese citizenship status on an equal level with Burmans, Shans, Kachins, Kayahs, and other "indigenous" minorities.

Resentment of colonial exploitation and maladministration contributed to the development of a nationalist movement in the early twentieth century, as Western ideas of nationalism, socialism, and communism found their way into Burma. A major nationalist organization was formed in 1919—the General Council of Burmese Associations (GCBA)—incorporating the Young Men's Buddhist Association, which had been conducting nationalist educational activities since 1906. During the 1920s the British granted a measure of self-rule, but a decade or so later, a group of intellectuals and Rangoon University students, disillusioned about Burma's circumstances and prospects, formed a revolutionary nationalist organization. This group, the Dobama Asiayone, launched a major strike at the university in 1936, in the process bringing to national prominence such men as Thakin Aung San, who was to lead Burma to independence, and U Nu, who was to become its first prime minister. Thakin Aung San was among the Thirty Comrades given military training by the Japanese, who occupied Burma during World War II. The recruits agreed to serve the Japanese in return for the promised postwar independence for Burma, but later, disillusioned with prospects for its realization, they switched to the Allied side.

Supported by the anticolonial principles of a postwar British Labour Party government, Thakin Aung San, by then a general in the Burmese army, became the architect of Burma's independence. Envisioning a union in which formerly separated peoples would be joined in a framework providing for a substantial degree of diversity, he won Shan, Chin, and Kachin agreement to join with the interim Burmese government. Karens declined to do so; Burman-Karen animosities had been inflamed by colonial policies that granted Karens a separate voting roll in the national election and had recruited Christian Karens into the Burma Army to put down Burman-led rebellions. Before the country's independence was declared, however, General Aung San was assassinated. His successors emphasized minority participation within a framework of political and administrative centralization.

Burma began independence as a parliamentary democracy under the leadership of U Nu. The 1947 constitution provided for a cross between a federal and a unitary system of government, and Shan and Kayah states were given the right to secede after 10 years. A coalition party organization, the Anti-Fascist People's Freedom League (AFPFL), had been formed in 1945, bringing together individuals and groups of various political persuasions—nationalists, socialists, and communists—who had shared in winning freedom for the country. Despite the all-embracing philosophy of the AFPFL, however, various groups and factions remained outside, gathering forces of resistance and opposition to the party and the state.

Given the difficulty of finding an acceptable solution to the problem of political and ethnic diversity, it was not surprising that the new leadership was unable to reconcile the differences and that the resilience of the newly forged union was tested almost immediately. Within several months of independence, communist bands were in armed rebellion, seeking to overthrow the central government. Several months thereafter, elements of the Karen minority—the largest of the discontented ethnic groups—launched their own revolt, as did members of other ethnic minorities, all seeking a territory for their own group and greater decisionmaking authority in matters affecting its future. Wholesale Karen desertions played havoc with Burma's armed forces, and dissidents soon occupied much of Lower Burma and spread elsewhere. By 1951, however, in part because the insurgents were never able to unify their efforts and in part because of U Nu's determined response, the reconstructed armed forces had brought the insurrection substantially under control, although insurgents continued to dominate much of the countryside. The infiltration into Shan State of remnants of Nationalist Chinese forces beginning in late 1949 compounded concern over domestically rooted subversion, arousing fears that Chinese troops might pursue their defeated opponents into Burma. Burmese government actions alleviated these pressures to some degree in the mid- and late 1950s. The government also succeeded in gaining increased loyalty among certain hill minorities; but Karens and Communists continued to feed government concern over national stability and to arouse fears among the grass-roots population for their own personal security.

Economic development made little headway. Overriding dependence on rice as a foreign exchange earner continued throughout the era of constitutional democracy (1948–62), leaving the country still highly vulnerable to fluctuations on the world market. The failure of AFPFL leaders to agree on plans and priorities inhibited efforts to carry out reconstruction.

In the late 1950s troubles for the new state mounted rapidly. The AFPFL was torn by internal rivalry as opposition strength mounted. Shan dissidents demanded greater autonomy, mobilizing for a secessionist movement. Under an 18-month military caretaker government they went into open revolt, as did Kachins, joining forces in some areas with Karen and communist insurgents. The military amended the constitution to limit some rights of Shan feudal chiefs and paid them to surrender others. Returned to power in national elections in February 1960, U Nu formed a new government that set about to formulate new economic plans and to strengthen the base for democracy. A conference was set for early 1962 in which representatives of all groups would convene to discuss domestic problems, especially the issues of federalism and succession. In the meantime, however, U Nu had made good on a campaign promise to reestablish Buddhism as the state religion, exacerbating existing tensions by further alienating Karen and other non-Buddhist minorities.

The most significant political event in independent Burma's history took place in March 1962, when forces under the command of General Ne Win assumed power in a bloodless coup. Calling itself the Revolutionary Council, the group suspended the 1947 constitution and began rule by decree, citing "economic, religious, and political crises with the issue of federalism [as] the most important reason for the coup." Military officers were put in place as department heads, while General Ne Win, as chairman, assumed full executive, legislative, and judicial powers. Moving quickly to consolidate its position, the council imprisoned U Nu, some of his cabinet ministers, and other presumed opponents, including regional separatists—generally without trial.

By early 1983 U Ne Win had been in power for some 21 years and, with open, organized opposition or criticism disallowed and dissidence other than among communist and ethnic insurgents seldom expressed, his authority was assured. The Revolutionary Council had been disbanded after the promulgation of the 1974 Constitution, according to which the government is divided into legislative, executive and judicial functions; the State Council is the top decisionmaking body. Having resigned from the military, U Ne Win served as chief executive from 1974 until late 1981. In August of that year, he announced plans to retire as president after the October elections. He was succeeded by U San Yu, a retired army general.

The real seat of power, however, continued to be the military-led BSPP, of which U Ne Win remained chairman. Making up the numerically dominant element in the party's Central Committee, the military manipulated the levers of power. An elite cadre organization in its formative years under the Revolutionary Council, the BSPP had been transforming itself into a mass party since mid-1971 as a means of broadening grass-roots support and political participation. The process had by no means been smooth, however. In 1973 and again in 1976 the party leadership had deemed it necessary to undertake mass purges of regular and candidate members, and an extraordinary party congress in November 1977 dropped more than 100 members of the Central Committee for "antiparty" and "antipeople" activities.

Backed by a powerful security apparatus, whose several arms possessed wide discretionary powers codified in a 1975 antisubversion law, the BSPP gave strong emphasis to the maintenance of internal security. Most opposition politicians and ethnic separatists imprisoned immediately after the military takeover in 1962, however, were released within a few years, and thousands of government opponents, including U Nu, returned to the country from exile or were released form prison under a general amnesty order in 1980. But student strikes at Rangoon University had been twice rigorously suppressed, most recently in 1975; and in the early 1980s, in its efforts to maintain political stability, the leadership continued to close off avenues of criticism and dissent.

As indicated in remarks by President San Yu read to Union Day delegates in 1983 by BSPP Joint Secretary General Brigadier Tin Oo, top political priority continued to be given to three long-standing objectives. These were consolidation of national unity, economic development through efforts by all Burmese in their respective territorial divisions, and elimination of insurgency through vigilance and continued cooperation with Burma's armed forces.

In the intervening two decades since its assumption of power, the leadership had already taken a number of measures to promote national solidarity. Not the least of these was the establishment of the Academy for the Development of National Groups. At the academy, minority customs and cultures were nurtured and encouraged, and minority students, educated in these traditions and in other academic subjects to imbue them with "union spirit," were trained to serve as teachers and to carry out development work in the border regions.

Another area of success in consolidation of support for national goals involved the *sangha*, whose members, reacting to the fall of the devout U Nu, had initially remained aloof from the military leadership. In 1965 the *sangha* refused to comply with the government-urged concept of membership registration. Its attitude shifted, however, as the BSPP and the government took measures to recognize the role of Buddhism in the society by various means, including the establishment of the governmental Department of Religious Affairs. Delegates to a mass Buddhist "purification" congregation in Rangoon in May 1980 agreed to the principle of carrying identification cards, as well as to form a national Buddhist council, which held powers to excommunicate monks who violated accepted standards of personal conduct and to discipline Buddhist orders judged to be teaching heresy.

Economic development under military rule can be seen as having taken place in two stages. Programs and policies of the 1960s focused on the growth of heavy industry in a program emphasizing state ownership of the means of production and discouraging private investment. A 1963 nationalization law removed Chinese and Indians from strategic positions in the economy (causing many Indians to leave the country), and a 1964 demonetization law targeted the elimination of private savings, further reducing the position of Indians and Chinese. Failure of the overall program, however—later attributed in part by the leadership to overly rigid implementation—brought hardship and despair, especially to the Burmese population in the central lowlands. In the cities the population rioted over commodity shortages.

A watershed was reached in 1971, according to Burma specialist David I. Steinberg, as a result of economic rethinking that took place during the First Congress of the BSPP. In the aftermath of the deliberations, a crucial decision favoring a liberalized approach to economic development was agreed on, which was given specific formulation in a document that continued to provide the basis for planning some 12 years later. Its pragmatic approach took cognizance of the plight of the consumer, stressed equity considerations, and envisioned greater stress on agriculture, mining, forestry, and fishing to reflect the country's natural advantages. A Twenty-Year Plan was developed to last until fiscal year (FY) 1993.

Economic performance was sluggish initially, but by the period of the incremental Third Four-Year Plan (FY 1978–81), the economy was definitely on the upswing. The average growth rate rose according to plan by more than 6 percent per year, the agricultural sector alone by more than 8 percent. Behind the growth lay successful efforts to increase rice production through improved inputs and a turnabout of former reluctance to accept foreign aid, now provided as direct assistance and concessionary loans by a consortium of Western nations.

This positive note was muted somewhat in 1983 by increasing concern over the foreign debt service burden and by lagging oil production. Over the long term there was reason for concern as well over various issues arising from the complex interaction between private and public production and marketing systems. The thriving shadow economy supplied a broad spectrum of society with consumer goods unavailable through legal channels, depriving the government of much-needed foreign exchange earnings and tax revenues. The migration of rural inhabitants to Rangoon and other urban centers, bringing additional pressures on an already overburdened job market, was an additional problem for authorities.

Goods from the black market were furnished in part by ethnic insurgents and by BCP dissidents. By engaging in smuggling and drug trafficking to supplement whatever funds could be obtained from foreign sources, antigovernment rebels were able to purchase arms and equipment for insurgency operations. Although well before early 1983 these operations had been confined by government forces to remote and sparsely populated border areas, they nonetheless constituted a steady drain on public resources. Alongside the insurgent groups were various warlords, supported by private armies, and common criminals who also engaged in smuggling, banditry, and drug trafficking motivated purely by greed or lust for power.

Burma's foreign policy under U Ne Win's leadership continued to be one of nonalignment, reflecting long-standing Burmese wariness of foreign entanglements. In September 1979 the country had withdrawn from the Nonaligned Movement, asserting that that body had deviated from its basic premise of strict neutrality. The leadership was committed to the establishment and maintenance of cordial relations with all countries on an equitable basis and exhibited a strong determination not to be drawn into any regional conflicts. While maintaining an independent posture and refusing assistance from either the United States or the Soviet Union on any significant scale, Burma was using to its advantage substantial help from a consortium of Western aid donors who offered both aid and concessionary loans. Burma still refused any form of private joint venture with foreign capital, however.

In 1982 the country appeared to have no major foreign policy problems. Relations with China, vastly improved since the low point reached after the anti-Chinese riots in Rangoon in 1967 and eased by the absence of reports in 1983 of Chinese aid to the BCP, were correct and cordial. India loomed large in Burma's foreign policy perspective, if only because of its relative size and because of historic Burmese fears of assimilation. Population pressures in Bangladesh had made Rakhine State an attraction for those of its citizens who lived near the Burmese border; Bengali residents in Burma had not been an issue between the two countries since 1978, however.

Much speculation centered in early 1983 on the related questions of post-U Ne Win leadership and the dimensions of possible policy shifts when the aging senior party official finally stepped down. In the meantime there was little doubt that U Ne Win enjoyed a considerable measure of popular support despite the authoritarian methods of his regime. The style of his rule was not out of keeping with traditional models of political authority in Burma and, whatever the case, many Burmese were grateful that their country remained independent and, unlike Afghanistan or Vietnam, had not been drawn into the orbit of superpower conflict. Beyond this, the strength of the BSPP, the absence of legitimate channels of opposition, and the significant economic strides of recent years worked in favor of the man who had succeeded in maintaining unity and viability for more than two decades.

May 1983

Shortly after the manuscript for this study was completed, Burma was jolted by the sudden announcement that Brigadier General Tin Oo, confidant and possible successor to BSPP chairman U Ne Win, was resigning from his important government posts. Observers concluded that for one reason or another the former intelligence chief and third-ranking party figure had fallen out of favor with the aging U Ne Win, the country's long-time supreme leader.

The action came amid a corruption scandal involving Tin Oo's close aide, Minister of Home and Religious Affairs Bo Ni, and charges that Tin Oo himself had indulged in lavish spending on a son's wedding. Tin Oo's quick defense of Bo Ni put his own case in a worse light. According to other widely reported rumors, the general's fall was attributable to his unpopularity with army field commanders or to disapproval of his zest for enlarging his own political power base. Many of the close supporters whom he had appointed to important positions were caught in the political shake-up that followed his resignation. By late July 1983, the BSPP had formally denounced Tin Oo, and the government prepared to take legal and disciplinary action against him. In early August he went on trial, charged with misusing the equivalent of US$250,000 in state funds and property.

Tin Oo's fate gave new significance to the long-standing succession question. While some Burma-watchers opined that the general should not be written off altogether in the country's political future, nearly all agreed that rivals in the top leadership, particularly President San Yu and General Kyaw Htin, had moved up in the power structure as a result of the affair.

However important, the circumstances on the domestic scene paled in comparison with another development in 1983—the October 9 terrorist bombing in Rangoon that killed 21 persons, including four cabinet ministers and other high officials of the Republic of Korea (South Korea). The South Korean diplomatic mission, headed by President Chun Doo Hwan, had been in the Burmese capital on the first leg of a five-nation Asian tour and had planned to lay a wreath at the Burmese Martyrs' Mausoleum where the explosion occurred. Delayed in arriving, Chun himself narrowly escaped assassination. The bombing was a source of major embarrassment and deep regret to Burma and to its people, who were sensitive to the country's failure to provide adequate security to a visiting foreign delegation and to the grievous consequences of the lapse.

Burmese security forces immediately mounted an all-out campaign to identify the perpetrators of the monstrous act and bring them to justice. Within a few days of the attack, they had pinned down three "Korean" suspects, one of whom was killed and the two others captured in exchanges between them and Burmese forces. Both of the captured suspects had sustained serious injuries from explosions of grenades they had detonated themselves. On the basis of a voluntary confession from one of the two and other evidence assembled through intensive investigation—in which Burmese authorities were aided by South Korean intelligence operatives—the Burmese government soon announced that it had definitely established North Korean responsibility for the bombing and immediately severed diplomatic ties with P'yŏngyang. South Korea welcomed the Burmese decision to break off formal relations. Meanwhile, trial proceedings got under way against the two surviving suspects—North Korean military officers—who in early December were convicted of murder and sentenced to death. At the United Nations nearly half the member delegations supported the findings of the Burmese government and its conclusion of North Korean responsibility for the bombing.

December 15, 1983

Frederica M. Bunge

Chapter 1. Historical Setting

More than 100 stupas, shrines, and other satellite structures surround Rangoon's great Shwedagon Pagoda established in the eleventh century or earlier.

BURMA CAN BE SEEN as divided into three distinct regions that have played different roles in the country's historical development. The coastal and river delta region—comprising the Tenasserim coast facing the Andaman Sea, the Arakan coast along the Bay of Bengal, and the Irrawaddy and Sittang river deltas (the later commonly referred to as Lower Burma)—has served as the gateway for overseas influences. The second region, the central Irrawaddy valley (known as Upper Burma), was the homeland of the Burmans, the country's dominant ethnic group, and was for many centuries the center of political power. The third region, the ring of hills and mountains that forms the border on all sides of the country, has been inhabited by ethnic minorities who, because of the terrain, have been able to maintain their independence and separate identities. Burmese historical dynamics has involved the interaction of the diverse peoples of these three regions who migrated into Burma from different parts of mainland Southeast Asia and Inner Asia.

Owing to the country's ethnic and ecological heterogeneity, national unity, though pursued by Burmese rulers for many centuries, has remained an elusive goal. Anawrahta of Pagan (1044–77), Bayinnaung (1551–81), and Alaungpaya (1752–60), all Burman kings, established unified kingdoms that covered the central, coastal, and delta regions and made vassals of the border peoples and even of peoples of the states beyond, such as Siam (Thailand) and Manipur (now a state of India). Periods of military strength and expansion, however, alternated with periods of civil strife and disorder. The British enforced their own form of unity on Burma after Upper Burma (actually Upper Burma and the northern border region) was annexed by them in 1886. Burma was made a province of British India, though constitutional revisions made it a separate colony in 1937.

Despite the centrifugal influence of heterogeneity, the Theravada Buddhist religion—introduced from India in very early times—has served as the central element of Burmese national identity. It has been the basis not only of personal faith and ethics but also of a social and political system in which the ruler and the *sangha* (Buddhist monkhood) supported each other in a symbiotic relationship. Buddhism continues to be the formative national influence, although Western ideas—socialism and parliamentary democracy—entered the country during the colonial period and formed the basis of a new Burmese nationalism.

When the country gained its independence in 1948 as the Union of Burma, a quasi-federal state, its prime minister, U Nu, combined Buddhist, socialist, and democratic themes in a sometimes contradictory attempt to create an enduring sense of

3

national unity. His successor, General Ne Win, who overthrew the parliamentary system and established a military government in 1962, has stressed a secular socialist program within the context of an authoritarian political system. Although the U Ne Win government retained control in the early 1980s over the coastal and central river valley regions, active insurgent movements continued in the border regions among some of the ethnic minorities.

Early Burmese Kingdoms

Because of the lack of reliable records, practically nothing is known of Burma's early history. Legends tell that a king of the Mons, a people who had apparently migrated into Lower Burma from the southeast, built the Shwedagon Pagoda on the site of modern Rangoon during the lifetime of the Buddha (ca. sixth century B.C.). Another legend—that the third century B.C. Indian emperor Ashoka, a devout Buddhist, sent monks to Thaton, a Mon settlement in Lower Burma on the gulf of Martaban—suggests that they had early contacts with the Indian subcontinent by sea. Indian ships docked at Thaton, Pegu, and other Lower Burma ports, and the region became an outpost of Indian civilization. India's most important contribution to Burmese culture was Buddhism, as the legends suggest. Over the centuries it was the axis around which Burmese life and national identity evolved. The loose network of Mon states in Lower Burma served as a bridge over which the Buddhist faith reached the Upper Burma heartland.

Third century A.D. Chinese records mention a people known as the Pyu, who lived in the central Irrawaddy River region of Upper Burma and had apparently migrated into the region from the Tibetan plateau. Chinese Buddhist pilgrims of the seventh century A.D. describe a Pyu city-state, known as Sri Ksetra (the "Pleasant" or "Fortunate Field"), near the modern town of Prome on the banks of the Irrawaddy. Sri Ksetra possessed over 100 Buddhist monasteries, and both the Theravada and Mahayana schools of Buddhism (see Glossary) were respected. Its greatest extant monument is the 50-meter-high Bawbawgyi Pagoda, built of brick in Indian style. According to Burmese chronicles, the Pyu gained supremacy over the Mons, sent ships to India, Ceylon (Sri Lanka), the Malay Peninsula, and the Indonesian archipelago, and claimed tributaries as far afield as the islands of Sumatra and Java.

Another state, or collection of states, was established as early as the fourth century A.D. in what is now Rakhine State (formerly Arakan State), facing the Bay of Bengal. The Arakanese were related to the Burmans of Upper Burma and had, because of their location on the coast, close maritime relations with India.

It is recorded that the Burmans, a people closely related to the Pyu, established settlements at Pagan on the banks of the

4

Irrawaddy in Upper Burma as early as the second century A.D. The earliest verifiable date for Pagan, however, is 849. Pagan was strategically located on north-south and east-west trade routes and near the irrigated plain of Kyaukse, which produced an abundance of rice. This provided the economic base upon which a powerful kingdom grew (see fig. 2). Nearby was Mount Popa, a extinct volcano, the summit of which contained a shrine sacred to the spirits (*nats*) of the Burman people (see The Burman World View, ch. 2). Mahayana Buddhism may have been brought to Pagan around the seventh century. A prominent sect was that of the Ari, who practiced magical Tantric rites similar to those of Tibetan or Bengali Buddhists.

The Pagan Dynasty, 1044–1287

King Anawrahta (1044–77), the founder of the Pagan Dynasty, was the first to bring Lower and Upper Burma under unified rule. Starting from Pagan, then only a confederation of small villages, he conquered the neighboring principalities of the central Irrawaddy valley. In 1057 he captured Thaton and gained control over Lower Burma.

Anawrahta brought the Mon king of Thaton and some 30,000 captives back to Pagan, introducing the still countrified Burmans to a refined literature and art. The most significant development, however, was Anawrahta's conversion to Theravada Buddhism, which was accomplished by a Mon monk, Shin Arahan. The king established himself as a patron of the faith and outlawed the Ari sect, conscripting Ari monks, described by one Burmese historian as "heavy-eating and arrogant," into the royal army. He assisted the Buddhist Singhalese kingdom on the island of Ceylon in its war against the invading forces of the Hindu Chola Dynasty of South India. The king of Ceylon reciprocated by sending Buddhist scriptures and a Buddha tooth-relic to Anawrahta, the latter being enshrined in the Shwezigon Pagoda near Pagan. Mon monks continued to play the central role in bringing Theravada Buddhism to Upper Burma.

Kyansittha (1084–1113), Pagan's second great king, carried on the work of Anawrahta, reunifying the kingdom after a series of revolts, holding off foreign invaders, and maintaining diplomatic and ecclesiastical ties with Ceylon. Although influenced to a certain extent by Hinduism, he saw himself primarily as a Buddhist king and built the Ananda Pagoda, considered the greatest example of Burmese religious architecture. Kyansittha was so impressed by the work of his architect that, in rather un-Buddhist fashion, he had him executed so that he could not reproduce the work. The Ananda Pagoda is approached in quality, however, by the Thatbinnyu Pagoda, at 61 meters the tallest in Pagan, built in the mid-twelfth century by King Alaungsithu.

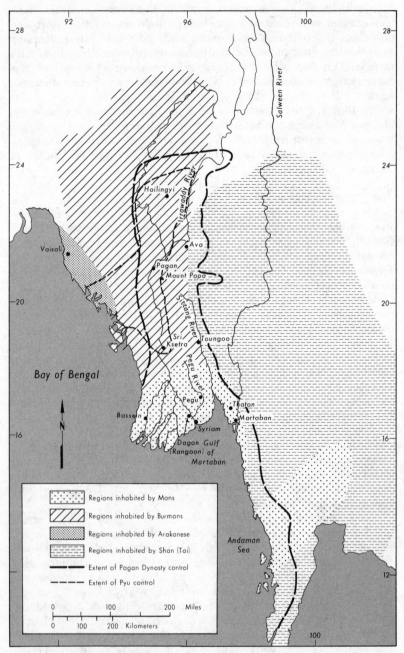

Source: Based on information from John F. Cady, *The United States and Burma,*
Cambridge, 1976, 20.

Figure 2. The Early Kingdoms

It is believed that as many as 13,000 pagodas, temples, and monasteries were built at Pagan before the dynasty's fall. Burmese historians claim that, unlike the Hindu-Buddhist monuments at Angkor Wat in Cambodia, the Pagan temples were built not by slave or corvée labor; instead, free laborers flocked to the construction sites, hoping to gain Buddhist merit through their work.

Pagan flourished for more than two and one-half centuries before being destroyed by the Mongol armies of Kublai Khan, invading Upper Burma from China in 1287. The last king, Narathihapate, fled south but was killed by his own son. He is remembered by the Burmese as the king "who fled from the Chinese," compared with the eighteenth-century king Hsinbyushin, "the king who fought the Chinese." The Mongol Yuan Dynasty and succeeding Ming and Qing dynasties established a strong military and administrative base in the Chinese province of Yunnan; thus Burma was exposed over the centuries to a new and powerful threat. The Mongol destruction of the kingdom of Nanchao in Yunnan led to the large-scale migration of Shan peoples (their Burmese name; they call themselves the Tai) into the eastern border region (now Shan State) and Upper and Lower Burma.

Disunity and foreign domination characterized the fourteenth to mid-sixteenth centuries. Upper Burma came under the control of Shan princes, though Burman kings ruled at Ava, near modern Mandalay, as Shan tributaries. In Lower Burma a Shan named Wareru (1287–96) established a kingdom at Martaban in 1281, subsequently gaining control of much of the Lower Burma region. There followed a golden age of Lower Burma culture. Binnya U (1353–85) established a new capital at Pegu. Dhammazedi (1472–92), a former Buddhist monk, was a model Buddhist king who promoted reform of the *sangha* through the introduction of orthodox ordination rites from Ceylon.

The Toungoo Dynasty, 1486–1752

In the sixteenth century a revival of Burman power took place at Toungoo, on the Sittang River. In 1280 there had been established a fortified town, which subsequently became a political center of some importance. After the capture of Ava by a Shan prince in 1527, many Burmans sought refuge there. Tabinshwehti (1531–50) established the second unified Burmese kingdom, whose ruling house was known as the Toungoo Dynasty, after its place of origin. He conquered Pegu in 1539, extending his control to Martaban and the coastal area as far south as Tavoy. Tabinshwehti captured Prome from the forces of the Shan conqueror of Ava; in 1546 he had himself consecrated king of Burma, making Pegu his capital. His invasion of Siam (what is now central Thailand), undertaken in 1548, however, ended in failure.

After Tabinshwehti's assassination and a subsequent revolt in central Burma, his brother, King Bayinnaung (1551–81) captured Ava in 1555, thus uniting Upper and Lower Burma. He then marched against the Shan principalities in eastern Burma and parts of modern Thailand and Laos and in 1569 captured the Siamese capital of Ayutthaya, located near the modern Thai capital of Bangkok. Plans to conquer the independent kingdom of Arakan on the Bay of Bengal coast, however, were never carried out. The reign of Bayinnaung's son, Nanda Bayin (1581–99), witnessed the beginning of the decline of Toungoo power. Siam reasserted its independence, and an Arakanese fleet laid siege to Pegu, capturing it in 1599.

Anaukpetlun (1605–28) restored for a brief time the unity of the kingdom. His brother, Thalun (1629–48), moved the capital from Pegu back to Ava, a decision some significance, for it represented the withdrawal of effective Burman power from Lower Burma and the consequent relative isolation of Burman kings from outside influences brought by sea. Ava became involved in Chinese dynastic struggles when the last prince of the Ming Dynasty, Yong-li, sought refuge at the Burmese capital, provoking Manchu incursions into Upper Burma.

Portuguese merchants and adventurers established a factory or trading station at Martaban in 1519, and their accounts of Pegu describe it as a rich city and international port. Yet Burma's products, which included rice, jewels, precious metals, "Martaban jars" used for storing water or rice, shellac, and teak, were of less interest to them and their later Dutch and English rivals than the spices of the Indonesian archipelago. Strong kings, such as Tabinshwehti and Bayinnaung, bought European firearms and employed Portuguese as mercenaries in their armies. When authority broke down in the delta region toward the close of the century, a Portuguese adventurer in the pay of the invading Arakanese, Philip de Brito, set himself up at Syriam and proceeded to carve out a kingdom for himself in Lower Burma. De Brito's career ended in 1613 when Anaukpetlun captured Syriam and executed him; his Portuguese supporters were exiled to Upper Burma. Portuguese pirates at Dianga raided the coastal villages of Bengal, providing captives for profitable Arakanese slave markets, until the region was taken from Arakan by the Mogul emperor of India in 1666.

The Konbaung Dynasty and the Anglo-Burmese Wars

Burmese history is often described in terms of the centuries-long struggles among ethnic groups, particularly the Burmans, Mons, and Shans. A number of historians have suggested, however, that although ethnic differences were not unimportant, the real dynamic at work was a particular conception of royal authority based on the Buddhist notion of karma. This phenome-

Historians claim that more than 13,000
Buddhist pagodas and shrines once stood on
the Irrawaddy Plain here at Pagan, the capital
of an early and powerful Burmese kingdom.

Platform of the Shwezigon Pagoda, near Pagan
Courtesy Catherine B. Ferguson

9

non first comes into clear focus during the Pagan Dynasty. A king was a man who had accumulated merit in past lives. This gave him *pon* (glory), a quality of skill, courage, and dynamism that attracted other powerful men who became his supporters. The support of the *sangha* was particularly important to the idea of kingship. World-renouncing Buddhist monks possessed a different sort of *pon* than kings, but the two formed a kind of symbiotic relationship. The *sangha* gave the ruler spiritual legitimacy, while the king provided the *sangha* with material support, giving the monks land and building monasteries and pagodas. As defender and promoter of the faith, the king had a wider mission: he was responsible for the welfare of his subjects, in order that they might have the material means and leisure to pursue their own salvation. This "welfare state" concept of kingship had a formative influence on the development of socialist thought in modern Burma (see The Emergence of Political Movements, this ch.).

Political authority was thus based on religious and universal, rather than ethnic or particularistic, criteria. Different rulers would establish competing centers of royal power. The outcome of their struggle was believed to depend on the winner's status as a *karmaraja*, a "karma king." In these contests ethnic lines were often confused, particularly in Lower Burma. Thus Tabinshwehti, a Burman, adopted Mon titles and usages when he had himself crowned king at Pegu in 1546. Although the population of Lower Burma was predominantly Mon in the early eighteenth century, the revolt that led to the fall of the Toungoo Dynasty was initiated by the royally appointed governor of Pegu, a Burman. He was killed by his own troops, and the local Mon population and the Gwe Shans—a people considered by some scholars to have been Karens—made Smim Htaw Buddhaketi, a Buddhist monk and a Gwe Shan, their king. The king's armies seized the ports of Syriam and Martaban in Lower Burma and marched as far north as Prome and Toungoo by 1743. Binnya Dala, a Shan, deposed Smim Htaw Buddhaketi in 1747; he marched into Upper Burma in 1751, capturing the royal capital of Ava and deposing the last king of the Toungoo Dynasty the following year. In this civil war—a contest to find a new *karmaraja*—Burmans, Mons, Shans, and Gwe Shans fought on both sides.

The Reigns of Alaungpaya and His Sons

The Toungoo king, his court, and as many as 20,000 prisoners were brought back to Pegu by Binnya Dala's forces in 1752; the outcome of the contest for royal power seemed decided. A new leader, however, appeared in Upper Burma and within eight short years unified Upper and Lower Burma and extended his power far beyond the borders of his country. This was Maung Aung Zeya, a Burman and district chief at Moksobomyo, a town some 95 kilometers to the northwest of Ava. After Ava's fall he built a stockade around Moksobomyo and organized the surrounding villages into a resistance movement. Defeating a detachment of Binnya Dala's troops, he proclaimed himself king of Burma and assumed the title Alaungpaya, or "embryo Buddha," the name by which he is known in history. Thus, he connected his royal aspirations to the powerful symbol of the Buddhist *karmaraja*. Renaming Moksobomyo as Shwebo, "Town of the Golden Leader," he built a royal palace and attracted supporters from all over Upper Burma.

Alaungpaya was the third of Burma's great unifiers, after Anawrahta of Pagan and Bayinnaung, and the founder of the Konbaung Dynasty, which ruled the country until the late nineteenth century. His swift successes seemed to validate his claims about the special nature of his karma. He captured Ava at the end of 1753 and defeated a large force sent into Upper Burma by Binnya Dala the following year. In 1755 Alaungpaya brought his forces down the Irrawaddy River in a large flotilla and occupied Dagon, the site of the greatly revered Shwedagon Pagoda. There he established a new town, naming it Yangon, or Rangoon ("the End of Strife"), the future capital of colonial and independent Burma. He captured Syriam, Lower Burma's main trading port, in 1756 and Binnya Dala's royal capital at Pegu in 1757.

Alaungpaya invaded Manipur, a small kingdom on Burma's northwestern border, in 1758; for more than two decades Manipuri horsemen had conducted raids deep into Upper Burma, looting and pillaging. The Shan kingdom of Chiang Mai was also brought under his control when he appointed a vassal as ruler. An insurrection at Pegu, however, drew the king's attention back to Lower Burma. Lower Burma Mons, reacting to Alaungpaya's harsh policies, massacred large numbers of Burmans before the revolt was suppressed. Scholars suggest that this marked the beginning of Mon-Burman ethnic polarization.

Alaungpaya demanded that the king of Siam recognize his status as an "embryo Buddha." When the monarch refused, Alaungpaya laid siege to Ayutthaya, the Siamese capital; but the siege was cut short when it was discovered that Alaungpaya was seriously ill with fever. His troops accomplished an orderly retreat back to Burmese territory, but the king died in May 1760.

Hsinbyushin (1763–76), the Konbaung Dynasty's second great king, captured Ayutthaya in April 1767. The city, which had been Siam's capital since 1350, was completely destroyed, and the Siamese king was killed. Thousands of prisoners and vast amounts of booty were taken. In the words of a Siamese historian, Bayinnaung had "waged war like a monarch," but Hsinbyushin conducted himself "like a robber."

Siam's ordeal was alleviated, however, by Hsinbyushin's entanglements with a far larger country—China. The Chinese were disturbed by Burmese expansion into the Shan states, Chiang

Mai, and Laos, which bordered their southwestern province of Yunnan and which were considered, along with the Burmese kingdom itself, to be part of their comprehensive "Tribute System." In 1766, when a dispute arose over the murder of a Chinese merchant at Keng Tung, a Shan state loyal to Hsinbyushin, the Chinese sent an army on a punitive expedition. The Chinese forces were defeated by the Shans with Burmese help. The Chinese emperor sent a second expedition, but this too was defeated; by 1767 two Burmese armies had entered Chinese territory. A third Chinese force, led by the emperor's son-in-law, Ming Rui, managed to get within 48 kilometers of Ava, which Hsinbyushin had restored as his royal capital. Ming Rui had overextended himself, however, and was cut off by Burmese forces. He committed suicide rather than face his father-in-law's wrath. The last Chinese invasion, taking place in 1769, was equally unsuccessful, and the Chinese commander sued for terms.

A peace treaty was signed at Kaungton in 1770, allowing for the withdrawal of Chinese forces, the restoration of trade between the two countries, and the sending of what the Chinese regarded as tribute missions by Burma to Beijing every 10 years. Historians D.G.E. Hall and Maung Htin Aung, who agree little on other things, both cite the wisdom and foresight of the treaty, which was negotiated by Maha Thiha Thura, the general who defeated the Chinese. The provision regarding tribute missions saved face for the Chinese emperor and prevented further threats from that quarter. This policy of moderation laid the foundations for good relations with China through the nineteenth century and served as an example to the leaders of independent Burma, U Nu and General Ne Win, in their relations with their sometimes-threatening northern neighbor. Hsinbyushin, however, was infuriated with Maha Thiha Thura for giving so many concessions to the Chinese and refraining from exterminating their forces. Nonetheless, hostilities did not break out again.

Even the nationalist historian Maung Htin Aung admitted that after the defeat of the Chinese "the Burmese as a nation became drunk with victory and grew arrogant and aggressive." The last six years of Hsinbyushin's reign saw few accomplishments. In Siam, Phraya Taksin, the half-Chinese general who became in his country a hero the equal of Alaungpaya in Burma, led a successful war of national resistance. After Hsinbyushin's death in 1776, his son and successor, Singu Min, ordered the withdrawal of Burmese armies from Siamese territory.

Singu Min ruled until 1781, when he was assassinated. His successor, Maung Maung, was king for only seven days. Badon Min, known better as Bodawpaya (1782–1819), the fourth son of Alaungpaya, seized power and commenced eliminating his opponents, including the old hero Maha Thiha Thura and all his own surviving brothers, save the youngest. A Mon rising in Lower

Burma in 1783 was harshly suppressed. King Bodawpaya was ruthless and marked with a streak of megalomania, but he combined these traits with great energy and intelligence—in the words of one English observer, "a masterful man who never hesitated to punish."

Bodawpaya carried out a successful conquest and annexation of the kingdom of Arakan. This country had been in a state of anarchy for at least half a century and was easily subdued; the Arakanese king, his court, and many thousands of prisoners were brought back as captives. The decision to bring back to Upper Burma the large bronze Mahamuni image of Buddha, the most precious of Arakan's national treasures, aroused considerable resentment. Along with the harshness of Bodawpaya's rule this action sparked rebellions among the Arakanese that would have portentous consequences for Burma's future, for Arakan bordered the Bengal territories of the British East India Company. In 1785 and 1787 unsuccessful expeditions were launched against Siam.

Internally, Bodawpaya's policies expressed both the practical and the more eccentric sides of his nature. Soon after establishing a new capital at Amarapura (near modern Mandalay) in Upper Burma, he initiated a complete survey of his kingdom, including the population, boundaries, and financial resources of each district and village, for taxation purposes. The study of law was encouraged, bandits were suppressed, and irrigation works were expanded. Yet the king used much of his tax revenues for the construction of innumerable pagodas. The largest, which would have been 170 meters high if completed, was started at Mingun near Amarapura. One-third completed, its vast bulk of brick and mortar—split by an earthquake—still looms over the Irrawaddy. Its bell, cast in bronze, is the world's largest except for the "Tsar of Bells" in Moscow. Bodawpaya became involved in controversies within the *sangha* between conservative and reformed sects. He sided with the former, defrocking the reformed-sect monk who had been appointed head of the *sangha* hierarchy (*thathanabaing*) by Alaungpaya. Bodawpaya also supported the establishment of an orthodox Buddhist sect, the Amarapura sect, in Sri Lanka. He claimed, like Alaungpaya, that he was an "embryo" or "future Buddha," but the *sangha* refused to acknowledge this.

State and Society under the Konbaung Kings

Historical records of invasion and war tend to obscure the fact that for the average Burmese, the overwhelming majority of whom were peasants, life was reasonably stable and predictable. After the country was reunified by Alaungpaya, the political order was rebuilt from the top down, and the institutions of royal power intersected with the system of grass-roots leadership exercised by district chiefs and village headmen on the local level.

At the apex of power was, of course, the monarch himself, residing in his palace, which represented symbolically the "center of the universe." He was advised by the Council of Ministers (Hluttaw), which was responsible for the administrative apparatus of the state and also functioned as the highest court in the land. Upper and Lower Burma were divided into administrative units, variously translated as districts, townships, or "circles." Their territory was rather extensive, particularly in regions at a distance from the capital, containing a main town and a large number of surrounding villages. Each district had its own governor, a royal appointee. The border regions consisted of small states that were in theory tributaries of the king, such as those ruled by feudal Shan *sawbwas* (hereditary chiefs) or the rajas of Manipur when it was subjugated. Royal power was naturally stronger in the Burman heartland than in the periphery. Lower Burma was restive, as the frequent Mon uprisings at the end of the eighteenth century attest, and the Shan states were a region of chronic instability. Among the tribal or clan societies, such as the Kachins and the Chins, the king and his officials had little or no influence.

Governors representing royal interests worked in cooperation with local district chiefs, who customarily inherited their offices. The chiefs' duties were broad: the collection of revenue from the district, the organization of corvée labor, the maintenance of law and order, the keeping of a district survey of families, and jurisdiction over petty criminal and civil cases. Below them were village headmen, whose posts were also hereditary. As elites on the local level, the district chiefs and village headmen formed the bulwark of national stability. They were politically of great importance: the leaders of the Konbaung Dynasty in the eighteenth century and of the struggle against British colonialism in the late nineteenth and early twentieth centuries came from their ranks.

Society was in theory hierarchical, composed of six principal status groups: the king and royal family, Brahmins, officials, men of wealth, merchants, and commoners. Within the stratum of commoners there was a class of slaves, including pagoda slaves, who were often criminals or their descendants, persons enslaved for debt who could redeem their freedom, and prisoners of war. Titles of rank and sumptuary regulations were precisely defined, so that the manner in which a person was addressed, clothing, housing, and personal implements revealed an individual's position in society. Infractions of these usages were severely punished.

Society was also divided into two of what historian Frank Trager calls "functional groups": *ahmudan*, or "crown service" groups, who served directly the needs of the king and his court (the palace guard and other military units, special classes of artisans, musicians, elephant tenders, boatmen, jailers, and the cultivators of fields where the king's own rice was grown) and were organized into discrete units outside the regular system of administration; and the *athi*, persons who lived in a single locality and were not bound in special service to the monarch. The status of the latter was generally considered to be lower than that of the former, given the former's close association with the crown.

Traditional Burmese society was not particularly rigid, however, at least compared with the caste system of India. Persons of ability could earn high status and its appurtenances, particularly because war, revolt, and foreign invasion offered opportunities for advancement. Although hereditary in most cases, the posts of district chief or village headman could pass from an incompetent first son to a competent kinsman, or even outside the lineage. The *sangha* offered another avenue of advancement for commoners. Most children were educated in monastery schools before the colonial period, and talented males could enter and rise high within the *sangha*. Moreover, the social position of women, as many observers have reported, was high, particularly compared to that of neighboring Asian countries. At the village monastery school they could learn, along with boys, reading, writing, and arithmetic, and many were active in running their own small businesses. They possessed property rights, and although cases of divorce in precolonial Burma were apparently rare, they could take their own property and half of the jointly owned property out of their former husband's household in such eventualities.

Land was, in theory, the property of the king, and part of his right to tax was based on the idea that all peasants were in fact his tenants. Certain lands, including those on which *ahmudan* cultivators grew rice for the palace, were his property in the ordinary sense of being at his disposal. Concerning other land, royal ownership entailed only the collection of revenue. Cultivators, in practice, could buy, sell, and inherit it. Given the large amount of territory in Burma and the small population, land tenure was not in general strictly defined. There was plenty of open land to be cleared, particularly in the river delta region of Lower Burma. A large amount of land was dedicated to Buddhist establishments by the king, and these were tax-exempt.

Expansion and Confrontation, 1784–1826

Ships of the British East India Company entered Burmese waters in the early seventeenth century. The British and French, based in the ports of Lower Burma and in competition with each other, played a role in the war between Alaungpaya and the rebel king of Pegu, Binnya Dala, supplying them with arms in return for trade concessions. Yet Burma remained largely peripheral to the interests of the company until it and the British-ruled Indian province of Bengal (including both modern Bangledesh and the Indian state of West Bengal) shared a common border along the

Naaf River after Bodawpaya's conquest of Arakan in 1784. Instability in the kingdoms south of the Brahmaputra River and east of Bengal (now in the Indian states of Assam and Manipur) provided an opportunity for Burmese expansion that also destabilized relations between the Burmese king and the company's governor general at Calcutta.

Bodawpaya's harsh policies in Arakan, including the drafting of thousands for forced labor in Upper Burma, drove large numbers of refugees across the Naaf River into British territory. Rebels used the Bengal side of this loosely defined border as a staging area for raids on Burmese garrisons in Arakan. The Burmese, claiming the right to cross the Naaf in "hot pursuit" of insurgents, caused increasing British apprehensions.

Burmese-British relations deteriorated, owing to the lack of established diplomatic communications after 1802. In 1811 an Arakanese insurgent leader, Chin Byan, assembled a large force from among the refugees in British territory, crossed the border, and seized Mrohaung, the old capital of Arakan. Although pushed out of Mrohaung and back across the Naaf River, Chin Byan continued his raids until his death in 1815. It infuriated the Burmese that the British, tied down at the time in a war in central India and having problems elsewhere, did no more to stop him.

Upon Bodawpaya's death in 1819, Bagyidaw, his grandson, became king. Although not a strong personality like his grandfather, Bagyidaw was apparently persuaded by his commander in chief, the general Maha Bandula, to pursue an aggressive policy both in the kingdoms of Assam and Manipur and on the Bengal border. Burmese forces marched into Assam, intervening in a succession struggle, which placed the British in a delicate position since both pretenders to the throne sought protection on British soil and organized resistance movements. Manipur was also invaded, because its raja was reluctant to become a vassal of the new Burmese king. Beset by refugees from Manipur, the raja of still another state, Cachar, fled to British Indian territory. In 1823 the British declared Cachar and a neighboring state, Jaintia, protectorates. On the India-Arkan border, Burmese troops seized East India Company personnel and an island in the Naaf River claimed by the British.

In January 1824 Burmese forces marched into Cachar and fought British troops, and fighting resumed on the Naaf River. Maha Bandula's strategy was apparently to invade Bengal with a double pincer movement, one force coming from the hill state and a second, commanded by him, from Arakan. There was some panic in Calcutta at this prospect; the British governor general, Lord Amherst, however, ordered his forces by sea to Lower Burma, and Rangoon was occupied on May 10. Maha Bandula was obliged to leave Arakan and return to Upper Burma.

In the First Anglo-Burmese War (1824–26) Burmese troops, led by Maha Bandula until his battle death in April 1825, put up a brave resistance. The British expeditionary force, however, was better armed and disciplined and able to push its way up the Irrawaddy River to within 72 kilometers of the Burmese royal capital. Peace was restored with the signing of the Treaty of Yandabo on February 24, 1826, providing for the cession of the territories of Arakan and Tenasserim to the British, an end to Burmese suzerainty over the Indian hill states of Assam and Manipur, an indemnity of £1 million to be paid to the British for the costs of the war, and the exchange of diplomatic representatives between Burma and British India. British troops left Rangoon in December 1826 after the full payment of the indemnity; however, the treaty was a shattering blow to Burmese pride. When representatives were exchanged, Bagyidaw tried to negotiate the return of Tenasserim, but in vain.

Dynastic Decline and the Second Anglo-Burmese War, 1826–53

The First Anglo-Burmese War had been, for the British, essentially a defensive war. The causes of the second and third were more complex, involving a number of different colonial and metropolitan interests. Commercial interests were tied to the promotion of trade and a free market in Lower Burma and elsewhere; "imperial" interests regarded the pacification, if not the annexation, of the Burmese kingdom as essential to the security of British India. Missionaries and the more ideologically inclined imperialists enunciated other interests that served as a sort of moralizing backdrop to more pragmatic economic and strategic concerns. The Buddhist Burmese kingdom stood in the way of Christianization, which Adoniram Judson, an American Baptist, had attempted to initiate as early as 1813. Most British, moreover, tended to regard Burma as an uncivilized country whose people would be only too grateful to exchange native "despotism" for the blessings of British rule (see fig. 3).

The Burmese monarchs between Bodawpaya and Mindon Min (1853–78) failed to establish strong, stable governments that could have responded effectively to British encroachments, and the royal succession became a free-for-all among contesting princes in which the losers often paid with their lives. In 1837 Bagyidaw, suffering mental illness and increasingly incompetent to rule, was overthrown by his brother Tharrawaddy. King Tharrawaddy attempted to curb corruption and abuses of the legal system; he also carried out a purge in which a number of former officials and court figures, including the crown prince, Bagyidaw's son, and Bagyidaw's principal queen, were executed. Revolts among the Shans and in Lower Burma in 1838–40 further undermined political stability.

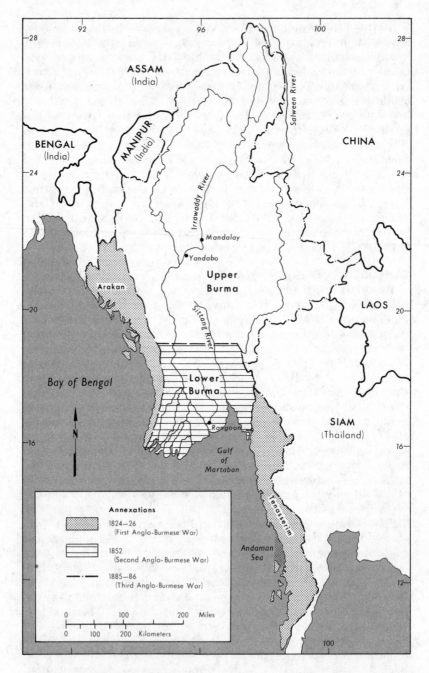

Source: Based on information from John F. Cady, *The United States and Burma*, Cambridge, 1976, 69.

Figure 3. Colonial Absorption of Burma, 1824–86

Tharrawaddy repudiated the Treaty of Yandabo and, impatient with what he perceived as the humiliating presence of a British resident, Henry Burney, in the royal capital, made life so uncomfortable for him and his successors that they were forced to leave. In 1839 the Indian governor general, Lord Auckland, ordered the residency closed and formal diplomatic relations severed. Although many, including the missionary Judson, cried for war, the governor general, preoccupied with Afghanistan and the Northwest Frontier, judged Burma at the time not a vital British interest.

Tharrawaddy died in 1846 and was succeeded by his son, Pagan Min. The new king was described in some accounts as a cruel tyrant and in others as merely an impractical doer of Buddhist good works having no interest in government. Whatever the case, he was particularly weak and allowed corruption and misrule to run rampant. In Upper and Lower Burma alike, the machinery of government was in a process of disintegration, while unrest continued in the Shan states.

A commercial treaty between Burma and British India had been signed in 1826, providing for unrestricted travel and trade by merchants of the two countries in each other's territory and uniform duties on imports. The immediate cause of the Second Anglo-Burmese War of 1852 was a dispute involving two British merchants who had been arrested by the Burmese governor of Rangoon for evading customs duties. Released after paying a small fine, they returned to Calcutta and claimed damages from the Burmese government totaling £1,920. It was unfortunate for the Burmese that the Indian governor general at this time was the Marquis of Dalhousie who, in the words of historian and former colonial administrator John S. Furnivall, "regarded the expansion of the British empire as a law of nature." In Dalhousie's eyes, this seemingly petty incident deserved serious attention, because British prestige in the East would suffer if the government "even for a single day" took "an attitude of inferiority toward a native power." In a classical case of gunboat diplomacy, he sent Commodore George Robert Lambert with an armed naval escort to Rangoon to demand compensation and the removal of the Rangoon governor.

Heavy-handed diplomacy on the part of Lambert, whom even Dalhousie labeled the "combustible Commodore," and the issuing of a stiff British ultimatum that the Burmese could not possibly accept led to the dispatching of a British expeditionary force in April 1852. The ultimatum had demanded a British resident in Rangoon, resignation of the Rangoon governor, a new indemnity of £100,000, and a personal apology from the king. Rangoon, Martaban, Bassein, Pegu, and Prome had been taken by October, though the Burmese staged a fierce, but futile, counterattack at Prome. On December 20, 1852, it was announced that Lower Burma would be annexed as a province of British India.

The Second Anglo-Burmese war not only gave the British all the ports at the juncture of the Bay of Bengal and the Andaman Sea but also left the Burmese kingdom shorn of its richest provinces. The boundary of the truncated kingdom and British Lower Burma was set along a line running through Myede on the Irrawaddy River, about 80 kilometers above Prome. Mindon Min, Pagan Min's half-brother, had opposed going to war with the British and in December 1852 staged a revolt at Shwebo, Alaungpaya's old capital. Pagan Min was deposed and forced into retirement in February 1853. The new king hoped to negotiate the return of Lower Burma but was disappointed in his efforts. Although he refused to recognize the annexation, he did not resume the war.

Diplomacy and Reform under King Mindon, 1853–78

Like his contemporary, the reformist King Mongkut of Siam (1851–68), King Mindon had spent most of his adult life in a Buddhist monastery before ascending the throne. He was a scholar and a peaceful man, perhaps the only Konbaung ruler to practice the Buddhist principle of *ahimsa* (non-harm), preferring to refrain from violence rather than repenting of it. This was revealed from the very beginning in his refusal to order a blood purge of Pagan Min's former supporters. His reign of a quarter of a century was characterized by a conciliatory attitude toward the British, a desire to extend diplomatic contacts to other Western countries, a program of modest reform, and an active promotion of the Buddhist religion. Like other newly installed kings, he moved his capital, this time from Amarapura to a location a few miles away at the foot of Mandalay Hill. At Mandalay, the "Cluster of Gems," an old prophecy held that 24 centuries after the Buddha, a center of Buddhist learning would arise and flourish. The king built a palace of teak enclosed by square walls two kilometers long on each side, and by 1861 the entire project was completed.

King Mindon's moderate rule was a welcome respite for Burmese and British alike after the vagaries of Tharrawaddy and Pagan Min. In dealing with the British, however, Mindon faced problems not known to his predecessors. Because of the annexation of Lower Burma, his kingdom was cut off from the sea, making economic and diplomatic relations with countries other than Britain extremely difficult. A mission sent in 1854 to Calcutta to raise again the question of the reversion of Lower Burma received Dalhousie's brusque reply that "as long as the sun shines, Pegu [Lower Burma] shall remain British." Commercial interests, now based in Rangoon, pressed more rigorously for the opening of the kingdom to increased trade, exploitation of its natural resources, and development of a river and land route to the supposed riches of southwest China markets. These, and the perceived threat of a growing French presence in Indochina, confirmed the British in their treatment of the kingdom as a denizen of that ambiguous region between independent status such as Siam enjoyed, with its own embassy in London, and the vassalage pure and simple of the Indian princely state.

Mindon felt that the future of his kingdom depended upon the modernization of its institutions and with the support of his most influential minister, the Kinwun Mingyi, initiated a reform program aimed at strengthening the position of the central government. One of his most ambitious measures was the establishment of fixed salaries rather than appanages for royal officials—instead of being supported by their districts they would receive remuneration from the central government. Regional governors were appointed to supervise the district governors, and the powers of the district chiefs and village headmen were curbed by giving their judicial responsibilities to provincial judges. Mindon established the *thathameda,* a tax on households with variable assessments to take into account years of bad harvest, fires, or natural catastrophes, in order to raise revenue for the reforms. Its success was impaired, however, by the opposition of the district chief and village headman "gentry" class and the determination of officials to continue being supported by their jurisdictions.

Mindon authorized a system of coinage to replace barter and payment in kind; a royal mint was established, and weights and measures were standardized. The overall economic policy that he envisioned could be described as a kind of state capitalism: royal monopolies on all exportable commodities would be maintained, and international trade would be controlled by the government. The profits from exports would be used to support the government, and historian Maung Htin Aung suggests that the king hoped that these would be sufficient in the future to relieve the people of all direct taxation. A "controlled" economy of this sort was clearly at variance with the ideas of British merchants in Rangoon; they were further rankled by his policy of buying goods directly and more cheaply at Calcutta rather than through them.

Mindon set up a ministry of industry, headed by one of his sons, the Mekkara Prince. A number of textile mills, rice and wheat mills, sugar refineries, and factories, producing small industrial goods such as glassware and pottery, were built. To improve transportation he purchased river steamers. A telegraph system was strung, linking Upper Burma to the outside world through the British system in Lower Burma. Telegraphers were trained, and a Morse code was devised for the Burmese language.

The king did not see modernization as inconsistent with a basic commitment to the Buddhist religion; its integrity seemed threatened by the spread of missionary activity in Lower Burma and the refusal of the British authorities there to grant patronage to the *sangha.* Mindon held annual examinations on the Pali scriptures, built a number of pagodas and monasteries in his new city, and supported both the orthodox Thudhamma sect and a group of reformist monks headed by the Shwegyin Sayadaw. He donated a *hti*, or jewel-encrusted golden umbrella, to be placed on top of the Shwedagon Pagoda in Rangoon but to his disappointment was prohibited by the British from coming down to dedicate it. Contacts that had been disrupted by years of war were reestablished with the *sangha* of Siam. His greatest enterprise, however, was the convening of the Fifth Buddhist Council at Mandalay between 1871 and 1874 to produce an authoritative text of the Pali Tripitaka, or scripture. The entire Tripitaka was carved on 729 stone tablets and displayed in the Kuthodaw Pagoda, east of Mandalay Hill. The council marked the zenith of his prestige as a Buddhist monarch, as the fourth council had been held more than 1800 years earlier in Ceylon.

Commercial and Diplomatic Relations

Although there was no official British representative at Mandalay during the first years of Mindon's reign, cordial relations were maintained with the commissioner of Lower Burma, the scholarly Major Arthur Phayre. Although the king continued to refuse to recognize the annexation of Lower Burma, he concluded a commercial treaty with the British, signed in 1862. It provided for the reciprocal abolition of some customs duties; the freedom of traders, both British and Burmese, to operate unrestricted along the coast of the Irrawaddy; and, most significantly, the posting of a British political agent at Mandalay.

A second commercial treaty, signed in 1867, had important strategic, as well as economic, implications and represented substantial concessions on the king's part. Remaining customs duties were further reduced, the export of gold and silver from the kingdom was permitted for the first time, and royal monopolies on all products except oil, timber, and rubies were abolished, thus cutting the ground from under Mindon's "state capitalism." A British residency was to be established at Bhamo, near the Chinese border, and the Burmese government agreed to assist the British in opening up an overland trade route to China. The British-owned Irrawaddy Flotilla Company was allowed to send ships up the river to Bhamo. These provisions, allowing for British activities within the Burma-China border area, seriously compromised the kingdom's independence, as did a further provision that the Burmese could purchase arms only with the prior consent of the commissioner of Lower Burma. Certain extraterritorial rights were also granted British subjects. Although there was opposition to the treaty, Mindon felt he had little choice but to agree to it. The year before, there had been an attempted coup d'etat, instigated by two royal princes, in which the heir apparent and members of the Council of Ministers were assassinated and the king himself narrowly escaped death. One prince fled to the

Karenni states (now Kayah State) to continue the rebellion there and was later interned by the British in India. Mindon's government was greatly weakened and, despite whispers of British involvement in the plot that were never substantiated, he desperately needed British arms and cooperation.

Owing to the kingdom's landlocked position, relations with Western countries other than Britain were intermittent. In 1856 a French mission had appeared at court, and a few years later the king purchased a French river steamer. Contacts with Italy, unified in 1871, were also fostered. The following year the Kinwun Mingyi led the first Burmese diplomatic mission to Europe, visiting Italy, France, and Britain. The Burmese hoped that, at long last, they would be able to establish direct diplomatic contact with London. They met Queen Victoria, traveled extensively through the British Isles, and enjoyed such Anglo-Saxon amenities as horse races and cricket matches yet they came no closer to having their kingdom recognized as a fully independent state. This was revealed by the fact that they were introduced to the queen not by the foreign secretary but by the secretary of state for India.

On the way home the delegation stopped at Paris, where a treaty of commerce and friendship was signed with the French government. This roused British suspicions, for it was thought that Burma and France had agreed to secret provisions, perhaps providing for arms and military training. Other issues poisoned Burmese-British relations. The British were accused of stirring up trouble in the Karenni states, still vassals of the Burmese king. There was talk of war, but Mindon opposed it, signing a treaty recognizing the neutrality of the Karenni states in 1875. That same year the Indian governor general ordered the Mandalay resident to cease observing the supposedly humiliating custom of removing his shoes when being received by the king. Unwillingness on either side to compromise on the "shoe question" led to the king's refusal to see any British envoys in person.

Thibaw and the Fall of the Burmese Kingdom, 1878–86

King Mindon died on October 1, 1878, and the 19-year-old Thibaw, one of his sons, was proclaimed his successor by the Council of Ministers. There were other, more talented princes who could have ascended the throne. The selection of Thibaw, however, was pushed by the ambitious Alenandaw, or Central Palace Queen, who hoped to marry her three daughters to the new king. It was also supported by "progressives" around the Kinwun Mingyi, who desired to establish a constitutional monarchy in which the king would serve as president of the Council of Ministers. This odd coalition believed that the young and pliable Thibaw would be a ready instrument for the achievement of the different aims.

No one had reckoned, however, with Supayalat, the Central Palace Queen's second daughter. She was married to Thibaw as his secondary queen but immediately moved to oust her elder sister as Thibaw's chief queen and even undermined the position of her mother. She grew to have such influence over Thibaw that he refrained from taking the many wives considered the king's prerogative. More significantly in terms of Burma's future, she collected a circle of supporters within the palace, of whom the principal one was a xenophobic government minister, the Taingda Mingyi, who blocked the reform plans of the progressives. The Taingda Mingyi engineered a massacre of royal princes and princesses, totaling around 40, on January 31, 1879, in order to stem possible revolt.

After Mindon's firm and moderate rule, Thibaw's reign was one of dangerous instability. Rumors were rife that one or more of the exiled princes was plotting to overthrow the king. These exiles included the Myingun Prince, one of the instigators of the assassination plot against Mindon, and the Nyaungyan Prince, who had escaped the royal purge in 1879. Terrified of assassination, Thibaw refused to leave the palace, thus cutting himself off from his subjects. Apparently, Supayalat and the Taingda Mingyi were convinced that the British, tied down in South Africa and Afghanistan, were stretched too thin to take effective action against a more independent policy. The directive on the "shoe question" made communication with the British resident very difficult; compromise on this touchy issue was evidently impossible. When the British resident at Kabul in Afghanistan was assassinated in September 1879, the Indian governor general, seeking to avoid a similar incident in Mandalay with all its attendant complications, ordered the residency shut down.

Although the records are tantalizingly ambiguous on the subject, it seems that Thibaw's government was seeking an alliance with France as a counterbalance to the British. A diplomatic mission sent to Europe in May 1883 negotiated a supplement to the 1873 Franco-Burmese commercial treaty, signed in Paris. At that time France was involved in a war with China over Vietnam and was extending its influence into the Laotian states of Vientiane and Luang Prabang. According to historian D.G.E. Hall, the French prime minister, Jules Ferry, admitted to the British ambassador in July 1884 that the Burmese wanted an alliance and military assistance. It was rumored that, among other things, the French had agreed to take over management of the royal monopolies, operate the Burmese post and telegraph systems, and open up a land route (some said a railroad) between Upper Burma and Tongking in French-controlled Vietnam. A strong French presence in Upper Burma was perceived as a strategic threat to India, which the British could not tolerate. Thus, a movement for the annexation of Thibaw's kingdom gained strength. It was supported by commercial interests in Britain who argued that annexation of Upper Burma would open up the supposedly rich markets of southwestern China and by those in Rangoon who were frustrated by the allegedly monopolistic policies of the Burmese government. Moral sanction was provided by British journalists who described in livid detail the further execution of alleged subversives, although it is unlikely that the number of victims approached that of the reigns of earlier kings, particularly Pagan Min.

In mid-1885 Burmese independence was a house of cards on the verge of collapse. The prerequisite puff of air was provided by the Bombay-Burma Trading Corporation (BBTC) case. This firm had a contract with the king .to extract teak from forests located just north of the border (this was still a royal monopoly). Following the complaint of Burmese foresters, the Council of Ministers in August 1885 served the corporation with a large fine (over £100,000) for defrauding it in the shipment of logs to Lower Burma. The British government complained that the Council of Ministers could not make an ex parte decision in the matter and requested that it submit the issue to arbitration. This the Council of Ministers refused in October, saying the issue had been settled. The Indian governor general, Lord Dufferin, sent an ultimatum to the king at the end of the month; it called not only for arbitration of the BBTC case but also for the reinstatement of the British resident at the capital with a large escort of armed men, Burmese cooperation in opening up a China trade route and, in light of the perceived French threat, an agreement that Calcutta would supervise Burma's foreign policy. The Council of Ministers replied with an assertion of its right to an independent foreign policy.

British forces sailed from Thayetmyo farther up the Irrawaddy in a flotilla of steamboats on November 17, 1885. The Third, and final, Anglo-Burmese War had begun. There was fighting at the Minhla fort, but the capital city of Mandalay fell without bloodshed on November 28 when an armistice was arranged. Some of Thibaw's ministers urged him to flee the capital to carry on resistance elsewhere, but he refused. He and Queen Supayalat met the British commander, and the following day they left the palace for a British steamer on the river. Burmese and British accounts alike describe the sorrowful spectacle of the royal couple riding down to the river in a lowly bullock cart, surrounded by British troops, while the populace wept. They were exiled to India, never to see their native country again.

The Indian government considered putting the six-year-old son of the Nyaungyan Prince on the throne and making Upper Burma a protectorate. Growing insurrection and the defiance of the Hluttaw, however, led to the decision in February 1886 to make the country a directly administered province of British India.

Colonial Burma, 1886–1942

After Mandalay fell into British hands, the most immediate task was the pacification of the countryside, a process that would take five years. Armed groups of bandits, which had sprung up before the fall of the kingdom—remnants of the old Burmese army and royal princes seeking the throne for themselves—all offered resistance to British troops and police, who numbered some 60,000 by 1890. Several local leaders attempted to imitate Alaungpaya, setting up their own royal courts. The chief victims of the fighting were the Upper Burma villagers. They were treated harshly by both British and rebels, thousands being killed before peace was restored. In Lower Burma there was also unrest. Ethnic antagonisms were deepened as the British recruited Karens, often led by Christian pastors or even Western missionaries, to fight Burman rebels who themselves were sometimes led by Buddhist monks who had laid aside their robes. By 1887 Burmans were no longer taken into the colonial army. The British felt the "loyal Karens" were more trustworthy as soldiers, along with—in later years—the Chins and Kachins. The Shan states were brought under British rule by 1889, the *sawbwas* retaining their traditional powers.

Under the Burmese kings there existed a top level of government consisting of royally appointed officials and a local level consisting of district or circle chiefs (such as Alaungpaya had been) and, below them, the headmen of the villages included in the districts. This local leadership was usually hereditary. Under provisions of the Burma Village Act of 1889, the districts were abolished in Lower Burma and district chiefs set aside; the village headmen were given many of their responsibilities. The village headmen's authority, however, was not based on personal prestige or village-level support, as had been the case under the traditional system. Instead, they were considered to be the lower level functionaries of the state bureaucracy who could be punished for incompetence or insubordination by their superiors. In 1907 these reforms were extended to Upper Burma.

The result of this reform was that the villages, largely autonomous units in precolonial times, lost much of their vitality and cohesiveness. Overall, the British chose to remove, rather than co-opt, national and local elites.

The role of Buddhist ecclesiastical hierarchy under the new colonial arrangements was an issue that stirred deep emotion. The king, though not head of the *sangha*, was expected to give it material support and promote its purification. Pious acts, such as the building of pagodas or the holding of examinations on the Tripitaka, mutually strengthened the *sangha* and the state. In India, however, because of its diverse religious communities, the British had developed a policy of religious neutrality. This was applied to Lower Burma after 1853, when they refused to appoint a *thathanabaing* with authority over the *sangha* in that territory.

Although Thibaw's *thathanabaing* was allowed to retain his office after 1886 and a successor was chosen by an assembly of monks in 1903, his authority was greatly weakened by the fact that the new state was secular, not dependent upon the *sangha* for its legitimacy; civil courts, moreover, absorbed many of his judicial responsibilities.

The discipline and quality of the *sangha* deteriorated, for practically any male could put on the yellow robes of a monk, and the ranks of the Buddhist clergy were infiltrated with troublemakers and criminal types. Village monastery schools lost their appeal as modern education, much of it sponsored by missionaries, spread, and the *thathanabaing* prohibited the teaching of secular subjects in the monasteries. Knowledge of the Buddhist scriptures and the Pali language also declined, though the government did sponsor examinations in these subjects.

Colonial Economy and Society

The development of efficient steamship transportation, the opening of the Suez Canal in 1869, and the construction of railroads (reaching Mandalay by 1889, Myitkyina by 1898, and Lashio by 1902), drew the country more tightly into the international economic system in ways that would have as far-reaching consequences as had the extinction of the Konbaung kingdom in 1886. The pace of economic development under British auspices was spectacular. Between 1870 and 1926–27 the value of exports increased 20 times and the value of imports, 15 times. Modern, large-scale Western enterprise was firmly established. Most important at first was the transportation sector (the Irrawaddy Flotilla Company and the railroad) and the teak-extracting and rice-milling industries. The mining sector, however, became increasingly important in the last decade of the nineteenth century. Although rubies, Burma's most exotic mineral resource, attracted foreign entrepreneurs, they were soon eclipsed by petroleum. The Burma Oil Company, working wells that the British government took over from the royal monopoly in Upper Burma, produced some 465,000 barrels of crude oil in 1898. By 1923 this had increased to 6.4 million barrels. In Asia, Burma's petroleum industry was second only to that of the Netherlands East Indies. Tin and tungsten mines were developed in Tenasserim Division, the latter becoming an important mineral export during World War I. When automobiles appeared in the early twentieth century, a system of paved roads was built.

"A Factory Without Chimneys"—The Development of the Lower Burma Delta

Before Alaungpaya unified Burma in the 1750s, the Irrawaddy River delta region of Lower Burma was inhabited primarily by Mons. During the first century of Konbaung rule, however,

Burmans migrated into the region from the drier heartlands, and the indigenous population was "Burmanized" by being obliged to adopt the Burman language and customs. Karens also moved into the delta from the headwater region of the Salween and Sittang rivers. Yet by the mid-nineteenth century, the river delta was still a thinly populated region compared with Upper Burma.

Burman migrants to Lower Burma had traditionally been subsistence farmers, but the British conquest of Lower Burma opened up new markets and incentives for surplus production. This spurred the transformation of the region into what British administrator Furnivall has called "a factory without chimneys"—a highly efficient system for the growing, milling, and distribution of rice to overseas markets in India, China, and Europe by the turn of the century. The British offered inducements to new settlers from Upper Burma, such as 12-year tax exemptions and low-cost, or free, river transportation. The king attempted to stem the flow by prohibiting cultivators from taking their families with them, but this restriction was easily evaded. Like the American and European settlers who were opening up the Great Plains of the United States and Canada at roughly the same time, the Burman settlers encountered considerable hardship, though of a different kind. The land with the greatest potential for rice paddy was covered with dense jungle or thick grass, which had to be cleared by hand. Poisonous snakes were always underfoot, and stockades had to be built to keep out tigers and other dangerous animals. Worst of all, fever, especially in newly cleared land where mosquitoes swarmed, was a cause of high mortality.

The enterprise of individual Burman settler families and the creation of a modern transportation network in the last decades of the nineteenth century produced a remarkable revolution in "industrial agriculture." According to Furnivall, the land under cultivation grew by 145,300 hectares between 1861 and 1870; between 1890 and 1900, however, rice land increased by 943,900 hectares. In the early 1870s the annual average of rice exported was 732,000 tons. This increased to 2.5 million tons by 1900 and 3.6 million tons by 1920.

The opening of the delta "rice frontier" involved a land rush in which laborers from Upper Burma or elsewhere would save their wages over a period of a few years, buy cattle and tools, and stake a claim to some open land. The first years of settlement, however, did not bring in a crop, so the settlers required investment capital. This was provided at first by the older and more estab- lished settlers who supported their relatives' settlement or who started up moneylending operations; but it came increasingly from Indian moneylenders, members of the Chettiar subcaste. The Chettiars, based in Madras in southern India, had a long history of commerce with the countries of Southeast Asia but had become particularly active with British colonial expansion into the region.

Though based in port cities, such as Rangoon and Bassein, they would send agents into the countryside to arrange loans with Burman cultivators.

The Tensions of a Plural Society

The growth of commercial rice cultivation and industries based on the extraction of natural resources fostered the development of a plural society. There was some Chinese immigration after 1852, but the great majority of immigrants during the late nineteenth and early twentieth centuries came from the overpopulated and famine-prone regions of Bengal and Madras in India. In Burma a great deal of labor was required during rice planting and harvesting seasons. Because the country could not supply sufficient labor, migration from India was encouraged. By the end of the nineteenth century, India supplied most of the workers for Lower Burma's rice mills and dockyards and in other modern industries. Most Indian migrants remained in the country for only a few years, long enough to acquire savings with which to establish themselves back home; yet natural catastrophes in Madras and Bengal would swell the volume of net migration. Furnivall notes that by 1918 some 300,000 laborers had come into Rangoon, making it second at that time only to New York as a port for immigration. The Indian population of Lower Burma increased from 297,000 in 1901 to 583,000 thirty years later, or from 7 to 10 percent of the total delta population.

Before the first decade of the twentieth century, however, the abundance of land, a shortage of labor, and good international markets for rice created a prosperity in which social tensions between Burmese and Indians were largely muted. The price per bushel of paddy rose steadily between 1875 and 1908. Burmese saw themselves as independent cultivators, possessing a relatively high standard of living. They shunned the low-paying migrant labor or mill jobs, which brought desperately poor Madrassis or Bengalis from the subcontinent. Chettiar control of capital was not seen as oppressive as long as the market for rice was good and loans could be easily repaid.

Society in colonial Burma assumed a "three tiered" structure in which the British and other Westerners occupied the top managerial, administrative, and professional positions. On the second tier, Indians and, to a lesser extent, the Chinese operated retail shops, held skilled and unskilled jobs in the modern sector, and dominated the lower levels of the engineering and medical professions. Railroad workers, telegraphers, telephone operators, and mail carriers were almost all Indian. Furnivall relates how the latter, ignorant of Burmese script, had to get villagers to read and point out addresses. Indians held more than 50 percent of all government jobs in Lower Burma in 1931. Travelers to Rangoon and other large cities would have had difficulty distinguishing them from cities on the subcontinent. Rangoon's population in 1931 was 50 percent Indian, with lower percentages of Chinese, Indo-Burmese, Eurasians, and Europeans. Burmese comprised only 36 percent. English and Indian languages, rather than Burmese, were spoken in the streets and offices. On the lowest tier the Burmese were found in the villages—unwilling, or unable to enter the modern sectors of the economy on even the most menial level.

This arrangement might have remained relatively stable if it had not been for a change in economic conditions. The "rice frontier" was being filled up, marked by declines in the amount of new delta land being opened up after 1902. Population growth began to outstrip economic growth, and fluctuations in the price of rice after 1908 created new and unstable conditions. Burmese cultivators, dependent on the Chettiars for loans, faced foreclosure with increasing frequency. The Chettiars, though themselves not agriculturists, acquired from their former debtors land that they operated as absentee landlords. These farms were often operated by Indian tenants.

As Burmese farmers fell in status from owner to tenant and migrant laborer, the colonial government attempted with limited success to shore up their position by restricting landownership by absentee landlords, regulating mortgage terms and rents, and establishing the cooperative bank and local cooperative societies to provide credit on reasonable terms. By 1915 there were some 1,250 local cooperatives, and 10 years later they had increased in number to over 4,000. The system was plagued by poor management, however, and by the end of the 1920s was virtually bankrupt. Foreclosures continued. Whereas in 1901 only 17 percent of the cropland had been owned by absentee landlords in the delta region, by 1930 this figure had increased to 30 percent, and by 1940 it was 67 percent.

In the best years of the private enterprise system, when the "rice frontier" was being opened up and the moneylenders, Burmese or Indian, had not become too oppressive, the people enjoyed greater freedom and mobility and a higher standard of living than they ever had under their own kings. Yet the system, as well as the administrative reforms contained in the 1889 Burma Village Act and the disestablishment of the *sangha*, eventually undermined village coherence and community. Under the traditional system, common lands had been maintained for the benefit of all. These now tended to be taken over by private owners for their own use. Elaborate methods of cooperation involving the use and maintenance of irrigation systems or mutual aid during planting and harvest time broke down. According to Furnivall, village cultural life suffered a decline as villagers neglected to support festivals, religious ceremonies, and the traditionally popular puppet and *pwe* (theatrical) performances. The most marked symptom of social instability, however, was the sharp rise in banditry and violent crime. British officials admitted that before the establishment of their' rule, Burmese villages and districts had been relatively peaceful. As traditional social restrictions broke down, however, the Burmese gained a reputation for violent crime— resorting to their razor-sharp *dah* (knives) to settle even the most trivial dispute.

The Emergence of Political Movements

The fall of the Konbaung Dynasty in 1885 and the removal of national and local elites from positions of power created a political vacuum, perhaps best symbolized by the British removal of the king's throne from the "center of the universe"—the palace at Mandalay—to a museum in Calcutta. Nationalism was initially reactive. There was a great fear that Burma, tied administratively to India by the British, would be overwhelmed both demographically and culturally by the subcontinent and its huge population. These fears seemed to be confirmed by increased Indian immigration and the continued reliance of the British on Indian personnel in government and modern enterprise. The focal point of early concerns, however, was Buddhism. It was generally agreed that national identity was summed up in the proposition that "to be Burmese is to be Buddhist." The government's stated policy of religious neutrality and the spread of Christian mission schools offering a modern education were seen as direct threats, and a number of nonpolitical organizations were established in order to revitalize the faith. These included a reformed Buddhist school set up at Moulmein in 1897, the Buddhist Missionary Association founded in Mandalay the same year, and the Ashoka Society, established in 1902 at Bassein. In 1904 a Student Buddhist Association was started at Rangoon College; the Baptist Judson College and Rangoon College were the only institutions of higher education in Burma at the time. A Young Men's Buddhist Association (YMBA), modeled on the Young Men's Christian Association and similar to one set up in Ceylon in 1898, was established in Arakan in 1902 and in Rangoon in 1906. The YMBA maintained student hostels, emphasized lay observance of Buddhist precepts, and sponsored seminars and discussions, which quite often touched on politics. It attracted members of the still small Burmese professional class—lawyers, journalists, and government clerks. The YMBA soon had 50 branches in towns throughout the country. A national organization, the General Council of Buddhist Associations, was set up and held annual meetings.

The "shoe question," which had bedeviled relations between Burmese kings and the British before annexation, resurfaced in a new form to spark a national controversy. Contrary to custom, British visitors to temples and pagodas did not remove their shoes. In 1916 a meeting of YMBA branches in Rangoon called for the government legally to sanction a ban on footwear in pagodas that would apply to Burmese and Europeans alike. This the government refused to do. The Ledi Sayadaw, a highly respected monk, wrote a book in the Burmese language, *On the Impropriety of Wearing Shoes on Pagoda Platforms*, which gained widespread support for the YMBA's cause. The issue came to a head in October 1919 when a group of Europeans wearing shoes was attacked by monks at a pagoda in Mandalay. Although four of the monks were arrested and punished, including one sentenced to life imprisonment, the government felt forced to compromise. It gave the custodians of pagodas the right to exclude persons wearing shoes from their premises. Exceptions, however, were made in the case of soldiers and police engaged in the maintenance of public order. This point continued to rankle Buddhists.

Two issues stirred nationalist movements in the period between 1918 and 1923. The first was the proposal to grant a very limited system of self-government, known as dyarchy, to British India. Legislative councils, including both elected and appointed members, would be given governmental responsibilities, though the most important powers would be retained by the London-appointed viceroy. In December 1917 a group of YMBA representatives had visited E.S. Montagu, the secretary of state for India who had formulated the plan, expressing the opinion that Burma should be separated from India. This, and the general impression that Burma was "the most placid province in India," led Montagu to recommend that political reforms such as dyarchy be postponed there indefinitely.

Despite continued hesitation about remaining a part of British India and wide criticism of the limited nature of dyarchy, the initial Burmese reaction to the recommendation, expressed through the medium of the YMBA, was to insist that Burma be included in the reforms. A delegation was sent to London to secure this end. Yet Indian independence leader Mahatma Gandhi's opposition to dyarchy, sparked by the Amritsar Massacre of April 17, 1919, in which unarmed demonstrators in that Indian city were killed by British soldiers, aroused considerable sympathy in Burma. The dyarchy system was implemented in Burma in 1923, and the nationalists subsequently organized an antidyarcy boycott that gained wide popular support. Thus, in the election for the Burma Legislative Council in 1922, only 7 percent of the eligible voters participated, though this did increase to 16 percent in the 1925 election and 18 percent in the 1928 election.

The General Council of Burmese Associations (GCBA) was organized in 1919–20 by YMBA members and other nationalists; it replaced the General Council of Buddhist Associations, drawing from a wider constituency that included Hindus, Muslims, and Christians. A faction of the new organization, identifying itself with the aims of Gandhi's Indian National Congress, led the

Nineteenth-century British engineers laid out downtown Rangoon's streets in a grid pattern, designating the Sule Pagoda as its focal point.

boycott óf the dyarchy reform and was the most important political group during the 1920s. It gained a following in the villages through its local-level *wunthanu athin* ("own race societies"; also translated as "national interest defender organizations").

The second nationalist issue involved education. Because there was a shortage of trained administrative personnel in Burma, the government decided to establish an independent, degree-granting Rangoon University; previously Rangoon College and the Baptist Judson College had prepared students to take degrees from the University of Calcutta. The new university was organized on the model of Oxford or Cambridge—a residential institution having a relatively small enrollment, high academic requirements, and a curriculum emphasizing the arts and humanities. The elitist nature of the new institution aroused the opposition of college students who organized a strike on December 4, 1920. They set up strike headquarters at the Shwedagon Pagoda, working closely with Buddhist monks and gaining widespread public support. Their ranks were soon swelled by high school students from the Rangoon area. They demanded that the university be made more open and called for the establishment of "national schools" that would teach Burmese history, literature, art, and technical subjects. A number of national schools were established between 1920 and 1922, largely in Buddhist monasteries, but most were soon disbanded owing to inexperienced management and lack of resources. Although the student strike, which lasted about a year, did not obtain its major objectives, it brought the students into the center of the political arena.

"Political" monks were another important force that appeared around this time. U Ottama, the most articulate of these, had lived in Japan and India and was familiar with Gandhi's methods of nonviolent civil disobedience. In 1921 he began preaching sermons in which he claimed that *nibbana* (nirvana—freedom from the endless cycle of rebirth) could not be obtained until the people were liberated from earthly slavery. Under foreign rule, which had allegedly corrupted people's minds, spiritual development was not possible. Although there was nothing in Buddhist doctrine to support a specifically nationalist ideology, or for that matter any form of political activity, memories of the traditional ties of king and *sangha* prompted monks to take the lead in opposing British rule.

The General Council of Sangha Associations (GCSA) was established in 1922 to coordinate the activities of "political" monks. This new "worldly" orientation surprised many observers, including some Buddhists. In fact, monks were almost ideally suited for political action. They were still highly respected by the general population, lacked the family ties that would counsel caution and moderation in other men, and lived in large monastic communities that could be easily mobilized. Monks were arrested for instigating violence and making seditious speeches. This put the British in the delicate position of having to imprison monks, their treatment becoming still another passionate issue. U Ottama spent much of the 1920s and 1930s behind bars, and a second political monk, U Wisara, became a national martyr in 1929, when he died in jail during a hunger strike undertaken to force the authorities to allow him to wear his Buddhist vestments.

Social Unrest and the Appearance of New Political Forces

The worsening economic position of the villagers was reflected in declining prices for paddy and an increased rate of foreclosure, particularly with the onset of the world economic depression in 1930. Hard times led to escalating communal tensions as Burmese cultivators found themselves at the mercy of Chettiar moneylenders and as laborers in the port cities competed with Indian immigrants for scarce jobs. In May 1930 there was a riot in Rangoon involving Burmese and Indian dockworkers. Violence against Indians and Chinese continued throughout the decade. In July 1938 renegade Buddhist monks led Burmese mobs through Rangoon in a rampage of violence in which about 200 Indians were killed. Colonial society, held together in good times by the incentive of mutual profit, was experiencing great strains.

A second wave of unrest had traditional roots. Since the annexation of Upper Burma there had been sporadic uprisings in the rural areas involving a savior-king, or Setkya Min, who promised to liberate the people from the British. The most widespread of these movements, however, appeared in 1930. In October of that year Saya San, a native physician and former member of the radical wing of the GCBA, proclaimed himself king, setting up a palace with royal insignia in Tharrawaddy District north of Rangoon. His agents contacted the *wunthanu athin* in both Upper and Lower Burma. By December revolt had broken out. Although Saya San had been a monk, his movement differed from that of U Ottama in that it drew on magical and animist symbols as well as on those of Buddhism. The peasant rebels, armed with swords and spears against superior British forces, were subdued by 1932, Saya San himself having been captured in the Shan states in August 1931. The revolt posed no real threat to British rule, but some 8,000 soldiers had been needed to suppress it.

During the 1930s nationalists were divided over whether Burma should continue to remain part of India. Those against separation argued that a separate Burma would not be able to take advantage of further political reforms evolving in India unless it were accorded self-governing dominion status, which the British were not prepared to grant. The British Parliament, however, voted for separation and approved a new constitution for Burma in 1935 over the strenuous opposition of many nationalists. Under the new system a British governor of Burma still retained extensive powers; a nine-member cabinet, appointed by the governor in consultation with an elected House of Representatives, had broader responsibilities than under the dyarchy arrangement. The majority party in the legislature would choose a prime minister. Elections were held in 1936, and when the new constitution was implemented in 1937, Dr. Ba Maw, leader of the Sinyetha (Poor Man's) Party, was chosen prime minister by a coalition of parties.

The Thakin Movement

The Dobama Asiayone (We Burmans Association) had emerged in 1930–31 during the Saya San Rebellion, in part as an urban response to that village phenomenon. Its members drew attention to themselves by calling each other *thakin*, or master. This was taboo in polite colonial society, because the word was customarily used by Burmese as a respectful term of address to the British, like the term *sahib* in India. The founders of the society claimed that the Burmese must develop a "master mentality" and reject the "slave mentality" that the British had imposed. Their appropriation of the term *thakin* was seen as a first step in this direction, and they were soon known to the general public as Thakins.

The Thakins gained national prominence through the medium of Rangoon University. After the student strike of 1920–21 the institution had become quiescent. Students, obliged to study subjects in an alien language, English, and preoccupied with passing examinations and gaining good positions after graduation, had little interest in politics. Discontent over the competitive examination system and the hardships of the depression, which affected even university graduates, began to change these attitudes. In the autumn of 1935 Maung Nu was elected president of the Rangoon University Student Union (RUSU) and Aung San the secretary. Both men, who were later to play the central roles in Burma's struggle for independence, were politically conscious and used the RUSU as a forum for the discussion of national issues. Maung Nu, who as a member of the Dobama Asiayone assumed the name Thakin Nu, got into trouble for publishing an article in the union's newspaper calling for the dismissal of a Burmese member of the faculty for alleged moral improprieties. Thakin Nu was expelled along with Thakin Aung San, the editor. Although this was purely a university issue, it provoked a student strike in February 1936, which quickly focused on a wider political context. As in 1920, strike headquarters were established at the Shwedagon Pagoda. Demonstrations closed down the campus, forcing the authorities to postpone examinations. The RUSU gained the support of Rangoon-area high school students through the All-Burma Student Union. Thakin Nu and Thakin Aung San were readmitted to the university but by this time had committed themselves to full-time political careers.

The Thakins succeeded in having two of their members elected to the legislature in the 1936 election. They attempted to organize dockworkers and oil field workers, leading a march of striking oil refinery workers from Syriam to Rangoon in 1938. When, in connection with this, a student was killed by police during a demonstration, a second university strike was called. Tensions escalated still further when, in February 1939, some 17 students and monks were killed during a large protest in Mandalay. In the eyes of the public, the Thakins were pushing parliamentary political leaders, such as Ba Maw and U Saw, and the more traditionally oriented nationalists out of the center of the political stage.

The Thakins had no single, consistent political ideology. They were greatly influenced by socialist thought, particularly welfare state "Fabian" socialism of the variety introduced to them by Furnivall. After the first university strike, Thakin Nu established the Nagani (Red Dragon) Book Club in 1937 in order to publish and distribute socialist and Marxist literature. Other influences included Sun Zhongshan (Sun Yat-sen), the Indian National Congress, European and Japanese fascism, and the Irish Sinn Fein movement. Overall, their thought was highly syncretic.

The Thakins were among the first to bring the demand for complete independence, expressed by the rural followers of Saya San, into the urban and university context. Politicians like Ba Maw, though not enamored of the British, had some stake in the political system established by the 1937 constitution. The students, however, operated largely outside the established political process. Unlike the political monks, who entered politics in order to defend the religion, the Thakins were primarily secular and noncommunal in their orientation. This was particularly true of Aung San, who defined independence in terms of Burmese rather than Burman nationalism (see The Nationalities Issue, this ch.). The Thakins retained close relations with the Indian National Congress and attempted to defuse communal tensions after the anti-Indian riot of 1938.

They did not, however, abandon tradition. One of the founders and guiding lights of the Dobama Asiayone had been Thakin Kodaw Hmaing, a former Buddhist monk and writer who at the age of 10 had witnessed the exile of the king and queen from Mandalay. Described by one scholar as "a living historical link between the Burmese revolution and the cultural traditions of the pre-British Burmese kingdom," he combined Western democratic and socialist thought with Buddhist themes. He wrote that in the earliest times there had been an "earthly nirvana," or paradise, but that men became greedy and acquisitive and were no longer capable of governing themselves; so they elected a "future Buddha" to be their sovereign. Thakin Nu argued that capitalism, engendering greed, precluded the attainment of salvation. In a socialist society the promotion of the people's welfare was not only a meritorious act for the ruler but it also enabled the masses to turn from material concerns to the attainment of their own spiritual enlightenment. Even the left wing of the Thakin movement, led by Thakin Soe and Thakin Than Tun, drew on Buddhist concepts and Pali terminology to introduce Marxist ideas to the Burmese. Although there were direct links with the ideas of U Ottama and the "political" monks, socialist concepts and a commitment to independence gave them the basis for a more positive program.

In February 1939 Ba Maw was replaced as prime minister by Tharrawaddy U Pu. In September of that year, as war broke out in Europe, Ba Maw's Sinyetha Party joined forces with the Burma Revolutionary Party, a Thakin group formed by Kodaw Hmaing and Aung San, to form the Freedom Bloc, a coalition committed to full independence. In September 1940 U Pu's government was replaced by one formed by U Saw, head of the Myochit (Patriot) Party. Described by historian Frank Trager as a "strange, self-educated, uncouth leader, who had won a following among the peasant masses," U Saw attempted to suppress Freedom Bloc activity and persuade the British to grant Burma full self-governing or dominion status.

War and the Struggle for Independence

The Allied proclamation of the Atlantic Charter in August 1941, which guaranteed "the right of all peoples to choose the form of government under which they live," raised the hopes of nationalists; they were disappointed the following month, however, when Prime Minister Winston Churchill stated in Parliament that this did not apply to Burma, which had its own program of political evolution. U Saw went to London to argue for dominion status, but on the way back to Rangoon he was arrested for attempting to make contact with the Japanese and was exiled to Uganda until the end of World War II.

The Japanese military became interested in Burma not only because of its strategic resources, particularly oil, but also because the Burma Road provided a route through which the Allies could supply the Chiang Kai-shek government in Chongqing. Its severance would speed a successful conclusion of the war with China. In 1939 Japanese agents contacted Ba Maw who, the following year, discussed the possibility of getting Japanese support for independence with his Freedom Block ally, Aung San. In August 1940 Thakin Aung San and a fellow Thakin were smuggled out of Burma on a ship bound for Amoy. Subsequently, they went to Tokyo to lay the groundwork for armed struggle against the British in concert with Japanese advances into Southeast Asia.

An intelligence organization, the Minami Kikan, was established by the Japanese military under an army colonel, Suzuki Keiji, to coordinate operations in Burma. Aung San returned to

Burma, contacted the Thakins, and arranged to smuggle 28 men out of Burma. These men, together with Thakin Aung San and his original companion, comprised the Thirty Comrades, who received military training from the Japanese on Hainan Island off the south coast of China. They formed the core of the Burma Independence Army (BIA), which was established in Bangkok in late December 1941. Commanded by Colonel Suzuki, the BIA consisted of the Thirty Comrades, some 200 Burmese resident in Thailand, and Japanese members of the Minami Kikan. Underground movements were organized within Burma. When Japanese forces began the invasion of the Tenasserium area along the Andaman Sea and other parts of Lower Burma in January 1942, the BIA aided their advance and occasionally engaged retreating British forced in combat. One of the Thirty Comrades, Thakin Shu Maung, infiltrated Rangoon in early February and organized sabotage activities. He would become better known by his nom de guerre, Ne Win, "Brilliant like the Sun." Rangoon fell in March 1942, British troops evacuated Mandalay, and the Burma Road was cut off in May.

A number of historians have suggested that had the Churchill government been more flexible on the issues of self-government, Burmese nationalists might have fought on the Allied side. Ba Maw relates in his memoirs, *Breakthrough in Burma*, his bitterness in perceiving that the principles of the Atlantic Charter applied to "white" nations like Poland but not to nonwhite colonial peoples. Japanese propaganda appeals for a common Asian struggle against "white imperialism" struck a responsive chord in many Burmese, despite the harsh realities of Japanese policies in China. The issue for the Thakins and other nationalists, however, was not a choice between Britain and Japan but which course of action would lead most quickly and surely to full independence.

The Japanese Occupation

When most of Burma was in Japanese hands, Ba Maw was made prime minister in August 1942 and Aung San commander of the 4,000-man Burma Defense Army, which succeeded the BIA. In January 1943 Japanese Prime Minister Tōjō Hideki announced that independence would be granted by the end of the year. In August Ba Maw was proclaimed head of state in a ceremony at Rangoon that recalled the traditions of Burmese kingship. General Aung San was designated minister of defense and commander of the new Burma National Army (BNA), and Thakin Nu, minister of foreign affairs.

Ba Maw's government had very little actual power. Nominally independent, Burma was seen by Tokyo primarily as an economic and strategic component of its all-out war effort. Aung San had been made fully aware of this when he visited Tokyo in March 1943; Colonel Suzuki, who apparently had a sincere commitment to Burmese independence, told him he had been disgraced for being too friendly to the Burmese. Japanese military authorities treated the Burmese people harshly, putting thousands in forced labor battalions. The Kempeitai, or military police, was universally dreaded. Although only a puppet leader, Ba Maw haughtily refused to cooperate fully with Japanese officers, and his assassination by the latter was apparently contemplated. He disliked the Thakins, especially Aung San, but did not betray them when they began to plan resistance against the Japanese.

Karen officers in the BNA who had connections with British officers still in Burma served as intermediaries between the Thakins and the British Special Operations Executive Force 136 in late 1943. Thakin Than Tun, who became a communist during the war, already had established contact with the Allies and the "inner circle" of Thakins in Ba Maw's government, which included Aung San. Resistance plans firmed up as secret meetings were held in August and September 1944 between BNA officers, socialists and communists, and Thakin Nu. The Anti-Fascist Organization, later to become the Anti-Fascist People's Freedom League (AFPFL), was set up. Aung San played the central role of coordinating diverse groups, such as the Karen National Organization, the Japanese-sponsored East Asia Youth League, former associates from Dobama Asiayone days, and the leftists.

Lord Louis Mountbatten, head of the South-East Asia Command, agreed to cooperate with Aung San. The 1944 Japanese offensive into India through Manipur had failed, and by the end of January 1945 Allied troops had reopened the Burma Road and captured Myitkyina. On March 27 Aung San, receiving a signal from Mountbatten, led a revolt of the BNA, which began attacking Japanese units. Rangoon was captured in early May, though fighting continued in various parts of the country up to and even after the Japanese surrender on August 15, 1945.

Steps Toward Independence

Because the cooperation of the BNA was needed for the recovery of Burma from the Japanese, Mountbatten was inclined to forgive and forget the events of 1942. At the end of May 1945 the BNA was officially recognized as a component of Allied forces and renamed the Patriotic Burmese Forces (PBF). At victory celebrations held in Rangoon in June, the "resistance flag" of the Anti-Fascist Organization—a white star on a red field—flew alongside the Union Jack. Mountbatten and British commanders in the field had come to respect General Aung San's commitment to independence and regarded him as the principle representative of Burmese national aspirations.

In London and in India, where the British government of Burma had been in exile during the war, attitudes were quite different. Aung San was still regarded as a turncoat who would

Below pagoda-studded Mandalay Hill, King Mindon erected his fabled nineteenth-century royal palace, fulfilling the long-held prophecy that on this site one day would rise a great center of Buddhist enlightenment. To the left of the moat is a section of the palace wall.
Courtesy Caroline M. Hufford

have no role to play in future developments. There were also divergent perceptions of what Burma's postwar political status should be. On May 17, 1945, the Churchill government issued a white paper enunciating a very conservative program: the 1937 constitution, with its elective prime minister, would be suspended; the governor, appointed by London, would retain all authority. Although what the British called "Burma Proper," where the population was predominantly Burman, would be given "full self-government within the Commonwealth" after 1948, the Shan states and the other border regions inhabited by non-Burman minorities would remain under British rule indefinitely. The white paper envisioned several years of economic reconstruction for war-ravaged Burma, and the prewar colonial firms were to play an important role in this. The white paper revealed little appreciation of the Burmese point of view. It granted less than the Japanese had, even though Ba Maw had been only a puppet leader; perhaps the most unpopular proposal was the idea that Chettiar moneylenders be allowed to retain their titles to land. During the Japanese conquest many thousands of Indians had left

41

with retreating British forces, including most Chettiars. The Japanese gained much peasant support by allowing the farmers to reoccupy their foreclosed lands.

Aung San initiated a campaign against the white paper at a mass meeting in Rangoon on August 19, 1945, demanding that independence be granted immediately. The AFPFL, a united front, was established to replace the Anti-Fascist Organization. The AFPFL's broad base of support, including the socialist and communist parties, and its control over a large armed force assured it a dominant position. General Aung San had resisted the demobilization of the PBF. Some 4,700 men were absorbed into the regular armed forces by December 1945, but another 3,500 refused to hand in their arms and comprised the new People's Volunteer Organization (PVO), which became in effect the private army of the AFPFL. The PVO established contingents all over the country, increasing to as many as 14,000 men.

The British governor who had headed the prewar colonial government, Reginald Dorman-Smith, sought to offset the influence of the AFPFL by supporting U Saw, who had returned from exile in East Africa; the governor also excluded members of the AFPFL from his executive council, which functioned as a cabinet, though he included U Saw and the conservative Sir Paw Tun. Conditions became chaotic as components of the AFPFL, led by the communist Thakin Than Tun, organized mass demonstrations and guerrilla operations in order to pull down the Dorman-Smith government. A general strike broke out in September 1946 involving government workers, police, laborers, and university and high school students. Because the country was dangerously close to rebellion and there were few troops at his disposal, Dorman-Smith's successor as governor, Hubert Rance, was obliged to come to terms with Aung San. A new executive council was formed; Aung San served as deputy chairman, and six of its 11 members were adherents of the AFPFL. The general strike came to an end on October 2, 1946.

In July 1946 Thakin Soe, leader of the Burmese Communist Party (BCP), broke with the AFPFL and with other communists formed an underground movement known as the Red Flag faction of the BCP. Hard on the heels of Rance's decision to include Aung San in the government, the communists remaining in the AFPFL under the leadership of Thakin Than Tun labeled Aung San a collaborationist. Aung San in turn expelled Than Tun and the latter's communist White Flag faction from the AFPFL. The White Flag faction thereafter adopted a policy whereby it opposed the government by all means short of armed struggle. Immediately after independence, however, the White Flag communists also took up armed struggle against the government; its large contingent of armed men and countrywide organization dated from the Japanese occupation, and the group proved a formidable foe of the independent Burmese government.

The British government in London, under Labor Prime Minister Clement Attlee since July 1945, was apparently encouraged by Aung San's break with the communists, believing that it could negotiate with him. In December 1946 the prime minister invited him and other political leaders to come to London. On January 27, 1947, Attlee and Aung San signed an agreement calling for full independence within a year, elections for a constituent assembly within four months, continued British aid, British sponsorship of Burma to membership in international organizations and, most significantly, the promise that the border areas would be included within the boundaries of the new nation.

The Nationalities Issue

During the Konbaung period, the Shans, Chins, Kachins, Kayahs, and other peoples had been linked to the royal court in a tributary relationship that did nothing to limit the local authority of their rulers. The British policy, developed first in India, was to interfere as little as possible in the internal affairs of the minority groups and to separate their administration from that of Burma Proper. Thus when the dyarchy system was introduced in 1923, the Burma Frontier Service was created with its own corps of civil servants. In the 1937 constitution "Ministerial Burma" (Burma Proper, which was included in expanded self-government) and the peripheral border areas were further segregated. The border areas themselves were divided into "Part I" areas, also known as Excluded Areas, which were under the direct control of the governor, and "Part II" areas, which were under the jurisdiction of the legislature. The governor could veto any bills passed in reference to these areas. Some Part I areas could elect representatives to the legislature. The rationale behind the separation of Burma Proper and the border areas was that the border peoples needed a period of political tutelage; the effect of the policy, however, was to exacerbate divisions in the country that would persist long after independence.

The situation of the Karens was somewhat different from that of the other minorities. They were tribal peoples who had migrated from southern China around the sixth or seventh century A.D. Karen nationality was in part developed through Christian missionary activity, for proselytization encouraged a feeling of common ethnic identity contrasting with that of Buddhist Burmans or Mons. Memories of harsh treatment under the Burmese kings led Karen leaders to form the National Karen Association in 1881, which promoted Karen unity and supported the establishment of British colonial rule. The Karen role in the British armed forces in Burma also prompted them to identify their interests with those of the British. Karens were treated harshly by the BIA during the

Japanese takeover; a large number of them were executed as British sympathizers. After World War II a number of Karen leaders agitated for the establishment of a Karen state within the Commonwealth of Nations but separate from Burma.

During and after the war Aung San had been diligent in forging links with minority leaders, including those of the Karens. The AFPFL included minority groups, but most remained unconvinced of the advantages of becoming part of an independent Burma rather than retaining a British-sponsored separate identity. In January 1946 Aung San went to Myitkyina to gain the support of Kachin chiefs. In March the first Panglong Conference was held, attended by 34 Shan *sawbwas* and representatives of the Karens, Kachins, and Chins. Thakin Nu represented the AFPFL, but his statements that it was the British who had fostered ethnic divisions through their separation of Burma Proper and the border areas met with general suspicion. Because the British at the time seemed determined to implement the white paper provision concerning separate minority areas, the AFPFL reasserted its claim that the Burmans and minority peoples should together form a single state. Aung San enunciated his own liberal concept of nationhood, which contrasted with the older, Burman-centered notions of other nationalists. The basis of nationalism, he argued, was not race or culture but a feeling of "oneness" that develops as different peoples share hardship and prosperity in common. A nation is a "conglomeration of races and religions [that] should develop a nationalism that is common with the welfare of one and all, irrespective of race, religion, or class or sex."

The British favored integration of the border areas with Burma Proper following the January 27, 1947, agreement, and a second conference was held at Panglong between February 7 and 12, 1947. It was agreed that Kachin State would be established in the north of the country, that the autonomy of the Shan *sawbwas* would be recognized within the separate Shan State, and that the Chins would also join independent Burma if promised material assistance. The Panglong agreement settled, for the time at least, the question of the border areas. The question of the Karens, however, remained unresolved, because the AFPFL rejected the proposal of the Karen National Union that a separate Karen state be established in the Thaton coastal region, where Karens were a minority. The union retaliated by boycotting the Constituent Assembly elections scheduled for April. The question of whether the Kayah would join independent Burma was still left open.

In April elections were held for the Constituent Assembly. There were a total of 255 seats, Burma Proper being allotted 210, of which 24 were reserved for the Karens and four for Anglo-Burmans, and the border areas were allotted 45. The AFPFL won an overwhelming victory, returning some 248 representatives, most of whom were socialists or members of the PVO. The assembly met on June 9, and Thakin Nu was selected as its president.

Aung San's Assassination

On the morning of July 19, 1947, gunmen entered the Secretariat building in central Rangoon and murdered Aung San and seven of his ministers. U Saw, left out of the political process after the January 1947 Attlee-Aung San agreement, had plotted the assassination, apparently nurturing the desperate hope that with Aung San out of the way, the British governor would turn to him to lead the country. He may also have been plotting a takeover by force. The crime was poorly planned, however; the gunmen were traced to his house by police, and he and his accomplices were immediately arrested.

The violent death of Aung San, at age 32 the architect of Burma's independence, stunned the nation. All that had been carefully constructed now seemed on the verge of collapse. Governor Rance, however, showed no inclination to use the assassination as a pretext to delay the independence process; he immediately appointed Thakin Nu, president of the Constituent Assembly and vice president of the AFPFL, prime minister. At a special tribunal held in October–December 1947, U Saw and his accomplices were convicted; they were executed in May 1948.

On September 24, 1947, the Constituent Assembly approved the constitution of the independent Union of Burma. It provided for a parliamentary system of government and a bicameral legislature. The upper house, the Chamber of Nationalities, had strong minority representation (72 out of 125 members were non-Burman); the lower house, the Chamber of Deputies, was elected from geographical constituencies defined by population. It nominated the prime minister, who was responsible to it. The president of the Union of Burma had only formal powers as head of state.

In accordance with the Panglong Agreement, Shan State and Kachin State were created. When a Karenni delegation was seated in the Constituent assembly in September, Karenni State was also established. (It would become Kayah State in 1948.) The autonomy of local Karenni and Shan rulers was guaranteed, though their regions would be under the supervision of union residents; Shan and Karenni states were given the right to secede from the union after a period of 10 years. The Chins of the western frontier were not granted a state, but Chin Special Division was established. Although a Karen state was not set up, a referendum on this issue was promised and the Karen Affairs Council created "to aid and advise the Union Government on matters relating to the Karens."

Although a critical Ba Maw said that the constitution created not one but "many nations, kept balanced and apart," one of its authors pointed out that the constitution, "though in theory federal, is in practice unitary." State legislatures were not separately elected but were composed of members of the union legislature from their respective states. Governors of the states were chosen by the union prime minister in consultation with the state legislatures and served as ministers in the union cabinet. The Supreme Court had jurisdiction over disputes between the union and state governments and between the states. The states could, however, pass laws as long as they did not conflict with union law. Burma Proper was ruled directly by the union government.

The 1947 constitution expressed a commitment to social justice and the establishment of a welfare state. The rights of people to employment, education, support in old age, and health were asserted. Although the right of private property was recognized, large absentee landholdings, such as had been maintained by the Chettiars before 1942, were prohibited. The state had the right, as the ultimate owner of the land, to redistribute land. The state was secular, and freedom of religion was guaranteed. Other fundamental civil rights included freedom of speech and assembly and equality before the law. Equality of the sexes was guaranteed.

On October 17, 1947, prime ministers U Nu and Clement Attlee signed a treaty formally recognizing the independence of the Union of Burma. The British agreed to cancel a £15 million debt and provide a military mission. The Burmese government claimed the right to expropriate British properties, though with adequate compensation for the firms involved. On December 10, 1947, the British Parliament over the strenuous opposition of Churchill's Conservative Party passed the Burma Independence Act. January 4, 1948, was set as the date for the transfer of power. That independence was achieved with a minimum of violence was a tribute to the moderation of AFPFL and British leaders. This contrasted sharply with the stubborn policies of the Dutch in Indonesia and the French in Indochina, where their futile attempts to block independence resulted in much bloodshed and hardship.

Parliamentary Government, 1948–62

Regarding the first two years of independence, Thakin Nu (known as U Nu after 1951) quotes, in his autobiography, the British proverb that "trouble never comes singly." The Red Flag communist faction under Thakin Soe was already underground, operating in the mountainous Arakan Yoma region; the Mujahadin— Muslim rebels—attempting to set up an independent Islamic state, were in northern Arakan near the border with East Pakistan (now Bangladesh). As the October 17 agreement between Britain and Burma was signed, the White Flag communist faction, led by Thakin Than Tun and H.N. Ghoshal, accused U Nu of settling for "sham independence." The communists organized strikes and demonstrations. In March 1948 a reconciliation of the government with the communists was attempted; when the attempt failed, Thakin Than Tun left Rangoon for Pyinmana and raised the standard of revolt. The White Flag insurrection spread through central Burma in the Sittang-Pegu Yoma region; at its height it involved as many as 25,000 rebels (see fig. 4).

In July 1948 the procommunist White Band faction of the PVO rebelled against the government, threatening the capital. The First Burma Rifles and part of the Third Burma Rifles also joined in the revolt, leaving the government dependent upon its Kachin and Chin troops, the loyalist Yellow Band PVO, and the Fourth Burma Rifles, commanded by General Ne Win.

A number of Karen leaders, embittered by what they perceived as British desertion of their people and uncertain of the future under Burmese rule, took advantage of the chaotic state of affairs to initiate their own armed resistance. In 1947 the Karen National Union had demanded that a Karen state be established with the right of secession and that its territory include large portions of Tenasserim, Pegu, and Irrawaddy divisions. An armed group, the Karen National Defense Organization (KNDO), was established. The government's failure to resolve the question of a Karen state and increasing communal violence between Burmans and Karens pushed the KNDO into insurrection in January 1949, and KNDO forces soon captured Insein, Bassein, Prome, and Toungoo. At the same time, Naw Seng, a Kachin commander involved in suppressing the communists in central Burma, joined forces with the Karens, capturing Mandalay on March 13, 1949.

The darkest days for the government occurred during February––April 1949, when insurrectionists controlled most of the countryside, and even parts of Rangoon were at times in rebel hands. Yet as the year wore on, the tide began to turn in favor of the government, in part the result of U Nu's determination. Mandalay was recovered from Naw Seng's forces on April 24. By autumn he had fled to China, to resurface in 1967 as leader of a reconstituted Burmese communist party. General Ne Win, commander in chief, organized thousands of "peace guerrillas" —civilian auxiliaries—to supplement the armed forces. The communists, Karens, and rebel PVO and army units were never able to coordinate their plans or objectives. By 1950 the KNDO was driven back into the trans-Salween area and parts of Tenasserim. The following year a constitutional amendment was passed creating the Karen state of Kawthule. Areas under communist control were significantly reduced, although the Red Flag faction maintained its base in the Arakan Yoma and the White Flag faction its base in the Pegu Yoma. The White Band PVO broke with the communists, and in July 1950 the entire PVO was disbanded. A government minister, speaking in 1951, however, admitted that less than half of the country was under effective

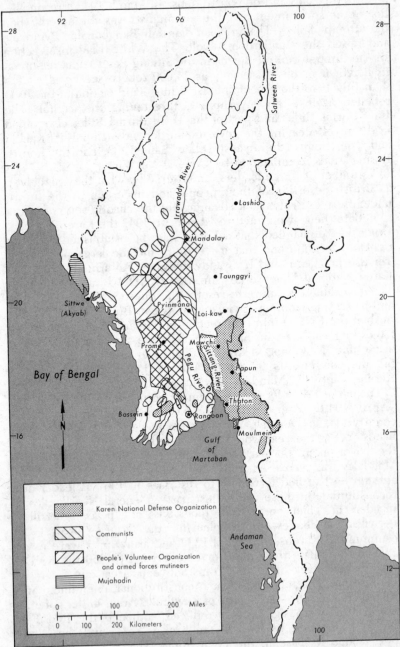

Source: Based on information from Hugh Tinker, *The Union of Burma*, London, 1961, 44.

Figure 4. Areas Dominated by Insurgents, February–May 1949

government control; in many areas its authority was limited to the daylight hours.

A new threat appeared in 1949 when the Chinese civil war spilled over onto Burmese territory. After Yunnan Province in southern China was taken over by the communist People's Liberation Army, Nationalist (Kuomintang) forces crossed the border into Burma and began using the border area as a base from which to attack the communist forces. Before long these troops in Burma, labeled the Chinese Irregular Forces (CIF), had entrenched themselves in Shan State, numbering as many as 12,000 in 1953, including Shan levies. They turned their attention from battling the communists to building up a profitable opium export business, extending their control over most of the Eastern portion of Shan State. Here, a system of warlordism flourished, which gradually extended into western Laos and northern Thailand, creating what would be known as the "Golden Triangle," a major world center for opium cultivation and export (see The Black Market and the Opium Trade, ch. 5). By 1953 some five-sixths of the Burma Army was tied down in fighting CIF groups; Chinese irregulars in southern Shan State even constructed a loose alliance with the KNDO. Although numerous offensives were launched against them during the 1950s, the CIF were never dislodged from their Shan State stronghold (see fig. 5).

AFPFL Politics and Issues

Between 1948 and 1958 Burma was a dominant-party state in which freedom of speech, press, and assembly, the principle of judicial independence, and the legal framework of parliamentary democracy were largely respected. Politics was dominated by the AFPFL, its popular support guaranteed through its historical role as the party of Aung San and the struggle for independence. It remained a coalition of diverse individuals and groups. Its members, who numbered 1.3 million at the third league congress in January 1958, included persons who belonged directly to the AFPFL, 488,000 at that time; the remainder were affiliated members, part of the league through their belonging to an AFPFL-affiliated group. These included a broad array of ethnic and vocational associations: the Burma Muslim Congress, the Karen National Congress, the Union Karen League, the Chin Congress, the United Hill People's Congress, the All-Burma Teachers' Organization, the All-Burma Women's Freedom League, the Youth League, the All-Burma Fire Brigade, and the All-Burma Federation of Trade Organizations. The Socialist Party and its affiliated organizations, the Trade Union Congress—Burma, and the All-Burma Peasants' Organization, were perhaps the most important component of the AFPFL, although the more Marxist-oriented socialists broke with it to form the Burma Workers' and Peasants' Party (BWPP; also known as the Red

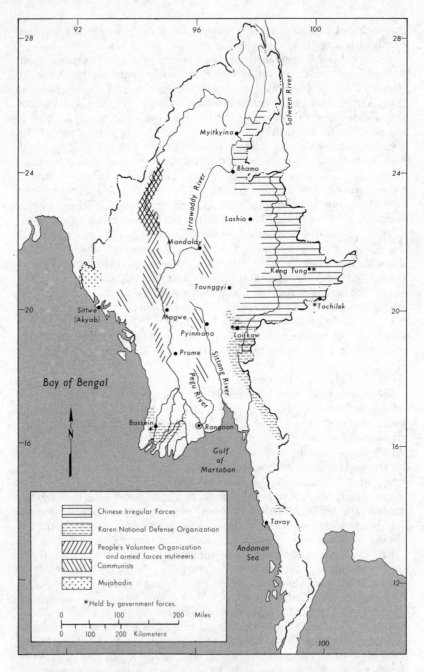

Source: Based on information from Hugh Tinker, *The Union of Burma*, London, 1961,
51.

Figure 5. *Areas Dominated by Insurgents and Chinese Irregular
Forces, 1953.*

Socialists). Socialist leaders U Ba Swe and Kyaw Nyein served in U Nu's cabinet, and the latter was the AFPFL secretary general.

The first national election for the Chamber of Deputies had to be postponed four times, owing to the insurgency. It was finally held in 1951–52 over a seven-month period as troops were moved around the country to guard the ballot boxes. The AFPFL won handily, gaining 200 of the 239 seats (counting candidates from affiliated groups); non-AFPFL opposition candidates came from the Marxist BWPP and the supporters of old politicians, such as Sir Paw Tun and Ba Maw.

Economic Policy

Land reform, nationalization, and socialist industrial planning formed the keystones of government economic policy. U Nu and other AFPFL leaders were committed to the goal of building a socialist welfare state. Nationalism, however, also provided a significant impetus. Nationalization was aimed at both Western-owned firms and enterprises owned by nonindigenous, particularly Indian, residents.

In line with the 1947 constitution's provisions naming the state as the ultimate owner of the land and prohibiting large, absentee estates, the Land Nationalization Act of October 1948 transferred absentee landholdings to the government, aiming to redistribute the land in parcels of up to 20 hectares to individual cultivators. The Ministry of Land Nationalization was created in 1952. Progress, however, was slow. By 1959 some 1.3 million hectares were acquired but only 587,000 hectares distributed to some 190,000 farmers. Forty-four percent of all farmers were still tenants in fiscal year (FY—see Glossary) 1961.

Nationalization proceeded in the industrial, transportation, and distributive sectors of the economy. In 1948 the Bombay-Burma Trading Corporation, the casus belli of 1885, lost its teak concessions and sawmills. The prewar oil companies were not nationalized but in 1954 were obliged to come into a joint venture with the government, which would hold a one-third interest. After 1955 there was some slowdown in nationalization, owing to the need to attract foreign investment into the country.

At the 1952 Pyidawtha (Welfare State) Conference in Rangoon, U Nu announced an ambitious eight-year program of development, drawn up with the assistance of United States and United Nations advisers. A target gross domestic product of K7 billion (for value of the kyat—see Glossary), the equivalent of US$1.5 billion, was set for 1959; K1 billion was to be invested in industry, mining, electrification, transportation, communications, and irrigation during the 1952–55 period. This could be accomplished, it was asserted, if the insurrections were quelled by 1954. The Pyidawtha program was to be financed through exports, principally rice. As long as international markets were good, it was even suggested that Pyidawtha might be funded without resort to foreign loans, and the public sector Agricultural Marketing Board took over rice export. The end of the Korean War in 1953, however, brought a collapse in international rice prices. Burmese rice, often of poor quality, remained rotting on the docks or in storage. In 1955 the eight-year Pyidawtha development plan was scrapped, and the more modest Five-Year Plan was proposed the following year. The government found itself increasingly dependent on foreign assistance, such as Japanese war reparations (the equivalent of some US$250 million), PL-480 grants (see Glossary) from the United States, and long-term loans from the World Bank (see Glossary), the United States, and other sources. The Soviet Union and other communist countries gave gifts and loans and agreed to buy Burmese surplus rice, despite its poor condition.

By 1960 many sectors of the economy had not returned to prewar levels. Rice production was only 93 percent of pre-World War II levels and exports only 64 percent. Petroleum and teak exports were even more severely depressed at 52 percent and 39 percent of prewar exports, respectively. Although agricultural exports other than rice were up 125 percent, Burma's position in the international economic system had deteriorated, even if the government could claim that the profits from exports were more equitably distributed. In the Four-Year Plan initiated in FY 1962, just before the military coup, many of the socialist orientations of earlier plans were dropped, emphasizing instead the development of the economy through encouragement of the private sector. This aroused the opposition of military officers committed to socialism, however, with serious consequences (see Military Rule under General Ne Win, this ch.).

Religion and National Unity

U Nu's personal commitment to Buddhism was a decisive influence in his career as prime minister. The connection of Buddhism to welfare state socialism, which had been developed by earlier Burmese thinkers, formed the basis for his rejection of Marxist socialism. In his words the doctrine of Karl Marx was "less than one-tenth of a particle of dust that lies at the feet of our great Lord Buddha." The identification of Buddhism and other religions with national development was stressed in a 1954 report on the Pyidawtha program: "The new Burma sees no conflict between the religious values and economic progress. Spiritual health and material well-being are not enemies; they are natural allies."

Like the pacific King Mindon, U Nu took seriously Buddhist prohibitions against doing harm. He was often accused of indecisiveness and an unwillingness to deal firmly, or ruthlessly, with his opponents. Buddhism formed an important element in his neutralist foreign policy, which evolved after 1949. U Nu also used the symbols of Buddhism and popular religion to strengthen his rule and foster national unity. As a Buddhist ruler, perhaps even a "Buddha-in-the-making" he participated in meritorious public acts, such as giving offerings to the *sangha*, building or restoring pagodas, venerating relics (including those brought from abroad), liberating animals, and cleansing and adorning Buddha images. He sponsored religious ceremonies, including those dedicated to the *nats*, Burma's national spirits, and took time off from his duties as prime minister to meditate at monasteries or holy places like Mount Popa.

U Nu took seriously the ruler's traditional role as promoter and defender of the faith. In 1954–56 he held the Sixth World Buddhist Council, commemorating the 2,500th anniversary of the Buddha's attainment of nirvana. Like King Mindon, sponsor of the fifth council, he called together thousands of monks and lay scholars to study and revise the Tripitaka: Mindon's revisions were compared with texts brought from Ceylon, Cambodia, Thailand, and the West. Government and AFPFL funds and labor were used to build the Kaba Aye (World Peace) Pagoda and the Maha Pasana Guha (Great Sacred Cave) in Rangoon, where the council was held.

Although U Nu drew on Buddhism both as a personal faith and as a basis for national unity, in contrast to Aung San's more secularist approach, he was careful to respect the rights of minority religions. In 1953 he refused to impose a ban that many Buddhists urged on the slaughtering of cattle by Muslims during a religious festival; this, he thought, was oppression of a minority by the majority, regardless of his personal feelings about the killing of animals. His suggestion that Christian and Islamic religious instruction be given along with Buddhism in state schools aroused the animosities of politically active monks in 1954. U Nu's reaction was to ban all religious instruction in government schools, a move that precipitated demonstrations by the *sangha* and laity throughout the country. He was forced to capitulate and allow only Buddhist instruction; one observer suggested that he was in a sense the victim of the very sentiments that, as a patron of Buddhism, he had fostered.

The most heated issue, however, was a proposed constitutional amendment making Buddhism the state religion. U Nu had committed himself to this as early as 1954 and strove to convince Christian, Muslim, and animist leaders that this would not lead to the oppression of their communities. There were violent confrontations, however, particularly between Buddhists and Muslims. On August 17, 1961, U Nu proposed the amendment in parliament, and it was passed and promulgated by August 26. Another amendment, however, was passed soon after; sponsored by U Nu, it guaranteed the minority religious communities the right to teach and propagate their faiths, a measure that provoked a violent reaction on the part of the political monks.

Neutralist Foreign Policy

Aung San had proposed in 1946 that Burma form part of a "United States of Indochina," including the other nations of mainland and insular Southeast Asia, for the purpose of mutual aid and security. Burma, he argued, could not stand alone in a dangerous international environment. U Nu's perception of the world was similar. Burma, he said on several occasions, was "hemmed in like a tender gourd among the cactuses." Unlike Aung San, he developed a policy of neutrality through which Burma would be, as far as was possible, on good terms with all countries and would avoid entangling alliances. U Nu distanced himself from Cold War confrontations, saying "we cannot allow ourselves to be absorbed into any power bloc." He attempted to serve as an intermediary between East and West, particularly the United States and China, with limited success. Intensely interested in foreign policy, he was, as a friend observed, "his own foreign minister" and became a prominent world figure in the 1950s.

As the communists attempted to seize power in the first two years of independence, U Nu's government—already tied to Britain through the October 17, 1947, treaty—was drawn closer to the West, from which it sought aid to combat insurrection. At this time the policy of neutrality was apparently not fully formulated. Strong and reliable allies were sought, but neither the Commonwealth nations nor the United States seemed interested in establishing mutual security arrangements, in part because U Nu's position seemed so precarious. In October 1949, the People's Republic of China was proclaimed. Burma was the first noncommunist nation to recognize the new Beijing government, on December 16, 1949, hoping in part to stem the perceived threat of Chinese aid to communists within Burma. The neutralist turn in Burmese foreign policy dates from this time.

Peaceful relations with China, historically Burma's greatest threat before the nineteenth century, was U Nu's greatest diplomatic triumph. The CIF question was a cause of great tensions, for the Chinese Nationalist irregulars continued to use bases within Burma to attack Yunnan across ill-defined borders. When it was discovered that United States money and arms were being piped to the CIF, U Nu canceled United States aid programs in protest in 1953 and took the issue to the United Nations. An airlift of some 6,000 CIF to Taiwan was carried out in May 1954.

A large number of irregulars remained behind, however, and continued to cause problems. In 1954 U Nu and Zhou Enlai, China's premier, met in Rangoon and agreed to mutual observance of the "five principles of peaceful coexistence." Yet the lack of a border agreement continued to be a vexing issue. The Chinese claimed large areas in Kachin and Shan states, and in 1956 Chinese troops entered these regions. In October 1956 U Nu went to Beijing to negotiate with Zhou. Chinese troops were withdrawn, and a temporary settlement of the border was reached by November. Final agreement on the Burma-China border, along with a treaty of friendship and nonaggression, was ratified on January 28, 1960. Although other issues, such as the domicile of Burmese communists in China, the entry of illegal Chinese immigrants into the country, and the status of overseas Chinese living in Burma, arose between China and Burma, they did not disrupt what were essentially friendly relations.

U Nu supported China's claim to Taiwan, urging the United States to pull its naval force out of the Taiwan Strait in order that the island be "peacefully liberated." He opposed the formation of the United States-sponsored Southeast Asia Treaty Organization (SEATO), claiming that it would increase the chance of war in the region. Yet Burma had supported the United Nations resolution against the Democratic People's Republic of Korea (North Korea) and its incursion into the Republic of Korea (South Korea) in 1950. Relations with the United States were not unfriendly, despite the CIF issue; in 1955, while visiting Washington, U Nu suggested that the United States and China begin talks, offering to serve as intermediary. He also became one of the founders and leaders of the nascent Nonaligned Movement and helped organize the first Afro-Asian Conference at Bandung, Indonesia, in April 1955.

1956 General Elections

The BWPP and the Justice Party allied to form the National United Front to oppose the AFPFL in the elections of 1956. Although the front won only 48 seats in the Chamber of Deputies (55 if its support in the states is counted) as against 173 seats for the AFPFL (including its support in the states), it received nearly 37 percent of the popular vote, with the AFPFL garnering 56 percent. Soon after the election U Nu stepped down from the prime ministership in order to devote his attention to revitalizing and reunifying the AFPFL. He had often threatened to retire permanently from politics, and three of his ministers, U Ba Swe, U Kyaw Nyein, and Thakin Tin, each took the opportunity offered by U Nu's temporary retirement to mobilize personal support for himself as eventual heir to U Nu's primacy.

When U Nu resumed the prime ministership in February 1957, the AFPFL was less unified than ever before. At the AFPFL national congress in January 1958, U Nu asserted that the league could no longer be simply a coalition or a united front but must be a unified political party with its own ideology, which he sought to formulate as socialist but non-Marxist. This was perceived by the socialists in the league as an attack on their independent and dominant position. A split in the AFPFL occurred in March. The "Clean" AFPFL was headed by U Nu and Thakin Tin, and the Socialist Party leaders, U Ba Swe and U Kyaw Nyein, led the

"Stable" AFPFL. The Stable AFPFL was the larger faction, owing to its socialist support; and when it moved into the opposition, U Nu had to win votes of parliamentary members from the National United Front and from minority communities in order to stay in office.

In addition to the competition between AFPFL factions for power within parliament, the growth of politico-military organizations that supported rival leaders and parties encouraged factionalism. For example, the Stable AFPFL had the backing of the Auxiliary Union Military Police, whereas Thakin Tin had the support of the so-called peace guerrillas of the All-Burma Peasants' Organization. In Rangoon a violent clash occurred between the newly established Union Labor Organization of the Clean AFPFL and U Ba Swe's Trade Union Congress, Burma. The split in the AFPFL also led to armed struggles between political rivals in the rural villages, each side seeking to gain control of the village defense forces that had been set up by the central government to help loyal villagers repel insurgents. The insurgent forces, which had been losing ground throughout the mid-1950s, seemed likely to benefit from renewed insecurity in the country unless a strong government took charge. In October 28, 1958, U Nu put forward a motion in the Chamber of Deputies that General Ne Win be offered the prime ministership of a caretaker government.

Caretaker Government, 1958–60

In his acceptance speech before parliament, General Ne Win promised to "do my best to hold fair and free elections within six months if the insurgency and crimes are brought to an end within the period." His cabinet was composed of former civil servants; party politicians were excluded.

The primary task undertaken by the caretaker regime was the establishment of law and order. Several hundred politicians were arrested, and thousands of rebels were killed, were captured, or surrendered. Town and village defense was reorganized and removed from the control of civilian politicians.

General Ne Win saw as the next most pressing need the restoration of order to the administration of government offices, enterprises, and services. To achieve this the general inserted military men into many government departments and turned over control of the state-owned industrial and commercial enterprises to the Defense Services Institute under the direction of a capable and dynamic subordinate, Brigadier Aung Gyi. Within a short time the Defense Services Institute was operating a large economic complex, including banks, factories, shipping, and numerous other commercial enterprises. Some had been taken over from private control, and others were newly established by the Defense Services Institute.

Pedestrians mingle with vehicular traffic against the backdrop of a public market whose design, in keeping with British colonial style, typifies that of many downtown Rangoon buildings.

The administration of the border states was brought into closer conformity with that of the rest of the union. The hereditary chiefs of Shan and Kayah states were induced to surrender substantial political and revenue powers—powers that they held according to the 1947 constitution but that had long been regarded by the union government as incompatible with a modern democracy as well as potentially threatening to the integrity of the union.

Politically, the caretaker regime tried to remain free of party labels, although government spokesmen frequently found occasion to attack members of U Nu's Clean AFPFL. The army did not form its own political party, but the armed forces established a National Solidarity Association in towns and villages throughout Burma that involved the cooperation of military and civilian personnel in security and social welfare projects and in demonstrations of loyalty to the union. These associations were continued by the armed forces after the civilian government was restored.

U Nu Returns to Power

In February 1960 General Ne Win began the process of reinstating civilian government by holding elections for parliament. U Nu, at the head of the Clean AFPFL, fought a highly effective campaign on the issue of democracy versus fascism and on a promise to establish Buddhism as the state religion if he became prime minister. For the first time in Burma's history, more than half the electorate (59 percent) turned out to vote, and U Nu won a massive victory. After taking office on April 4, 1960, U Nu reorganized his party and renamed it the Pyidaungsu (Union League) Party. The Stable AFPFL was the major opposition party, and after the election it dropped the prefix from its name. The National United Front, although it contested many seats, did not win any.

While campaigning, U Nu had hinted at the possibility of separate Mon and Arakanese states' being formed. Several small revolts had flared up in Shan State in 1959 after the *sawbwas* had relinquished their authority, and because more than 10 years had elapsed since the constitution had come into effect, it was legally possible for the Shans and Kayahs to consider seceding from the union. In february 1962 U Nu called leaders of the semiautonomous states to Rangoon to discuss minority problems. They considered the possibility of replacing the present constitution with one that provided for "pure federalism."

Internal divisions within U Nu's Pyidaungsu Party became severe during the national congress of the party in January 1962. As a result, U Nu had to retire from his position as party president. The economy and the efficiency of government were deteriorating. In addition, the business community of Rangoon was unhappy with the announced decision of the government to nationalize all foreign trade as of March 1, 1962.

Military Rule under General Ne Win

On March 2, 1962, the military under General Ne Win seized power. The demands of some minority leaders for "pure federalism" and the animosities sparked by the amendment to make Buddhism the state religion were perceived by the military as a threat to the union's very existence. U Nu's wavering commitment to socialism also alarmed the military. Prominent political leaders, including U Nu, were arrested and held without trial. The 1947 constitution was suspended, and parliament was dissolved. The Revolutionary Council, consisting of high-ranking military officers and headed by General Ne Win, was established and given the responsibility for administering the state. General Ne Win, by a collective decision of the Revolutionary Council, assumed "supreme legislative, executive and judicial authority."

On April 30, 1962, the council issued a 21-point basic policy statement, "The Burmese Way to Socialism," outlining long-range goals. Speaking as "we, the working people of the national races of the Union of Burma," it expressed its commitment to building a new nation. One central objective was the creation of a socialist economy—the "planned, proportional development of all the national productive forces," aimed at eliminating the exploitation of man by man and creating a more prosperous and "morally better" society. A clean break with the parliamentary institutions of the past was announced. The "Burmese Way" stated that "parliamentary democracy has been tried and tested in further-ance of the aims of socialist development. But Burma's 'parliamentary democracy' has not only failed to serve our socialist development, but . . . lost sight of and deviated from the socialist aims." The council promised to establish "mass and class organizations" based "primarily on the strength of peasants and other working masses who form the great majority of the nation."

After the coup, local and regional administration was brought under the control of the military through the creation of a system of Security and Administrative Committees (SAC). The Central Security and Administrative Committee, responsible to the Revo-lutionary Council, administered laws and directives, coordinated government projects, and was responsible for maintaining public discipline. Below it, there was a four-tiered hierarchy of state and division, district, township, and village SAC; their chairmen on all levels were military officers.

Although in control of state administration, the military leader-ship saw the necessity of creating its own political organization in order to gain popular support. In May 1962 an attempt was made form a single, united party drawing on those Pyidaungsu, AFPFL, and National United Front politicians who were not in jail. This effort failed, for only the last group agreed to cooperate. On July 4 the military established its own party, the Burma Socialist Pro-gramme Party (BSPP—see Glossary). In March 1964 the Law to Protect National Solidarity banned all political parties except the BSPP, and Burma became a one-party state.

In January 1963 the BSPP published *The System of Correlation of Man and His Environment*, a detailed exposition of its ideology based on a theory of human nature and society. Although its author has never been officially identified, one scholar suggests that it was most likely U Chit Hlaing, a Marxist during World War II and member of the BSPP Central Executive Committee as late as 1981, who had received a traditional Buddhist education. The document is a somewhat vague and confusing mixture of Buddhist and Marxist themes. The first chapter, dealing with the "three worlds"—the material world, the animal world, and the phenome-nal world—is drawn from Buddhist metaphysics and concludes that "matter and mind in man are inseparably linked on the ever-turning wheel of change." There are discussions of "The Determining Role of the Working People" and "The Laws of Process and the History of Society," which reveal the influence of Marxist concepts. Yet the significance of *The System* is its ultimate rejection of Marxist theory. This is apparent, first, in its denial of the reality of fixed laws of social change, such as Marxist dialectical materialism. Although there is a "law of dialectics" (a Buddhist term in Pali being used to denote this), it, like everything else, is subject to change according to the "law of impermanence" (a basic principle of Buddhism). Second, although the human mind and spirit are dependent on a material substratum, they attain a degree of independence (in contrast with Marxist economic determinism), which places the responsibility for social change and improvement on human will and cultivation of mind rather than on an impersonal process of evolution. Thus, the much-emphasized maxim, "Man Matters Most."

The System rejects a "vulgar materialism," in which "some so-called 'leftists' appear to pay scant heed to mind and mental factors." It also embraces, in line with its affirmation of the "law of impermanence", a pragmatic point of view, asserting that the BSPP would examine and make use of any "progressive ideas, theories and experiences at home and abroad" that would benefit the Union of Burma. In a section entitled "Our Attitude to our own Ideology," it states that the party's ideology ought not to be regarded as complete and final, that it is constantly undergoing a process of formulation and reformulation in a manner consistent with the idea that "things in this universe are transient and every period in its own life is all too brief."

Student and Sangha Reactions

Popular reaction to the coup had been one of passive compliance, tinged with a sense of relief that the military had seemingly stopped the deterioration of national unity that had occurred during the last days of U Nu's rule. Yet in July 1962 the military confronted the Rangoon University Student Union. Union protests against strict new university regulations turned into a riot on July 6; General Ne Win ordered in the army, which fired on the students, killing at least 15. The following day the Student Union building, the stage for the fateful student strike of 1936, was demolished by the military. Protests continued, and the university was closed down by the government. It was clear that it would no longer tolerate the students' political activist role (see Public Order in Central Burma, ch. 5).

The government moved quickly to establish control over the media and education. The Printers' and Publishers' Regulation Act required that all publications apply for an annual government license. Opposition papers, such as the *Nation* of Rangoon, were shut down. A government newspaper, *Working People's Daily*, was set up. The importation of foreign books and periodicals was placed under the control of a government firm. The 1963 Private Schools Registration Act laid down textbook and curriculum requirements for these institutions, which carried much of the burden of educating the country's children. In December 1965 all private newspapers were banned. The pluralistic society of precoup Burma was gradually brought under state control.

Despite the reliance of *The System* on Buddhist concepts and its rejection of Marxist dialectics, General Ne Win was secular in outlook, believing that the government ought not to favor any particular religious community. The military did not support the recognition of Buddhism as the state religion and sought to distance itself from religious affairs. This proved extremely difficult, given the traditional closeness of state and *sangha*, which U Nu had promoted. Many monks were suspicious of the government's intentions. One fear was that the Revolutionary Council's program of nationalization of the economy, labeled "communist," would make it impossible for people to donate funds for the support of monastic communities. One monk, U Kethaya, a leader of the pro-AFPFL Young Monks' Association, began preaching against the military in late 1963, even predicting that U Ne Win, like Aung San, would be assassinated. The government, fearing *sangha* ire, dared not arrest him. Overall, it followed the precarious course of, on the one hand, carrying out the disestablishment of the *sangha* and, on the other hand, of restraining the monks from taking an active role in politics. In January 1965 the 1949 Ecclesiastical Courts Act, vesting authority in *sangha* judges, was repealed, along with other measures providing for state support of Buddhist missionary activities and education and examinations in the Tripitaka. Yet the government in April 1964 ordered all *sangha* groups to register with the government. This measure was taken in order to purge it of "political" monks.

In March 1965 some 2,000 representatives from all sects gathered in Rangoon to discuss the government's proposal that a new Buddha Sasana Sangha Organization be established by the clergy to regulate its affairs. Widespread opposition within the clergy was spurred by the proposal that the organization issue identity cards for all monks. There were massive demonstrations in Mandalay, and 92 leading monks, as well as over 1,000 Buddhist laymen, were arrested. Although the organization was established, its impact on the *sangha* was minimal. After 1965 there were no confrontations, and an uneasy truce existed between the government and the monks.

A Nationalized Economy

Despite the emphasis on pragmatism and flexibility expressed in *The System of Correlation of Man and His Environment*, the military established a state-controlled economic system that resembled in many ways those of Eastern Europe. This course seems to have been initiated in February 1963 after the resignation of Brigadier Aung Gyi, a key figure in the coup, from the Revolutionary Council. Aung Gyi had advocated a mixed public-private sector economy. Thereafter, the influence of Brigadier Tin Pe and U Ba Nyein (a civilian), both doctrinaire socialists, was predominant. There followed a wave of nationalizations, beginning with the British-owned Imperial Chemical Industries in August 1962 and the Burma Oil Company in January 1963. Banks, both domestic and foreign, were nationalized in February 1963; that same month the Enterprise Nationalization Law decreed that all large-scale industrial enterprises would come under state control by June 1, 1963. In fact, nationalization of large enterprises, including foreign-owned ones, continued through 1964 and 1965. In September 1963 the People's Store Corporation was set up to take responsibility for retail distribution of imported and domestic goods. The Defense Services Institute, a military-run enterprise involved in a number of activities ranging from shipping and hotels to the sale of *ngapi* (fish paste, a staple of the Burmese diet), was made a state enterprise in October. Overall, some 15,000 enterprises were taken over by the government between 1963 and 1972. The government also invested more than K1 billion in an ambitious industrialization program during this period.

On May 17, 1964, the Demonetization Law was promulgated. This declared that K50 and K100 notes were no longer legal tender. The law required persons to turn them in to the authorities (to receive a maximum refund of K500 in smaller notes), and there were heavy penalties for noncompliance. In August a special tax was imposed on bank accounts of a certain amount (the equivalent of US$882) and above. These laws had the effect of undermining the dominant economic position of Indian and Pakistani traders and retailers. Responding to government pressures, some 97,000 out of a total of 109,000 Indians and 12,000 out of 26,000 Pakistanis had left the country by July 1965.

Despite the growing resemblance of the management of the economy to that of communist countries, the government made no real attempt to collectivize agriculture. The Union of Burma Agricultural Marketing Board, similar to the Agricultural Marketing Board established by the U Nu government, was placed in control of purchasing paddy from the farmers and exporting it overseas. The government moved to abolish tenancy. In 1963 laws were passed both prohibiting the seizure of land or animals following the nonpayment of debts and the setting of levels of rent, to be paid either in cash or in kind. In April 1965 the government turned to what General Ne Win called "unfinished business which mocks our declaration that we will not . . . permit the exploitation of man by man." The Tenancy Act was amended, to abolish rents on farmland.

A number of sympathetic observers pointed out that the military's economic policy during the first decade of its rule was designed to promote equity and put an end to foreign (including both Western multinational and resident Indian) exploitation of the country, rather than economic growth. Stagnation of the state-controlled economy, however, resulted in practically everyone's getting smaller—though perhaps more equal—slices of the pie. Per capita income in constant prices rose modestly between FY 1962 and FY 1972, but it was still below prewar levels. Although paddy production grew from 6.7 million to 8 million tons within the same period, this barely kept pace with population growth. Rice exports declined precipitously. Their value in FY 1965 was the equivalent of US$134.5 million, falling to US$52.7 million in FY 1972. Because of the government's emphasis on rapid industrialization, public investment in agriculture declined.

Lack of consumer goods and price-fixing by the Agricultural Marketing Board gave the farmer little incentive to produce more; his best rice was often hidden from government buyers and sold for a good price on the black market. The quality of rice exported by the board thus declined, resulting in fewer overseas buyers and less foreign exchange. In the cities, shortages of goods in the People's Stores, the shelves of which were often bare, and high inflation eroded the standard of living. Consumer goods were often available only on the high-priced black market. An American observer in the early 1970s discovered that in the Zegyo Market in Mandalay, a half-empty bottle of "Horlicks," a British powdered health drink, sold for the official equivalent of US$12, and aspirin was available neither there nor in Rangoon's People's Stores. The capital, once known for its brightness and gaiety, began to take on the woebegone aura of a Soviet provincial city transported to the tropics, though lively crowds still frequented the Shwedagon Pagoda and its precincts.

The government initiated a major reversal in policy at the First Congress of the BSPP, held in June-July 1971, when it approved the document "Long-Term and Short-Term Economic Policies of the Burma Socialist Programme Party." This represented a less doctrinaire approach to planning, calling for the abandonment of Soviet-style rapid industrialization and giving top priority to the agricultural, consumer goods, and mining sectors, in that order. The mistakes of the past and the plight of the consumer were acknowledged, and the role of material incentives in development was stressed over ideological mobilization. The congress recommended the acceptance of limited economic assistance from abroad, without compromising Burma's neutralist foreign policy stance. It also approved the Twenty-Year Plan (fiscal year [FY] 1974–93), projecting growth targets of 5.9 percent gross domestic product (GDP) per year through to FY 1993, when Burma would have developed into a "socialist industrialized state."

The Nationalities Issue and Insurgency

Given the military's perception at the time of the 1962 coup that national unity was threatened by the demands of restive minorities, it was not surprising that the Revolutionary Council radically transformed the quasi-federal structure of the country. The state legislatures or councils, the office of minister and head of the states, and the separate state administrations were abolished and replaced by a system of state councils under the direct control of the central government. The military-controlled SAC hierarchy was extended to the states as well as to Burma Proper.

In February 1964 the government issued the "Declaration of the Conviction of the Revolutionary Council on the Question of Union Nationalities." It declared that both economic and social development were tasks to be undertaken by the nation as a whole. Minorities were cautioned that divisive movements would not be tolerated. Minority autonomy was limited to the area of culture: languages and literature, national customs, visual and performing arts, and religion. Minority cadres were trained at the new Academy for the Development of National Groups, founded at Sagaing and later moved to Ywathitgyi; (ironically in the heartland of Burman culture in Upper Burma). According to political analyst Josef Silverstein, these measures in fact represented the Revolutionary Council's commitment to the "nationalization of the society and the Burmanization of its culture."

In June 1963 the Revolutionary Council issued an invitation to the various communist and ethnic insurgent groups to come to Rangoon and discuss peace terms. Safe conduct was guaranteed, even if the negotiations failed. Between June and November, delegations from the Red and White Flag communist factions, the Karen National Union, the Karenni National Progress Party, the New Mon State Party, the Kachin Independence Organization, the Chin Group, the Shan State Army, and other groups appeared in the capital to talk with the government. Initially, there was optimism that peace might be achieved; by mid-November, however, the talks had broken down. One small Karen group had agreed to demobilize, but the only lasting result of the parley was the creation of the National Democratic United Front (NDUF) by the rebels, a loose coalition including both communist and ethnic groups, which fell apart in the early 1970s.

Although none of the insurgent groups, or coalition of groups, was strong enough to seize power, the role of China in the communist movement in the late 1960s posed a new threat. In the mid-1960s the White Flag faction of the BCP, based in the Pegu Yoma, was in the process of carrying out a "cultural revolution" purge similar to the one going on in China at that time. Thakin Than Tun, the organization's leader, had purged most of the old leadership but was himself assassinated in September 1968. As a result of a Burma Army attack on the White Flag stronghold that disrupted radio contact with Beijing, a new leader, Thakin Zin, was chosen without consulting China, which favored the selection of another BCP leader, Thakin Ba Thein Tin, then living in China.

Relations between Rangoon and Beijing worsened after anti-Chinese riots in June 1967 (see Neutralism and Seclusion, this ch.). In response, China began to give material support to communist insurgents in Burma. Rather than aiding the White Flag faction, which was located too far from the China border to be readily accessible, the Chinese recruited veteran Kachin rebel Naw Seng—living in China—to form a new insurgent force. Naw Seng was made a member of the BCP White Flag Central Committee and later of the BCP Politburo; in reality the new insurgency, known as the BCP Northeastern Command, was quite separate from the original White Flag movement. It was directly dependent on China for training, aid, and support, and its personnel consisted primarily of ethnic Kachin, Shan, and Wa minorities; the Burman contingent was virtually nonexistent, in contrast with the original Red Flag and White Flag factions.

Naw Seng's army of some 1,000 strong began attacking villages in northern Shan State and southern Kachin State in early 1968; by the time he was killed in the early 1970s, the center of BCP insurgency had shifted to these areas. In November 1970 the Red Flag insurgency had been critically weakened by the capture of its leader, Thakin Soe, by government forces; the White Flag faction was virtually eliminated in March 1975 when Burma Army troops killed Thakin Zin and other leaders in combat. Thakin Ba Thein Tin, who had previously switched his allegiance within the party to the Northeastern Command, was then elected chairman of the entire BCP, encompassing both the Red Flag and the White Flag remnants and the insurgency in the northeast. The latter had diversified at that time into several components. It made alliances with ethnically based groups, such as the Kachin Independence Organization, the Shan State Army, the United Pa-O Organization, and the Shan State Nationalities Liberation Organization.

Another insurgent group was established by U Nu following his departure from Burma in 1969. Called the National United Liberation Front, a coalition of his Parliamentary Democracy Party and ethnic groups, it operated along the Thailand-Burma border. The movement gradually lost momentum, however, after U Nu resigned as its president in January 1972.

Neutralism and Seclusion

Foreign policy represents the strongest line of continuity between the parliamentary and military periods. The very day of the coup, the Revolutionary Council announced its "adherence to a policy of positive neutrality," guaranteeing "the continuance of the existing cordial relations with all countries."

Neutralism, however, was combined with a new element, a policy of seclusion. This was, in part, a reaction to the perceived threat of external involvement in the insurgent movements. Another element in the country's isolationism—the result of attitudes going back to the colonial era—was fear of foreign economic domination and the desire to create, as far as possible, an autarkic socialist economic system. A third element was cultural. When the government took control of the media and the school system, it sought to eliminate sources of "decadent" Western influence. Foreign agencies, such as the Asia Foundation, the Ford Foundation, the British Council, and the library of the United States Information Agency, were shut down. Western missionaries were expelled and foreign tourists and scholars excluded from the country.

Burma continued to refuse to align itself with either of the superpowers and kept aloof from regional associations, such as the Association of Southeast Asian States (ASEAN), which was formed in 1967. Relations with China were initially excellent, as signaled by the friendly visit of President Liu Shaoqi in April 1963. The radicalization of China that took place during the great Proletarian Cultural Revolution of 1966–68, however, led to a sudden worsening of relations. The Chinese embassy in Rangoon began encouraging local Chinese to participate in Cultural Revolution-style activities in 1967, much to the distress of the government. An especially touchy issue was the wearing of red badges showing pictures of Chinese Communist Party Chairman Mao Zedong, which the government prohibited. Resident Chinese students protested, and there were violent confrontations with Burmese students on June 27, 1967. This led to attacks against Chinese shops, houses, and automobiles and against the Chinese embassy. One Chinese aid official was killed by Burmese mobs. When the government refused to give a full apology and punish the perpetrators, the Beijing official press began calling for the overthrow of General Ne Win, labeling him a "fascist military dictator." Burma and China withdrew their ambassadors, and Chinese aid programs were suspended. Support at this time was given to the creation of the communist insurgent movement in the northeastern border area. By March 1971, however, relations were restored and subsequently were good, though Chinese support of the BCP would continue to be a point of irritation.

Burma's relations with its other neighbors remained cordial, though distant. A problem arose with India concerning the nationalization and demonetarization decrees, which affected Indians resident in Burma and led to the repatriation of thousands, but was settled amicably by the mid-1970s (see Relations with Selected Countries, ch. 4). Relations with Thailand were strained for a time by the presence of U Nu's forces on the border, but he was expelled from Thailand in 1973. Burma remained outside of the vortex of the Vietnam Conflict, though there is evidence that there was cooperation between the BCP insurgents in training communist Pathet Lao forces on the Burma-Laos frontier.

The Socialist Republic of the Union of Burma

In line with the Revolutionary Council's determination to transform the BSPP from a cadre to a mass party, a new party constitution was drafted in November 1969, laying out clear-cut party organizations on the regional and local levels, requirements for party membership, and specific intraparty decisionmaking procedures, based on "democratic centralism." The Revolutionary Council promised a transition from rule by a close-knit military elite to a "socialist democracy" having a broader base of popular participation. In this spirit General Ne Win and 20 other military leaders resigned their commissions in April 1972; U Ne Win continued, however, as prime minister and head of the BSPP.

At the First Congress of the BSPP, held in June–July 1971, the party constitution was officially adopted, and a committee was set up to draft a new state constitution, headed by Brigadier San Yu, a member of the Revolutionary Council. Its 97 members included 33 military officers and representatives of workers', peasants', and ethnic groups. At the October 1973 Second Congress the committee's draft constitution was approved. In a referendum held in late December, the document received overwhelming popular approval (90.2 percent of the 13.3 million eligible voters participating), though participation and approval rates were lower in the states than in the divisions. The Constitution was promulgated on January 3, 1974; in March 2, 1974, the Revolutionary Council dissolved itself, transferring power to the newly elected People's Assembly (Pyithu Hluttaw). U Ne Win became president of the new Socialist Republic of the Union of Burma.

The preamble to the 1974 Constitution states the new socialist republic's commitment to "socialist democracy" and "a socialist economic system." It recognizes only a single political party, the BSPP. The People's Assembly, a unicameral legislature popularly elected for a four-year term, "exercises sovereign power on behalf of the people," although administration is the responsibility of the State Council and the Council of Ministers, both of which it nominates (see Constitutional Framework, ch. 4). Below the national level is a three-tiered administrative structure, encompassing people's councils at the state and division, township, and ward and village-tract levels. The councils are structurally analogous to the national legislature and choose their own executive committees. The different levels are linked through the principle of "local autonomy under central leadership." On the regional level there are seven divisions and seven states, the latter including Karen State, Chin State, Rakhine State, and Mon State, as well as the states created at the time of independence.

The most striking contrast between the 1947 constitution and the 1974 one is the status of the national minorities. The quasifederal structure and the specifically ethnic character of the states were abolished on the principle, enunciated by U Ne Win at the

1969 Party Seminar, that "our Union is just one homogeneous whole. A Chin, for instance, can go wherever he likes within the Union and stay wherever he likes. So, too, a Burmese [Burman]. Everyone can take part in any of the affairs, whether political, economic, administrative, or judicial. He can choose his own role." Given this assumption, U Ne Win argued, "we will not need to have separate governments within the Union."

During the decade of the 1970s national unity and "socialist democracy" remained elusive goals. In May 1974 there was a strike by oil field workers at Chauk demanding higher wages; the following month far more serious disturbances occurred as workers struck the railroad yard at Insein protesting food shortages and high prices. The strike soon spread to some 42 other state enterprises. Riots followed, and at least 22 persons were killed by police, although unofficial sources give a much higher number. In December university students and Buddhist monks demonstrated over what they perceived was the government's refusal to give appropriate honors to U Thant, a close associate of U Nu and former United Nations secretary general, who had died on November 25, 1974. They seized his body and held their own funeral at the site of the demolished Rangoon University Student Union. Government troops recovered his coffin, reburying it near the Shwedagon Pagoda. There followed riots throughout Rangoon, and students and monks called for the overthrow of "one party dictatorship." Martial law was declared; nine people were killed and some 1,800 arrested. A new law forbidding antistate activities was passed in early 1975 (see Crime and the Criminal Justice System, ch. 5).

In July 1976 opposition appeared within the ranks of the military itself as a number of younger army officers plotted a coup d'etat and the assassination of U Ne Win, U San Yu, and Colonel Tin Oo, director general of the powerful National Intelligence Board (see Intelligence Agencies, ch. 5). Members of the coup group were apparently disgruntled over the resignation of another popular military officer, Defense Minister Brigadier General Tin U, in March and were committed to reforming the socialist economic system, which they saw as condemning the country to ever-deepening poverty. They were put on trial in September along with Tin U, who apparently knew of the plot but did not inform the government. The coup leader was condemned to death, and the others were given prison terms.

Insurgency continued, and activities by more than a dozen major groups were recorded in 1977. These occurred in the north and northeastern border regions, where the BCP continued to pose the greatest threat when allied with smaller groups and posed a lesser threat in Rakhine and Mon states (see Revolutionary, Separatist, and Warlord Groups, ch. 5). The gradual withdrawal of Chinese support from the BCP Northeastern Command led it to engage more actively in the lucrative opium trade.

A stagnant, high-inflation economy in which growth in GDP (see Glossary) barely kept pace with population growth and in which exports declined continued to worry government leaders. In November 1976 the Burma Aid Group had been formed under the auspices of the World Bank (see Aid, Credit, and Investment, ch. 3). This group, which included Japan, the Western nations, and multilateral lenders, such as the World Bank and the Asian Development Bank, approved increased aid for Burma and recommended reform of the socialist economic system.

At the Third Congress of the BSPP in February 1977 there was a purge of the Central Committee, and the socialist economist U Ba Nyein and 40 others were obliged to resign. The congress concluded that the faulty implementation of policy, rather than the "Burmese Way to Socialism," was responsible for the bad state of the economy. BSPP Secretary General U San Yu called for changes in the management of state and cooperative enterprises and better incentives for private producers. He also proposed the acceptance of a greater volume of foreign aid and suggested the possibility of the government's forming joint ventures with foreign firms. The Right of Private Enterprise Law was promulgated in September 1977 (see Public and Private Enterprises and Markets, ch. 3). It guaranteed against the nationalization of a wide spectrum of sectors until FY 1993, the end of the Twenty-Year Plan.

The inflow of foreign aid and investment, the growth of a small-scale private enterprise, and improvements in the state's methods of procuring rice from farmers contributed to an improvement in the economy after the Third Congress in 1977. In the 1978–81 period GDP growth rates averaged 6.2 percent (adjusted).

In February 1978 government officials began registering the Muslim inhabitants of the northern region of Rakhine State, arresting and detaining a number as illegal residents. This caused a panic among the Muslims, resulting in the flight of some 200,000 across the border into neighboring Bangladesh. Fears that the government was embarking on an anti-Muslim policy were quelled after negotiations with Bangladesh were concluded, providing for the repatriation of the refugees. Burma's remaining Indian minority, which included both Muslims and Hindus, looked with some apprehension on the expected passage of a new citizenship law, drafted in 1980, which denied nonindigenous citizens (those whose forebears had not lived in Burma before 1824) certain political and economic rights (see Constitutional Framework, ch. 4).

Burma's resignation from the Sixth Nonaligned Summit Conference, held in Havana in September 1979, represented a departure from the country's usual low profile in the international arena, though not from its stated policy of independence and neutrality. The Burmese delegation protested the pro-Soviet orientation of the conference, pushed by Cuba, as a violation of the movement's basic principles. According to Foreign Minister U Mying Maung, "the principles of the Movement are not recognizable any more; they are not merely dim, they are dying . . . there are those . . . who deliberately exploit the Movement to gain their own grand designs" (see Foreign Policy Environment, ch. 4).

In May 1980 the government sponsored the First Congregation of the Sangha of All Orders for Purification, Perpetuation, and Propagation of the Sasana, held at Rangoon on the site of U Nu's Sixth World Buddhist Council of 1954–56. The 1,218 representatives of the various *sangha* communities agreed to establish a new institutional structure for the monkhood that would promote order and self-discipline and prevent imposters from infiltrating (see Recent Political Developments, ch. 4; Public Order in Central Burma, ch. 5). An ecclesiastical court system was also revived. Some observers considered the congregation as the beginning of a new relationship between the state and *sangha*, similar to that which existed under the Burmese kings. Although the government did not abandon the principle of the separation of church and state embodied in the 1974 Constitution, it was perceived that U Ne Win, now an old man, was taking on the aura of a traditional Burmese ruler and patron of Buddhism. Thus he ordered the construction of a new pagoda, to contain Buddhist relics donated by the king of Nepal, near the Shwedagon Pagoda in Rangoon.

On May 28, 1980, the government announced a general amnesty to last 90 days. It also established an honorary order, the Naing-Ngant Gon-Yi, to be given to those who had participated in the independence struggle, including opponents of the government who took advantage of the amnesty. A cash award for these now-aging heroes was also established. On July 29 U Nu returned to Burma under the amnesty's terms, saying that he would devote the remainder of his years to religious scholarship.

In August 1981 at the Fourth Congress of the BSPP, U Ne Win announced his plan to retire as president following the October elections to the People's Assembly. He was succeeded after the election by U San Yu, former BSPP general secretary, although he retained his post as leader of the BSPP.

* * *

Extensive discussions of early Burmese history can be found in G. Coedès' *The Indianized States of Southeast Asia* and in the opening chapters of John F. Cady's *The United States and Burma*, Maung Htin Aung's *A History of Burma*, and D.G.E. Hall's *A*

History of South-East Asia. Michael Aung Thwin's "Jambudipa: Classical Burma's Camelot," published in *Essays on Burma* (1981), describes the ideological and institutional bases of traditional Burmese kingship, focusing on the Pagan period.

For information on the Konbaung and colonial periods, D.G.E. Hall's treatment in *A History of South-East Asia* is considered by many to be definitive. Maung Htin Aung's *A History of Burma* and *The Stricken Peacock: Anglo-Burmese Relations, 1752–1948* are passionately nationalistic but provide a needed balance to Hall's perspective, which is that of the British colonial official. Charles L. Keeton's *King Thebaw and the Ecological Rape of Burma* fails to develop fully its thesis on the role of the ecology in history but provides a fascinating account of the last years of the Burmese kingdom. On the colonial economy and society, the best analyses are provided by John S. Furnivall's *Colonial Policy and Practice: A Comparative Study of Burma and Netherlands India* and Michael Adas' *The Burma Delta: Economic Development and Social Change on an Asian Rice Frontier, 1852–1941*. Interesting discussions of the evolution of Burmese social and political thought, especially as related to Buddhism, are provided by E. Sarkisyanz' *Buddhist Backgrounds of the Burmese Revolution* and Trevor Ling's "Burmese Philosophy Today" in *Asian Philosophy Today* edited by Dale Riepe. Maung Maung's *Aung San of Burma* and U Nu's autobiography, *U Nu: Saturday's Son*, provide vivid portraits of these national leaders.

Hugh Tinker's *The Union of Burma*, the third edition of which was published in 1961, is a good discussion of the postindependence period. Regarding Burma after the military takeover, Josef Silverstein's *Burma: Military Rule and the Politics of Stagnation* and *Burmese Politics: The Dilemma of National Unity* are valuable. Recent developments are traced in the February issues of the monthly *Asian Survey*, the yearbook *Southeast Asian Affairs*, and the Far Eastern Economic Review's *Asia Yearbook*. (For further information and complete citations, see Bibliography.)

Chapter 2.   The Society and Its Environment

Members of the sangha carrying their bowls for collecting alms

THE LAND OF BURMA has long supported a thriving agricultural society. Three major rivers flow from the ranges of mountains in the far north, and lesser streams drain the hills and mountains that form the country's eastern and western borders. In the central lowlands of the country live the Burmans, who control the society and are basically farmers speaking the Burmese language and practicing Theravada Buddhism. In the southern part of the central lowlands, wet-rice agriculture is typical, but in the drier areas dry-rice farming is necessary, mixed with other crops, such as millet.

Surrounding the Burman majority, and sometimes intermixed with them in lowland settlements, are a host of ethnic minorities, each of which may have its own history, language, religion, and life-style. These minorities have interacted with Burmans for so many centuries that whenever they opt to do so, they may assume Burman ways for strategic reasons. In the southwest are the Buddhist Arakanese, speaking a form of Burmese but having a proud historical independence until the late eighteenth century. North of them in the plains and mostly in the hills are the Chin peoples, who have their own language and religion and live a mountain life in contrast to their Buddhist lowland neighbors. Still farther north are the Naga and Kachin hill peoples, having a distinct language and culture, most preferring the safety of the mountains but others settling in the valleys with Burmans or another minority, the Shans. The Shans (or Tai, as they call themselves) are usually rice farmers, have their own language and customs, and practice their own variants of Theravada Buddhism.

Along the eastern borders of Burma are still more complex groups of peoples, including a large population of valley Shans in the eastern Shan Plateau. In eastern hill and mountain areas also may be found Kachins, Was, Akhas, Lisus, Palaungs, Kayahs, Karens, and many others, groups of whom may prefer to stress their distinctness or separateness from the Burmans or decide to throw in their lot with lowland, "civilized" life. In the southeast of the country, in addition to the Karens, are the Mons, descendants of a once-powerful southern kingdom of Mon-speaking Buddhists who were conquered by the Burmans in the late eighteenth century. To make the society of Burma even more complex are thousands of Muslims, Hindus, Chinese, and others originally from neighboring countries who live in urban settlements or are found scattered about the countryside.

All these ethnic peoples are "Burmese," that is, part of the modern nation of Burma, but they are not "Burman," a term referring only to those who have elected to become part of the mainstream, speak Burmese, practice Theravada Buddhism and, now, Burmese socialism. To be Burman implies a certain amount of genetic consistency, but other ethnic peoples may become Burman by making a cultural conversion. Many ethnic groups in modern Burma refuse to make that conversion to a world view that harmonizes with those Burmans controlling the government.

Social control in Burma, as well as in other parts of Southeast Asia, has classically involved attempts by a central source of power to integrate disparate groups within radiating rings of influence, like a circular mandala (see Glossary) that is most intense at its core but weakens as its concentric lines fade and finally disintegrate at its farthest reaches. Political mandalas of power rise and fall according to the capital's ability to extend its rings of control. At the edges of such systems—Burma since independence in 1948 being a prime example—ethnic minorities, particularly in the hills and mountains, have managed to maintain a fair degree of independence; thus they have resisted the establishment of modern boundary lines, which has made them de facto citizens of a nation they have never permanently acknowledged. In the early 1980s the modern nation of Burma was attempting to impose a military-led socialist mandala of power from its Burman capital of Rangoon. Like earlier mandalas, its reach was weaker the farther one moved from the capital; at the fringes, or border areas, non-Burmans have been able to assert their independence by mounting armed rebellions, preserving their ancient languages, dressing differently, retaining ancient non-Buddhist religious beliefs, or simply by following a different life in the inaccessible hills or distant valleys. Ethnic identity in modern Burma has not only been partially a genetic consequence of history but increasingly also entailed a conscious choice to be culturally non-Burman. The Burmans, nonetheless, work hard to create national unity out of such diversity.

Physical Environment

Burma has an area of about 678,000 square kilometers, sharing boundaries with Bangladesh and India in the west and northwest, with China in the north and northeast, and with Laos and Thailand in the east and southeast (see fig. 6). Land frontiers consist for the most part of a ring of hills and rugged mountains, making overland transportation between Burma and its neighbors very difficult. In the south and southwest the country faces the Bay of Bengal and the Andaman Sea along an extensive coastline. Internally, communication is facilitated by the Irrawaddy River system that drains the greater part of the country, arising from its source in the forested mountains of northern Burma and flowing southward through the country's central lowlands toward an expansive delta, where nine mouths of the river empty into the Bay of Bengal.

The central lowlands lie between a range of mountains known to the Burmese as the Arakan Yoma on the west and the Shan

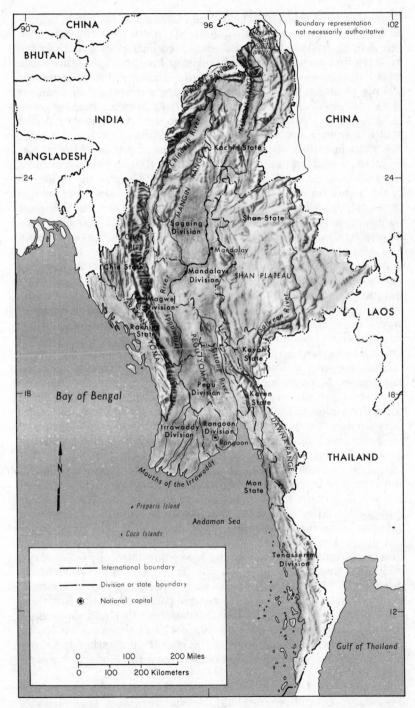

Figure 6. Topography

Plateau in the east. The folds of the plateau and the ranges of the Arakan Yoma are aligned in a generally north-to-south direction, the deeply dissected Shan Plateau extending southward into the Tenasserim coastal region of the Malay Peninsula. Another large river, the Salween, flows across the plateau; this is generally steeply rolling terrain, having an average elevation of 984 meters above sea level and at certain places rises to twice that height.

The climate of the country is under the influence of the southwest monsoon, which blows off the Indian Ocean and divides the year into three seasons: a rainy season, from late May to late October; a cool season, from late October to mid-February; and a hot season, from mid-February to late May. Despite the influence of the monsoon over much of the country, the amount of rainfall varies sharply by area. Along the coastline, where the west monsoon winds are forced to rise and cool, annual rainfall is very heavy. In drier upland areas annual precipitation is considerably less.

Always somewhat protected and isolated by the formidable ring of mountains on its borders, Burmese society has developed in its unique manner, never unaffected by the larger nations of India and China but always able to develop in a particularly Burmese way. The variety in the physical environment in Burma itself has ensured that a people unusually close to nature in their ways of living would develop a society itself complex and varied.

Those seeking to develop an understanding of Burma are often encouraged to begin with comprehending the difference between the wet-rice-producing tropical lowlands and the drier hills. These contrasts are often not as simple as they first may seem, but as an introduction, the valley-hill dichotomy is useful.

Blessed with huge rivers flowing southward from the heartlands of Asia, Burma has collected for millennia rich, alluvial soil that has been the base for a tropical panorama of life and a promise, sometimes achieved, of an agricultural bonanza. The drenching monsoons inundate the plains and even help the drier uplands during the rainy season of roughly three months. Trapped in ancient irrigation canals—low earth dikes—this life-giving water has supported centuries of ricegrowers in what is often called Lower Burma (approximately the lower one-third of the country), including the coastal and river delta regions that, particularly during the last hundred years, were opened up to cultivation. Lower Burma may also refer to the area annexed by the British in their second war against the Burmese in the mid-nineteenth century. In general, it may be thought of as the wet-rice region that is not the historical heart of the country but rather the more modern agricultural rice-basket centering on the modern-day capital of Rangoon.

In actuality, Lower Burma includes not only the whole Tenasserim coastal region along the Andaman Sea, encompassing intricate islands stretching down toward Malaysia, but also the areas around Moulmein and Pegu, traditionally the ancient home of the Mons, a people whose ancestry certainly rivals or surpasses in antiquity that of those known as the Burmans. Centuries of political maneuvering in Lower Burma can be traced in the settlement patterns today around the deltas of the great Irrawaddy, Sittang, and Salween rivers, where peoples such as the Mons and Karens have been made into citizens of the modern state of Burma but proudly hold memories of a separate ethnic identity that modern politicians find difficult to meld into a single national will.

North and upriver of the wet-rice plains are the drier heartlands of Upper Burma, where the classical civilizations of Burma developed. For about a thousand years, kingdoms, based on control of central Burmese agriculture and manpower, shifted their capitals to fulfill predictions of good fortune (see Early Burmese Kingdoms, ch. 1). As these kingdoms and their urban centers rose and fell, the villages of outlying farmers survived, and through much adversity and forgotten predictions the villages have endured, not without memories of royal fortunes that have impinged on their tested and trusted rural ways. The medieval city of Pagan and the last royal capital of Mandalay still somehow manage to retain a mood of greatness and past glory that radiates into the countryside. Because a national sense of pride developed in a riverine environment so far from the sea and so seemingly protected by the mountain ranges about it, Upper Burma at moments of greatness believed it was indeed the special heart of the world, the center of everything important. The fact that the Chinese, Japanese, and British had at one time swept over the land, leaving ruins in their wake, has not dimmed the conviction that Upper Burma remains the guardian of traditions and truths of considerable cosmic import.

While kingdoms rose and fell in the plains and village farmers perfected the art of surviving palace coups and foreign invasions, the people in the hills also became quite adept at keeping out of the way when the armies raged and sought recruits. Like mountain dwellers everywhere, Burmese hill groups have prized their freedom and right to live less luxuriously than their valley neighbors. Since the rivers of Burma tend to run from north to south, with ranges of mountains in between, the rivers, roads, and trails from east to west or west to east have to pass through rugged mountain terrain, making it difficult for the valley peoples to reach and thereby control the ethnic groups perched in their sky-top villages. Before the government used helicopters for search missions, the mountains were a retreat where various activities— including growing opium poppies, feuding, counting the loot from valley raids, slave trading, smuggling, and other time-honored customs—could be pursued with relative impunity. Unique religious beliefs and practices, special ethnic dress, a myriad of dialects, treasured kin and marriage rules, shifting cultivation (see Glossary), and a host of delicately tuned hunting traditions have also remained a part of life in these areas. Never isolated from the plains but always watching and interacting from their high settlements, the hill peoples, such as the Chins, Kachins, and eastern Karens, have forged their own ethnic identity and pride, not always in harmony with the modern notions of nationhood that emanate from the valley and the delta.

Beyond the western portion of the ring of mountains, on the coast, are the Arakanese people. Neither a hill society nor traditionally enclosed within Burma Proper (see Glossary), the Arakanese, by accident of conquest, find themselves also embraced in the grip of the modern phenomenon of Burma's nationbuilding. Another onetime rival of the Burmans are the Shans, who live in the eastern plateau, where they have for centuries farmed their valley rice plots and formed their own small kingdoms. Once rulers of Burma, the Shans, like the Arakanese, have lost their royal power and are now subsumed in modern Burma.

Burma, then, is a nation cartographically defined with the fixed borders so revered by the colonial mentality that carved the world into neat pieces of pie not necessarily related to natural or societal divisions. If the Naga people in northwestern Burma happen to be sliced into two sections, one in Burma, the other in India, or if the Karens straddle the eastern border with Thailand, the cartographer does not worry. The lines are drawn and boundary commissions have moved whole Kachin villages that were not on the correct side of a given China-Burma line. Burma in the early 1980s was faced with the formidable task of finding an acceptable rationale for calling a cartographer's dream a nation, and it was not at all surprising that armed rebellion and disorder have plagued every government since the British colonialists left the area.

Few visitors have departed from Burma without having acquired a lifelong fascination with the land. As of mid-1983 travelers were restricted to seven-day visas and had precious little time to explore the ecological wonders; continual insurgency in many areas had closed the countryside to visitors, who were carefully protected by the Tourist Burma offices (see Insurgency in the Periphery, ch. 5). Thus most hill and delta districts had not been visited by foreigners since 1962. Nevertheless, much can be said in general, subject to correction if and when visits to the countryside are allowed.

The fundamental contrast is between the untamed jungle—whether in the lowlands or the mountains—and the land manicured by farmers. In the jungle are creatures such as tigers and elephants. Sometimes the increasingly rare birds are more often heard than seen. Deer, boar, and bear are hunted in the hills, and fish may be trapped or stunned with poison in mountain streams. In the jungle the wild may be tamed, or conquered temporarily, but the tropical world is just as likely to use its primal energy to overcome humans if not dealt with carefully according to strict traditions. Hill tribal priests and hunters follow careful procedures; religious hermits in the jungle are especially held in esteem, for it is widely believed they tame the surrounding fierceness with their Buddhist presence. The jungle also gives sanctuary to dangerous humans as well—outlaws and fugitives, insurgents, and rebel armies. Yet uncontrolled by society, the jungle or forest remains a resource and source of strength for the country.

The contrast between wild and tame is nowhere better illustrated than by the typical scene of a huge water buffalo pulling a plow in a rice paddy, duplicated in neat fields as far as the eye can see to the surrounding hills. Humped Indian cattle pull wooden carts on rutted, dusty roads, as pigs and chickens scavenge under the houses built on stilts. Nets of all kinds are used to harvest fish from the rivers and ponds in the valley. Except for an occasional cobra or another of Burma's many poisonous serpents, the jungle has been pushed back and domesticated in a primarily Buddhist atmosphere of benevolence and practicality.

The essence of the forest, its teak and bamboo trees, has been converted and transformed into house posts, flooring matting for walls, water pipes, fences, buffalo bells, or images of the Buddha. Jungle fruit, such as durian, is nationally craved. Domesticated flowers from the rain forest are set in a woman's coiffure or reverently placed on an altar. Rubber trees are made to grow in plantation rows to facilitate the gathering of sap.

The land has been highly productive; Burma was once the world's leading exporter of rice and is still conscious of its potential. The hill peoples can persuade their sometimes brittle ecology to yield dry rice, millet, maize, beans, garden vegetables and, of course, opium for instant cash. In the modern age the lowland farmers have the option of growing high-yielding rice varieties, which, despite fertilizer and irrigation requirements, can benefit both the planter and the government. The potential is there for surplus if the farmer can be persuaded to sell to the government and if the latter has developed the capacity to buy at a fair price and to store, process, and market the crop properly.

Production and marketing problems involve other natural resources in Burma, such as petroleum and minerals. Largely self-supporting in oil owing to low usage, reflecting lack of equipment, Burma may yet discover further deposits offshore, despite recent disappointments in exploration. Hidden in the backcountry and particularly difficult to reach are unknown quantities of tin, lead, tungsten, antimony, iron, and silver. Ironically, the very isolated areas of the ethnic minorities may prove to contain much of Burma's natural mineral resources, a factor not lost on leaders of minorities concerned that they might not receive proper economic compensation for such exportable treasure. Of more than passing interest are the ruby, sapphire, and jade mines, which the government, as in the past, controls subject to the ever-present traffic in such items that the black market inspires. So great is this unrecorded trade that since 1962, evaluation of the country's wealth through government statistics has been almost useless. Jade and tin move in the black market and in private, unreported sales, as does much of the country's ecological treasure.

The Burmese seem in no hurry to exploit their bountiful land. Wary of foreign helpers who are difficult to control and suspicious of "progress" that leaves congestion and pollution as a wretched legacy, the Burmese proceed slowly. Accordingly, Burma remains a uniquely unspoiled country, where there is no compelling public pressure to modernize at the cost of the land's traditional charm.

Elusive Social Unity: The Population Mixture

Probably no one knows how many people lived in Burma in 1983, but sources suggest about 36 million. Dominating the scene are the Burmans—primarily defined as Burmese-speaking Buddhists. Under socialist military control since 1962, the government of Burma has sought an elusive social unity for the country.

The quest for unity is not new. The ancient, unperfected stratagem of royalty was to create a kingdom from the inside out, that is, to radiate as much power as possible from the center of the realm, attempting to control as many people as feasible. In this system, control at the center was absolute and impressive, but in the hinterlands the king was more a symbol than a reality. The king claimed to rule the entire would and was so treated, but a few hundred miles away another monarch might be successfully persuading his subjects to believe that he was the world emperor. Villagers tried vainly to stay out of the way of both sublime beings. Although such royal states usually collapsed owing to palace violence and warfare, a few managed to expand enough to include most of modern-day Burma, creating the cultural template for the modern notion of unity.

Another sort of unity was forced by the colonization of all of Burma by the British at the end of the nineteenth century. Through superior weaponry the British put the entire area under direct or indirect control. From Rangoon and Calcutta the colonial bureaucracy and mentality spread even to the hill peoples, some of whom resisted "pacification" as late as the 1930s. The British used the fringes of the center against the center itself, that is, recruiting hill peoples into armed units to control lowland Burmans or importing Indian soldiers to help keep the colony in line. Delicately courting the minorities, Britain created a precarious unity held together by the awe of the military might behind the system, much as matters had stood under a very strong king. Burma became a country by colonial definition, not by organic social evolution. In a sense, therefore, Burma was still a fragile mandala or, more accurately, a series of them, since the British encouraged considerable self-rule among the Chins, Kachins, Shans, Kayahs, and Karens. When the source of colonial power departed after World War II, the illusion of unity was again shattered (see The Nationalities Issue and Insurgency, ch. 1; fig. 7).

Postcolonial leaders, such as General Aung San and U Nu, had brief moments of success in bringing the new nation together in some kind of common cause, but at the edges of the country and within ethnic minorities in the deltas and the cities there was no lasting consensus. Even in the flush of independence, communist and secessionist leaders were planning divisive campaigns. In 1961 the declaration of Buddhism as the state religion in an Asian democracy provoked the minorities to rebel, which was used as one of the justifications for the military coup in 1962 (see Military Rule under General Ne Win, ch. 1).

The coup leaders have labored to create a national party system and to fashion a socialist, military-led mandala (see National Unity, ch. 4). On paper the system bespeaks successful bureaucratic party control over every section of the country. One thousand years of Burmese history, however, suggest that in practice, such conclusions may be subject to challenge. In the early 1980s the center was Rangoon, and the Burmans, backed by military power, dominated the Burma Socialist Programme Party (BSPP—see Glossary) hierarchy. Despite organizational charts that show a rationally unified country balancing seven divisions—containing mostly Burmans—with seven states featuring various minority peoples, true unity may remain elusive. The 14 administrative units are represented by 14 stars in the national flag.

The Seven Divisions

The segments of Upper and Lower Burma that constituted the seven divisions made up the core of Burma in terms of population and political power. Government control was more secure in these areas, where in the early 1980s an estimated 64 percent of Burma's inhabitants lived, than it was at the fringes. The divisions were the Buddhist strongholds, which were also the areas where Burman education and the arts have flourished for centuries. As kings came and went, the divisions were most often under Burmese administration, although the Mons and others often managed to challenge the system. The divisions shared a basic world view, culture, language, religion, and royal tradition that could be reasonably called Burmese. Beyond the boundaries of

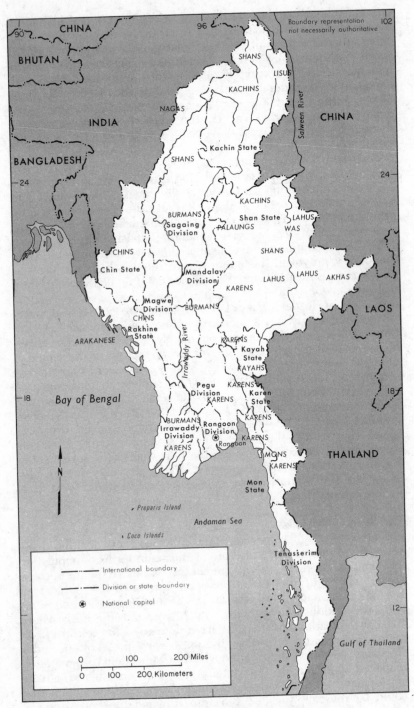

Figure 7. Distribution of Major Ethnic Groups

these seven divisions, matters became much more complex and capable of varying interpretations.

According to a report in the government-run *Working People's Daily* in May 1981, the seven divisions had a combined population of approximately 23.1 million, based on the most recent census. This was distributed as follows: Irrawaddy Division, 4.5 million; Mandalay Division, 4.2 million; Sagaing Division, 3.5 million; Rangoon Division, 3.5 million; Pegu Division, 3.5 million; Magwe Division, 3.1 million; and Tenasserim Division, 800,000.

Rangoon Division

Rangoon Division included the modern capital of the country, the largest city in Burma. The division was primarily composed of the capital, its sister town of Syriam, and towns on both sides of the Rangoon River for about 100 kilometers upstream. The small size of the division was more than compensated for by its political dominance, and in modern times Rangoon has rivaled Mandalay in terms of cultural importance.

Rangoon showed clearly its colonial heritage in the form of old British bank buildings still standing—sometimes with the original signs intact—many decades after independence. The size of urban Rangoon and its multiethnic population gave it a sophisticated atmosphere unlike most of the rest of Burma. Recent economic hard times have left their mark on the condition of the buildings, the struggling transportation system, and the standard of living. Every foreign visitor legally entering the country must disembark at Rangoon, and comparisons with other capitals are inevitable. Rangoon has not modernized rapidly but has barely maintained the necessary fundamentals, owing to the ingenuity of its people, who have kept in functional condition equipment that would be museum pieces elsewhere.

Above all mundane materialistic matters in Rangoon rise the beautiful Shwedagon and Sule pagodas, revealing the deepest values of the Burmans. The care and wealth lavished on these and other Buddhist symbols of Burman pride provide the clue to a people's priorities, no matter what the current economic situation might be. The Shwedagon Pagoda also serves as a major pilgrimage goal for many southern or Theravada Buddhists from abroad. As such, it represents Burma's bond to millions of believers outside its borders.

In the early 1980s most vital decisions were made in Rangoon; in addition to being the largest city in Burma, it was also its busiest port, the center of publishing and cinema, and the hub of economic power. Because the heart of the bureaucracy was there, it was difficult for any part of Burma to be uninfluenced by the policies and rules determined at the capital.

Mandalay Division

Mandalay Division evoked memories of a glorious precolonial past before Burma turned more outward and commercial and its capital was moved downstream. In this division were some of the old royal centers: Mandalay, Amarapura, and Pagan, as well as the old British hill station, Maymyo, where colonialists vacationed and where U (formerly General) Ne Win maintained a summer home. In the early 1980s the prestige center of the country was still Mandalay, despite Rangoon's status as the nation's capital.

The division stretched almost 300 kilometers north and south, from the rare gem mines in the north at Mogok to Pyinmana on the Sittang River to the south. To the west it was bounded by the Irrawaddy River and to the east by Shan State. At its center was the Kyaukse area, historically important for its rice production, using ancient irrigation systems that supported many Burmese royal centers.

Despite the bid of those at the Kaba Aye Pagoda complex at Rangoon to assume the leadership role for the *sangha* (Buddhist monkhood), the monasteries at Mandalay continued to retain traditional respect as centers of scholarship. The secular university at Mandalay played a similar role within the state-controlled education system. Whether creating images of the Buddha at Mandalay or fashioning fine lacquerware at Myinkaba near Pagan, traditional artists in Mandalay Division were thought to be the best. Upper Burma in these cases assumed a role of superiority over Lower Burma, which was seen as tainted more by Western ways under a longer British rule than was imposed upon the northern divisions. Although the dry crops of Upper Burma were usually successfully produced and harvested, the area was not able to support itself with enough rice and had to import from the more productive southern divisions. Thus the rivalry continued between these mutually dependent areas, each having something the other needed, and such ancient tensions between various sections of Burmese society were part of the spice of life in Burma.

Irrawaddy Division
Lying west and northwest of Rangoon, Irrawaddy Division included the mouth of the Irrawaddy River and the area upriver to Kyangin, south of Prome. Dominated by the second busiest port in Burma, the city of Bassein, the division bustled with commercial activity, such as jute shipping, rice processing, umbrella manufacturing, potterymaking, fishing, and turtle-egg collecting on Diamond Island. Although the dominant population was Burman, there were many Karens and also some Arakanese. Ethnic harmony has been difficult to maintain, and the delta area was not always considered secure enough for tourists to visit. Because the division bordered Rakhine State (formerly Arakan State), it was affected at times by tensions involving Arakanese restlessness under Burman rule. The Karen-Burman relationship in the division has been uneasy since early 1942, when nationalist

Burma Independence Army (BIA) forces took into custody and executed Karen hostages in the Myaungma District in the delta region, invoking Karen retaliation against the Burman population. The government has since made a considerable effort to minimize such ancient rivalries, but peace has remained elusive.

Pegu Division

Pegu Division included primarily the area north of Rangoon Division between the Irrawaddy and Sittang rivers. Its most famous centers were Pegu, Prome, and Toungoo—all three cities capitals of kingdoms in earlier times.

The southern part of the division evoked vivid memories of the Mon kingdoms at Pegu and the total destruction of their capital by the founder of the last Burmese royal dynasty, Alaungpaya (see The Reigns of Alaungpaya and His Sons, ch. 1). Local pride in past glories was expressed at Pegu in the towering Shwemawdaw Pagoda and in its large reclining Shwethalyaung Buddha. Although Mon power was broken almost two centuries ago, the importance of the Mons now and yesterday is never forgotten, because old rivalries have continued in modern guise, although usually with a typical Burmese politeness, if possible. Also numerous in the southern area were the Karens, whose own state formed the eastern border of the district.

Northwest of Pegu is Tharrawaddy, an area where the charismatic Burmese leader Saya San raised his rebellion against the British in the nearby jungles in the 1930s (see The Emergence of Political Movements, ch. 1). Still farther north is the city of Prome on the Irrawaddy, the center of various Mon and Burmese kingdoms that were often pawns in north-south struggles. Prome is also the location of the ancient ruins of Sri Ksetra, one of the most important archaeological sites in Burma because it was possibly one of the capitals of the Pyu peoples between the fifth and ninth centuries. Interest in Burma about the Pyu was strong because of their early Buddhist culture and because the government had, as the result of encouragement in high places, strongly urged research on these early inhabitants of the country.

Sagaing Division

Sagaing Division began just west of Mandalay and continued north until it reached the Ledo Road (made strategically important by World War II) coming out of the high mountains of India. At its southern end the division was nationally revered for its spirituality at beautiful Sagaing, where for centuries Buddhists have retreated for meditation and peace. In many ways Sagaing was the religious capital of the country, not in the sense that it was any kind of bureaucratic center of the *sangha* but rather in the role it played as a national resource of persons withdrawn from society and thus believed to possess heightened insight.

The Chindwin River flows through the western section of the division, which touches Chin State. As the river is traced into the mountains northward, it leads to some of the least known areas of the country, where the Naga peoples, who live on both sides of the Burma-India border, reside. Once famous for head-hunting, the Nagas living in India have been embroiled with its government in a struggle for guarantees of increased autonomy. Reports on their status in Burma were few, but a Naga separatist group was believed to be operating in Sagaing Division during the early 1980s. On the eastern borders of the division are Kachin and Shan states; therefore, the ethnic mix of the northernmost area is considerable, and the degree of governmental control is often problematic.

Magwe Division

Magwe Division (formerly Minbu Division), southwest of Mandalay, was part of the dry-crop zone of Burma on both sides of the Irrawaddy. In the western highlands the district bordered both Rakhine and Chin states. On the eastern side of the Irrawaddy the district met the southern portion of Mandalay Division. The natural resources of the area included numerous oil deposits, which were handworked for centuries and have since become important national assets, particularly those at Chauk and Yenaungyaung. As part of the traditional Burman heartland, the Pakokku monasteries to the north of Pagan command nationwide respect as centers of learning, and the town of Taungdwingyi to the south is famous for its literary figures.

Tenasserim Division

The least populated of the seven essentially Burman divisions in 1983 was Tenasserim, which stretched down the long coastline of the Andaman Sea, bordered on the east by Thailand. Although some rice was grown in its short valleys, Tenasserim was better known for its pearl fishing, sea cucumbers, edible bird's nests, and tin ore. It was also a problem area to the government because of the busy smuggling trails to Thailand across which were transported daily everything from tin to Buddhist sacred art. In its many archipelagic islands a seafaring life has existed for centuries, as practiced by the sea gypsies. In 1983 dreams of offshore oil existed to boost the national economy.

The Seven States

According to the same government publication that provided data for the divisions based on the most recent census, the populations of the states were as follows: Shan State, 3.2 million; Rakhine State, 1.9 million; Mon State, 1.5 million; Karen State, 1 million; Kachin State, 814,000; Chin State, 350,000; and Kayah State, 145,000.

Inhabitants of a village near Mandalay draw
water for household use.
Courtesy Frederica M. Bunge

At first glance the observer might be tempted to believe that the ethnic populations in each state match the names of the state, but such is not the case. For example, although there were many Kachins in the state of the same name, there were also many Burmans, as well as Shans and other minorities. Not all those in Mon State were Mons; many were also Burmans and Karens. Thus, the states were geographic areas in which largely symbolic recognition was given to a group that historically has lived in close relationship with Burmans but has periodically charted its own destiny. The endemic rebellions in most of these areas for centuries testify to the perdurability of their independent spirit.

Shan State

Once the masters of the Burmans when they ruled after the collapse of the Pagan-based monarchy, the Shans have no historical inferiority complex. In the centuries after the Pagan period, the Shans developed their own monarchies where Shan mandalas of power oscillated constantly as more powerful Burmese and Thai kings contested each other. Deference to outside royalty was a small price to pay for considerable Shan independence internally.

The Shans in 1983 were basically rice farmers, skillful traders, and a valley people. In matters of governance, historically they have allowed an aristocratic elite to rule them. Much like their

Burman neighbors and linguistically and genetically very close to the ethnic majority in Thailand, they nevertheless have maintained a uniqueness. The Shans have preserved customs and beliefs long since forgotten by their neighbors, for their society fosters such fidelity. For example, a Shan scholar has referred to the range of their monastic practices as "a living museum of ancient sectarianism" because nowhere else in Burma have people so cherished and preserved the diversity of their Buddhist heritage. Under policies and programs of early Burmese nationalists and later of military socialists, however, Shans have shed diversity more and more each year.

Certainly, the Shan era of the *sawbwa* (chieftain) was gone forever, and with the era's demise also departed much local feuding and many traditional graces. The fierce independence that each local world emperor engendered, however, had not likewise departed. Whether or not one accepted the belief that Shan plans for possible independence from Burma helped to motivate the army coup in 1962, one had to recognize that many Shans still believed they deserved more than token statehood or representation in the Union Day parade at Rangoon each February 12. If they were to be caught permanently in the web of nationbuilding, then many Shans wondered whether the nation planned simply to take more from the Shans than it would ever return, as traditional Southeast Asian village wisdom has always maintained is inevitable. Trapped in such a web, the Shans then could turn to the ancient arts of obfuscation, insurgency, and armed insurrection as options, or perhaps accept funding from outsiders who would like to harness internal discontent for international purposes. Another obvious alternative was to become a "bornagain" socialist, join the mass party, and seek fortune and fame with the Burman majority.

Assimilation in the Burman majority was a painful decision, as would be a similar process if Shans were absorbed into Thailand, where minorities were not tolerated as separate entities but were put under constant pressure to become Thai in language, dress, religion, and politics. Faced with unwelcome pressure to assimilate by both the Burmans and the Thai, many Shans sought to establish whatever symbolic or real uniqueness they could manage. Peculiarities of language and script were preserved, their form of Theravada Buddhism was different in many subtle ways from that of their neighbors and, most importantly, historical evidence for their right to independence was not allowed to be forgotten.

A few Shans have become involved in the smuggling and opium trade as a means of generating income and power. Fragile alliances have been made with Chinese-backed communist groups, descendants of the Chinese Nationalist troops, or with other ethnic groups in rebellion, such as the Karens, Was, or Kachins.

Using trails and a centuries-old smuggling network, Shans could move great quantities of material into Thailand. Much Burmese Buddhist art reached Bangkok by that route, and a Chinese-controlled smuggled jade business thrived as part of the same network. In the early 1980s the smuggling and drug traffic continued, despite decades of sporadic army efforts on both sides of the border to eliminate it or persuade the people to grow other crops or raise bees. The smuggling traffic also brought back into Burma the consumer goods for the thriving black market that provided what Burma's economy could or would not produce. The entire illegal system provided funds that would be used to keep alive Shan hopes for more autonomy.

Such hopes were not very realistic if most outside observers of the Burmese scene are correct. BSPP committees in Shan State were carefully fashioned by the military-controlled, unity-conscious leadership in Rangoon, whose ultimate goal was an integrated society tightly controlled by a central government, not a loose federation of states with a strong leader at the center of each. In such an environment it did little good to evoke the memory of the old Panglong Agreement days where national hero General Aung San had forged a bonding spirit that gave the Shans and others hope of more autonomy. Moreover, under the BSPP programs, the natural wealth in agricultural products, teak, ore, hydroelectric potential, or precious stones in Shan State was to be harnessed not so much for itself as for the higher goals of the socialist development of the entire country.

Perhaps the greatest danger to Shan autonomy would come when young Shans, indoctrinated in a highly controlled public education system, began to believe that the old Shan *sawbwas* were truly the archetypal aristocratic villains of socialist lore, whose demise was a victory over the forces of evil and a blow struck for the freedom of the masses. If Rangoon rhetoric succeeded in discrediting the *sawbwas* as oppressors of its peasants and workers, then the BSPP enticements of socialist power and plenty might yet have genuine appeal and efficacy, because the *sawbwas* in the early 1980s were vital symbols of Shan political identity, as they had been for centuries. The official attitude was that minorities could have their cultural unity within the framework of political unity. Minority identity would then become harmless theatrics epitomized in the Union Day parade at Rangoon, when the Shan minorities marched in their proper alphabetical place for a majority Burman crowd. Because many Shans rejected this role, Shan rebellions continued, other Shans dragged their feet in the nationalizing process, and still others cooperated with the socialist system either because they believed in it or because they hoped it might yet be possible to assert unique Shan claims in the People's Assembly.

Rakhine State

As Burma has developed into a predominantly Buddhist country, the Hindus and Muslims in its midst have had difficult roles to play. Buddhism claims a superiority over Hinduism. The great Hindu gods of Brahma, Siva, and Indra are reduced to godlings who must be reborn as Buddhist humans to achieve a release from further rebirths. One of the eight victories of the Buddha involves his teaching a Brahma that union with him is not the final goal but merely a stop on the way to final release from rebirth. The caste system is socially rejected. Hindus are referred to as *kala* (black people) in a derogatory fashion. Brahmin priests may have advised the kings of Burma, but they are classified by Burmans as inferior to Buddhist monks, despite their skills in astrology and other mystic arts. Memories of British troops using Indian soldiers to colonize Burma had not been allowed to fade. Muslims have fared little better, often assigned to butcher roles, for Buddhists disdain taking the life of the animals they eat. Colonial memories die hard, and the recollections of massive foreclosures on farms by Indian moneylenders in Lower Burma were still painful in the 1980s. Currency regulations enacted in the mid-1960s undermined the dominant economic position of Indian peoples living in Burma and resulted in the exodus of tens of thousands of them (see A Nationalized Economy, ch. 1). In such an atmosphere Rakhine State, bordering Bangladesh, naturally embodies certain minority tensions, particularly involving Bengali Muslims who had moved back and forth over the border.

Although Shan State represented approximately 10 percent of the nation's population in mid-1983, Rakhine State accounted for only about 6 percent. Until its capture by King Bodawpaya in the late 1700s, Arakan managed to maintain itself as an independent kingdom, speaking a variant of the Burmese language and practicing Buddhism. Bodawpaya, haunted by world emperor dreams, carted off to his capital the Arakanese Mahamuni statue of the Buddha with all its reputed powers of supernatural protection, and it resides in splendor in the Arakan Pagoda sanctuary south of Mandalay. The statue and a huge cannon were part of the loot acquired by the Burmans and were exhibited as physical proof of Burmese powers in nationbuilding, despite the formidable mountain ranges that had previously given security to the Arakanese. Having lost the symbols of a glorious past yet retaining the massive ruins of their former capitals, the Arakanese nationalists submitted to Rangoon only because of the fickleness of history.

Statehood for Rakhine was a tribute both to its historical independence and to its international position with reference to volatile relationships with nations to the west. Because many southern Chins impinged on its foothills and plains to the north, Rakhine also had the typical minorities mix of many of the seven states. Despite all these complexities, Rakhine was one of the more peaceful states, and parts of it around Myohaung and the capital of Sittwe (Akyab) had been opened in the early 1980s to foreign visitors; the beaches at Sandoway were opened by 1983. Physically separate from the Burman heartland, Rakhine was not in the mainstream of national life but like Shan State had its own history and concept of its special destiny.

Mon State

The third state in terms of population in mid-1983 was Mon State. Its center was Moulmein, the third largest city in Burma and once the British administrative center in the first half of the nineteenth century. To the east was Karen State, and many Karens lived on both sides of that border. There were also many Burmans included in Mon State, just as there were many Mons in Pegu Division. Historically, the Mons established kingdoms with capitals at Thaton and Pegu, the latter not part of the present state. Rivalry between Burmans and Mons (sometimes referred to as Talaings) has been a major factor in the dynamics of Burmese history, and bitter memories remain of the final destruction of the capital at Pegu by King Alaungpaya in 1757. The long struggle between the Mons and the Burmans was so destructive of life and property that many Mons migrated into Thailand for safety. Certainly, relationships with Burmans were not improved when Mons helped the British in the Anglo-Burmese wars, and tensions from such historical events continued to surface in modern group relations.

Although the Mon language is not akin to Burmese, the Mon religion is Theravada Buddhism, and tradition in Burma assigns to the Mon form of Buddhism a strong role in keeping all Burmans close to orthodoxy. Mon contributions to the arts, architecture, and literature of Burma are also legendary and can be particularly noted at Pagan. Interspersed with Burmans since the eighteenth century, many Mons have lost their language and some of their customs, becoming more and more like their neighbors, except that Mon nationalists retain a sense of identity. In the early 1980s Mon State was still not open to foreign visitors owing to the smuggling problems and various Mon-Karen independence movements.

Karen State

Karen State, once called Kawthule, included most of the border areas adjacent to Pegu Division and Mon State. East of it was the Thai border, and many Karens lived in Thailand as well, some crossing the border constantly. Historically, the Karens have found safety and semi-independence in the hills, where they have developed their own languages, religion, customs, dress, and political systems. Many migrated to the plains, where they took up rice farming, usually living near other Karens in an enclave.

Plains Karens, such as the Sgaw and Pwo Karens, were not located in their state at all but were found in many areas of Lower Burma, where they often adopted Buddhism and lived lives very much like those of their neighbors.

Those in the hills generally lived by the slash-and-burn system of clearing hillside patches of land—burning them and planting crops, such as rice, maize, and vegetables, in the soil and ashes. Although the government of Thailand has officially taken a dim view of this use of land, Burma apparently has not shared that negative view; neither government has had enough manpower to interfere. In Thailand the Karens were officially squatters, but they were definitely not so considered in Burma, and Karen State was no simple tokenism.

The Karens historically did not play a role equivalent to the Mons or the Arakanese; even in their own oral histories, they saw themselves as usually outdone by the Burmans. Seldom organized beyond shifting groups of villages loyal to a charismatic leader, the Karens have no glorious memories or archaeological ruins of past Karen kingdoms, but they have been prone to enthusiastic beliefs in millennial leaders who would bring them the boons of a kingdom to come.

It has been fashionable to call the traditional religion of people like the Karens a form of animism, or "spirit worship." The word never does justice to such beliefs, which may be as complex and lofty as those of the major religions of the world. Traditional Karens, like so many other peoples, believe that both matter and spirit are realities, each possibly inhabiting the same entity at a given time or perhaps later separated but still linked. The natural world of plants and animals is filled with the spiritual components of each thing, just as the spirits of humans must be dealt with, whether still joined to a living body or not. Living very close to both nature and one's living and dead kin involves traditional Karens with obligations to spiritual forces about them. A common Western bias is that if a people worship gods, they are more civilized than if they worship spirits, but in Southeast Asia the more distant the god, the less important the spiritual influence of that force. There are Karen gods, rituals, and oral religious traditions so impressive that early missionaries toyed with the belief that the Karens were a lost tribe of Israel. Traditional Karen religion has a strong tendency to ascribe a supernatural component to all forms of life and everyday experiences. In that respect they share much with their Buddhist neighbors.

Always alert to ways to strengthen themselves for the perpetual competition with more powerful neighbors, the Karens welcomed the advent of the British in the last century, and many turned to Christianity as a means of establishing links to the Western world. Others eagerly sought education under British and American Baptist missionary guidance. When the British staffed army units with hill tribe peoples and Indians to control the Burmans, who were denied the right to join the colonial armed forces, the Karens joined with eagerness. Understandably, the Burmans did not look kindly on what they considered misplaced loyalty. In all these areas Karens seem to have sought means to avoid assimilation with the Burmans, and separatist movements were endemic among the Karens.

The most impressive Karen insurgency took place after World War II when, in alliance at times with Mon nationalist and communist groups, Karens and others took over parts of Burma, including Bassein and Mandalay. Nothing on that scale has occurred since 1949, but the fighting has never stopped for long, despite numerous amnesty campaigns and many frank talks with insurgent leaders. One of the basic problems not addressed by the creation of Karen State has been that the vast majority of Karens live outside it.

No matter where Karens live, they characteristically have a strong sense of ethnic pride. With a script developed with missionary help, for example, they published their own newspaper as early as 1841 in Tavoy, and Karens continued to publish Christian and secular material in the early 1980s. At Rangoon University and Judson College, they strove hard for upward mobility while competing with Burmans in both studies and sports. Because many Karen leaders have been Christian, they have sought to maintain contact with Westerners almost as a way of obtaining more security, but because outside missionaries have been banned from Burma in recent decades, the opportunities for outside contacts have diminished. The Karens' turn to insurgency may in part represent yet another method of making sure they are not altogether forgotten in a mass of Burman socialists.

Kachin State

Kachin State accounted for only under 3 percent of Burma's population in the early 1980s, including many plains Burmans and Shans. The Kachins have never been bashful about making themselves known as willing to fight hard to preserve a certain amount of independence from Burmans, Shans, Chinese, and even the invading Japanese in World War II. Inhabiting the northeast border area of Burma, they have historically preferred the hills to the plains, but some have also left the mountains to become wet-rice farmers in "civilized" fashion.

Of all the minorities in Burma, the Kachins have the greatest reputation for resorting to arms to assert what they believe are their rights. The British discovered this when they tried to "pacify" the area, which some say was not firmly under Pax Britannica until the 1930s. A few years later the Japanese found it impossible to conquer the area. Since independence, the Burmese government has done little better; the Kachin Independence

Organization and elements of the insurgent Burmese Communist Party have located in the north, where it was possible to maintain contact with both militant Shans and China (see Revolutionary, Separatist, and Warlord Groups, ch. 5).

Kachins (known more accurately as Jingphaws, Marus, or Lashis) have never had Shan-style small kingdoms but have created loose groupings of village chiefs who have acted in concert when mutual interest has been served. Prone to avenge wrongs, Kachins have often feuded. They have also exacted safe-passage fees from trade caravans moving through their territories. Before colonial times they traded in slaves across the northern expanse of Burma. In their attitudes toward plains people, the Kachins may certainly have appreciated the more complex civilization below them, but they also felt a certain pride in being mountain people. The British army recruiter Major C.M. Enriquez, who much admired the Kachins, was given the following Kachin statement in the 1920s: "I feel my own size up here . . . . In Mandalay I am only as big as my finger. In solitude everyone is important. A crowd is a herd of small people." Such an attitude might be said to epitomize the feelings of most hill peoples.

Christian missionaries long worked in the Kachin hills, but without the degree of success they had expected. During British rule, missionary schools could be used for a bid for language skills and social contacts, which some Kachins developed to become leaders of nationalistic causes. The traditional Kachin religion is deeply related to their intimacy with the mountains and a combination of their hunting concepts and hill agriculture. The religion also provides a symbolic explanation of their complex kin, marriage, and feasting systems in which those who aspire to the most status have to validate themselves by giving elaborate feasts at which wealth is redistributed for increased prestige. The fate of traditional Kachin culture, like that of all hill peoples, is little known outside of Burma.

Chin State

Even less populous than Kachin State in the early 1980s was Chin State, which represented about 1 percent of the total population. Chin peoples, who are identified by a bewildering number of names, live in the mountainous regions between Rakhine State and central Burma. On the western border, Chin State touches Bangladesh and India, where many Lushai Chins live. Always self-defined, like so many other hill peoples, by reference to lowland wet-rice Buddhists, historically Chins have found an ecological niche where their hillside villages existed in relative independence from Burmese administration. Because no east-west roads connect their territory with the outside world, historically they have been able to trade, make war, conduct slave raids, hunt, feud, and compete with each other without direct outside control or much interference.

Village leaders, as in other hill groups, may have momentarily commanded a regional following, but nothing resembling a state has apparently ever developed. Turbulent, competitive, legalistic, and yet very social, the Chins did not take to Christianity as well as did the Karens. Like the Karens, those who are Christians (possibly one-quarter of the population) have hoped to use their new faith to link with outside powers to protect their people from being engulfed by Burmans. The traditional religion was undergoing changes long before the area was closed to outside observers in 1962, and it may not have survived into the early 1980s in its former state. Chin religion, in which the door to paradise is opened by hunting done in the proper way to honor and contend with the spirits of what is killed, can be seen in contrast to the Buddhism of their neighbors, where taking life is normatively scorned. Animal sacrifice, so common among hill peoples, is likewise condemned by valley Buddhists. While hill and valley people share a common conviction that the most interesting explanations for phenomena are spiritual or supernatural speculations, they differ sharply on matters of sacrifice.

Although Chin nationalist groups have at times been formed to promote Chin causes, insurrections have not apparently been at all common. Little information was available, but one could assume that Arakanese and Muslim disturbances nearby have not been without influence on militant Chins, and in the early 1980s a very small Chin separatist movement was believed active in Chin State. Burman kings historically exacted levies on Chins, who were used as warriors; the British used Chins in their armies because of their fighting ability and their loyalty, and Burman commanders have used Chin units for similar reasons. The combative spirit is certainly not lacking in the Chins, but perhaps the drive for complete independence is. Their quest is, and has always been, for coexistence with the majority, not complete separation.

Kayah State

More a token nod to a Karen subdivision than a recognition of any substantial political power, Kayah State represented slightly over 0.4 percent of the national population in the early 1980s. Nestled between Karen State to the south and Shan State to the north, with Thailand on its eastern border, the Red Karen, or Karenni (also called Kayahs), have managed to differentiate themselves enough from their neighbors to carve out a special status with Burman kings, Shan princes, British colonialists, and Burmese socialists. It is possible that the secret of their success has been that no major power has really cared enough about their territory to integrate it thoroughly into a larger mandala. To distinguish themselves from other Karens, Kayahs historically established Shan-like small kingdoms that were more symbolic than actual. In the early 1980s their state was part of the complex Thailand-Burma border culture that involved the shadow economy and Karen and Shan insurgency, but up-to-date information was sparse.

Chinese, Indians, and Other Minorities

The seven minority states by no means, even on a symbolic basis, do justice to the ethnic mix that is modern Burma. Centuries of Chinese immigration have affected Burmese life, from national tastes in food to religious customs. Most Chinese, like their counterparts in Thailand, have tried to assimilate over the years to avoid the anti-Chinese violence that occurred in Indonesia and Burma in the 1960s. Always aware of its giant neighbor to the north, the government has constantly encouraged goodwill visits while keeping Burmese troops active against Chinese-backed insurgents. Chinese businessmen, proverbially sharper and more successful than Burmans, have been subdued more in Burma than in neighboring Thailand, but a few still manage to obtain wealth and high status. Perhaps the most enduring Chinese influence on Burma has been on the Burmese socialist revolution itself which, with its mass programs and rhetoric to mythical workers and peasants, seems to have its roots in the Chinese Revolution as much as in its Soviet counterpart—almost as if the Burmese are saying that it is not necessary for the Chinese or Soviets to take over Burma because the Burmese have already had their revolution.

Peoples from India, Burma's other large neighbor, have had an obvious and profound influence on Burma's religion, law codes, medicine, royal traditions, nationalist movements, education system, and economy. Tensions between the Burmans and Indians were greatly increased when the latter were able to gain access to the country under British colonial auspices, soon gaining power in the commercial, military, and civil service sectors, much to the annoyance of the Burmans, particularly in Lower Burma. By the early 1980s Indians were most often found in the urban areas and had lost most of the power they once had in Burma.

Muslims, particularly in Rakhine State in Lower Burma and in parts of Upper Burma, also have been important in Burmese society. The historically porous border between Burma and Bangladesh and India has been the source of perpetual movement of Muslims back and forth in response to their various political fortunes. The First Anglo-Burmese War involved such border clashes, and U Ne Win has found it advantageous to moderate immigrant issues involving Muslims in Rakhine State in order not to alienate militant Muslims in the world community. Although the potential was always there for Buddhist-Muslim confrontation, in general the two groups have managed to live peaceably side by side but without much interaction.

Since 1962 the Burmese government has been unreceptive to efforts of most non-Burmese Westerners who have tried to live in the country, including those married to Burmese. Anglo-Burmans having Burmese citizenship, on the other hand, have been accepted as members in good standing. The frustrating seven-day visa limit so long imposed upon foreign visitors mirrored on a small scale Burma's neutralist and somewhat isolationist policies on the international scene.

In 1982 the government passed a new citizenship law that included as full citizens groups of "nationals," such as the Kachins, Kayahs, Karens, Chins, Mons, Arakanese, Shans, and members of those ethnic groups that had lived in Burma before 1824, the date of the First Anglo-Burmese War. Others could apply to become citizens, "associate citizens," or "naturalized citizens." Those in the last two categories could lose their status if they showed "disaffection or disloyalty" to the state in any way. Only time would show how the law would be applied to Indians, Muslims, Chinese, and others. The good behavior clauses gave the government considerable leeway in controlling foreigners to whom it granted some form of citizenship, and it was yet to be learned whether the government would make all Indians, Muslims, and Chinese citizens. No provision was made for refugees. Many who had come into Burma since colonial times were not defined as citizens but had to apply for citizenship. A foreigner could not become a citizen simply by marrying one, but offspring of such a union might apply for naturalized citizenship. The law, in other words, gave full citizenship only to the descendants of "nationals" who had been in residence since the time when the British colonial conquest of the country could be said to have begun. Many minority peoples had settled in Burma since that time and were not considered full citizens.

Mention should also be made of some of the many other minorities who have neither symbolic state status nor sizable population but who are nevertheless given their place in the Union Day parade, where some 67 "national races" are officially listed, including those assigned separate states, as well as the Burmans themselves. A "race" seems to be determined by a wide variety of criteria, from linguistics to social identity. From Shan State comes perhaps the greatest variety of minorities: the Shan Tayok (Chinese Shans), whose men wear distinctive turbans and blue trousers; the Akhas (also called Kaws), devotees of elaborate silver decorations; the Was from the China border area, once famous for head-hunting and now deeply involved with opium and border politics; the Lahus, whose women wear long black dresses draped with ropes of silver; the Lisus, whose women wear long multicolored skirts; and the Palaungs, who are Buddhist hill peoples speaking a Mon-Khmer language. From the Loi-kaw area of Kayah State come the "giraffe" women who sport rings about their necks. All these examples of the ethnographic variety in Burma only suggest the complexity of the task facing any government that tries to build a unified modern state out of cartographic Burma.

In the early 1980s the government was seeking to broaden its network of social services activities and to train and inspire people to serve in the "hardship" areas. To meet such goals it had established the Academy for the Development of National Groups in 1964 at Sagaing (later moved to Ywathitgyi), where mutual understanding and government-sponsored concepts of unity were taught. The main problem seemed to be that graduates were reluctant to serve in the hardship border areas, the same problem that the government has had with doctors. Because power is centered in Rangoon, people who wish to improve their status seek work there, not in the fringe areas where most of the minorities are. For many in the periphery, therefore, the governmental stick was seen more often than the carrot. More tempting for the minorities were smuggling, the opium trade, or paid insurrection, and for such reasons the border tensions were unlikely to be solved in the near future.

Overseas Burmese

One regrettable outcome of the events since 1962 has been the exodus of many talented and patriotic Burmese from the country because they could not accept, or be accepted by, the new leadership. To these overseas Burmese, the loss of their country has been a painful experience. To prevent a "shadow nation" from growing outside its borders, the government has required each citizen who leaves the country for any reason to post a sizable bond that their relatives and friends are bound to pay if the citizen does not return to Burma. Many have had to leave their family's life savings and belongings behind, while others have spent many years in jail for opposition political activities.

In recent years offers of amnesty have been made, and some exiles have returned, the most famous being ex-premier U Nu who, with his well-known dedication to Buddhism and literature, was presumably enjoying his native land once again as a nonpolitical Buddhist scholar. In the return of U Nu, himself a former insurgent leader against the man who ousted him from leadership, the enigmatic character of contemporary Burmese society was well illustrated. A military socialist revolution occurred that often has been relentless in its application, but it was a revolution carried out by once-colonized Buddhists, who were likely to remember both the principles of how to treat the loyal opposition and the virtues of the Buddha's message of compassion.

The Burman World View

Centuries of living together have produced for Burma's ethnic groups a certain core of culture that is characteristic of the whole civilization. Although ethnic minorities in the hilly border areas may celebrate and preserve their distinct ways, the lowland, Burman view of the world is well known, if not as a counterpoint to "tribal" ways then as an alternate, higher status ethos. The way the dominant society sees the world distinctively can be called their world view, which is not completely unique to the Burmans; aspects of it may be shared with other ethnic groups in the country and without. The important point is that the attempt is made to focus on what the majority in the country, the Burmans, practice and believe. Certainly the dominant aspect in their world view is Theravada Buddhism (see Glossary).

The Buddhism of Burma

Burmese follow "the path of the elders"—that form of Buddhism known as Theravada or Hinayana (the "small" vehicle), in contrast to Mahayana (the "great" vehicle—see Glossary) in China, Japan, Korea, and elsewhere. The Theravada faith is followed in Sri Lanka, Burma, Laos, Kampuchea, and Thailand, and for thousands of years its sacred texts have come down in Pali, an ancient Indian language. Theravada Buddhists differ from other Buddhists primarily because they emphasize only Gotama the Buddha, the original teacher of the sixth century B.C. in India, and not a host of other Buddha-like beings called bodhisattvas, who exist in heaven to aid the faithful, as they also did for the Tantric Buddhists of old Tibet and elsewhere. In strict orthodox Theravada Buddhism, Gotama was merely a human being; he does not exist anywhere to hear people's prayers. His words are left in the sacred books and can be learned from his "sons," the living Theravada monks, who exist today as the Buddha once instructed the first monks to live. All Burmans share in this heritage and follow some semblance of the strict orthodox teachings. The Buddhism of the Pali scriptures, however, often differs from actual religious beliefs and practices in modern Burma.

Nonattachment

In terms of each persons' daily plan and lifelong ambition, a major quest is for nonattachment to the sensate world, which everyone must quit eventually. In the early years and in the flush of adulthood, attachments to kin, sensate pleasures, career, society, and self are seen as naturally strong; nonetheless, one should try to lessen the bonds. Rational thought should conclude in harmony with the Buddha's teachings that the stronger the attachment, the worse the eventual suffering when all must be released at the end. Each person will vary tremendously in the ability to control desire, and human weaknesses undermine many sincere efforts. For example, because the Buddha condemned alcohol as a substance that prevented rational thought, Buddhists

*Pagodas and temples throughout Burma reflect the
ethos of a society permeated by Theravada Buddhism.
Monks—even the very young who may just be novices
in the order—are accorded great deference.
Photograph opposite page, top right,
courtesy Caroline M. Hufford; photograph
bottom left, courtesy Catherine B. Ferguson*

try not to drink alcohol, but some lack the will to avoid it, though they usually are the first to explain that they are wrong to indulge. The more sensate pleasure a person can deny, the more Burman Buddhists honor that person. Slaves to attachments, however, are merely normal humans, not sinners.

The Burmans most honored are monks and nuns (few in number), for they control their desires as lay people try to do but cannot. Because almost all male Burmans from their youth onward spend some time in a monastery striving for nonattachment, their self-control is tested; if they cannot control their desires to eat often or be sexually active, for example, they return to normal life, and no stigma will be attached to them. The worst possible behavior would be to accept public honor for being a monk but to cheat and secretly give in to desires, for then the Burman's most respected institution, the *sangha,* would be sullied. Most monks therefore abide by all 227 rules under the watchful eyes of one another and the members of society at large who support them. Those monks who need the least are, in such a system, given the most honor and act as exemplars for the society, for they embody a daily reminder of the Buddha's teachings. Lay persons simply do their best to be moderate. Of course, the older one gets, the closer one gets to death and, as in the Indian tradition, the first gray hairs signal that less attachment might be a good idea as the shadows fall. On holy days, older people therefore naturally predominate at the rituals and seek more ardently to practice the wisdom that since youth they have been taught but could not always follow.

Rebirth, Giving, Merit, and Demerit

Rebirth in some form is assumed, the form of life to be determined by the quality of one's previous existence. Any living creature (the cycle does not involve vegetation) can be seen as a being like us, that is, involved in a cycle of rebirths in which the most fortunate birth is as a human, a male, and a monk. Strictly, since the self is ultimately seen as an illusion in Theravada Buddhism, it is the consequences of ones' actions that are reborn, not a soul or personality. Most Burmans act on an easier concept to grasp—that of some form of self that returns. The Buddhist quality of this life determines the conditions of the next. Between rebirths there is time to be punished in any one of eight hells or rewarded in any one of 32 heavens.

Burmans believe that the best way to ensure a better future life is to give as generously as possible to Buddhism rather than to secular charities or causes. Buddhist giving is noted in golden books kept by heavenly beings and is called "merit." The more merit earned, the better the rebirth. The more one has, the more one should give, but intent is very important, and a simple flower from a sincere poor farmer is said to earn more merit than a disdainful cash donation by a rich merchant. Merit is usually shared or can be entirely transferred. When a boy enters a monastery for the first time, he traditionally transfers the merit he earns to his mother. It is customary to share merit with all beings in this world, in hell or in heaven. Merit is a concept difficult to convert into secular channels. Buddhists do not see themselves earning any merit by paying taxes for a welfare state or by giving to hospitals or the poor. Some socialists wish ardently that they could transform Buddhist merit earning into social improvement projects, but there are strong reasons why Theravada Buddhists do not do so.

Each person, poor or rich, sick or healthy, intelligent or otherwise, is the product of whatever merit or lack of it was earned in previous lives. Each is, in a sense, spending in this life the fruits of merit earned previously. There is no one to blame if this life is difficult; each deserves what was earned before. Others will feel compassion for another's suffering, but ultimately each is responsible for one's own fate. Under such a system, riches are one's just reward; poverty, conversely, is the just consequence of what is called demerit.

Demerit is recorded on dog-skin books by supernatural beings, and the record may include the killing of a mosquito as it bit, a drinking party, or perhaps adultery. The standard five precepts include not lying, not taking intoxicants (including alcohol and narcotics but not tobacco or coffee), not committing adultery (some exclude males who use prostitutes) not killing any creature, and not stealing. The orthodox maintain that each demeritorious act must be paid for first in one of the eight hells before moving on to one of the heavens to delight in the rewards for the worthy, but others lull themselves into believing that demerit can be reduced by application of merit earned or transferred. The human wish to use an accounting system explains the sudden, conspicuous religiosity of some notoriously wicked individuals in Burma. Although many may hope their merit record will give them a trip to a sensually exquisite heaven before their next rebirth, the ultimate Theravada goal is final, total release from any more rebirths. This permanent transcendent state of freedom from the entire cycle is known as nirvana, a condition reached only by the Buddha and those who live at the highest levels of Buddhist accomplishments.

Meditation and Truth

One way of seeking nirvana is through an inward exploration of consciousness known as meditation, which helps to confirm the belief that what is conveniently conceived of as self or person is actually a coalition of parts creating the illusion of existence. Burmans follow particularly a form of introspection and insight that stresses components of consciousness, such as breathing.

Some monks specialize in this search for ultimate truths, and in modern times laypersons join centers that teach the arts of meditation in peaceful settings. Burmans in meditation seek not only Buddhist paths to truth but also the benefits of mental and physical health that accrue from the process, for tensions are reduced at many levels.

Buddhists also believe that in the process of discovering inner truths through meditation, a person, particularly a monk, gains supranormal power, such as the ability to see and hear things far away or the power to travel in air. A monk must not claim such powers, nor is he to use them, but his lay followers may let it be known that indeed he has them, and many stories are told of remarkable disclosures made by meditating monks about matters that Western science cannot explain. Burmans will often deny to outsiders that they believe in psychic or magical phenomena, but many, if they meet with an understanding listener, will be quite willing to explain how supranormal powers are manifest.

Truth is comprehended at various levels, only one of which is scientific in the Western sense, whereas there are many religious paths to enlightenment or wisdom. The only orthodox path is through the *sangha*, because thousands of strict teachings and rules have kept the realms of *nats* (spirits) and magic in their proper places. Outside the *sangha* are various other religious practitioners, such as hermits, wizards, alchemists, astrologers, shamans, mediums, and folk experts of all kinds. All of these will usually operate under an umbrella of Theravada Buddhism but are not considered on the right path by the strictest monks. A *nat*, whether in the heavens or on earth, is ever present. Only Buddhism is said to master the spirit hosts, but many non-monks also try hard to control them. Everyone seeks to comprehend as much truth as possible, some only through orthodox means, but many also seek the exciting and dangerous, if less noble, paths.

Prophecy and Hope

In Burma some hill Karens and many Burmans share hopes that some day a leader will come to prepare the world for the next Buddha. The last Buddha lived 2,500 years ago, and life is believed to become worse as more and more people forget the last Buddha's teachings. Life will deteriorate further, so the prophecy goes, and then a charismatic king will come to Burma (or to the Karens if they express the hope), and under his reign there will be a paradise on earth in which the next Buddha will preach, and all who hear him will be assured of nirvana. Many charismatic historical people, like Alaungpaya, the founder of the last Burmese dynasty, have been seen as this future king or world emperor. Although scriptures can be quoted to prove that the world must wait 5,000 years from the death of the last Buddha for such events, various experts are always on hand to recalculate and to prophesy that the future emperor is indeed imminent or actually here, as the tempestuous King Bodawpaya claimed. Since potential "kings," such as Saya San, can cause serious rebellions, the present government strongly discourages such belief, but as life becomes more difficult, old prophecies are recalled nevertheless.

Spiritual Power as National Treasure

Convinced that they carry on truths that could save the world from its present path, Burmans welcome visitors sympathetic to their religion. Those who admire rationality strip Theravada Buddhism to a philosophy or mental science that proudly proclaims a longtime understanding of the insubstantiality of matter or the essence of relativity. Those who prefer the supranormal to the logical welcome visitors who are bored with science and seek to explore other explanations for phenomena. In between these two groups are millions of Burmans who believe that the Buddha's teachings are the only sensible guides to handling modern life as it increasingly caters to creature comforts.

Any visitor to the massive Shwedagon Pagoda or to the public ceremonies at Kaba Aye Pagoda in Rangoon, which honor the hundreds of monks who have won prizes for scholarship in Pali, will quickly realize how important Buddhism is to national life. What is true in Rangoon is valid in this case at every Buddhist village. The village pagoda may be much smaller and the monastery inhabited by one or only a few adult monks, but the meaning and importance are the same. With much effort and pride, the teachings of the Buddha are honored not because he was a god but because he was a deeply respected, very wise human being. The more one donates to Buddhism, the more one demonstrates that respect, and the more others in the society respect the donor. No matter what the standard of living may be in Burma in comparison with other countries—and few would argue that it is anything but very low—the society never fails to give generously to its religion. The thousands of ancient pagodas around the countryside built in honor of the Buddha's memory are never torn down for a hotel site or building materials. They remain as testimony to the spirit of Buddhist giving, as do the massive buildings at Pagan. Such is the Burmans' national treasure, preserved and honored through the ages.

Men of Prowess

Those who have earned a great deal of merit in previous lives benefit in this life with visible marks of success, such as power and wealth. The greater the splendor, the more the reserve of merit gained in previous existences. Historically, the monarch claimed the best merit balance, and because he had the most wealth, he was expected to be the most generous donor to Buddhism in the society; thus medieval Pagan was built.

Popular belief, however, has asserted that once a person's account is exhausted of previous merit, then that individual will have to "spend" the store of demerit previously earned; that is, misfortunes in a row will strike, signaling the exhaustion of good fortune and the beginning of bad. The smallest signs might be the fatal clue, such as a bad fall or the appearance of an evil omen. Followers and supporters might suddenly evaporate in fear that the leader's unfortunate fate will doom them also. Because Buddhism has stressed that nothing is permanent, even the universe itself, the downfall of a brilliant leader is only further proof of the law of impermanence. Swift changes in fortune are likely to be explained by such reasoning in all walks of Burmese society.

Leaders, therefore, are watched carefully for merit balance indications. Neither king nor military hero is expected to be able to defeat the law of impermanence. Those who rule by force, especially through war, are amassing great quantities of demerit, but their success is nevertheless heralded as proof of a previous good life. Kings, the rebel Saya San, the martyred general Aung San, and General Ne Win are examples of men who clearly had a massive merit balance. Such secular men of prowess are also expected to continue to work on their cosmic merit balance by giving to Buddhism at some point. The new pagoda that was being constructed under Ne Win's guidance was conceived by many as his bid for recognition as a leader in the old style of the kings at Pagan.

The law of impermanence thus can manifest itself at any time. A person who dies suddenly or is brought down by disaster can also become a *nat*, held in awe and fear by many. Such spirits may then inspire a body of followers who appease the particular spirit to protect themselves from any harm it might do to them or to receive any powers it may be able to dispense. Over the centuries certain spirits, known as the Thirty-Seven Nats, have attracted considerable public attention and inspired ritual treatment by mediums possessed by these spirits. In socialist Burma the official government position discourages belief in spirits, but in the society at large such beliefs are widespread. Even those who succeed in a brilliant fashion may be thought to have supernatural help from spirits, not necessarily from the classic *Thirty-Seven*, but from any of countless beings, from Brahmas in the most ethereal heavens to Indra (the spiritual counterpoint of earthly monarchs).

Powerful leaders, therefore, become the focus of a number of ambivalent public beliefs and emotions. If they are like the old kings, then they may be one of the traditional five evils one prays daily to escape. If the country experiences good fortune during their regime, then all may rejoice in the blessings of their accumulated merit. If assassination or sudden death strikes, then the ancient Buddhist law of impermanence is proved once again. If stories of supranormal events are told about a person after death, he may be thought of as some form of spiritual force that must be reckoned with seriously. The standard wisdom in Burmese society stresses the proverb "When the buffalo fight, the grass gets trampled." Thus those who are the grass should hope they are not present around the powerful ones, for fight they always will.

Social Status

In any Theravada society, the highest deference is given to Buddhist monks; even a mother bows deeply to her young son, who may be just a novice in the order, for in his orange robe he has become a living symbol of the Buddha. One's head must be kept below that of a monk. Upon entering a monastery, one bows three times deeply to the statue of the Buddha, then to the presiding monk. When leaving, one bows to the monk first and then to the image. The highest ranking military officer or politician in the country must so behave, for monks are even more respected than kings. In Thailand, for example, the king ritually bows to his head monk.

If a monk is especially revered by the people because of his nonattachment and character, women, to show their respect, may bow in the street so that he walks on a "carpet" of their hair. Respect often involves an emotional feeling akin to love. Monks so revered may be honored with gifts, which they are too nonattached to use, thus inspiring still further gifts, which are usually given to the needy.

Because anyone who is mentally and physically sound and who is not a fugitive from legal responsibilities may join the *sangha*, any male may become one of the most highly respected members of Burman society. Consequently, the *sangha* becomes a vital ingredient in social mobility. Because monks move about the country seeking new teachers, a country boy from a poor home has the same basic options as does his opposite.

Although the ideal monk is given much status because of nonattachment, there are monks who do not always leave the world behind them and dabble in secular affairs. Any good village monk is a counselor, adviser, and consultant on village affairs, but he is expected to be apolitical, particularly regarding national issues. In the turbulent 1950s and 1960s, for example, many monks became involved in mass politics, much to the embarrassment of all "good" Buddhists. The "purification" efforts of the early 1980s by the government to rid the *sangha* of false monks ostensibly have sought to defrock those who used the robe as a disguise. A monk may only eat and use what he has been given; therefore his lay supporters traditionally have been able to register their disapproval through reducing their giving. The *sangha* has lasted 2,500 years because of this simple method of control, but it is traditional in Burmese society for strong rulers to claim the power to purify; thus U Ne Win is making his timely bid.

Kings of the past and socialist military leaders have been naturally a bit uneasy to see untaxed wealth pouring into the *sangha*. King Bodawpaya was almost obsessed with the problem and threatened to defrock every monk in the kingdom, but the monks stayed out of sight until the king simmered down. Monks are clearly not always saintly, and donors are sometimes seeking to evade taxes or influence monks to action. Monks by definition must not rouse their followers to political action, and if monks must become political they must leave the *sangha* voluntarily. Political monks invite lay control, and much of the sectarian activity in Burma in the last century has been owing to self-reform movements within the *sangha* to improve their respect in the public's eyes. Despite complex developments within the *sangha* to cope with modern instability in Burma, the monk continues to receive the most respect the society can give.

In Burman society the aged are revered also. Although the aged bow to the monk, everyone else bows or at least should show some sign of respect to older people, such as raising joined hands to the head. To have one's first gray hairs is to be approaching the period in life when deference will be given with affection. In village life the ultimate authority usually resides in the elders, whose knowledge of their neighbors is used to foster the spirit of compromise in a mature fashion. Persons with cool heads have mastered their passions. Typically, headmen are younger spokesmen for the leaders to the outside world or token leaders for their silent, older superiors within the village. Burmans, though they admire youthful movie stars, dancers, or athletes, do not ascribe wisdom to the young, nor do Burmans attempt to hide their age, as do so many Westerners.

In the *sangha*, leadership is also in the hands of the most senior person, that is, the monk with the greatest number of years in the order. Elsewhere in society decisions also flow from the top, and attempts to rule by committees and voting in a democratic fashion go against ancient custom. In the Burman way the person with the highest status, often the oldest person, is asked before the meeting what to do. After informal discussion, agreement is reached privately; then in public, after perhaps perfunctory discussion, unanimity is announced. Attempts since colonial times to overthrow the system of seniority and hierarchical control have met with very little success. So deeply ingrained is the system that among siblings, each always honors older brothers and sisters no matter how powerful one may become outside the home. At Buddhist rituals the family sits in hierarchical order based on age within male and female groups.

Western models of social organization in Burma, of course, are deeply rooted in both communism and socialism, and both ideologies, like democracy, have been transplanted to Burmese soil that has always been more conducive to other, more ancient, systems of interrelationships. Western ideas are so firmly planted that the government keeps touting and counting the number of committees of peasants, workers, or whomever the revolution has inspired. To a traditionally oriented Burman, however, serving on a committee is a grim form of torture. Much more comfortable is governance by seniority or hierarchy; when each person is made equal by fiat on a committee and expected to vote in a democratic fashion, then the typical result is the release of aggression normally held in check by the usual chain of command. The society has been structured too long by seniority to change easily. Thus no matter how much socialist rhetoric flowed from government presses about the voice of the masses, the decisions in modern Burma still emanated from a hierarchy.

In a Buddhist society that offers high status to nonattachment and age, wealth is nevertheless respected. In modern socialist Burma, capital has been difficult to acquire because so many private industries have been nationalized. The heralded government goal has been to reduce the contribution of the private sector to about one-fourth of the gross domestic product (GDP—see Glossary) by fiscal year (FY—see Glossary) 1983, but achievement of that end was doubtful. Observers of Burmese economics and markets in the early 1980s were convinced that wealth through ownership of large landholdings had been sharply reduced through land reform, although not entirely eliminated. Wealth through agricultural success was difficult to achieve in a controlled economy concentrating on food production. Even the casual observer of Burma could note the signs of private wealth; thus methods obviously existed for achieving it, but outsiders could only speculate on the means. Allusions to the shadow economy or corruption in the bureaucracy were easily made but not possible to verify. There apparently remained ways to gain financial leverage. Conspicuous consumption was clearly not a good idea, but giving generously to Buddhism was still much admired. The wealth that produced the most status was that used to feed and support monks, build a monastery or pagoda, or support Buddhism in general.

Wealth could be manifest in the form of a government car, a free airplane ride for relatives, better housing, a job for a cousin, or any other benefit from government influence. These marks of success were difficult to transfer to the *sangha*, and to the degree such schemes prospered at the expense of transferable wealth, the old society would gradually change.

Without doubt, the army and police had great status. Having power that few could challenge, they were both feared and respected for the sheer exercise of force, but whether they were admired was another question. Burmans have retained bitter

111

memories of the exclusion of their people from colonial armies and the use of minorities to enforce the will of the raja. The training of the Thirty Comrades by the Japanese as heroic soldiers to help "liberate" the country from the British has assumed the quality of a national epic because generals Aung San and Ne Win and many other major leaders emerged from the experience (see The West, ch. 5). Independence, a regained national pride, and the appreciation of the need for restraint of factionalism all could be related to the growth in status of the soldier. Hierarchical military control appeared to fit many social patterns better than did chaotic democracy. Still, lean and self-sacrificing soldiers look better to the populace when liberating a country than when assigned to a desk and running a university library; and when the soldier hero tries to tell the villager how to grow and sell rice or becomes a militant enforcer of socialism, he begins to take on qualities of the buffalo that tramples the grass.

Police with or without uniforms also have status but are not granted any of the admiration the military may have earned since independence. Although reputedly less corrupt than police in other Southeast Asian countries, they are instruments of a military rule, and their procedural methods are at times authoritarian and highly intrusive (see The People's Force, ch. 5). They fairly effectively jail the government's opponents and harass unwanted Burmese into exile. From the socialist viewpoint they are vital agents of the necessary revolution.

Burmese bureaucrats probably much resembled their counterparts the world over; whether driven by party zeal, a craving for petty power, or the dream of the ultimate in job security. When they controlled a successful project, their status was considerable and quite different from how they were perceived when they were simply making or enforcing rules that did not work. For example, bureaucratic operation of the high-yielding rice program was fairly successful because farmers had found that the rice worked for them and therefore took an interest in local committees that administered the new source of income (see Farm Modernization, ch. 3). With mass interest comes success for the bureaucrat who then can report the welcomed response to government leaders.

A government job was a precious possession for any person, particularly for one not formerly in the military or the police. To retain such a position, one had to support the Burma Socialist Programme Party (BSPP) and accommodate the bureaucrats. The job provided a certain kind of status but one that was never secure because determination of socialist loyalty took precedence over the quality of one's work.

The revolution in Burma has been hard on teachers, scholars, artists, writers, and other creative professionals. The socialist government has sought to harness all intellectual activity for service to the state. In doing so, the state has attempted to influence individuals conventionally having high status in society. Many have become silent or left the country while others have struggled to find a permitted outlet of expression.

Education was under the exclusive control of the *sangha* until colonial times. Most literature and art were Buddhist inspired, if not always generated in a monastic compound. Secular and Christian education to train the civil servants of the British Empire changed all that, and the new lay teachers simply inherited the mantles worn by the monks. In independent Burma one's teacher is still highly respected, just as one's parents and older relatives are honored. Even those learning are given a certain deference, thereby partially explaining why student strikes generated such popular support in the nationalist period. The university degree remains perhaps the most prized goal of any aspiring Burmese family. For these reasons the BSPP leadership has kept a watchful eye on all those involved with education and the arts. U Ne Win's apparent strategy has been to close the universities or tighten censorship whenever an outpouring of criticism neared the point of expression.

In Burma one should treat any book or manuscript as though it were the words of the Buddha. Such is the influence from the past that putting something written on the floor is offensive to many Burmans. Those who write books are highly honored, and traveling authors are greeted by throngs when they arrive in the countryside to read from their works. The author's status is immense, and the government has sought to require permits for authors to read to the public, for such communication otherwise bypasses the constant censorship of publication.

An expert in any field has status, but physicians have more than most. For centuries folk medicines and rituals were used to battle disease and illness. In colonial times and in later years, people began to learn of injections and other miraculous inventions of modern medicine. Hospitals continued to be regarded as places where one goes to die, but physicians were rare and held in awe. When few Burmese were allowed to depart from Burma in the 1970s, physicians were allowed to leave to study special topics. The physician-to-patient ratio was low; thus physicians were expected to serve a huge area in a rotating system that was hard on them but that many understood to be necessary.

In sum, certainly the socialist revolution has attempted to change the society, but monks, old people, wealthy donors to Buddhism, the miliary, teachers, writers, artists, and doctors continue to enjoy the highest status; however, the BSPP chiefs and leaders undoubtedly have made inroads on the traditional networks of respected roles. To the degree the party figures have enforced unpopular policies, they really did not compete with any of the well-established, high-status roles. To the extent they were seen as helpful, however, they did.

Anade

Accompanying the traditional system has always been an aspect of the Burman mentality for which there is no adequate English term. The behavior pattern or emotion is called *anade* by Burmans. Rather than suffer a direct affront or embarrassment, Burmese prefer to withdraw or avoid a situation entirely. Rather than cause such a feeling in another, a Burman may completely avoid an encounter. Among good friends or family, expected behavior is that a person will never bring up matters that would bring shame or reduction of status to another. The concept of *anade* is so broad that it can also refer to reluctance to enter a relationship that creates a debt one does not wish to have. Thus, offered kindness can be rejected by a person not willing to reciprocate. If *anade* is pleaded as an excuse for inaction, others are always expected to honor it.

Most importantly, *anade* implies a superior-inferior relationship that does not harmonize well with democratic social machinery. To vote down a minority in a committee is not allowing for any face-saving, whereas in a hierarchical order the person in the inferior position is not necessarily made to feel inferior. Knowing where one stands, one can avoid demeaning confrontations with authority, but if everyone is made equal and forced to interact through committee structure, then individuals will publicly risk embarrassment if they lose. Representative government becomes a dangerous business where the traditional harmony of *anade* observance contends with the conflicting demands of constituents. For three reasons a "committee" of monks or party members seldom resembles democracy or socialism in action but more likely a dutiful group of followers doing what their leader expects them to do.

Keeping the appearance of harmony is an important goal that *anade* serves, and debate is neither encouraged in the typical education process nor common in public life. Politeness is to be maintained by avoiding direct expression of disagreement.

The Sense of Uniqueness

Burmans, despite colonialization and the travails of independence, have never lost a certain sense of having a special culture in which they take much pride. Historically, the kings of Burma really did believe they were the world emperors, and even the glorious future king was expected to create his paradise first on Burmese soil.

Burmans are never tired of recalling their ancient history, particularly to illustrate how vast their conquests were and how far back their Buddhism can be traced historically and archaeologically. Buttressed by their thousand-year history, the Burmans are not all that impressed with western nations so recently arrived on the scene. Such pride often underlies the overbearing attitudes that an occasional government official may show.

When Western nations proudly acclaim some new achievement, the Burmans often point out that they have been doing the same thing for centuries. A case in point involves the Western women's liberation movement. Burman women have always been powerful. By remaining close to their mothers, female relatives, and daughters, they always have a strong support team. Equal inheritance of land and wealth with brothers gives them financial power, which is often enhanced by their managing family finances or carrying on a business. Although Buddhism assigns superiority to males, the powerful female is quite often aware that the superiority is a token that men seem to need for self-esteem. As one very successful Burman lady explained, "Let him go first. That is where the snakes are." When a woman wished to divorce a man, the proverbial story was that she put his things outside the house for him to see when he came home. By feeding the monks, women were their real supporters and thus have always had much social influence and power. Although seldom given as much formal education as a man, they predominate in chanting Pali responses on holy days because they often have formed their own study groups. They may treat their husbands with the greatest deference, keeping their heads below their husband's, walking behind them, eating after males have finished, or following other ancient customs, but they are in actuality still very dignified and formidable beings. A man may strut as he plays his part on a stage that makes him superior, but the woman is so powerful she needs no theatrics. Some women who have been educated abroad may feel that some improvements in their status should be made, but most are proud and satisfied to be what they are.

Burmans also take pride in their positive attitude toward living, particularly when times are bad. Their sense of humor is almost indestructible, and visitors to the country have always been treated by the people with great hospitality and friendliness, particularly if one makes even the slightest attempt to speak their complex tonal language or read their unique script. Because minute changes in tone create new words, the foreign visitor attempting a few Burmese phrases often makes outrageous or unintentionally obscene statements, much to everyone's delight. Burmans realize foreigners may not understand the country's greatness, but they naturally are very pleased when guests show any knowledge of things Burmese. Social reciprocity is a matter of honor, and a favor returned at any cost or danger.

When Burmans are able to talk about their current situation without fear of reprisal, they can be very realistic and rationally critical. When they talk about history, they are neither. Their history is filled with legends and often meaningless lists of data that pass as scholarship. Historical analysis or historiography is very rare; therefore Burmans use history to express national pride and their special sense of destiny. The past is remembered in terms of archetypes that carry the culture, and the socialist government has carefully combed the past for examples that show how peasants and workers have heroically created the country or how strong leaders have been unifiers. History, in any case, is less a record and more a creation shaped for specific ends, which are usually to foster the sense of Burman uniqueness, often called the "Burmese Way," whether socialist or not.

Finally, Burmans share the conviction that they preserve the true faith. In a different political climate, the Burmans might expect a host of foreign Buddhists seeking the true purity which is being maintained by their best monks. At an elaborate ritual, often called a synod (*sangayana*), or council, the Burmese periodically rededicate themselves to the primal Buddhist purity they believe resides in their traditions. Texts are scrutinized for error, heretics are purged, thousands of monks are assembled at great expense, and the secular leader of the state plays the role of the royal sun with his necessary moon, which is the disciplined and rejuvenated *sangha*. This national ritual was performed by most of the kings in the last dynasty, by U Nu, and has been the fascination of U Ne Win. No other country in the past century has claimed the ritual. It is a Burmese specialty and is characteristic of their sense of unique destiny and responsibility.

The Socialist Transformation

The world view of the government of the early 1980s was a most complex blend of ancient Burman notions, British socialism, and Leninist beliefs concerning the supremacy of the state. The country was primarily run by the military establishment, which saw itself as following a credo established by the hero, General Aung San. Without the military, the government believed, chaos would break out in the country. To create a strong, self-reliant, and independent Burma, the military believed that a middle way could be found that would escape the evils of multinational big business and communist domination. The middle way was "The Burmese Way to Socialism."

Central to this vision was a unified Burma—by persuasion if possible, by force if necessary. According to this view, because the totality takes precedence over the parts, the minorities ultimately have no choice. They are simply proclaimed units of the nation-state, and if resistance arises, it has to be quelled to make the vision of total control by the government in Rangoon a reality.

When socialism became the official policy of the state in the early 1960s, the country was subjected to a borrowed template that postulated the vital role of the worker class. Actually, there were very few industrial workers (only 7 percent of the work force) to lead the revolution, for the country was mainly agricultural. State promotion in the early days featured the "model workers" who were sent for special vacations to the old colonial resorts and given socialist seminars. The military, following the borrowed socialist rule book, was convinced that heavy industry would energize the new nation to prosperity. Burma's nationalized industries, however, were viewed by many in the early 1980s as inefficient and unproductive. Outside observers may see the Burman as a better capitalist venturer than corporate executive or worker. Clearly, by the 1970s the revolution was not going to be achieved if Burmese workers had to provide the impetus. Thus the government turned to the "peasant."

Just as workers were a bit scarce, so were true Burmese peasants. There were millions of cagey, individualistic farmers but very few classic peasants waiting for the signal to string up the landlord on a banyan tree. Wary farmers in their villages— descendants of survivors of the rapacity of the Burmese kings— care about the economic policies, not the rhetoric, emanating from Rangoon. Artificially low rice prices (because a farmer was required to sell to the government) were just taxes in disguise. Mass peasant support was therefore scarce until the government had its "miracle" rice to distribute. Volunteer army units helping with the harvests are to a farmer just so many inspectors to reduce his illegal private sales. Village farm wisdom has never before seen the central government as anything but a dangerous force that takes more than it returns. Land reform and loans have been somewhat successful programs of the government, however, and certain agriculturists appreciated the state services. As commercial fertilizer or pesticides become more necessary, then the new farmer will have to turn increasingly to the state. Even so, more demands on the state do not necessarily create revolutionary socialist peasants out of Burmese farmers.

Socialist Media and Education

Art for art's sake was obviously not the belief of the socialist military; all media in Burma were to be dedicated to the socialist revolution. One typical socialist movie showed how an upper class, long-haired, guitar-playing effete young man from Mandalay met a pretty, revolutionary, socialist girl who was bitten by a cobra as she was in a rural area on a literacy program drive. After saving her life and falling in love, he cut his hair, abandoned his guitar, and was last seen tutoring delighted, but illiterate, aged peasants. Western decadence was once again overcome; besides, the girl was very beautiful.

Socialist Rationality

While the average Burman takes scrupulous care of his shrine to Mahagiri, the national protective *nat*, and is also likely to change his name if astrological calculations suggest trouble, the military socialists like to think of themselves as rational arbiters of the nation's destiny. In a country where it was once traditional and is still common to heed prophecy from a number of sources, the socialist government seeks to project an image of being "modern" in the sense that it collects statistics and information upon which it sets up its "plans." Ever since the caretaker government days of the late 1950s, when the military brought order to social chaos, socialist military officials have offered the public a rational world view.

The present government has discouraged books and publications on *nats*, wizards, witches, ghosts, and supranormal powers in general. In terms of Buddhism proper, the official position has stressed the scholastic side of monastic endeavor, not the meditation aspects which reputedly are accompanied by extensive mystical power. The implication is clear: modern socialists should be more rational and scientific in making decisions on economics and politics, and the public may very well agree with that position.

The military as individuals, however, are well-known supporters of the occult, if only to harness whatever protective magic a practitioner may be able to provide to those who must take military risks. Charms, tattoos, spells, and protective alchemical mercury balls may help in moments of danger, and the theory prevails that it is better to be safe than sorry. While a twenty-year economic plan may well be thought best if designed rationally without astrological help, one's own life is a different matter because the law of impermanence perhaps can be somehow averted. Thus, the soldier may have a curious ambivalence toward all things occult. On the jungle trail, open to snipers, a military socialist may hope his tattoo works, but behind a desk in Rangoon he may deny publication rights to a book on *nats*.

On a higher level, the military socialist dreams of a better world for his people, which rational government policies will create, yet much of the country's limited wealth constantly goes toward merit-making Buddhist activities. On the one hand, the socialist can only wish more funds were available for more railroad track or roads or for medical care; on the other hand, the socialist planner, if Buddhist, knows that his people do not put such goals first because merit-making holds that place securely. The dilemma is painful and frustrating for the government because the ambivalance a soldier feels toward the occult is there also for a colonel when he thinks of Buddhism. At the philosophical level, Buddhism prides itself on being the most rational of the world's religions. On the popular level, Buddhists earn merit and try to avoid disasters, not always in ways that socialists would define as rational. Attempts to combine Buddhism and socialism into one consistent rational system have often been tried, but with most confusing results, to Western minds.

In mid-1983 Burma produced its own movies and imported foreign films that were edited considerably to reduce the amount of sex and violence. The first television transmission in Burma

*Student ascends steps of the library
at Rangoon University*

*Pupils enjoy a break in a Mandalay schoolyard.
Courtesy Frederica M. Bunge*

took place in 1980; a limited number of daily programs were being shown in 1983. Less than 10 percent of the villages had electricity, however; thus the impact of television would be minimal. Radio programming was controlled by the government-operated Burma Broadcasting Service. Because radio music was screened, cassettes of Western music that were available on the black market became very popular, and the latest hits from Western capitals could be heard soon after they were released abroad. Burma did not abide by any international copyright law; therefore copies of taped music could be made quickly and then sold for a good profit.

Since 1962 all private newspapers have been closed or taken over by the government. Newspaper editors who have been judged as not contributing properly to "socialist construction policies" have been imprisoned. In the early 1980s two papers in English were published daily, the *Working People's Daily* and the *Guardian.* In Rangoon there were also four Burmese-language daily newspapers. All publishing activities were strictly controlled by the government, and perpetual shortages of paper and newsprint made it very difficult to meet the demand for printed books. The most popular form of literature, therefore, was the short story or essay, which could be found in the many magazines that could be published more readily than full-length books. Books had to go through a maze of tedious and time-consuming bureaucratic procedures administered by the Press Registration Board. For example, four copies of a typewritten book manuscript had to be submitted, and in Burma, where typewriters and copying machines were scarce, that requirement was very difficult to fulfill. Thousands of independent publishers still existed and had licenses, but they tended to stress inexpensive pulp magazines rather than books, which were scrutinized more closely by the government.

The government has stressed literacy campaigns and has participated in United Nations (UN) literacy programs. A new Burmese dictionary project has been promoted heavily by U Ne Win and others. Seminars and awards for writers have been encouraged. Some have suggested that modification of classical Burmese language and script might be a good idea, but the official policy seems to have been that traditional Burmese grammar and spelling should be retained.

Best selling books overseas were constantly pirated without copyright restrictions; they were very popular and lucrative for the translators, because no royalties had to be paid. In the field of scholarship, all writers realized that they had to avoid politics and matters that might offend the military or the socialist leaders. U Ne Win personally closed down the *Journal of the Burma Research Society,* which had been a venerable research outlet for English articles for over half a century. The journal clearly represented to U Ne Win a colonial legacy that he no longer felt he had to tolerate, and such a decision could not be appealed. Because journalistic or scholarly freedom did not exist, Burmese publishing was swamped with adventure tales, spy and detective stories, and the eternally popular love sagas.

Despite these problems Burmese authors managed to publish a few literary novels each year, and the National Literary Committee selected a best work to honor annually. Few of these have ever been translated into Western languages; thus, the modern literature of Burma was little known to Western readers.

Modern socialist statistics echo old Burman ways. Buddhism insists on breaking up illusory wholes into still more illusory parts; the tendency to count and number the pieces is irresistible. Buddhists have constantly stressed the number of this and the number of that, almost overwhelming the mind with subdivisions, units still further subdivided until existence itself becomes little more than a statistical fantasy. Such Buddhist training seems to have left its inescapable mark on Burman chronicles that relish dates and endlessly list names and places, the significance of which has long been lost, even if verification had once been possible. Pleasure seems to come from the laborious listing and preservation more than from the meaning of the data.

In time-honored tradition, statistics poured constantly from every branch of the government in the 1980s, but their reliability was dubious. Did anyone really know how many people live in Rangoon or how many Muslims live in Burma? Probably no one did. Some Western social scientists who worked in Burma when permission for such endeavors could still be obtained found that obfuscation was rife. In one case, a head monk himself filled out the questionnaires for all the monks in his entire large monastery. In another case, a social scientist spent months with Rangoon land records trying to determine how much land was under monastic control, but he was utterly defeated by the superb obfuscation that, of course, made matters just as difficult for tax collectors.

The government, realizing the role that students have played historically in nationalistic movements and well aware of the key part played by students in the overthrow in 1973 of the government of Thailand, has kept a sharp eye on the universities. Any sign of student activism has been dealt with severely; in 1962 a student leader was executed and the Rangoon University Student Union demolished by government troops (see Student and Sangha Reactions, ch. 1). Between 1962 and 1978 the universities and institutes were closed down for security reasons for about one-fourth of the time. Nevertheless, Burmans continued to seek a university degree as a golden passport to success.

To decentralize and deemphasize the old university system, several changes have been enacted. Liberal arts have been given less attention, and science and technology have been touted as more useful subjects to study for the nation's needs. Regional junior colleges have been organized that feature a two-year curriculum stressing vocational skills, allowing for an optional third year if students do not pass an examination for entrance to a university or institute after the second year. Half of these regional college students were found in Mandalay and Rangoon areas, however, and regional colleges have evolved to become stepping-stones to university entrance; fewer and fewer students enroll in vocational programs. To open up access to the university degree, there has been established a correspondence course system that leads to a degree at Rangoon University. A similar degree can be obtained at the Defense Services Academy at Maymyo, which offers not only military status but also tuition-free education. So important is education to Burmans that people's cooperatives have been known to raise money to help local schools when state funding is inadequate. A further development in Burmese education has been the growth of private "cram" schools, where tutoring for university entrance is given to those who can pay. In general, the government's various plans to convert higher education into training programs for workers useful to the socialist state have been defeated by the determination of so many families to obtain a university degree for their children, male or female, at any cost.

As of mid-1983 education was free in the elementary and intermediate schools, covering grades one through four and five through eight, respectively. Vocational schooling was also free. High school students in grades nine and 10 paid K5 to K6 per month (for value of the kyat—see Glossary). Universities charged tuition to those fortunate students who survived the intense competition for admission. Figures for the academic year 1977–78—the most recent available—gave a total of about 22,000 state elementary schools having 3.8 million students, 1,260 intermediate schools enrolling 825,000 pupils, and 585 high schools having 189,000 pupils. Burmese was the medium of instruction; English was a required subject in the high schools.

Education has always been strong in learning by rote rather than analysis, for in Buddhist education the oral tradition has always been dominant. Student monks were told to memorize long passages of Pali and not to worry about the meaning, which could come later. Every once in a while a monk was discovered who had memorized all the Theravada Buddhist scriptures, and such a person was always honored as a national treasure. The emphasis was on keeping the traditions alive by memory, and even in the modern university, professors found students memorizing lectures rather than understanding them. Similarly, BSPP members were more likely to commit to memory party doctrines rather than to understand them, much less apply them to new situations. In such an intellectual atmosphere, "scholarship" often became repetition, listing of names and data, and pages of statistics that often did not have internal consistency, much less objective value. The political climate was such that little encouragement was given to students to think for themselves, express new ideas, or learn to be critical.

The touchstones became key socialist words that ran like a litany through government prose—words such as "sincere," "correct," "frank," "bold," "honest," "solidarity," "hardworking," "progress," "right". Negative words, for example, included "exploitive," "nepotism," "arrogant," "patronizing," "personalism," "opportunist," "decadent," or "incorrect." All these terms merely directed party members into the mental paths that promoted altruism or selfless service to the state. Those who wished to succeed had to learn to express themselves using the "correct" terms. How deeply, under these conditions, the meaning of socialism had penetrated the minds of average Burmans was impossible to determine.

The government has spent much energy in promoting its literacy campaign, and the latest estimate in 1983 was that 67 percent of the entire country was literate. In Upper and Lower Burma before independence, the rate was 83 percent, a most respectable figure, although colonialists used to say that 95 percent were literate and that Burma had one of the best rates in the world. In any case, the government had encouraged volunteers to fan out into the rural areas to act as tutors. The UN has cooperated with this program, and it undoubtedly has had a beneficial effect on the country and has helped to improve the government's image.

Medical Programs

A major governmental effort has been launched to improve medical conditions. Since 1962 the number of hospitals has almost doubled; the same rate of progress was true for the increase in rural health centers. In the same period the number of physicians registered has more than tripled, and the number of health assistants and female health visitors has grown by almost the same rate. There were about five times as many nurses and midwives in the early 1980s as there were in 1962. To train personnel there were three institutes of medicine (two in Rangoon and one in Mandalay); the Institute of Dental Medicine and the Burma Dental University; a paramedical personnel school; a health assistant school; and 16 nursing and midwifery schools. In addition the popular Traditional Medicine Institute and Hospital, where indigenous curing methods and substances could be studied and applied, was opened in Mandalay.

This impressive improvement nevertheless had to be counterbalanced by a host of serious medical problems. The contamination of fresh water and the existence of poor waste disposal habits have exacerbated the incidence of gastrointenstinal diseases, such as typhoid, dysentery, and cholera, as well as that of dengue, poliomyelitis, typhus, and yaws. Malaria and filariasis are persistent problems, spread by stubborn mosquito populations.

Tuberculosis, influenza, venereal disease, leprosy, otomycosis (ear infection), plague, and trachmoma are also serious health problems. The World Health Organization has helped to develop programs to fight a number of these diseases.

Burmese physicians were not paid well, and many had to moonlight to make ends meet. Naturally they tended to seek employment in the urban areas, but even salary bonuses to those serving in hardship posts did not attract enough doctors to the border areas. Another problem was an insufficient supply of medicines. Despite these difficulties, the government had succeeded in proving that it was dedicated to improving conditions, and this effort was not lost on the populace.

Land Reform

In the early 1980s it was possible to learn what the government claimed to have done in land redistribution, but it was not possible to determine what had actually evolved in land practices during the past 20 years. In 1977 almost 60 percent of all farms had been under four hectares, and less than 1 percent were near 20 hectares or more. Tenancy was supposed to have been abolished, but evidence was conflicting. According to government edict, all inheritance of land had been abolished, and all belonged to the state. No outside observer believed that such pronouncements changed the way farming families developed their own farms and passed them on to descendants; no one, however, was sure what actually had happened (see Land Tenure and Organization, ch. 3).

Land reform may have made some friends for the leadership, but enforced low rice prices had not. When the government introduced high-yielding rice strains and enabled farmers to make more money, rural Burma became more interested in socialism. As governmental programs switched from courting the workers and dreaming of heavy industry to celebrating the peasant and agricultural potential of the country, peasant councils were formed, allegedly involving millions of Burmese in grass-roots socialism. If true, then the conversion of agricultural individualists and rural capitalists into eager socialists would be a miraculous revolution indeed. Judgement should clearly be withheld on the matter.

Instead of encouraging birth control, the government officially took the position that the land was underpopulated; therefore contraceptive devices were not made available at clinics or hospitals, and abortions were not encouraged. In 1974, however, 42 percent of all hospital admissions were related to abortions, and contraceptive devices were easily available on the black market. In this situation, quite clearly the government and the masses were not in agreement.

The Shadow Economy

Official pronouncements lauded the achievements of socialist workers and peasants, but consumer goods from the shadow economy supplied the otherwise unavailable luxuries. Because the Japanese were waiting in the wings to sell every Burmese a complete electronic nirvana or a pair of plastic sandals, the BSPP found it best to ignore the black market's ubiquity. By defining the shadow economy as evil, the government saw itself as philosophically consistent by discouraging consumption of Western clothes, music, cosmetics, Mercedes-Benz carburetors, home remedies, suggestive calendars, or old copies of *Playboy*.

The government was also on record as seeking eventually to abolish private ownership of business, and nearly all firms hiring over 100 workers had been nationalized. Such policies would always collide with the ancient alternative of trying to make a small business venture work. Operating in the street or under a simple awning, many private entrepreneurs having little capital to invest nonetheless put everything into their business inventory.

Marketplaces throughout the land enable people to sell their goods at minimal overhead, because the food or merchandise display is often staffed by many members of the family so that business is kin oriented and social. Relatives are hired first, if anyone is to be paid a salary, and the old and the very young all help. Business is labor intensive, and Burmese are ingenious in keeping machinery working long after its time. Nothing remotely useful is thrown away. Ostentatious display is rare; instead a business may seem very modest or even run-down as seen from the street but actually be quite lucrative. Because there is little in the way of a Western social net of welfare programs, successful private ventures are critical to the survival of entire families. If one prospers beyond the demands of family survival, then the Buddhist virtue of meritorious giving always beckons. Because Burman society has been so structured for centuries, strict socialist thinking works against the grain in many ways. Thus, "The Burmese Way to Socialism" will necessarily evolve its own forms that will take into account the old ways and will never be purely socialist.

Purification of the Sangha

Although in the 1960s the military exerted its power over every other segment of Burmese society, it had failed to force members of the *sangha* to submit to registration and to carry identity cards. By the early 1980s the government was secure enough to attempt what it had failed to do earlier. Identity cards have been accepted in principle, and a few monastic court trials were heavily publicized in the press. At the Kaba Aye complex in Rangoon, an English magazine—the *Light of the Dhamma*—has come to life again, and some of the Buddhists who had been denied an international voice for years were finding themselves once again in print. A few prestigious monks had even been allowed to make brief visits to the United States and Europe, where they encouraged Buddhists and others to form Burmese Buddhist centers. Numerous monks also have been honored with titles. To cap off the new direction in government policies, a new pagoda was being built near the Shewdagon in Rangoon under the watchful eye of U Ne Win.

All these changes in official attitudes toward Buddhism signaled first a belief on the part of the military that purification of the *sangha* would be possible because of the government's strength. Second, U Ne Win himself seemed to have determined that, as a true Burman, he should do something about his own merit balance. The latter explanation might be specious, but in any case, his actions constituted good politics and certainly helped the public image of the military in its leadership position.

Attitude Toward Foreign Influences and Entanglements

Wary of involvement with any foreign power, Burma continued in the early 1980s to pursue what it called a nonaligned foreign policy (see Foreign Policy Environment, ch. 4). Japan had been able to establish an influence because of war reparations and because of development assistance. But in general, Burma was determined to avoid foreign entanglements of any kind, almost as though *anade* operated at a national level of consciousness. Better to avoid unnecessary contact with stronger powers than to have to give them a say in how the country was to be run—so the reasoning might be. Isolation, self-imposed, was better than feeling inadequate or threatened in relations with others. As Buddhists, many Burmese probably believed that communism would destroy their culture, but neither did they wish to become agents of the West and risk their own destruction. As socialists they associated capitalism with exploitive colonialist firms that froze out Burmese. Modern technology did not seem to bother them as much as the systems that produced such improvements.

Only a few years ago U Ne Win personally and dramatically put a stop to a rock dance in Rangoon. He believes that much more enters a country than just the noisy Western music. More a traditionalist than his socialist speeches might lead one to believe, U Ne Win, with the support of many others, likes to wear the *longyi*, or wraparound long skirt, and the *gaungbaung*, a turban-like headgear. Burmans do not like miniskirts, shorts, or blue jeans. Public display of affection between the sexes is not approved and, although prostitution is not uncommon, premarital sex is not expected. Nightlife and bars are almost nonexistent, sex in cinemas is not explicit, and drug use is not all that common. In general, many modern Western customs are seen as potentially disruptive of Burmese society. Burmese, although not puritanical, seem to wish to preserve their time-tested ways of living, and much of what the global village offers is very seductive but also dangerous socially.

Those Burmese who wish to advertise their rebellious nature wear tight jeans and Western hairstyles, learn the latest dances, and listen to their imported cassettes. They often seek out the young tourists and identify with them, but they are not as numerous as some visitors might think.

The Non-Burman World View

Although many socialists in Burma would like to believe that the essence of being Burman is being a socialist, not a Buddhist, they are not being very realistic. Minorities in Burma face a Buddhist majority, and Christianity remains an option for asserting one's distinctness, not only for the Karens or Chins, for example, but also for those who have had a genuine Christian conversion and for others who retain a fierce loyalty to all things British. On a visit to Mandalay, a visitor attempting, however ineptly, to speak Burmese should not be surprised to have an impeccably dressed older man watch for a while with a smile and then speak in exquisite English with a perfect Oxford accent. The same elderly gentleman will also finish his days as an ardent Christian. No revolution will convert him into either a Buddhist or a socialist. Among many Burmese there is a curious ambivalence toward the British, particularly since the departure of the latter has not solved all their problems by any means.

Just as British rule has left its mark on language taught in school, Christian churches here and there, sports—such as soccer and horse racing—architecture, and a certain sense of fair play, so also have the other major civilizations and religions had their influences. Mosques are found in Arakan, Rangoon, and in all areas where the Muslim community is strong, some of these groups having established themselves in Burma centuries ago. Like the Hindu and Chinese populations, Muslims have to keep a low profile in terms of asserting their ethnic identity in order to avoid the racial antagonism that has often flared up in the past.

Aggressive group ethnicity was not a good strategy in Burma in the early 1980s; however, maintaining one's personal faith, customs, and special dress was possible and was widely in evidence, particularly in urban areas. The socialist government had in theory tried to follow a separation of church and state and therefore had sometimes pointed with pride to religious diversity, but its attempt to purify the monkhood had brought it closer to mainstream Buddhist concerns.

Although no outside observers were allowed into the border areas, if tendencies observed up to 1962 were still in operation in the early 1980s, religious change was proceeding apace in the hills. The classic choice between the traditional religion and either Buddhism or Christiantiy was not the only set of options; the traditional religion could also change. Prophets might appear telling of new visions and revelations that perhaps offer a revitalized deity, a millennial hope, a charismatic leader, less reliance on traditional priests, or perhaps an escape from rituals believed demanded by ancestral spirits. In Thailand, for example, one Karen group has adopted a special tattoo that frees the believer from ancestral spirit control. In such cases minority groups can be seen maintaining their ethnic boundaries by self-adjustments in their traditional religion rather than by assuming the faith of outsiders who may want to change and eradicate a minority's traditional ways of life.

Nothing is more troublesome to the bureaucracy than a group of hill people who pack up and move all the time. Even more problematic is the minority notion that national boundaries are porous and do not apply. Perhaps as irritating is the belief that no one really owns the hills of Southeast Asia and that certain groups should be free to wander about in the mountains at will. When hill peoples actually dare to believe that they themselves control the hills, then those at the center of the mandala become most upset. All these minority beliefs have existed for centuries, and no one has been able to change them.

Those who live by the slash-and-burn method of growing their food find that, depending on the soils and crops planted, they must abandon the fields to lie fallow every five to 15 years. They may never move their homes but simply use new land, or they may pack up and travel to a new hill. Over a period of many years such peoples may appear to be nomadic but are actually using a fairly limited home range. Many Chins, Kachins, Karens, and Shan hill peoples follow such a pattern and do not accept the concept that they are fairly recent nomadic intruders on Burman soil. They may be vaguely aware that various lowland "unifiers" since King Anawrahta in the eleventh century have claimed jurisdiction over the mountain areas, but over the centuries the land has been theirs by custom, if not title. When a logging team from a government-run group comes in with chain saws and a proprietary air, then the issue of ownership suddenly comes alive, and tempers flare.

In the early 1980s still other groups moved over considerable distances across porous national borders, such as the Meos, Akhas, Was, and Lisus, their movements tolerated by modern governments that in distant border areas had neither the manpower nor the will to stop them. What the hill peoples may have seen as the exercise of freedom, the governments may have seen as smuggling, insurrection, or some other illegal activity. A more sophisticated charge leveled at hill peoples was to say they ruined the environment, a notion that conjured up visions of huge stands of virgin teak ablaze in forest fires or eroded hillsides sliding into muddy streams. Another lowland scheme, used more in Thailand than in Burma, was to create massive state parks or forest reserves out of border areas in which hunting was not allowed or timbering prohibited without permission. All these stratagems were merely aspects of minority-majority problems endemic to Burmese politics.

Communism in Burma

In the nationalist days before World War II, many students at the university called themselves "communists" and defined it as they saw fit. Perhaps it meant giving the university president an argument at every turn or being jailed for bravely speaking against the British, or perhaps it meant organizing a strike at the oil fields. In those heady days, fellow students like U Nu and Aung San moved in and out of a confusing array of secret groups, playing national and personal politics at the same instant. Friends one moment and rivals next, the future leaders seemed driven not by a firm and clear political credo but by quests for personal fulfillment.

Communism, like socialism, may have been an almost scholastic textbook adventure for some, but for others it meant alignment in global struggles that would deliver Burma into a Soviet or Chinese camp. Recourse to violence may have characterized the commitment of still others. In the long run the deepest commitment has been to the nation's independence from the Soviet and Chinese spheres, as well as from any others. The tolerance for the loyal opposition that some old communist friends may have been given when they acted as good socialists has never prevented U Ne Win from purging them from his party if their ultimate loyalty was not for *his* revolution, Burmese style.

Communist support and encouragement along traditional fissure lines in the fragile society of Burma may have at times motivated fairly large groups of common people to side with armed rebels, but the local goal was always Burma oriented, not international. Mass communist support seems highly unlikely among Burmans but is still tempting for some minority groups seeking leverage in the northeastern area.

The Future of Burmese Society

Although the government certainly has tried hard to modernize the Burmese economy, thus far it has had limited success. Rapid growth therefore has been one problem the society does not have to battle. Improvements in living conditions were coming slowly enough to be integrated well into the total fabric of the society. Not enough buses, cars, or trucks existed, or were in working order on a given day, to pollute Rangoon's air, in contrast to other Southeast Asian cities. Burmese officials returned periodically from Honolulu and Bangkok with the conviction that paving Burmese cities with macadam and cement for tourist buses and automobile commuters was not the modernization the country desired. Burmese have a deep affection for the country, the beauty of which they appreciate the more they see how other countries modernize.

In the early 1980s Burmese fears of becoming another Vietnam, Laos, or Kampuchea seemed to have been reduced somewhat by the rapproachement between the United States and China. But even the retreat of the communist insurgents to the northeastern corner of the country did not signal the end of fighting. Burmese still worried about the cold war of ideas that was introduced whenever foreign libraries opened, books flowed in and out of the country, intellectuals jousted, journalists and editors bid for the reader's attention, or foreigners stayed too long. Little immediate change was likely in these areas, and information flow and exchange were unlikely to increase. Signs were increasing, however, that as government sought to involve more of the populace in the process of governance, more low-level expression of opinions on how socialism was working would be tolerated, although certainly no criticism of the system itself would be welcome or possible.

The government sought to modernize the economic base of the society, but most outside observers agreed that the heavy hand of military officers at all levels of planning and administration had created a cumbersome bureaucracy that hindered development. By not harnessing the profit motive in private business, the government, to improve the society economically, had to rely on its nationalized corporations, cooperatives, and committees, where the bureaucratic attitude prevails. Local and private ingenuity therefore functioned under very difficult odds, although both areas had managed to survive. More state control and increased local dependence on the state would seem to be likely outcomes in the future, without necessarily any improvement in the standard of living.

Increased use of international loans, which Burmese pride themselves in always repaying, may be the socialists' main hope, but the investigations necessary for these loans intrude into Burmese isolation, and the dependence on outsiders grates on Burmese pride. Experience has shown the Burmese how to avoid external pressures from international powers, and they should be able to integrate outside funding into their society without fundamentally changing it.

Under U Ne Win, the country has been free of dictation from outsiders—if not free within, at least "free" as Westerners define freedom. His government, however, is certainly no harder on the society than most of the nation's previous monarchs. Burmese religion and culture developed in close interrelationship with monarchy, and therefore the Burmese have learned well how to survive under difficult conditions and find a modicum of happiness each day. Perhaps Burmese find more delight in living than many others have found in the electronic global village around them, with its modern freedoms and social rights. U Ne Win has kept out much of the outside influence that has ruined the societies of other small countries. If he were not in charge, there are many Burmese who certainly would open the gates wider to the outside world, and the Burmese would soon be consuming more than they could pay for. Like a true Burman, U Ne Win has preached less attachment to the pleasures of this world and more dedication to the national goals he has set. Quite likely he will be admired in history by Burmese who complain now but will be grateful later. Whether he and his successors can succeed in creating a permanent unified nation is debatable but likely.

* * *

Standard and still-useful nineteenth-century works in English on Burmese society include James G. Scott and J.P. Hardiman's *Gazetteer of Upper Burma and the Shan States*, Scott's *The Burman: His Life and Notions*, and numerous accounts of various colonial visitors, clergy, and administrators, such as Albert Fytche, Michael Symes, P. Bigandet, and H. Fielding Hall. Modern general anthropological works include *The Golden Road to Modernity* by Manning Nash, Melford Spiro's *Kinship and Marriage in Burma*, and articles and theses by David Pfanner. Burman religion is treated by Michael Mendelson in various articles and *Sangha and State in Burma*, by Spiro in *Burmese Supernaturalism* and *Buddhism and Society*, and by John Ferguson in articles and theses. Art, architecture, and archaeology are treated by Gordon Luce in many articles and *Old Burma-Early Pagan*, by Aung Thaw in *Excavations at Beikthano* and *Historical Sites in Burma*, and by John Lowry in *Burmese Art*.

Modern Burmese literature is discussed by Anna Allott and U Thaung in articles; colonial education, by L.E. Bashawe; music, by Muriel Williamson; and social psychology, by Sarah Bekker. Literature on minorities in Burma before 1960 includes books, monographs, and articles by the following: Leslie Milne (Shan), Harry Marshall (Karen), H.N.C. Stevenson (Chin), Edumund Leach (Kachin), O. Hanson (Kachin), and W.R. Head (Chin). More recent work has been done by Sao Saimong Mangrai (Shan), Charles F. Keyes (Karen), Theodore Stern (Karen), F.K. Lehman (Chin, Kayah, and general), H.L. Shorto (Mon), Maran La Raw (Kachin), Brian Foster (Mon), Uma S. Singh (Indians in Burma), Nalini Chakravarti (Indians in Burma), and Moshe Yegar (Muslims in Burma). Overviews of minorities in Burma are found in *Ethnic Groups of Mainland Southeast Asia* by Frank Lebar et al., Julian Steward's *Contemporary Change in Traditional Societies*, and *Southeast Asian Tribes, Minorities, and Nations*, edited by Peter

Kunstadter. Josef Silverstein in books and articles has concentrated on Burmese minorities under the present government. Highly personalized, but informative on Burman life-styles, are U Nu's *U Nu: Saturday's Son*, Mi Mi Khaing's *Burmese Family*, Kenneth Sein and J.A. Withey's *The Great Po Sein*, and Edward M. Law-Yone's article "Dr. Ba Maw of Burma." Much information on the physical environment in Burma is given in the mimeographed "Environmental Profile of Burma" by Robert Varady. Travel books useful to the general reader are Ulrich Zagorski's *Burma: Unknown Paradise*, Anthony Wheeler's *Burma: A Travel Survival Kit*, and the thorough and beautifully illustrated *Burma* by Hans Johannes Hoefer et al. (For further information and complete citations, see Bibliography.)

Chapter 3.   The Economy

Villagers setting out rice seedlings. Water buffalo are used as draft animals.

SMALL-SCALE AGRICULTURE and other primary industries continued to dominate Burma's economy in 1983. Farming, forestry, and mining activities employed over two-thirds of the labor force and produced nearly half of the gross domestic product, which at the equivalent of US$180 per person in 1981 was one of the smallest in the world. Manufacturing consisted chiefly of the simple processing of rice, oilseeds, teak, tin, tungsten, silver, and other primary products, which have been exported from Burma since the colonial era (1886-1948). Facilities for construction, power, water, transportation, communications, banking, trade, and social and government services have been expanding but were still poorly developed. Since 1977, however, led by the agricultural sector, the economy has performed very well, growing by over 6 percent per year on average through 1981.

The Burma Socialist Programme Party, the only political party, has been somewhat successful in its attempt to improve economic performance and the basic welfare of the people; most of the progress has occurred since the late 1970s. The main accomplishment has been the introduction of high-yielding varieties of seeds, chemical fertilizers, and intensive cropping patterns to increase the supply of rice and other agricultural commodities for both domestic consumption and export. The quantity of exports, however, remained far below that achieved in the colonial era. Other measures of economic and social progress of which the government could be proud were the improved rates of literacy and life expectancy.

Remembering the indignities of the colonial past, the government has been strongly committed to the ideal of economic independence and self-reliance. For more than a decade after coming to power in 1962, the government, under the leadership of U Ne Win, experimented with radical measures to insulate the country from the influence of the world's major economic powers. Burma continued to trade with the rest of the world but accepted little or no foreign economic assistance, and it nationalized all foreign-owned enterprises. Since the mid-1970s, however, the government has modified its policy and has actively sought foreign assistance to support a vastly expanded investment program. Nonetheless, the government has refused to allow foreign enterprises to invest directly in the economy.

The official commitment to socialist ideals, espoused more or less continuously since the nation's independence in 1948, supported the nationalization programs. At one time or another after the military took over the reins of government in 1962, publicly owned enterprises or state economic agencies dominated nearly all aspects of industry and trade. Managerial inefficiencies, however, caused the government to lift periodically its controls on private enterprise. By the early 1980s the government had relaxed many of the legal restrictions on private enterprise but continued to supply little support to its development. The official economic plans still emphasized the expansion of public and cooperative enterprises, which together contributed more than 40 percent of the gross domestic product in the early 1980s. In the dominant agricultural sector, moreover, where private farms accounted for almost all of production, government agencies and public enterprises were exclusively responsible for supplying the needed technologies and financial incentives to expand production.

Another of the ruling party's socialist objectives was the elimination of economic inequalities, and the distribution of wealth in Burma has probably become more equitable than in other low-income developing countries. Nevertheless, economic conditions in the areas inhabited by the Burman ethnic majority seemed to be better than those in the mountainous border regions, where antigovernment insurgency on the part of ethnic minorities was also a problem. The farmers of the wet-rice plains and rice-growing heartlands benefited most from the agricultural modernization programs, while the cultivators in the border regions continued to utilize unproductive traditional technologies; some resorted to the illegal cultivation of opium poppies. Likewise, the transportation, communications, and industrial infrastructure was better developed in Rangoon, Irrawaddy, Pegu, Magwe, Mandalay, and Sagaing divisions; simple mining, forestry, and handicraft manufacturing predominated in the administrative subdivisions inhabited chiefly by the ethnic minorities.

The most problematic economic issues arose from the complex interaction between public and private forms of production and marketing, which continued to exist side by side. The government channeled almost all investment into publicly owned enterprises, some of which suffered from poor management or the constraints imposed by the government's unrealistic pricing schemes. The much-heralded cooperative program languished because of a lack of funding, expertise, and popular enthusiasm. Meanwhile, private enterprises have continued to flourish, despite the lack of official support, creating private marketing arrangements that paralleled those of public enterprises. Most private economic activities were legal, but the production and sale of contraband—including drugs and a wide variety of smuggled consumer goods—as well as the resale of items purchased at controlled prices were illegal. Insurgent ethnic minorities played a major role in the illegal activities, which nonetheless formed a thriving black market that was virtually indistinguishable from the legitimate private market. One estimate suggested that 80 percent of all consumer goods sold in Rangoon were traded at uncontrolled prices, whether legally or on the black market.

Government measures to interdict the black market were halfhearted, except for those related to the drug trade; in the eyes of many Burmese the black market was essential to the smooth functioning of the whole economy. Yet the dichotomy between controlled and free market activities entailed certain economic costs. Not only did the discrepancy between official and free market prices reduce revenues for the tax authorities and public enterprises, but it also impeded economic analysis and planning. At the same time, the government was missing the opportunity to tap the dynamism of private enterprises, which outnumbered public enterprises and employed the largest number of laborers. Because their development costs were generally lower than those of public enterprises, private enterprises offered better prospects for reducing the ranks of unemployed or underemployed workers, whose increasing number was becoming an important social and political concern.

There were many other economic issues for the 1980s. Associated with the problem of distributing more economic investment to the less developed regions, which the government claimed to be doing since the promulgation of the 1974 Constitution, was the question of decentralizing planning and management. As of 1983, however, most of the decisions on investment and production were made by the central government. Among the technological issues facing the nation, improvement of the production of petroleum from domestic wells was perhaps the most important. In the early 1980s declining productivity had led to an energy crisis that threatened the economy's growth prospects. The need for technological development underlined the problem of obtaining cost-effective technical assistance from overseas. The government's reluctance to allow private foreign investment in the economy was becoming all the more costly as the nation's technological needs became more pronounced.

Patterns of Development

The March 1962 military-led coup ushered in a program of radical economic policies designed once and for all to rid Burma of capitalist exploitation and foreign domination. During the next decade the U Ne Win government reorganized over 15,000 private firms into public enterprises, and most foreign capital was expropriated and nationalized or left the country. The leadership also renewed the national effort to complete the land reform initiated by the pre-1962 government and went so far as to set up a few model collective farms. At one time or another nearly every aspect of the nation's distribution system was taken over by government agencies, including all import and export trade. About 109,000 Indians and Pakistanis who had been resident aliens in Burma since the colonial era and who had dominated private industry and trade found these policies intolerable and fled the country. (See A Nationalized Economy, ch. 1).

The result of these policies was hardly the success hoped for by the Revolutionary Council, which had been set up by the military leadership in 1962. Economic growth during the 1960s was slow and erratic, the nation's gross domestic product (GDP—see Glossary) barely kept pace with population growth. Per capita food production, especially that of the important rice crop, declined substantially after 1964 and did not recover until well into the next decade. Despite the emphasis of public investment on industry, manufacturing output grew even more slowly than agriculture, revealing serious inefficiencies in the management of publicly owned industries (see table 2, Appendix). Shortages of consumer goods at the government-run stores led to the rapid growth of the black market. Although the government occasionally deregulated private trade, the overall thrust of economic policy was not conducive to private initiative and investment.

As of the early 1970s Burma was a hermit nation to most of the rest of the world, and inside the country concern over the chronic economic stagnation intensified. In 1971 the First Congress of the ruling Burma Socialist Programme Party (BSPP) had announced the formulation of a Twenty-Year Plan to guide the economy until fiscal year (FY—see Glossary) 1993. By late 1972 the ruling party had completed what analyst David I. Steinberg calls a "reassessment of priorities." In September 1972 the Central Committee of the BSPP approved a document entitled "Long-Term and Short-Term Economic Policies of the Burma Socialist Programme Party," a critical appraisal of past policies and a program for the future.

Looking back on the poor economic performance of the past, the BSPP catalogued numerous problems. Foremost was the neglect of agriculture, forestry, fishing, and mining, where most of the natural wealth was concentrated, and the failure to develop consumer goods and exports based upon these resources. The BSPP also decried the poor economic planning and coordination among government agencies and enterprises, the lack of discipline among both managers and laborers, the inability of public enterprises to employ sound business and accounting procedures, the waste of skilled manpower, and the "weak" relations with foreign countries. The policy initiatives designed to counteract these problems—namely, a balanced investment program, commercialization of public enterprises, promotion of private initiative and investment where necessary, and borrowing of funds and technology from overseas—did not represent an abandonment of socialism. Public and cooperative modes of production were still to lead the drive toward economic modernization.

Once again, however, the government's policies were poorly implemented, and the changes were slow and ineffective. Major crises struck the economy because the government was unable to procure enough rice to feed the urban population in 1973, despite an excellent harvest, and severe weather destroyed much of the crop in the following year. The official index of prices soared by over 25 percent per year from FY 1973 to FY 1975, prompting student protests and worker strikes. The First Four-Year Plan (FY 1972–75) was cut short a year earlier than planned, and halfway through the Second Four-Year Plan (FY 1974–77) economic growth rates were running well behind the targets.

In 1976 the government quickened the pace of economic reform and became more receptive to suggestions from a newly formed consortium of foreign lenders known as the Burma Aid Group (see Aid, Credit, and Investment, this ch.). A reform of the tax system in April followed by a major revision of pricing policies resulted in increased government revenues for investment and a narrowing of the gap between controlled and uncontrolled prices for many items. The government set up the Export Price Equalization Fund and in May 1977 devalued the currency by another 10 percent (there had been a 30 percent devaluation in 1975) in order to promote exports. Also during 1977 the government instituted more flexible budgetary procedures for state enterprises and departments and undertook a major investigation of the entire budgeting process.

Two developments in particular had far-reaching consequences for the economy: the nationwide program to introduce high-yielding varieties of rice and the unprecedented inflow of foreign funds to bolster the public investment program. In FY 1977 the government launched the Whole Township Extension Program, which by FY 1980 was providing new rice seed, fertilizer, and other modern inputs to farmers in 72 of the nation's major rice-producing townships; over 45 percent of the rice-growing area was cultivated with the new seeds. Meanwhile, a major decision reached at the Third Congress of the BSPP in February 1977 increased the amount of long-term capital imported by the government from bilateral and multilateral sources by almost 100 percent per year from 1977 to 1980; the amount of direct grant assistance increased more than sevenfold.

The result of these changes was a significant upturn in the rate of economic growth from 1976 onward (see fig. 8). After the disappointing start to the Second Four-Year Plan, the GDP growth rate for the plan period as a whole averaged out to just above the initial target of 4.5 percent per year. In particular the forestry, mining, power, construction, communications, financial, and social services sectors expanded more rapidly than planned, while the other sectors were just under the targeted rates. According to preliminary data for the Third Four-Year Plan (FY 1978–81), the

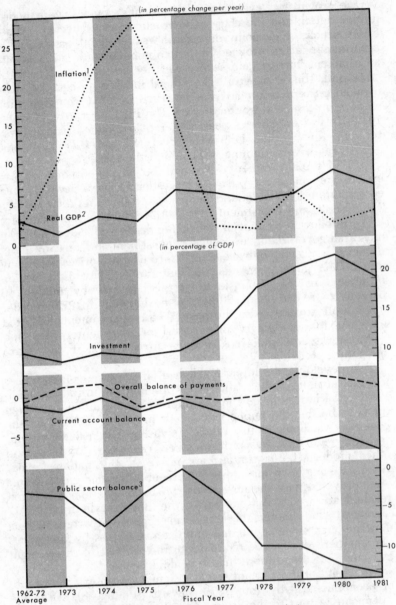

(in percentage change per year)

(in percentage of GDP)

NOTE– Data for FY 1980 are provisional; data for FY 1981 are preliminary estimates.

[1]Changes in the GDP deflator, a broad measure of inflation at official prices and excluding prices on the private market.

[2]Gross domestic product (see Glossary).

[3]FY 1968-72 average instead of FY 1962-72 average. Through FY 1973 government accounts consolidated on a different basis that excludes payments on the public debt.

Figure 8. Key Economic Indicators, FY 1962–81

average growth rate rose to 6.6 percent per year as planned, led by the agriculture, forestry, construction, finance, and social service sectors. Especially remarkable was the 8.6 percent growth performance of agriculture, which accounted for over one-third of the total growth rate.

Despite the economic turnaround, there has been little so-called modernization of the basic structure of the economy. The major development was the increase in the share of agriculture, forestry, and fishing from some 34 percent of GDP in FY 1962 to about 47 percent in FY 1981 (see table 3, Appendix). The shares of production attributable to industry and services have declined on average. Burma's recent economic growth has relied, therefore, on the revitalization and technological improvement of the traditional agricultural sector. The expansion of industry, usually considered the hallmark of modernization, had yet to begin.

The labor force likewise showed little structural change, according to official estimates. Although part of the labor force of 13.8 million, which has been growing at a rate of about 2 percent per year since FY 1972, shifted from agriculture to other sectors, in FY 1981 nearly 67 percent of all workers were still employed in agriculture, forestry, or fishing. The mining, manufacturing, power, and construction industries together accounted for only 10 percent of the work force. The most rapidly growing sectors of the labor force were mining, at over four times the growth rate for the whole work force, and social and administrative services, at two and one-half times the average growth rate. Employment in manufacturing and power expanded by more than 3 percent per year during the 1970s. New employment opportunities, however, did not develop as rapidly as necessary, and officially reported unemployment rose rapidly to 528,000 in FY 1979, or 4 percent of the labor force that year.

Although most Burmese households in early 1983 could meet their basic needs of subsistence, however lacking in comfort and convenience, there persisted several symptoms of economic malaise. The utilization of existing industrial capacity was low despite some improvement in recent years, and there were often shortages of crucial inputs, such as spare parts and petroleum. The oil sector, which almost single-handedly accounted for the growth of the mining industry in the FY 1977–79 period, was suffering a decline because of a lack of technological know-how. Of great concern to the international community was the large national debt; Burma's repayments of its foreign debt exceeded 28 percent of the value of its exports in FY 1981, about 10 points above the level of conventional prudence. The black market continued to expand its area of operations as many consumer items remained scarce.

The most far-reaching and potentially destabilizing problem facing the economy was the apparent waste of human resources.

141

Outside observers estimated that unemployment reached 6.7 percent of the work force in FY 1981, and so-called underemployment—the crowding of workers into unproductive jobs beneath their capabilities—was probably extensive. More and more skilled Burmese laborers were leaving the country altogether, despite a strong reluctance to do so, and many qualified individuals who remained found employment only outside their area of expertise. Reports from observers in Rangoon noted conspicuous unemployment among able-bodied and well-educated youths, who crowded the urban cinemas. Other impressions suggested that increased urban in-migration from the countryside was swelling the ranks of the urban unemployed. Official data, however, neglected to record these disturbing trends.

Public and Private Enterprises and Markets

The enduring socialist objective of the government was to change the structure of the economy so that by the end of the Twenty-Year Plan in FY 1993 public enterprise would contribute about 48 percent of the value of GDP while cooperative and private enterprise would each produce 26 percent. Since it first began nationalizing most of the large-scale economic enterprises in the 1960s, the government has been able to accomplish about 80 percent of its goals for the development of publicly owned enterprises. The goals for the cooperative sector, however, were still far out of reach, and private producers continued to thrive. The complex network of public and private—legal and illegal—distribution channels created a system that almost defied description and analysis. Bill Blake, a journalist visiting Rangoon in mid-1981, conjured up an image of two separate Burmas: "one a never-never land where prices, exchange rates, rules and regulations create a fantasy world of order and prosperity; the other a harsh marketplace governed only by the relentlessness of supply and demand." There was little information available concerning private marketing and even less about private production outside of the farming sector.

State enterprises accounted for the largest share of production in the power, mining, manufacturing, construction, communications, finance, and social services sectors (see table 4, Appendix). Some 45 nonfinancial state corporations, each affiliated with a particular government ministry or agency, owned and operated most of the large-scale factories and business establishments—more than 97 percent of all those factories employing over 100 laborers in FY 1981.

Until the mid-1970s the government ministries maintained central control over all aspects of the management of these corporations. In May 1975, however, it was decided that the management committees organized at each corporation would be given greater authority over production and sales. The new

"Guidelines for Operating on Commercial Lines" stipulated that the government would no longer automatically subsidize the deficits accumulated by inefficient enterprises and urged their managers to distribute rewards and punishments to increase productivity. The government also reorganized the 22 state-owned trading corporations, merging them into 11 enterprises having only the responsibility to retail imported items and to export.

The activities of cooperatives contributed only 4 percent of the value of GDP in FY 1981, well behind the government's plans. The Cooperative Societies Law was passed in 1970 primarily to reorganize the system of wholesale purchasing and retail selling. The majority of the some 21,400 cooperatives in existence in FY 1981 therefore were the retail cooperatives organized at the ward and village-tract level (see Local Administration, ch. 4). The village-tract cooperatives purchased agricultural products for various state agencies and sold farm inputs and consumer items to a membership of some 4.5 million people. Other cooperatives served the urban areas, the armed forces, and the police. There were few producers' cooperatives, whose number would have to be expanded enormously if the government was to achieve its objectives. Progress was slow primarily because of the lack of skilled managers and financing (see Land Tenure and Organization, this ch.).

Throughout the 1960s the government tried its best to discourage private industry and trade by nationalizing many firms, restricting bank credit to state and cooperative ventures, and controlling the prices of most essential commodities. After the policy changes initiated at the first and second congresses of the BSPP in 1971 and 1973, however, the government signaled its intent to allow more scope for private economic activity. In July 1973, for example, the government pledged that it would not nationalize the larger of the private rubber plantations for at least 30 years and in September announced that private investment would be allowed in some 268 industries, when it did not conflict with state enterprise. In response to continuing bottlenecks in the transportation system in 1975, the government sold some of its state-owned equipment to private entrepreneurs, who were urged to repair and expand the use of these vehicles. In September 1977, just before the extraordinary congress of the BSPP, the Right of Private Enterprise Law was enacted to allow private enterprises to operate "in fields not yet taken over by the State or cooperatives, and within the framework of the socialist system."

In FY 1981 private enterprise produced almost all of agricultural output and altogether about 58 percent of the value of GDP. According to comments from some private entrepreneurs in late 1982, however, many were reluctant to expand the scale of their operations out of fear of nationalization. The provisions of the Right of Private Enterprise Law, moreover, were vague, implying no guarantees against nationalization beyond FY 1993. Private enterprises still had virtually no access to bank credit and had limited access to raw materials (see Industry and Services, this ch.). Many private enterprises also dealt illegally with the distribution of black market items.

The distribution and marketing system operated in a complex network of controlled, decontrolled, and black market prices. State-run enterprises procured and distributed about 39 percent of the value of all goods and services sold in the domestic economy in FY 1981, including all legally imported items. Cooperatives handled about 16 percent of this volume, and private business marketed over 45 percent.

Because public and cooperative enterprises marketed their goods and services at controlled prices that were lower than those prevailing on the private market, many items found their way to the hands of black market traders (see The Black Market and the Opium Trade, ch. 5). Although precise data were unavailable, the volume of black market activity was highest when the gap between controlled and uncontrolled prices was widest in the 1960s and the first half of the 1970s. In 1976 and 1977 substantial increases in official prices, along with the implementation of a turnover tax on all commodities, narrowed the ratio to about two-to-one on average. Given the fact that some 80 percent of consumer items purchased in Rangoon Division came from the private market, however, black market trade remained significant in the early 1980s. Most foreign-made consumer goods that were available could be purchased only on the black market.

Most people traded on the private market, whether legally or illegally, if they wished to receive timely service, and the government seemed loath to crack down on any illegal traffic other than the drug trade. Privileged officials and managers had access to special stores that sold scarce consumer items—produced domestically or imported—and could in turn make enormous profits on the private market. It was the dream of many parents to have their sons become seamen working for an international shipping company, for seamen could legally import automobiles and other costly items that could be sold on the private market at home.

Some sample prices prevailing in the official and private markets in late 1982 may give an indication of the interaction of these markets. A household could purchase a ration of 16.3 kilograms of rice per month at a cost of K20 (for value of the kyat—see Glossary) at the official rate or pay K160 to K200 for an equivalent amount on the free market. The better quality rice almost inevitably was sold on the private market. Each individual or company that operated a motor vehicle was assigned to an official pump, where gasoline could be purchased at about K1 per liter. The price on the free market, however, was between K9 and K11 per

Open-air markets, bazaars, and small shops provide services and offer a variety of food and other commodities for sale.

liter, more in line with the value of petroleum in the world economy. As a result, gasoline had to be rationed at les than 12 liters per day per person, the pumps had long waiting lines, and the daily ration was almost immediately resold on the black market. Most pharmaceutical drugs and nearly all foreign-made consumer goods were available exclusively on the black market.

State Planning and Finance

The government remained committed to centralized state planning. The discrepancy between this ideal and a system stressing the importance of market interaction was nowhere evidenced more clearly than in an editorial appearing in one of the government's English-language newspapers in August 1982. This article stated that "mills and factories must give priority to producing goods as approved and prescribed by the Pyithu Hluttaw [People's Assembly] in full accord to the targets, for it is found that some of the mills and factories produced goods which would be profitable and which are in good demand rather than those which they had coordinated with the respective departments and organizations concerned."

The ultimate objective of the BSPP was "to lay the economic, social, and political foundations of socialism" by the end of the Twenty-Year Plan (FY 1974–93). Unlike the plans promulgated in the previous decade, the one-year and four-year plans were to be consistent with this long-term plan and were much heralded in the press in order to galvanize public support. The noisy rhetoric notwithstanding, they remained practical documents, designed on the basis of objective economic data compiled by the Central Statistical Organization for the Ministry of Planning and Finance, the formulator of all plans. The published plans contained only the broadest targets for the growth of investment and output in the various economic sectors.

Only scant information was available about planning procedures and implementation. The planning process was initiated by the Council of Ministers, which sent work programs to the executive committees of the state- and division-level people's councils as well as to the economic ministries. The ministers and deputy ministers of the relevant ministries, the deputy prime minister in charge of the Ministry of Planning and Finance, and the chief executives of all the states and divisions then met together as the Economic Coordination Committee of the Council of Ministers, under the chairmanship of the prime minister, in order to finalize the plan proposals. These were sent to the Ministry of Planning and Finance for final formulation and then presented to the People's Assembly for approval (see Central Government, ch. 4). In 1981 an amendment to the 1974 Constitution allowed the term of the People's Assembly to be adjusted to enable the swift promulgation of the Fourth Four-Year Plan (FY 1982–85) before the end of FY 1981.

The published provisions of the Fourth Four-Year Plan, like the others, were extremely general. Since public investment represented almost all investment activity in the economy, however, the government's control over investment decisions gave it the most influence in the economy. In the formulation of priorities for investment, the government has increasingly employed analytical techniques favored by the World Bank (see Glossary) and other aid donors. The central government departments were staffed with competent economists trained at the Institute of Economics in Rangoon.

How deeply this competence ran in the lower levels of the government bureaucracy and the state economic enterprises was questionable. More problematic for even the most competent of central planners were the inaccurate available statistical data and the unrealistic official prices used to analyze investment decisions. The low price for oil, for example, seriously impeded the true determination of economic costs and benefits for competing projects. Because seemingly profitable projects proved to be wasteful, it was likely that pressures would build for a more rational price structure.

Government economic strategy was best reflected in the pattern of public investment, which more than doubled from FY 1962 to over 22 percent of GDP in FY 1981. Although during the FY 1964–73 period less than 9 percent of all public investment went to agriculture, livestock raising, and fishing, this percentage rose to about 14 percent during the Second Four-Year Plan and averaged over 16 percent of all investment in the Third Four-Year Plan. Mining, which had been neglected during the 1960s and early 1970s, accounted for more than 11 percent in the Third Four-Year Plan period. Even though manufacturing investment increased to more than 36 percent of the total during the Third Four-Year Plan, about one-third of this investment was for industries that either supported agriculture or were based on agricultural raw materials (see table 5, Appendix).

The actual investment pattern differed substantially from the targeted pattern. During the Third Four-Year Plan, for example, more funds were required for mining, construction, transportation, trade, and social services than anticipated. Many important projects, moreover, were implemented outside of the framework of the plan on an ad hoc basis. While the broad targets for economic performance have been achieved, by no means did the economic plans rigidly control the flow of investment.

The guidelines for the allocation of investment during the Fourth Four-Year Plan again stressed the importance of agriculture, although the target of 20 percent for farming, livestock raising, and fishing was lower than in previous plans. Part of this decrease may be because of more realistic assumptions about the ability of the government to implement investments in these sectors. Investment in social services, particularly in health services, was expected to rise significantly in order to reverse the decreasing trend in real per capita health expenditures during the 1970s. Mining was to maintain its high priority during the new plan period, but a major shift away from investment in manufacturing was to finance expansion in other sectors.

Fiscal Policy and the Budget

Finding sources of funds for its investment program without stimulating inflation was a major preoccupation of the government. Before the April 1976 tax reform, the government's fiscal performance had deteriorated for about a decade; current revenues plummeted from about 25 percent of GDP in FY 1966 to only 9 percent in FY 1975. The reform levied new income and profit taxes on private households and cooperatives and increased fees for the use of state-owned lands and resources. The major change, however, was the consolidation of excise taxes into a single commodities and services tax to be applied for the first time to goods and services sold by state corporations. The state enterprises were also required to turn over a share of their profits to the government, while the Export Price Equalization Fund also became a source of budget revenue (see Foreign Economic Relations, this ch.). The effect of the reform was almost immediate; revenues increased to nearly 14 percent of GDP in FY 1977 and averaged about that level through FY 1980.

The rapid increase in state expenditures during the Third Four-Year Plan, however, caused the deficit in the consolidated public sector budget to increase from 3 percent of GDP in FY 1977 to more than 12 percent in FY 1980 and to an estimated 15 percent of GDP in FY 1981 (see table 6, Appendix). In general, the government was able to contain its current expenditures during the Third Four-Year Plan period by keeping salary increases to public sector workers to an average of 5 percent per year. A 12-percent raise in government salaries in FY 1981 to make up for the increased cost of living, however, caused public savings—the current account surplus—to decrease from over 6 percent of GDP in FY 1977 to about 4 percent of GDP in FY 1981. Other drains on state revenue included the weak financial position of some state enterprises, the cost of servicing the outstanding public debt, reduced customs revenues because of smuggling, and the high current expenditures on defense to counteract domestic insurgency.

The current deficits of some state corporations were the result of the government subsidies for the prices of fertilizer, rice, petroleum products, hardwood, electric power, and transportation services. The government was also losing revenues from the resale of goods bought at official prices in private markets. As of early 1983, however, the only change in the revenue system was the implementation of a modest water and irrigation tax. There has been no significant increase in official prices for most commodities since 1976 and no increase in taxes. Customs duties, which supplied about 13 percent of total central government revenues in FY 1980, remained relatively low for the capital and raw material imports that made up the bulk of imports.

Monetary Policy and Banking

Because public sector revenues have been unable to match the growth of capital expenditures, both domestic and international borrowing have increased substantially. As of March 1981 some 87 percent of the total domestic credit outstanding was owed by the public sector. Almost all of this debt came from state corporations. The central government had paid off most of its domestic debts (accumulated from the early 1970s), but its external debt had reached the equivalent of about US$2.7 billion in FY 1980 (see Aid, Credit, and Investment, this ch.).

The banking system was nationalized in 1963, when the government took over 10 foreign and 14 private domestic banks to form the Union of Burma Bank, the central bank, having an initial capital of K80 million. The central bank was the sole source of domestic credit until the Banking Law of 1975 reorganized the bank's three divisions into autonomous affiliates: the Myanma Economic Bank (having an initial capital of K80 million), the Myanma Agricultural Bank (K40 million), and the Myanma Foreign Trade Bank (K30 million). All of these banks were state owned, and overall control of the banking system was still the responsibility of the central bank and the Ministry of Planning and Finance.

The central bank handled all financing of the central government and managed the domestic and external debt. It also set interest rates for the entire banking system. The Myanma Economic Bank provided short- and long-term credit to state enterprises, cooperatives, and local governments and agencies for all nonagricultural activities. It also accepted deposits—including all those of state enterprises—and managed the lucrative pawnbroking business. The Myanma Agricultural Bank provided credit to some 2.5 million farmers each year as well as to the state and cooperative enterprises engaged in farming activities. The Myanma Foreign Trade Bank handled all foreign exchange transactions and the Export Price Equalization Fund (see Trade Patterns, this ch.). The profits of the trade bank jumped some 256 percent from FY 1977 to K221 million in FY 1980. The K229 million of profits realized by the Myanma Economic Bank in FY 1980 were the highest of all banking institutions.

The rapid increase in the lending volume since FY 1977 has led to an expansion of the money supply that threatened price stability. The total currency in circulation and demand deposits on hand at the banks expanded by almost 12 percent per year from

FY 1976 to FY 1980. To prevent this additional liquidity from raising the price level, the central bank increased interest rates for deposits of more than three years' maturity from 8 to 10 percent and that for 12-year savings certificates from 11 to 20 percent. All income from savings deposits and certificates, moreover, was exempted from the income tax. One unfortunate side effect of this policy was for many local agencies to tie up their funds in deposits rather than to embark on needed capital construction projects. Overall, however, the 400 percent increase in savings deposits generated during the FY 1977 to FY 1980 period succeeded in preventing the official consumer price index from rising by more than 1 percent. The official index did not account for price increases in the private market, which were probably substantial and which absorbed much of the new liquidity.

Agriculture, Fishing, and Forestry

Although rice has dominated Burmese agriculture for centuries, the nation's diverse resources and traditions supported a variety of activities, such as the production of oilseeds, pulses, plantation crops, livestock, teak, and other tropical hardwoods. The inland rivers and 3,060-kilometer coastline afforded good fishing grounds. Altogether, these activities produced over 47 percent of GDP in FY 1981 and 92 percent of the value of exports in FY 1980; the production of farm crops alone accounted for 38 percent of GDP and 55 percent of exports.

According to government estimates for FY 1981, the cultivated land area totaled some 8.5 million hectares; another 1.8 million hectares were left fallow, and some 8.6 million hectares of cultivable wasteland remained unexploited, making Burma one of the most land-rich countries in Asia. Portions of the arable land area, however, were highly susceptible to flooding and erosion; and partly because of the difficulty of protecting this land, there has been only a modest 6 percent expansion of the area cultivated since FY 1971. There were an additional 32.1 million hectares of forests, in which only limited farming and grazing were possible; the remainder was built-up or otherwise unsuited to agriculture.

Rainfall, topography, and soil conditions formed three general agricultural zones: rich, alluvial lowlands; drier but fertile uplands; and the hill or plateau regions. The lower valleys of the Irrawaddy, Sittang. and Salween rivers and their deltas and some parts of the lowland areas of Rakhine (formerly Arakan) and Mon states were most affected by the monsoon and received the heaviest rainfall (see fig. 9). Farmers in these areas traditionally practiced wet-field paddy cultivation, planting rice during the monsoon season, which lasted from May to October. Heavy flooding occurred during July and August, and extensive drainage systems were required to prevent flood damage. Because of the nature of the soil, the traditional farmers did not usually plant second crops.

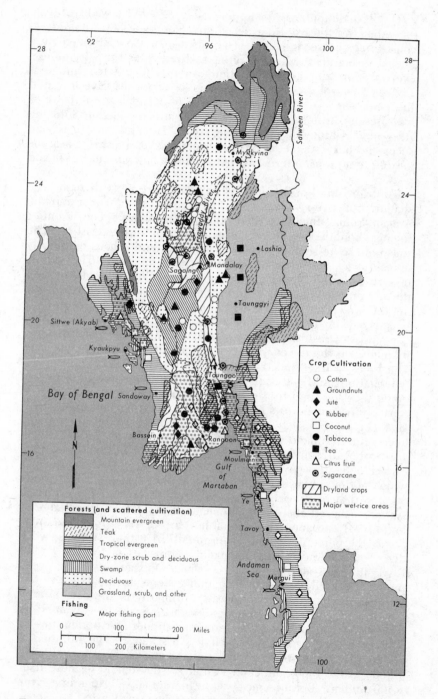

Figure 9. Agricultural Activity, 1982

The 160-kilometer-wide upper valley of the Irrawaddy River, extending northward from Thayetmyo for over 300 kilometers, constitutes the second kind of farming area. Characterized by a long dry season, the area is often referred to as the "dry zone," even though annual precipitation can exceed 100 centimeters. Living in fear of drought, the farmers for centuries have irrigated the land, especially the portion north of Mandalay where water was diverted from the lesser rivers and streams feeding into the Irrawaddy, Chindwin, and Sittang rivers. Hopeful for at least one successful harvest, the farmers developed several growing seasons for different crops, alternating between rice and various beans and peas.

The third kind of farmland is physically the most diverse. The shallow but steep valleys and ridges of the Pegu Yoma and the Arakan Yoma, the Shan Plateau, and the mountainous frontier regions nonetheless share some important characteristics. The soils tend to be shallow, subject to erosion, and exhausted quickly unless strict conservation measures are followed. The ethnic minorities in the border areas, sometimes called hill tribes, traditionally practiced forms of shifting cultivation (see Glossary), clearing the forests and scrub grass to plant upland rice, maize, millet, buckwheat, or opium poppies in rotation. Lawlessness and insurgency in the eastern border areas have limited the government's influence on the development of agriculture in these regions (see The Black Market and the Opium Trade, ch. 5).

Irrigation and flood control were the traditional means of developing the land, and the Irrigation Department of the Ministry of Agriculture and Forests has continued to improve and expand the area served by such systems. In FY 1981 some 1.1 million hectares of farmland were irrigated, compared with 840,000 hectares in FY 1971 and only 536,000 hectares in FY 1962. Since that earlier date, the government has engaged in over 270 projects, which not only irrigated additional areas but also controlled flooding and drainage on about 760,000 hectares of land. Government systems covered about 570,000 hectares of the total irrigated area in FY 1981 and about 1.1 million hectares of flood-protected area. Some 60 percent of the government irrigation systems were diversion schemes along the major tributaries of the Irrawaddy River in Pegu and Mandalay divisions. Village diversion, well, pump, windmill, and other irrigation systems unaffiliated with the Irrigation Department were located primarily in the dry zone.

In the mid-1970s the Irrigation Department vastly expanded its operations, stimulated by government support for agriculture as well as foreign capital and technical assistance. The number of authorized irrigation personnel tripled from FY 1973 to well over 19,000 in FY 1980, and capital outlays grew tenfold to more than K400 million. Because most of the potential for expanding river diversion projects in the dry zone has been exhausted, the construction program has shifted to the development of dam and reservoir storage systems. Three multipurpose schemes—located at Madaya on the Chaungmagyi River (Sedawgyi Project), at Myittha on the Panlaung River (Kinda Project), and at Loi-kaw on a tributary of the Salween River (Mobye Project)—will also produce hydroelectric power (see Utilities and Construction, this ch.). Dam and reservoir schemes covering 140,000 hectares were under construction and scheduled for completion in the early and mid-1980s; over 1.4 million hectares of additional project areas were proposed or under study. Some 160,000 hectares of drainage projects were being constructed in the lower Irrawaddy River area, and 322,000 hectares were proposed for coverage. Future river diversion projects will probably be located in Shan and Kayah states.

Despite the heightened level of government activity, irrigation development in Burma lagged behind that of its Asian neighbors. Not only was the irrigated area small by comparison, but also less than 14 percent of the irrigated land was cropped more than once a year. The government was also struggling to find an effective means to improve private irrigation schemes and management at the lower level. Shortages of fuel oil and equipment exacerbated the high costs and long periods of gestation associated with modern irrigation schemes. The evidence of the recent past, moreover, suggested that in Burma surprising gains could be achieved in rainfed agriculture by applying better cropping methods, modern fertilizers, and quality seeds (see Farm Modernization, this ch.).

Land Tenure and Organization

The issue of land reform has been a source of political controversy since the colonial era, but it was not until the 1970s that the worst aspects of landlordism were apparently eliminated. In 1948 the government nationalized all lands belonging to absentee owners and prepared to redistribute them to tenant or landless households. Amendments to the legislation and a reorganization of the bureaucracy and procedures during the 1950s impeded the pace of land reform, and by FY 1962 over 1 million tenant households remained—some 44 percent of all farm households, occupying 36 percent of all holdings. The new government passed a Tenancy Act in 1963, together with the Peasant's Rights and Protection Law, and amended the former law in 1965 to prohibit the payment of land rent of any kind. As late as FY 1970, however, official statistics still classified nearly 36 percent of all farm households as tenants; the proportion was more than 50 percent in Rakhine State and parts of Pegu and Sagaing divisions and was over 65 percent in Irrawaddy Division. Since that year the government has not published statistics concerning land tenure, but unofficial reports suggested that sharecropping continued.

In theory and according to the 1974 Constitution, the state is the ultimate owner of all of the nation's resources, including the land; individual ownership was restricted to small stands of tree crops in early 1983. The assignment of cultivation rights was the responsibility of village land committees, made up of local residents and officials. The committees also adjudicated land disputes, collected the land tax, and implemented the government's land reform policies. The committees typically allocated cultivation rights of deceased farmers to sons or other family members. The Settlement and Land Record Department of the Ministry of Agriculture and Forests supervised the operations of the local committees.

In practice, however, Burma continued to be a nation of smallholder, peasant farmers because they worked virtually the same lands as always. Some 4.3 million peasant households occupied and managed 9.8 million hectares of land in FY 1981. By contrast, official data seemed to indicate that only from 400,000 to 600,000 hectares were cultivated by state-owned or cooperative ventures. Over 61 percent of all farm households occupied less than two hectares of land, and the government was concerned about the continuing subdivision and fragmentation of landholdings in the densely populated paddy farming areas (see table 7, Appendix). Peasant smallholders produced 98.5 percent of the total value of farm crops.

Under the Twenty-Year Plan, cooperative farms were to account for 26 percent of agricultural assets and for 50 percent of production by FY 1993, but in FY 1981 they produced what one editorial called a "paltry" 1.2 percent of the total agricultural output. There were only 101 cooperative farms and 1,065 pilot cooperative farms—far fewer than the 12,557 village-tract cooperatives. The government was clearly concerned about the slow development of producers' cooperatives and had enlisted the aid of the International Labor Organization to improve the training programs for cooperative managers. The position of state farms in the crop-producing sector was even less significant than that of cooperatives; they farmed only 0.3 percent of total production in FY 1981.

Cooperatives and state farms were more influential in livestock and dairy farming, forestry, and fishing. About 2 percent of the total output of the livestock and fishing sector, which was undifferentiated in official data, was produced by state farms and another 1.7 percent by cooperatives. State farms were in charge of raising and disseminating pedigreed livestock and of hatching quality fish. State enterprises produced 40 percent of the value of timber extracted in FY 1981, while cooperatives accounted for 3.5 percent.

Although the progress of the producers' cooperatives has been slow, the BSPP has fared better in organizing the peasantry in to

Plowing rice fields with water buffalo, Shan Plateau
Courtesy Catherine B. Ferguson

the Peasants' Asiayone, or Peasants' Association (see The Burma Socialist Programme Party, ch. 4). Founded in 1977, there were 269 formal Peasants' Asiayone and eight informal organizing committees at the township level, as well as some 13,300 units at the village-tract or ward level in August 1981; the total membership reached 7.8 million by October 1982. The purpose of the Peasants' Asiayone was to encourage farmers to implement the government's agricultural extension programs, sell their produce to the state-run agencies according to production quotas, and promote rural health and literacy.

Farm Modernization

The introduction of modern cultivation methods and farm inputs began in earnest only in 1977, when the Whole Township Extension Program was launched. Using high- and quick-yielding varieties of rice seed developed at the Yezin Agricultural Research Institute in Pyinmana, the program spread to 23 townships in its second year and reached an estimated 78 townships in FY 1981, incorporating some 2.6 million hectares of paddy (see table 8, Appendix). Motivated by specially trained extension agents, many of them cadres of the BSPP, the participating farmers quickly adapted to the tight discipline required to cultivate the new seeds. Special committees made up of township officials and representative farmers administered the operation of the program. At least one observer of the Burmese scene has suggested that moves to implement the program in the insurgent areas, particularly in Karen State, were in part politically motivated.

The success of the Whole Township Extension Program prompted the government to introduce high-yielding strains for 20 other crops, including varieties of oilseeds, groundnuts, cotton, wheat, corn, pulses, sugarcane, potatoes, sorghum, and jute. In FY 1981 high-yielding varieties of these crops were planted in 61 townships. Altogether, the government planned for 169 townships in FY 1982 to receive new seed varieties for rice and other crops. Extension agents hired by the Agricultural Corporation, the state agency responsible for administering most aspects of agricultural modernization, spread information on how to plant and care for the new varieties. The Agricultural Corporation had 6,693 village managers in FY 1981, who supervised an average of 1,318 cultivated hectares each. It cost the government about K3,362 per manager or a little over K2 per supervised hectare in FY 1981, one-third more expensive than in FY 1977.

The Agricultural Corporation also had an Applied Research Division that ran 24 seed farms and 18 other central farms responsible for experimentation, demonstration, and training. The Yezin Agricultural Research Institute, also run by the Agricultural Corporation, trained specialists and conducted research for the state farms and local extension projects.

The new varieties of seed required additional modern inputs, such as chemical fertilizer and insecticides. Both have been scarce inside Burma but were provided to farmers and cooperatives at subsidized prices by the Agricultural Corporation. Although more than one-half of the nation's supplies of chemical fertilizer had to be imported in FY 1981, the total consumption had grown by over 15 percent per year since FY 1977, reaching nearly 240,000 tons. Even so, some estimates suggested that optimum usage would be 50 or 60 percent higher. Fertilizer was used more intensively for the high-yielding varieties of rice, sugarcane, and groundnuts. During the same five-year period, Burma's consumption of chemical insecticides had more than tripled to 1,078 tons.

Mechanization of farming operations has proceeded more slowly than other forms of modernization in Burma, despite indications that the quick maturation of the newer seeds has created periodic labor shortages. In many areas police, army, and civilian units have been mobilized to plant or harvest the crop. Nevertheless, the Agricultural Mechanization Department maintained 3,770 tractors at 88 stations around the country and managed to till 725,000 hectares of farmland in FY 1981, a 118 percent increase over FY 1977. Cooperatives owned 3,853 other tractors. Most of the existing fleet consisted of aging Czechoslovak tractors, assembled locally but lacking spare parts. Power tillers, threshers, pumps, and other equipment were available from the Agricultural

Corporation. Well-drilling machines, rice transplanters, and rice harvesters became available for the first time in FY 1981.

Agricultural credit from the Myanma Agricultural Bank was yet insufficient to finance all farm equipment purchases and capital construction but was extremely important. Farmers and cooperatives received loans at a 12 percent rate of interest repayable at the end of the harvest. Medium-term loans for the purchase of draft animals and equipment were available only on a limited basis. The size of the loans varied according to the crop. Farmers in the Whole Township Extension Program could receive loans of K346 per hectare of high-yield rice, twice the allotment for nonparticipants, starting in the FY 1981 monsoon season. Total loans during that season exceeded K1 billion, and the loan recovery rate was reportedly excellent. Many farmers and extension workers believed that about K500 per hectare of credit would be needed for the program to be completely successful. In addition to bank credit, state corporations provided advance purchase payments for certain industrial crops, such as jute, cotton, sugarcane, and tobacco.

Farm Production and Procurement

The production of rice was essential to the daily subsistence and cash incomes of the majority of farmers, and its procurement by the government was vital to the well-being of the inhabitants of urban and rice-deficient areas, as well as to the nation's ability to export and maintain financial and political stability. Until the mid-1970s there was almost no improvement in the average yield, but after the widespread introduction of high-yield varieties in FY 1976, the average yield increased by over 9 percent per year to an estimated 2.9 tons per hectare in FY 1981. By contrast, the average yields per hectare were only 1.6 tons in FY 1962 and 1.7 tons in FY 1972. The best yields were achieved in areas already having extensive irrigation and drainage networks. Government procurements bottomed out in the early 1970s at less than a quarter of the crop but improved to an average of about 30 percent of the harvest in the late 1970s and early 1980s. The volume of exports likewise increased, and exports in FY 1981 were nearly five times those in FY 1973, although less than half the average for the 1950s and early 1960s (see table 9; table 10, Appendix).

The ability of the government to procure a sufficient share of the crop was directly related to the ratio of free market to official market prices for rice. This price ratio averaged over two to one for most varieties of rice in the early 1970s and FY 1978, when procurement was lowest. Evidently, farmers were finding it more profitable to divert their harvest to private middlemen than to sell it to official purchasing agents at fixed prices. Prices paid to farmers for the ordinary rice crop were raised by an average of 50 percent in FY 1974 but remained unchanged through FY 1981. Prices paid for quality seeds and export quality rice have been adjusted upward further, however, to ensure sufficient supplies for the government extension programs and for export.

The government has also reorganized the system of rice procurement and brought in the armed forces to aid both as manpower and as supervisors in certain areas. The government introduced a quota system in FY 1973, under which the local-level people's councils assigned each farm a certain portion to sell to the state, depending on the size and quality of the landholding. The next year special bonuses, almost equivalent to the free market price, were paid for any portion of the crop in excess of the quota. The bonus system proved generally successful and was still in use in 1983. In FY 1977, however, the procurement system broke down after several successful harvest seasons, and the armed forces were called in to confiscate stocks. Since then the armed forces have been involved each year in "volunteer" programs to help the farmers bring in the rice crop. It was difficult to determine how much the soldiers were aiding the farmers by their labor or ensuring that government sales quotas would be met.

The major problem in the early 1980s seemed to be finding the warehouse space to store the increased supplies of rice. Declining world prices for rice have increased the domestic surplus further, and the poor quality of the rice procured by the government has also reduced the export prospects. In response to these problems, the government's objectives for the Fourth Four-Year Plan were to grow more high-quality varieties for export; to improve the currently low ratio for converting rough paddy to marketable rice; to build bigger and better storage facilities; and to improve procedures for grading, packaging, and handling export rice. The rate of increase in rice production would probably decline as the new seed varieties and planting methods were introduced into the less fertile areas, but the government hoped to make Burma once again one of the top three exporters in the world by the year 2000.

The other major cereal crops, maize and wheat, grown for both food and fodder, were cultivated on only 2 percent and 1 percent, respectively, of the total cultivated area in FY 1981. The area planted with maize has more than doubled since FY 1971, and the Agricultural Corporation procured 22,000 tons of quality maize seed in FY 1981. Use of the better seed has improved the average yield per hectare from 0.9 tons to 1.3 tons since FY 1978. Likewise, the wheat yield has more than doubled since FY 1978 to over 1.1 tons per hectare. In FY 1982 the Agricultural Corporation planned to double the area under wheat cultivation by expanding the state and cooperative farms in Shan State and Mandalay and Sagaing divisions. Increasing the domestic consumption of wheat products, a major government objective, would free more rice for export. About 20 percent of the wheat crop was procured by the state to be processed and distributed by state enterprises.

Oil-bearing crops, such as groundnuts, sunflowers, and sesame occupied some 21 percent of the cropped area in FY 1981; groundnuts and sesame accounted for over 90 percent of this area. Since the introduction of improved seed and cropping methods, the average yield for most of these crops has increased dramatically. By FY 1981 the average yields per hectare were 25 percent higher than the maximum yield achieved by FY 1978 for sunflowers, some 20 percent higher for groundnuts, and about 5 percent higher for sesame. Most of the gains resulted from the introduction of oil-bearing crops into the farming cycle in Irrawaddy, Rangoon, and Pegu divisions during the dry winter season. Burma's farmers also planted soybeans, which were not processed into oil.

Chick-peas, butter beans, and other pulses or legumes were a major part of the Burmese diet and were exported as well. They were grown all over the country, usually in rotation with a cereal crop. After a long period of stagnation that lasted through FY 1975, production increased by more than 11 percent per year. More than half of the increase resulted from higher yields, especially for butter beans, which together with chick-peas represented the largest share of the total crop of pulses.

Other important food crops included potatoes, onions, chilies, garlic, other vegetables, and fruits of many varieties. Most of the horticultural crops and temperate fruits were grown in the drier uplands and hilly border regions. Equatorial fruits were cultivated in Tenasserim Division, but bananas, mangoes, oranges, and other subtropical fruits were also produced in parts of Rakhine and Kachin states and other states and divisions.

Cotton and jute were the major fiber crops. Average yields for cotton, produced chiefly in Mandalay Division, grew by nearly 65 percent from FY 1978 to FY 1981 after the distribution of quality seeds, primarily of the long-staple variety. Jute, grown chiefly in the low-lying areas, experienced generally increasing yields during the 1970s, which nonetheless declined remarkably in FY 1981 because of shortages of diesel fuel to run the irrigation pumps. Jute was an important export item but was increasingly in demand for domestic production.

Rubber and sugarcane were the most important of the other industrial and commercial crops. Most of the rubber trees were planted in Tenasserim Division but were aged and unproductive. The government was replanting and rehabilitating these plantations only slowly, and production had yet to respond favorably in FY 1981. In 1982 Malaysia agreed to give Burma 780,000 rubber tree seeds for these programs. By contrast, sugarcane production has improved remarkably because of better varieties and increased fertilizer use, although the conversion to refined sugar remained inefficient. Tobacco and tea were important upland crops, and coconut and oil palm were significant in the lowland areas.

Animal husbandry was a secondary farming activity but, given the lack of mechanization, extremely important to the rest of agriculture. Progress during the Third Four-Year Plan period was good; the stock of draft cattle—including young water buffalo and cattle—increased by over 3 percent per year, compared with less than 1 percent per year during the previous plan period (see table 11, Appendix). Excluding water buffalo and ducks, the population of livestock averaged higher than targeted. The number of poultry increased quickly, especially on the cooperative or state-run farms located near the urban centers in the delta region. Meat production was growing but reached only 4.3 kilograms per capita per year in FY 1981. The production of fresh milk approached 10 kilograms per capita per year in FY 1981, nearly double the production for FY 1972.

Since FY 1978 the government has established township and village-tract livestock development committees to promote the expansion and better management of the livestock population. The Livestock Development and Marketing Corporation, however, failed to meet its targets for introducing pedigree breeds from its farms around the countryside during the Third Four-Year Plan, and only 14 of 42 planned new breeding farms were established. The Department of Veterinary and Animal Husbandry did carry out its program of artificial insemination and disease control, receiving aid from the World Bank and the United Nations Development Program (UNDP). The state corporation received important assistance from the Japanese and Canadian governments and the UNDP for developing state farms.

Fishing

Fish and shellfish were the most important sources of protein in the Burmese diet and were used in a variety of dried and cooked forms and in sauces and pastes. Per capita production, however, was low: about 17.6 kilograms in FY 1981, or less than half of that in neighboring Thailand. About one-fifth of the annual catch came from freshwater fisheries, slightly more from coastal grounds, about 30 percent from nearby waters, and the rest from the deep sea.

Small inland lakes, ponds, and floodlands—both natural and man-made—accounted for most of the freshwater catch. Aquiculture ponds covered 1,871 hectares in FY 1981, a 23 percent increase since FY 1977, and produced 3,108 tons of fish and prawns. Private or cooperative laborers fished about 3,500 of 3,700 freshwater fisheries that had to be leased from state or local agencies and produced another 71,000 tons. Open freshwater fisheries and floodplains produced the rest of the total 88,000 tons of freshwater fish. Most of the freshwater grounds were located in

Irrawaddy, Mandalay, and Sagaing divisions. In FY 1981 the Department of Fishery distributed 7,500 fingerlings of freshwater carp from its more than 100 hectares of hatcheries. The state-run People's Pearl and Fishery Corporation accounted for only about 6 percent of the freshwater catch.

State-owned vessels were more important in the marine fisheries, where they accounted for over 8 percent of the total catch of 290,000 tons. Loans from Australia, Denmark, and Britain enabled the state-owned fleet to expand from 42 trawlers and 17 carriers in FY 1977 to 79 trawlers and 47 carriers in FY 1981. Other loans went to the construction of cold storage, jetties, and other onshore facilities in Rakhine State and Tenasserim Division, where the major fishing bases were located. As the name implied, the state corporation cultured some 11,100 pearls in the Mergui Archipelago of Tennasserim Division and was experimenting with culture grounds in Rakhine State.

The vast bulk of the fishing fleet consisted of small, antiquated vessels. Private individuals and 643 fishing cooperatives operated about 5,000 powered craft and over 98,000 motorless vessels in FY 1981. Projects scheduled for the Fourth Four-Year Plan period, however, were concentrating on improving the state-owned fleet, shore facilities, and the fishery survey facilities.

Forestry

Burma is the world's largest producer of teak, and forestry continued to be a leading sector in the Third Four-Year Plan period, growing by nearly 8 percent per year on average. Production in FY 1981 reached some 925,000 cubic meters of teak and 2.4 million cubic meters of other tropical hardwoods. The state-run Timber Corporation produced all of the teak extracted each year and over 60 percent of other hardwoods. Private producers and cooperatives extracted hardwoods primarily for fuel and construction materials. The government included the production of bamboo, cane, resins, honey, bat guano, birds' nest, and other sundry commodities in the statistics on forestry production, which represented over 7 percent of the nation's GDP in FY 1981.

The tools and equipment used in forestry production ran the gamut from elephants and water buffalo to modern cable-logging equipment. The increased extraction during the Third Four-Year Plan, however, was primarily the result of new equipment purchased under foreign loans. These operated at major forestry projects located near Prome, in Sagaing Division, in West Bassein Township in Irrawaddy Division, and in the eastern Pegu Yoma. A Canadian loan financed the construction of an equipment repair depot at Pyinmana in Mandalay Division.

Forest conservation has been a major concern of the government since the late nineteenth century, and the Forest Department continued this tradition in the 1980s. The area designated as reserved forest, i.e., that which is carefully managed and protected by the government, was almost 10 million hectares in FY 1981, or 31 percent of all forests; this was an 11 percent increase in the reserved forest area since FY 1962. Even in the public, nonreserved forests, the extraction of certain species was restricted. Unlike Thailand, Burma has prevented the elimination of its valuable teak reserves. The Forest Department had the sole responsibility for teak girdling—removing a strip of bark to dry out and kill the teak tree. The number of teak trees planted each year has more than quadrupled since the late 1960s to an average of 640,000 per year in the FY 1979–81 period; the planting of other hardwoods increased more than 500 percent to an average of 848,000 in the same period. The Forest Department was also surveying and researching the nation's forest resources and needs under a grant from the UNDP.

Two problems were affecting the forestry sector. First, the government had less than adequate control of the private extraction of hardwoods in farming areas. About 56 percent of the forest cover was located in areas of shifting cultivation or near permanent farms; the average rate of deforestation during the late 1970s was about 95,000 hectares per year and was expected to increase to 105,000 hectares per year in the first half of the 1980s. Second, as much as 20 percent of the teak felled each year was lost to thieves who either smuggled the logs across the Thai border or processed them for sale in Burma. Although the latter had no effect on the conservation of the forest resources, it reduced the government's substantial forestry revenues.

Industry and Services

Besides the general lack of technical sophistication, the two main features of the industrial sector at the start of the 1980s were its overwhelming concentration in a few central administrative divisions and its dominance by state enterprise; the same could be said of the infrastructure and service sectors as well. The only exceptions to the geographical pattern were in the mining and power industries, where the availability of resources dictated the location of some investments. Private enterprise flourished only in small-scale and sometimes illegal business activities. Above all, the transportation and communications networks demonstrated clearly the isolation of the peripheral states and divisions from the heart of the economy.

Because of its access to transportation, communications, and government services, Rangoon Division was the obvious center of industry and produced some 55 percent of the total industrial output in FY 1981. Since the promulgation of the Constitution in 1974, the government has vociferously declared its intention to decentralize economic activity as much as possible, especially in industry. No information was available in 1983 to judge defini-

*Logs being floated down the Irrawaddy
River, destined for export. Burma is a major
world producer of forest products.*
Courtesy Frederica M. Bunge

tively the progress of this policy, but there was little evidence to
suggest that a major reallocation of investment resources had
occurred.

Official regulation and law tightly circumscribed private industrial activity, although the Right of Private Enterprise Law of 1977
stipulated that private industrial concerns would be allowed to
operate in a number of sectors at least until the end of the
Twenty-Year Plan. Most light industry and the less important
mineral and chemical industries were open to private enterprise.
All important minerals, foodstuffs, garments, pharmaceuticals,
chemicals, transport equipment, and machinery were produced
by state enterprises and their affiliates. Private enterprises,
moreover, had to purchase most of their raw materials from public
producers. In order to set up contracts for such materials, private
companies had to disclose information about their finances to the
government, which they were often reluctant to do.

The BSPP organized most industrial workers into the Workers'
Asiayone (Workers' Association) in 1977, and by December 1982
the total membership reached 1.6 million laborers (see the Burma
Socialist Programme Party, ch. 4). Organized at each factory but
under centralized guidance, the Workers' Asiayone took the place
of labor unions, representing the workers' interests to the enter-

163

prise managers. They also urged the workers to fulfill production targets set by the government, chose model workers to be heralded in the press, encouraged workers to join the BSPP, and ran some welfare facilities.

Mining

Leading the effort to exploit Burma's diverse mineral resources and promising the best hope for reducing the nation's indebtedness was the petroleum industry—one of the oldest in the world. When production of crude oil peaked at more than 21,000 barrels per day before World War II, the country ranked fourteenth in the world. After a long postwar decline, the nation finally exceeded this level of production in FY 1976, but by then the rest of the world had forged far ahead. Nevertheless, the extraction of crude oil and the recovery of natural gas were crucial to the government's modernization program. At the same time, the government remained proud that most of the post-World War II exploration and production has been accomplished without foreign assistance.

Maintaining this posture of self-reliance in the oil industry was becoming more and more costly as the productivity of the older onshore fields declined and the longevity of the newer fields proved to be ominously short. Offshore, where the government has invited foreign concessionaires, drilling has not uncovered any significant fields. One independent consultant estimated Burma's total reserves to be 102 million barrels of oil and another 30 million barrels of natural gas, converted to its equivalent in oil. The government, however, remained sanguine and estimated total recoverable reserves to be 2.1 billion barrels of crude oil and 860 million barrels of natural gas. Reports of serious shortages of oil in 1983 tempered this optimism.

Crude oil production, according to official estimates for FY 1981, averaged 33,000 barrels per day, a figure that was probably biased upward because it did not exclude the water contained in the oil at the well site. Over 90 percent of the total production came from the Mann field in Magwe Division. The overpuncturing of the wells in this field reportedly led to the shortfall in FY 1980 (see table 12, Appendix). Other reports indicated that actual production in 1981 was less than 26,000 barrels per day, a 9 percent decline from the previous calendar year.

The state-owned Myanma Oil Corporation announced the discovery of three major new oil fields in late 1981, the largest of which was located just south of Pagan in sand layers similar to those of the older fields. The two others, located near Kyangin in the northern part of the Irrawaddy Delta and near Kyonpyaw right on the delta, were the first to be found in limestone layers; the government claimed that there were over 35 similar configurations of limestone around the country. Drilling in the Kyonpyaw area reached a depth of 4,100 meters—the deepest ever for Burma and a significant achievement, given the lack of trained engineers to run the two deep-drill rigs purchased only in 1979 and 1980. Most analysts believed that the best oil finds would come from a level of 5,500-6,100 meters. In the past, however, the government's announcements of new oil finds have proved to be overly optimistic, and there was every possibility that oil imports would resume in the mid-1980s.

Natural gas production has shown a continuous and impressive expansion, reaching an average of 1.8 million cubic meters per day—equivalent to 11,000 barrels of oil. Production has nearly doubled since FY 1979, and over 20 percent of the increase came from one field near Kyangin, which has been in production since FY 1978. Foreign demand for liquid natural gas prompted the Japanese to establish a joint venture with the Myanma Oil Corporation in 1982 to explore four blocks of promising offshore areas in the Gulf of Martaban. In February 1983 a gas flow of about 1.1 million cubic meters per day was reported for the first test boring.

Coal production supplemented the energy derived from oil and natural gas only minimally. The estimated 38,000 tons of coal extracted in FY 1981 represented, however, one-third more than the previous post-World War II high achieved in FY 1977. The increase occurred as the result of mine expansions around Kalewa in Sagaing Division. The Number Three Mining Corporation was responsible for coal production as well as for the production of iron and nonmetals. The government did not provide an estimate of total coal reserves, but extensive deposits were believed to be located in the Shan Plateau. The Department of Geological Survey and Mineral Exploration was conducting exploratory surveys for coal and other minerals with the aid of a UNDP grant.

Lead, zinc, and silver resources were abundant, but production in FY 1982 was less than one-fifth of the historical high achieved in FY 1939. The country's major mine, at Bawdwin in Shan State, had a history dating back to the eleventh century and was once one of the world's largest. A project to improve open-pit mining methods and the recovery of low-grade ore had raised production at Bawdwin during the Third Four-Year Plan period. The depletion of high-grade reserves has also occurred at the other major mines at Bawzaing, where renewed exploration had led to increased production. The Number One Mining Corporation was responsible for these and other nonferrous metal mining, except for tin and tungsten.

Tin and tungsten deposits were the most numerous of all mineral sites and provided excellent resources for future development. The largest mines were run by the Number Two Mining Corporation. The Mawchi mine in Kayah State was once the largest tungsten producer and second largest tin producer in the world and still had minable reserves of about 800,000 tons in

1982. Some 67 percent of all production, however, came from numerous smaller sites in Tenasserim Division, especially around Tavoy. Offshore dredging operations had yet to be developed, but a survey conducted with UNDP assistance revealed significant deposits in the Gulf of Martaban.

There were over 20 reported occurrences of copper throughout the country, and the chief mine, being developed at Monywa in Sagaing, had a planned output capacity of 12,000 tons per day of copper-bearing ores. Iron ore was found in some 20 known locations, but only the sites in western Shan State and at Maymyo in Mandalay Division have been developed. Antimony, nickel, and gold were also mined.

Burma continued to be a major producer of precious stones, especially of jade and rubies. Kachin State was the principal location for jade and amber mining, and Kamaing, northwest of Myitkyina, was the only known source in the world of a semitransparent variety of jade known as Imperial Jade. Mogok, in Mandalay Division, was the center of mining for rubies, sapphires, and other gems. In addition to these precious nonmetals, barites, gypsum, and limestone were mined on a large scale, primarily for the production of cement.

Processing and Manufacturing

The performance of the manufacturing sector during the Third Four-Year Plan was sluggish. Even according to provisional data, which were usually optimistic for industry, the average growth of the value added to GDP from this sector was only 6 percent per year, or less than one-half of the targeted rate. The production of some important consumer items, such as the ubiquitous *longyi* (traditional Burmese dress for men and women), was even less in FY 1981 than in FY 1969. To the credit of the government's policies, however, the supply of foodstuffs and industrial materials has risen rapidly (see table 13, Appendix). During the FY 1971–81 period, the government's quantum index of manufacturing production rose at an average of 4 percent per year, and most of the growth was concentrated in the latter part of the decade. About 69 percent of the increase came from light industry, another 19 percent from the manufacture of materials, and the remainder from the equipment-manufacturing and miscellaneous industries.

Light industry, including the processing and manufacturing of foods, beverages, textiles, personal and household goods, and printed materials, represented over 71 percent of the gross value of manufacturing production in FY 1981, almost the same as it did 10 years earlier. There were over 26,700 private, 524 cooperative, and 330 state-run factories and establishments producing these products, and 30 other state-run facilities were under construction. The processing of food and beverages and the manufacturing of textiles, accounting for over 90 percent of light industrial output, had the least amount of state ownership. The Ministry of Industry (I), one of two ministries responsible for nonmineral manufacturing, supervised the production of light industrial commodities and the manufacture of some chemicals, building materials, and light equipment.

Rice milling and the production of edible oils dominated the food processing industry, the former located in the major rice-producing areas and the latter in Magwe Division. The completion of three 50-ton rice mills and partial construction of thirteen 100-ton mills helped to increase the production of rice during the Third Four-Year Plan. In addition, the Food Industries Corporation constructed an integrated sugar mill in Pyinmana and expanded the nation's major brewery in Mandalay Division. Textile production was located in Rangoon, Pegu, Irrawaddy, Magwe, and Mandalay divisions, and, to a lesser extent, in Mon State. The major projects in the Third Four-Year Plan period were the construction of a jute mill in Myaungmya and the expansion of the major textile mill at Shwedaung. Most of the textile facilities were small-scale, traditional weaving establishments for the production of cotton and silk fabrics.

Raw materials production was less centralized than light industry. The most scattered was the forest products industry, which included sawmills, and factories for producing resins, turpentine, and plywood. The Timber Corporation constructed its fourth plywood plant during the Third Four-Year Plan period. The Ceramic Industries Corporation produced cement at factories in Thayetmyo and Kyangin along the Irrawaddy River and was expanding the latter and building a new plant in Pa-an in Karen State. The same corporation ran important glass works in Bassein. Mineral processing, which came under the purview of the various mining corporations affiliated with the Ministry of Mines, was expanding after the completion of the first sponge and pig iron plant at Maymyo.

The Petrochemical Industries Corporation, which together with most heavy industry was under the guidance of the Ministry of Industry (II), operated three oil refineries that produced gasoline, kerosine, diesel oil, and heavy oil. Expansion of the Syriam refinery near Rangoon and the opening of a new refinery at the Mann oil field seemed to be in vain, however, until the shortages of crude oil from the wells could be remedied. Burma's production of fertilizer—all of it urea produced from natural gas—was increasing as the capacity of the main plant at Sale was expanded to 83,000 tons a year in FY 1981. A second plant was located at Kyunchaung, and a third was under construction. The expansion of the Sittang pulp mill also improved the output of chemical products.

The equipment industry, which was growing rapidly from a small base, was dominated by the Heavy Industries Corporation.

Factories assembling tractors and other agricultural equipment were located in a major center of heavy industry at Sinde, near Prome in Pegu division, and in Minhla Township in Magwe Division. The only major projects of the Third Four-Year Plan, however, were a pump and nozzle plant and a tire manufacturing facility, both financed by loans from Czechoslovakia and both just beginning construction after a delay.

Utilities and Construction

Electric power contributed only 14 percent of the commercial energy produced in Burma in FY 1979, but the nation's excellent hydroelectric potential, estimated to exceed 100,000 megawatts of capacity, offered a distant hope to electrify the entire country. In FY 1981, however, the 695 megawatts of installed capacity were sufficient to provide only 273 towns and 711 villages with electricity. Over three-quarters of the existing capacity came from the network run by the Electric Power Corporation; the remainder was produced from plants attached to particular factories for industrial power. Of the estimated 1.4 billion kilowatt-hours generated by the Electric Power Corporation in FY 1981, some 61 percent came from hydropower facilities, about 30 percent from gas-fired plants, some 5 percent from thermal plants, and the rest from diesel-fired facilities. Leakages along the power lines totalled 31 percent of production in FY 1980 and 28 percent in FY 1981—extremely high by industry standards.

There were three main systems in place at the start of the 1980s. An integrated grid connecting the major hydroelectric dam at Law-pi-ta in Kayah State to two thermal stations near Rangoon and to the gas turbine station at Kyunchaung in Magwe Division served the largest area. The second system centered on the gas turbine station at Myanaung and connected to substations in the Prome area. The third network was based at the Mann oil fields. The total capacity of these integrated systems was approximately 408 megawatts. In 1981 construction was under way for three gas turbine stations, two multipurpose hydroelectric projects, one thermal station, and seven small-scale hydroelectric plants, which altogether would supply nearly 200 megawatts of additional capacity in the mid-1980s.

Although much of the activity of the power corporation concerned the construction of smaller facilities to meet rising demand and the replacement of worn-out lines to reduce losses from the system, there were plans to build much larger hydroelectric facilities. Over 23 sites have been investigated in the tributaries of the Irrawaddy, Chindwin, Sittang, Salween, and lesser rivers and streams, having the potential to produce over 8,000 megawatts of capacity. The most likely candidates for construction in the 1980s, however, were the Panglaung I project along the Sittang; the Baluchaung I project near the existing Law-pi-ta Dam on a tributary of

Children pose with sugarcane press.
Courtesy Catherine B. Ferguson

the Salween; and on the Pegu River as part of a water project for Rangoon. The total capacity of these projects would only be 350 megawatts, some 300 megawatts from the Panglaung project alone. The isolation of many of the sites raised the costs to develop them substantially, and except for multipurpose irrigation projects and small-scale projects to serve smaller townships, construction of new networks would proceed only slowly.

Some problems have arisen from the low electricity prices, especially for the state-run industrial enterprises. The Electric Power Corporation has encountered substantial losses, and many state enterprises have not been given any incentives to improve the energy efficiency of their factories. The government was studying how to improve the pricing structure to eliminate these problems but as of early 1983 had taken no action to increase prices.

State enterprises accounted for 83 percent of the gross value of all construction projects during the Third Four-Year Plan period, and over half of the state-run projects were built by the Construction Corporation. Most of the new construction was for industrial buildings, workshops, schools, hospitals, offices, and residential buildings for factory workers, but about 22 percent was for transportation projects. The Construction Corporation built facilities on contract to other state enterprises and agencies but deferred to the technical expertise of enterprises, such as the mining and railroad companies, to complete their own construction programs.

Transportation and Communications

By the government's own admission, the transportation networks were poorly developed, especially in the peripheral states. The existing system, a mixture of state and private transportation by river, road, and rail, provided good transportation from Mandalay to Rangoon but poor service from east to west and to the mountainous periphery. Water transportation made up for the lack of land facilities in the Irrawaddy delta area and along the Tenasserim and Rakhine coasts. The demand for transportation services has been growing rapidly, primarily because of the increased output of agricultural goods.

Five state corporations, coordinated under the Ministry of Transport and Communications, provided the only transportation services about which there was adequate information. The Central Movement Coordination Committee, a special government committee, was responsible for allocating transportation responsibilities among the state corporations and for contracting private and cooperative carriers to fill in gaps in the state system. In FY 1980 it was estimated that about 8 percent of the bulk freight trade was transported on state carriers—all of the railroad freight, about 5 percent of the road traffic, and 8 percent of the coastal and riverine freight. In addition, about 13 percent of the road traffic and 17 percent of waterborne freight were transported by minor public carriers. One-third of all freight was still transported only short distances on small boats, carts, or beasts of burden. Information comparing state-run and private passenger conveyances was not available.

The Burma Railroad Corporation dominated state-run land transportation, averaging 65 percent of all passenger distances and 53 percent of all freight distances clocked during the FY 1979–81 period. In FY 1981 the nation's meter-gauge railroad track extended for some 4,385 kilometers—a 5-percent increase since FY 1971 and 15 percent longer than in FY 1962. The track running between Rangoon and Pyinmana for some 464 kilometers along the major trunk route to Mandalay was double tracked (see fig. 10). A major railroad rehabilitation project begun in FY 1977 was concentrating on the replacement of outdated rolling stock. The number of diesel locomotives rose by 20 percent to 213 in FY 1981, while the aging steam engines have diminished to 123. Many of the diesel engines, however, were frequently out of service because of a lack of spare parts, and the average number of kilometers traveled by the available diesel locomotives declined from 232 kilometers per day in FY 1971 to 175 kilometers in FY 1979, when information was last available. Although the number of passenger wagons expanded by 5 percent to 1,345 during the

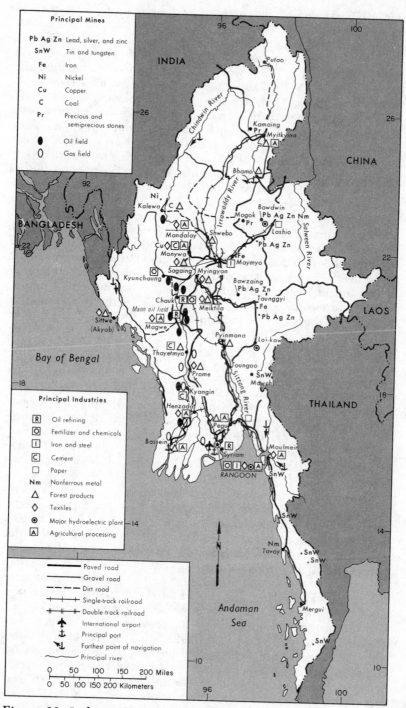

Figure 10. Industrial Activity and Transportation, 1982.

FY 1977–81 period, the number of freight cars declined by 1 percent to 9,144.

The system of major roads extended some 22,732 kilometers in FY 1981, a modest 1 percent increase since FY 1977 and 5 percent longer than in FY 1973, when the government reclassified the system. Since FY 1964 the length of so-called Union Highways, which were paved, has remained at 2,452 kilometers. As of FY 1977, however, less than 19 percent of the remaining system was paved, and more than one-third consisted of unimproved earthen roads. Although this situation probably improved somewhat during the Third Four-Year Plan, investment on road construction and improvement was lower than in other developing countries in the region. The stock of road vehicles was expanding but aging at the same time. In FY 1981 the Road Transport Corporation operated less than 11 percent of the 25,917 trucks, about 18 percent of the 7,682 buses, and only 620 of an unknown number of taxis. Transportation cooperatives owned less than 4 percent of these vehicles, and the rest were privately owned and operated. Most rural inhabitants traveled by cart, by bicycle, or on foot.

The Inland Water Transportation Corporation owned 500 of the largest and most modern of some 1,500 ferries, barges, and other vessels available for river transportation in FY 1981. Cooperatives owned an additional 791 nonpowered ferries. The Irrawaddy River carried the majority of inland water traffic along the 1,450 kilometers of navigable waterway from its mouth to Bhamo in Kachin State. Likewise the Chindwin River was navigable for some 800 kilometers above its intersection with the Irrawaddy River. The Sittang and Salween rivers flowed too swiftly in their upper reaches to allow boat traffic and were used primarily for floating logs. A major canal connected the Sittang to the Pegu River, however, providing an important route to Rangoon. The Twante Canal, linking Rangoon to the Toe River, was the busiest in the country.

Coastal and international sea transportation was based primarily at Rangoon port, the only legal depot for incoming foreign goods. Located on the left bank of the Rangoon River about 34 kilometers from the Gulf of Martaban, this port handled 55 percent of all coastal exports, about 35 percent of coastal imports, and some 85 percent of all international exports. Bassein, the most inland of seaports, was the second largest port and an important center for the rice trade. During the Third Four-Year Plan the major port development project undertaken by the Burma Ports Corporation was the further dredging of the Rangoon River to accommodate vessels as large as 15,000 deadweight tons. The Burma Five Stars Shipping Corporation monopolized Burma's share of international shipping with 12 freighters, but its 10 coastal freighters represented less than 4 percent of the available craft. The Burma Dockyards Corporation ran the major dockyard facilities.

Burma Airways Corporation maintained a small fleet of 15 turboprop and propeller aircraft and three helicopters in FY 1981. The Department of Civil Aviation operated 45 airfields around the country, the major facility being the international airport at Mingaladon outside of Rangoon.

The major issues facing these corporations and the planners at the Ministry of Transport and Communications were to improve the efficiency of operations, increase state revenues, develop the private transportation systems, and repair the infrastructure. Most measures of efficiency deteriorated until FY 1977, when the import of spare parts, improvements in the telecommunications network, and better management led to the more efficient use of the stock of transportation vehicles. Some of the state corporations suffered a decline in real revenues, however, because the government was reluctant to raise fares. The private sector, moreover, played such a large role in the provision of transportation services that the lack of government credit for the purchase of spare parts and the investment in modern equipment could not help but cause bottlenecks. The government's priorities during the Third Four-Year Plan were to replace the outdated equipment owned by the state transportation corporations to the neglect of the infrastructure, particularly of roads. The preliminary guidelines for the Fourth Four-Year Plan seemed to address this latter issue.

The communications network was also poorly developed, but projects financed by the World Bank seemed to be rapidly improving, especially the telecommunications system. In FY 1981 there were 14 telephones per 10,000 people compared with fewer than 10 telephones per 10,000 in FY 1969. During the Third Four-Year Plan period, the Posts and Telecommunications Corporation installed four times as many telephones as originally targeted, completed automatic exchanges in 13 towns, opened five microwave channels to remote areas, and built an overseas satellite communications facility. This corporation also increased the number of telex facilities to 70, more than double the number in FY 1974. Postal and telegraph facilities expanded only slowly; there was one post office per 31,450 inhabitants in FY 1981 and one telegraph office per 320,000 persons.

Foreign Economic Relations

Since FY 1977 the influx of foreign capital to finance the government's investment program has kept the overall balance of payments in surplus—the equivalent of about 0.7 percent of GDP on average through FY 1981 (see table 14, Appendix). The current account, however, where capital transactions are excluded, has been in chronic deficit, averaging about 5.5 percent of GDP during the same period. Because exports have failed to cover imports, foreign loans and direct economic assistance have been required to prop up the nation's reserves of foreign currency. One consequence has been for the repayment of interest and principal to foreign creditors to rise dramatically from 13 percent of foreign exchange earnings in FY 1977 to over 25 percent in FY 1981, according to government estimates, and even higher according to outside observers. Part of the current account deficit and higher debt-service ratio could be attributed to the general decline in the world economy and rising international interest rates at the start of the 1980s. In recognition of these adverse world trends, the International Monetary Fund (IMF—see Glossary) granted Burma a loan equivalent to US$28 million in January 1983 from its special fund for compensating countries experiencing unpredictably sudden drops in export revenues.

Trade Patterns

Before slowing down in 1982, the real growth of merchandise exports during the Third Four-Year Plan averaged more than the targeted 10.8 percent per year. Over 60 percent of the increase from FY 1977 to FY 1980 came from the expansion of rice and teak exports, traditional leaders of the economy. Although rice has in the past made up as much as three-quarters of the value of commodity exports, its share decreased to a low of 13 percent in FY 1973. The international commodity price boom of 1973 and 1974, however, shielded Burma from the worst effects of the drop in export volume. Increasing production led to exports equivalent to about 43 percent of the value of merchandise exports in FY 1980. Because of the volatility of the international price for rice, the government was trying to diversify its agricultural exports as much as possible. Meanwhile, the nation's teak exports revived from some 84,000 tons in FY 1977 to 130,000 tons in FY 1980, or one-quarter of the total merchandise export value. Future increases in the export volume would depend on the ability of the government to expand its reforestation projects and to divert teak away from domestic consumers, currently one-third of total production.

Exports of pulses and beans, jute, rubber, oil cakes for animal feed, and maize represented about 12 percent of the value of merchandise exports in FY 1980, virtually unchanged from the situation three years earlier. The export of pulses continued to rise as Japan became a major importer, and the long-term prospects for trade in pulses seemed to be very good. The volume and value of rubber and jute exports also increased in response to higher domestic prices, but the export price of jute had to be subsidized by the government, while a major rehabilitation of the rubber plantations was needed to expand exports further. Exports of oil cakes and maize, required more and more for domestic use as fodder, showed only modest increases during the Third Four-Year Plan. As the high-yield variety programs expanded to oil-bearing crops and maize, however, the export potential was growing.

The performance of mineral exports, such as tungsten, lead, zinc, silver, heavy petroleum oil, and cement also improved during the Third Four-Year Plan. Their share in the total value of exports rose from about 8 percent at the outset to over 12 percent in FY 1980; gems and precious stones added another 2.5 percent of the total value. Exports of crude oil rather than heavy petroleum oil, begun for the first time in FY 1979, were discontinued the following year because of shortages. Other mineral commodities, however, were expected to become even more important in the future as improvements at the existing mines and the construction of a copper mine took effect.

Fishery products, especially prawns, and hardwoods other than teak were new to Burma's export trade at the start of the Third Four-Year Plan but accounted for 2.5 percent and 2.3 percent, respectively, of the value of merchandise exports in FY 1980. Tropical hardwoods showed promise for expanding their share in total exports. The expensive capital investments required to modernize the fishing fleet, however, were perhaps an insurmountable barrier to rapid expansion. Emerging exports for the future included processed wood products and clothing. The Timber Corporation was receiving technical and marketing assistance from a Hong Kong company to develop a small furniture factory, and the Textile Industries Corporation began producing some men's shirts for export to a West German trading company in 1982.

The most significant government effort to promote exports began in 1976 upon the establishment of the Export Price Equalization Fund, managed by the Myanma Foreign Trade Bank. Almost all export items contributed to the fund in 1983. The purpose of the fund was to use the profits from traditional exports to subsidize the sales of newly developed commodities. The leading profitmakers have been rice products, forest products, oil cakes, heavy petroleum, rubber, and mineral commodities. Some of the foreign exchange earned by these items was distributed to the state corporations that exported fish products, jute, cement, and other items whose domestic price was above the international market price. The corporation exporting these products could receive up to 50 percent of the domestic price as a subsidy. They also received an incentive to come up with new, profitable export items because they were allowed to retain all profits during an initial period before paying into the fund.

The government's control of the foreign exchange rate has also tended to promote exports. In comparison with other countries, the rate of inflation in Burma seemed to be slowing, which would normally cause the currency to appreciate in value. The exchange rate for the Burmese kyat was fixed to a basket of international currencies at a constant rate, however, making the currency and hence the nation's exports appear all the more attractive to foreign buyers. At the same time, distortions in the domestic pricing

175

system made it impossible to evaluate the real costs or benefits to the economy of exporting certain commodities.

In 1983 the Ministry of Trade was also establishing a new Trade Information Service with the aid of the United Nations Conference on Trade and Development. In addition to the Myanma Export-Import Corporation, which handled the export of most agricultural commodities, each state corporation engaged in export trade was creating its own marketing section to tie into the new service. The purpose of the new system was to provide sophisticated marketing information to the various corporations as quickly as possible.

Despite these promotional efforts, the nation's foreign exchange earnings covered less than two-thirds of the payments to other countries in FY 1980, and the value of commodity imports has more than doubled since FY 1977. Almost all of these imported items were the capital goods, raw materials, and spare parts necessary to the functioning of the domestic economy. Consumer goods represented only 6 percent of the total. Imports in FY 1980 were more than twice the value of capital goods sold by state corporations to cooperatives and private enterprises and two and one-half times that of raw materials sales. In addition, Burma's payments for travel, insurance, and other international services exceeded receipts by over 40 percent, despite the tripling of tourist receipts since 1977.

The dominant trading partners in the nation's export trade were Japan, Indonesia, and Singapore, while the major suppliers of imports were Japan, Singapore, Britain, and the Federal Republic of Germany (West Germany), in deceasing order of importance. Much of the trade registered through Singapore, however, was indirect trade with third countries. The statistics on trade between Burma and Thailand did not reflect the enormous traffic in smuggled goods across the border, estimated by one unofficial source in 1980 to be over 9 percent of the total two-way commodity trade with all trading partners (see The Black Market and the Opium Trade, ch.).

Aid, Credit, and Investment

One-third of the increase in foreign financial support for the economy during the Third Four-Year Plan came from the suppliers of imported commodities and international banks at commercial rates of interest, but 70 percent of the foreign debt contracted during this period consisted of concessionary loans. About three-quarters of all grants and concessionary financing came from the members of the Burma Aid Group, an informal association of donors formed in 1976 to coordinate the lending program. In 1982 the members of this group, ranked by their share in the total outstanding debt as of March 1981 were Japan (29 percent); the World Bank (13 percent); the Asian Development Bank (11 percent); West Germany (10 percent); and France, Britain, Canada, Australia, the United States, and the IMF (altogether contributing less than 3 percent of the total). The UNDP also was a member and gave direct grant assistance, and Belgium, Italy, Finland, Norway, Switzerland, the European Economic Community, and the Organization for Economic Cooperation and Development were observers to the group and accounted for about 2.4 percent of the total debt altogether.

Important creditors outside of the Burma Aid Group included Czechoslovakia (6 percent of outstanding credit); China (5 percent); and the Organization of Petroleum Exporting Countries (OPEC), Denmark, the German Democratic Republic (East Germany), the Democratic People's Republic of Korea (North Korea), the Soviet Union, and Yugoslavia (2 percent collectively). Suppliers' credits made up the rest of the debt, chiefly from Japan, Britain, Yugoslavia, France, and Australia. Outside of the Burma Aid Group, only China, OPEC, Czechoslovakia, North Korea, and Yugoslavia were active in providing credit during the Third Four-Year Plan.

The gross disbursements of foreign grants and medium- and long-term loans from overseas during the first three years of the Third Four-Year Plan were equivalent to about 9 percent of GDP and some 60 percent of all investment. Data showing the distribution of loans and aid by economic sectors were available only on a commitment basis, which tended to bias them upward, but represented the following percentages of total public investment in each sector: crop cultivation (16 percent), fishing (23 percent), forestry (35 percent), mining (34 percent), manufacturing (44 percent), utilities (66 percent), transportation and communications (40 percent), construction (10 percent), financial services (24 percent), and public administration (48 percent). There was no indication at the start of the 1980s that these high levels of foreign support would diminish.

Burma continued to accept no direct foreign investment in 1983 and, as a result, would probably need the equivalent of some US$1 to US$2 billion each year during the 1980s. The only foreign ventures ever allowed to take place were in the offshore oil industry, and there was a report that the first such venture in five years had been established between the Myanma Oil Corporation and a Japanese consortium in late 1982. Whether similar ventures would result in other sectors of the economy as the nation's external debt mounted was a matter for speculation, especially given the government's fierce commitment to economic nationalism.

Living Conditions

Macroeconomic indicators of the quality of everyday living in Burma are often contradictory. The per capita GDP was around

K1,234 in FY 1981—a 40 percent real increase since FY 1962, yet only 22 percent higher than in FY 1938. The apparent consumption of rice had risen by over 53 percent since FY 1962 to 161 kilograms per person of unmilled rice, but this was 19 percent less than in FY 1938. National statistics suggested that the average minimum nutritional requirements of the population were being met in the late 1970s. Still, government surveys in selected townships of Rangoon Division during the FY 1979–81 period covering pregnant women, power-plant workers, and primary-school students found that some persons in these selected areas were malnourished. There was little doubt, however, that the provision of basic health and education needs had expanded since the 1960s; the number of physicians had more than doubled to over two per 10,000 people, and the student-teacher ratio had decreased by one-half to 20 to one in FY 1981. The problem with most of these statistics was that they did not take into account distributional aspects, by region and by income class.

Rural household incomes were almost impossible to estimate because of the lack of survey data. One very crude method of estimation would be to attribute the value added to GDP from the cooperative and private sectors in agriculture, fishing, and live-stock farming to different groups of farm households classified by the size of their holdings. Following this procedure suggests that the average annual income for some 2.6 million households working plots smaller than two hectares in FY 1981 was about K1,926—a level barely adequate to purchase the minimum nutritional requirements for a family of six. Another 1.1 million households obtained an average income of K5,930 per year, just above the subsistence level. Only 609,000 farm households earned enough income to live in relative comfort. Real household incomes for the lower income groups increased by 2.7 percent per year in the 1970s, about twice as rapidly as during the previous decade. Government development projects, moreover, improved the lot of many, although rural development expenditures averaged only about K3 per household. Those families living outside of the range of government services and projects, particularly among the ethnic minorities in the hill areas, were probably the poorest in the nation.

One new government program to improve the lot the peasantry was a life and accident insurance scheme launched by the Myanma Insurance Corporation in 1980. By June 1982 nearly 4.8 million policies had been sold. The low premium of only about K12 per year for K1,000 to K5,000 of coverage made the policies both attractive and affordable. Such insurance was previously available only to industrial workers.

Urban households earned generally higher incomes than rural households, and there were some survey data to substantiate this difference. According to a survey of nine urban areas in FY 1975, converted to FY 1981 prices for comparison, only 6 percent of urban households had incomes below K2,026 per year, and over 50 percent of the total had incomes between this minimum and K6,073. Nonetheless, the 1975 data suggest that over 80 percent of the urban population lived at or below subsistence level, not much better off than their rural compatriots. Since 1975, however, the increasing availability of farm produce and the burgeoning underground economy that could not be accounted for in income surveys had probably raised urban incomes substantially. Many workers had one or more part-time jobs in addition to their main occupation in order to make ends meet.

Workers in the towns and cities had better access to government services, including the social security system. About 30 percent of urban households had access to safe water, compared with only 13 percent in the countryside. Access to health, education, transportation, and communications services was undoubtedly easier than in the countryside.

* * *

The most comprehensive and coherent analysis of Burma's economic development, within an otherwise inadequate literature, is David I. Steinberg's *Burma's Road Toward Development: Growth and Ideology under Military Rule.* Among the same author's other useful works is the informative "Burma under the Military: Towards a Chronology." The *Far Eastern Economic Review,* in its yearbook and weekly periodical articles, provides a more fragmentary chronicle of economic events, although Paisal Sricharatchanya's cover story in the October 8, 1982, issue is an up-to-date overview of the entire economy. The annual articles in *Asian Survey* are good sources for general policy trends. The English-language dailies published in Rangoon, the *Guardian* and *Working People's Daily,* render the official story, and their editorials are particularly interesting. The Ministry of Planning and Finance's annual *Report to the Pyithu Hluttaw on the Financial, Economic, and Social Conditions of the Socialist Republic of the Union of Burma* is the definitive, though occasionally erroneous, source of economic statistical data. (For further information and complete citations, see Bibliography.)

Chapter 4.   Government and Politics

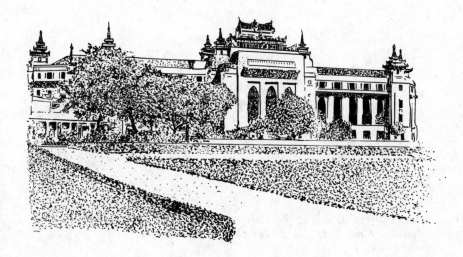

Government building in Rangoon, reflecting a combination of British colonial and Burmese architectural styles

IN THE EARLY 1980s government and politics were under the control of the Burma Socialist Programme Party (BSPP), or Lanzin, as the organization was called in Burmese. Founded by the military as a political instrument after it seized power in a coup in 1962, the BSPP's aim was to establish "a socialist democratic state" based on a set of guiding principles initially identified as "The Burmese Way to Socialism." In this socialist state the welfare of peasants and workers was to be promoted as a major national priority. The most dominant figure in the BSPP's effort to create a new Burma was U Ne Win, who had led the 1962 coup and headed the all-military Revolutionary Council until 1974 when military rule was replaced by a new system of rule under the Constitution of 1974. His current four-year stewardship as chairman of the ruling party will expire in 1985—barring unforeseen circumstances.

The BSPP is mandated, under the Constitution of 1974, "to lead the State." As "the sole political party" of the nation, it continued to provide the only lawful channel through which the masses of the people could express their political sentiments. Any attempts to undermine the BSPP in all its manifestations were banned under a law promulgated in November 1974. As a result, competitive politics in a conventional sense were not manifest in Burma. The political scene was calm, as had been the case since the mid-1970s. Principal actors in the pre-1962 parliamentary politics faded from the public arena because of old age, the government's political crackdown, and the dominance of the military-led BSPP. Students were once active as protesters, as were some Buddhist monks, but given the successful government effort to depoliticize them, there were no reports of unrest among students and monks after the mid-1970s. Participation in antigovernment activities was made difficult by a measure whereby anyone criticizing the government's leadership in any form would be subject to arrest. There was also an extensive network of neighborhood surveillance developed initially as part of a counterinsurgency campaign. All mass media were owned and operated by the government, thus effectively denying would-be dissidents any means of expressing their political grievances in public.

Opposition to the one-party system came from insurgents who had been waging antigovernment activities since 1948. Active in border regions adjoining China, Laos, and Thailand, the armed rebels had different motivations. The first insurrectionists were indigenous communists who sought to establish their own form of a Marxist state; others wanted to carve out ethnically separate autonomous states for themselves. Among these separatists were the Shans, Karens, Kachins, and others who wanted to achieve their aims by force of arms, convinced that the government would never accede to their demands. The insurgencies continued to pose a threat to internal security and political order.

Based on the Constitution of 1974, the governmental mandate is renewed every four years through elections. Under the Constitution the government is headed by the president, who chairs the State Council. The powers of the state are divided into the executive, legislative, and judicial spheres. They are centralized, and all political subdivisions below the national level—states and divisions, townships, and wards and village-tracts—serve as administrative arms of the central government.

Nearly all key government positions were filled by military officers, both active duty and retired. These officers were concurrently party officials, often with overlapping membership on the government's top decisionmaking body, the State Council, and the BSPP's top organ, the Central Executive Committee. Military officers also held many key posts at the state and divisional level and, to a lesser extent, at the township level.

In mid-1983 Burma continued to follow what it called an independent and active foreign policy. Nonaligned and determined to stay clear of all foreign entanglements, the country maintained friendly relations with other nations. The traditional fear of the Chinese menace and economic pragmatism were important considerations in the conduct of foreign relations.

Constitutional Framework

The Constitution of 1974 replaces the country's first basic law proclaimed in 1947; the latter was suspended in the 1963–73 period during which the military-dominated Revolutionary Council ruled by decree. The current Constitution is framed to rectify what it calls "the ill effects of capitalistic parliamentary democracy"—an allusion to the multiparty politics of pre-1962 years. In seeking to eliminate "the power and influence of feudalists, landlords, and capitalists," the Constitution provides for a political structure in which the grass roots are expected to play a significant role at all levels of governing hierarchy. It is clear, however, that the process of popular participation is to be directed by the BSPP (see Glossary).

The Constitution, effective since January 4, 1974, proclaims Burma to be a "socialist state of the working people"—the Socialist Republic of the Union of Burma. This republic is called on to establish a socialist economic system, as well as a socialist democracy. The sovereign powers of the nation are to emanate from the people of "all national races whose strength is based on peasants and workers." They are vested in and to be exercised by the popularly elected People's Assembly (Pyithu Hluttaw), the highest organ of state power. The state is defined as the "ultimate owner" of all natural resources and is directed to nationalize the means of production. But the state may permit cooperatives to own and operate "suitable enterprises." Private enterprises may also be allowed so long as they do not undermine the socialist economy of the nation.

Citizens are equal before the law irrespective of race, social status, sex, or religion. The Burmese citizenship law enacted in October 1982 provides for three classes of citizens: citizens (born of parents both of whom are citizens by birth); associate citizens; and naturalized citizens (see Public Order in Central Burma, ch. 5). The right to education, rest and recreation, health care "as arranged by the state," and benefits derived from labor are also included in the constitutional guarantees. Burmese is to be the common language of instruction, but other languages of the minorities may also be taught in schools. Burmese is to be used also as "the official language for the purpose of uniformity and clarity in communications" among government organs but without prejudicing the use of other languages if possible.

Religion and religious organizations are not to be used for political purposes. This stipulation is aimed at a strict separation of religion and state because a constitutional amendment in 1961 establishing Buddhism as the state religion proved to be politically divisive. The amendment was resented by followers of other religions found mostly among ethnic minorities (see The Seven States, ch. 2). The issue became complicated when a second amendment sought to provide government protection of other religions—a measure strongly opposed by the *sangha* (Buddhist monkhood), in a predominantly Buddhist society.

Privacy and security of the home, property, correspondence, and the freedom of residence are protected. No citizen is to be held in detention for more than 24 hours without due process of law, and no penal law may be enacted retroactively. The citizens are granted the right to seek redress from the state for grievances unjustly caused by any public official or government agency.

The citizens are duty bound to protect nationalized property, cooperative-owned property, and other public property and to strive to their best ability for "socialist capital accumulation." Additionally, they are called on to strengthen the defense capability of the nation and to enhance the living standards of the people. Rights and freedoms may be restricted by law, however, in situations that can adversely affect national security, the integrity of the socialist system, the unity and solidarity of the national races, public order and peace, or public morality. Restrictive laws must be "regularly reviewed and modified as necessary" so as not to encroach on civil liberties.

A motion for constitutional amendment may be initiated by members of the People's Assembly or a local people's council. In the latter case it must be approved "stage by stage from the lower to the higher levels" culminating in the People's Assembly. Certain important provisions concerning the socialist character of the body politic, "local autonomy under central leadership," political subdivisions, the People's Assembly, and the procedure for constitutional amendment can be changed in two stages: a prior approval by three-fourths of the members of the People's Assembly, to be followed by a popular referendum requiring a majority vote of more than one-half of the electorate. Other provisions can be amended, however, with a majority vote of three-fourths of all the members of the People's Assembly.

Central Government

The powers and functions of state organs are set forth in the constitution under appropriate headings. Among the basic principles relating to the government is that "the organs of state power at different levels shall function in accordance with socialist democratic practices." Such practices are described as "mutual reporting, mutually offering, accepting, and respecting of advice and wishes, collective leadership, collective decisionmaking, abiding by collective decisions, lower organs carrying out the decisions and directives of the higher organs which in turn respect the views submitted by the lower organs." Another principle concerns the relationship between the government and the BSPP. Article 205 states, "The Burma Socialist Programme Party, mass and class organizations formed under its leadership, and the working people may submit suggestions and advice to the organs of state power at different levels, on legal matters, economic planning, the annual budget, and other matters."

People's Assembly

The national legislature is the unicameral People's Assembly, which is elected by direct universal suffrage for a term of four years (see fig. 11). Under the constitutional amendment adopted in March 1981, the term may be shortened or extended. The most recent parliamentary elections were held in October 1981 to fill 475 seats in the assembly. The legislature may delegate executive and judicial powers to central and local government bodies. It may enact laws relating to economic plans, budget, and taxation; declare war and peace; and hold a national referendum when necessary. Furthermore, it may dissolve any of the local people's councils on the grounds of inefficiency, actions harmful to national unity or political stability, or violation of the Constitution and laws of the People's Assembly.

The assembly meets briefly twice a year in regular sessions—in March and October. During the intervals, its functions are discharged by the State Council, which in effect acts as the standing committee of the assembly. The council may convene a special parliamentary session and may issue ordinances having the force of law on any matters other than those concerning economic plans

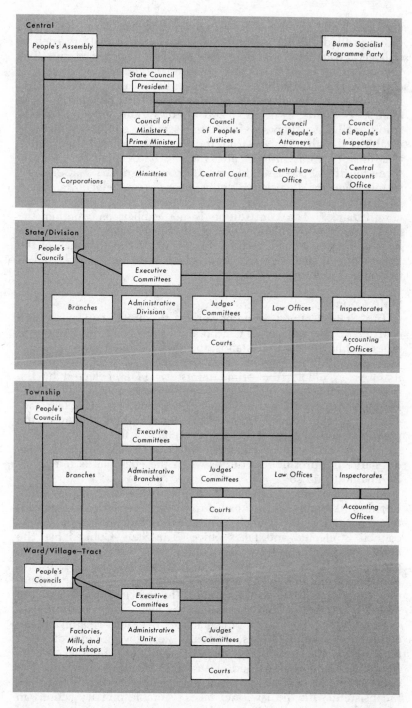

Figure 11. Governmental Organization of the Socialist Republic of the Union of Burma, 1983

and fiscal affairs. The People's Assembly may form legislative groups called "affairs committees" to deal with matters such as finance and national planning; cooperatives, agriculture, livestock breeding, and forestry; commerce; industry and natural resources; construction, transport, and communications; science and technology; public administration; foreign affairs; legislation; social affairs; peasants, workers, and youths; and national races. Additionally, a national defense and security committee may be established with members from the State Council and the Council of Ministers. Substantive matters are to be decided by a vote of three-fourths of the assembly members and ordinary matters by a simple majority. Legislative deliberations are privileged, and parliamentary immunity may be withdrawn only under special circumstances. The constitution is not explicit on whether the laws, rules, and regulations passed by the People's Assembly can be modified or vetoed. Article 80 states that the chairman of the State Council shall sign the laws, which must be promulgated in the official gazette.

State Council

The State Council is empowered "to direct, supervise, and coordinate" the work of all central and local government units and other public services. It stands above the cabinet and judiciary. The council is composed of 29 members, one of whom is a member ex officio (the prime minister); 14 are elected by the state- and division-level people's councils and another 14 by the People's Assembly from among its own members. Its chairman, elected by the council from among its members, becomes the president and head of state. The secretary of the council, who is second in order of precedence and who is also elected, may discharge the presidential duties when the chairman is temporarily unable to do so.

The term of office of the State Council is the same as that of the People's Assembly, but in order to ensure legislative and executive continuity the council continues to function until a new council is elected and takes office. The State Council has the authority to interpret the laws other than the Constitution, to promulgate them, and to submit to the People's Assembly lists of nominees from among the assembly members so that the legislature can elect officials to the cabinet, the judiciary, the Council of People's Inspectors, and the assembly's own affairs committees.

In addition, the State Council makes decisions relating to the conduct of foreign affairs, appoints key government officials, decides on the temporary suspension of any member of the People's Assembly charged with high treason, abrogates the decrees of the central and local government bodies if they are inconsistent with the law, and takes "suitable military action" in case of external aggression. It may also declare a state of emergency, promulgate martial laws in affected areas or in the entire nation, and order national mobilization. Such emergency measures must be reported to the next session of the People's Assembly for endorsement.

Council of Ministers

The cabinet or Council of Ministers, is a top executive arm of the state, second only to the State Council, to which it is responsible. The Council of Ministers has broad responsibilities for the management of administrative, economic, financial, social, cultural, and foreign affairs, as well as internal security and national defense. It must submit economic plans (long-term, short-term, and annual), annual budgets, and semiannual reports on the state of the administration to the opening session of the People's Assembly. It must also draft bills to be enacted by the assembly.

The Council of Ministers is headed by the prime minister who, along with other cabinet ministers, is elected by the People's Assembly from among its own members. Deputy prime ministers are elected by the cabinet from among nominees of the prime minister, and deputy ministers are appointed by the State Council from among the members of the People's Assembly nominated by the cabinet. All cabinet members serve a term of four years, and they may concurrently serve on the State Council.

As of January 1983 the cabinet was composed of the prime minister, two deputy prime ministers (each of whom had a ministerial portfolio), and 17 ministers. The 17 ministerial portfolios included agriculture and forests, construction, cooperatives, culture, defense, education, foreign affairs, health, home and religious affairs, industry (1), industry (II), information, mines, planning and finance, social welfare and labor, trade, and transport and communications.

Government ministries depended on career civil servants to discharge their functional responsibilities. The civil service came under the jurisdiction of the Public Service Commission, which was subordinate to the State Council. Although recruitment was based on competitive examination, personal ability alone was not enough to gain entry. There was no statutory requirement that a candidate be a party member, but party membership and demonstrated party loyalty were important considerations especially if senior positions were involved. Appointment to such positions required prior scrutiny by the BSPP. Information was not readily available concerning the size of the civil bureaucracy, but evidently nearly all government posts above the bureau or departmental chief levels were filled with either active-duty or retired military personnel, who predictably were members of the BSPP.

Council of People's Justices

The highest judicial authority of the land is the Council of People's Justices; it is responsible for supervising all judicial organs and courts. The nine justices of the council are elected for a term of four years by the People's Assembly from among its members, who are nominated by the State Council. They are not jurists, as was the case until 1972 when a sweeping judicial reform was instituted to bring about a more efficient and expeditious administration of justice. Under this reform as constitutionally formalized in 1974, all court proceedings at the central and local levels are now presided over by elected lay judges, and professional jurists serve in an advisory capacity. The judicial authority at the state and division, township, and village-tract and ward levels is exercised by judges' committees, elected by local people's councils (see Local Administration, this ch.). Lay judges include peasants, workers, ordinary citizens, retired personnel, teachers, and government employees.

For purposes of trial or appeal hearings, a rotating panel of three justices from the nine-member Council of People's Justices constitutes the Central Court. Below the Central Court are the state and division courts, township courts, and village-tract and ward courts. If the number of elected members of the local judges' committees is not sufficient to form the necessary courts, then appropriate members of the local people's councils may form courts under the direction of a member of the judges' committees concerned. "Other suitable citizens" may be included in such courts, however, "if the people's councils are unable to do so because of shortage of personnel." Presumably, the suitable citizens in question were appointed by the judges' committees of appropriate levels.

Council of People's Attorneys

Prosecution comes under the purview of the Council of People's Attorneys and its subordinate units: the Central Law Office, the state and division law offices, and the township law offices. The Constitution does not provide for these offices at the village-tract and ward level. The members of the council are elected for a four-year term by the People's Assembly from among its members, but the personnel of the law offices are appointed by the council.

The duties of the Council of People's Attorneys are to protect and safeguard the socialist system, as well as the rights and privileges of the working people, to tender legal advice to the State Council and to the Council of Ministers, to report to the State Council any unlawful acts committed by the central and local government agencies and other public institutions, and to undertake any other duties prescribed by law. The Council of People's Attorneys is responsible to the People's Assembly and to the State Council when the assembly is not in session, but the law offices at various levels are independent of the local people's councils and report directly to the Council of People's Attorneys.

Council of People's Inspectors

The "highest organ of inspection of public undertakings"—the principal fiscal watchdog of the government—is the Council of People's Inspectors. The council supervises the work of its local counterparts, called inspectorates, at the state and division and township levels. The members of the Council of People's Inspectors are elected by the People's Assembly for a four-year term. Their duties are to determine whether the activities of all governmental and other public organs are consonant with the interests of the public and to report their findings to the People's Assembly through the State Council. Inspectorates at the local levels perform similar functions. The hierarchy of inspectors operates through the Central Accounts Office at the national level and local accounting offices at the state and division and township levels.

Local Administration

Burma is composed of seven states and seven divisions at the top of a three-tier structure of administration; names of the states correlate with those of seven major ethnic minorities (see fig. 1; The Seven States, ch. 2). The middle tier consists of 314 townships, which divide into the lowest tier of village-tracts in the rural areas and wards in the urban areas. The administrative structure is uniform throughout all 14 states and divisions. All local governing bodies are ultimately accountable to the People's Assembly in Rangoon. The assembly's local counterparts are people's councils elected locally for a term of four years. The administrative and judicial arms of these councils are executive committees and judges' committees.

The Constitution stipulates that "local autonomy under central leadership is the system of the State." Evidently, given the multiethnic and multicultural character of Burmese society, this stipulation reflects an official attempt to strike a balance between local self-rule and the overriding need for centralized government control. The basic law states that local affairs should be solved "as far as possible" at the local levels, but on balance the principle of local autonomy is far outweighed by the principle of uniformity and centralized direction (see National Unity, this ch.). In theory, the people's councils are the major vehicle through which to define and act on local issues, but in practice their activities are closely supervised by the central government. For example, the State Council may overrule local decrees if they are considered to be inconsistent with the law or policies of the government. It may also bypass the people's councils by appointing "suitable citizens" to local administrative and judicial bodies "if the situation is not yet ripe" for the election of any of these local councils.

Electoral System

Elections provide the principal means of ensuring popular involvement in affairs of the state. They are held ordinarily every four years to legitimize the mandate of the government. Under the constitution elections were held in 1974—the first since 1962—and again in 1978 and for the third time in October 1981, rather than in January 1982. This was done to give the government more time to prepare its economic plans to be submitted to the opening session of the People's Assembly in March 1982.

Because only one party—the BSPP—is involved in the elections, expenses are borne by the state. Elections take place concurrently for both national and local organs of representation under the supervision of a commission appointed by the People's Assembly six months before the assembly's term expires. Voting is not compulsory, but voter turnout is consistently high. Citizens over the minimum age of 18 may go to the polls, except members of the *sangha* and others disqualified by law. Buddhist monks are not allowed to vote as part of the government policy of keeping the *sangha* protected from outside political influences (see Recent Political Developments, this ch.; The Socialist Transformation, ch. 2).

Office seekers must be at least 20 years old to run for election to the village-tract, ward, and township people's councils, 24 years of age for the state and division people's councils, and 28 for the People's Assembly. Candidates need not be members of the BSPP but in most instances belong to it. They are nominated by the BSPP but in most instances belong to it. They are nominated by the BSPP on the basis of party loyalty, good character, and competence "in consultation with mass and class organizations" and with "the electorate of the constituency concerned." According to the BSPP, good character is placed above competence, the assumption being that a person of good character can be trained to become competent.

Each township is assured by law of at least one deputy to the People's Assembly and a second member if the township population exceeds 100,000. Also by law, states and divisions having fewer than 10 townships and fewer than 1 million people are allocated additional seats; these provisions are designed to minimize underrepresentation. Thus, in the elections of October 1981 to the People's Assembly, there were, in addition to 314 members representing townships, 152 deputies elected on the basis of population and nine more deputies chosen according to other criteria.

Elections at all levels are valid only if more than half of the voters in different constituencies cast their ballots. The principle of majority rule applies also to individual candidates, who must receive more than half of the votes in their respective constituencies. In 1981 more than 90 percent of the 17.4 million eligible voters went to the polls. Seats left vacant for various reasons are filled through by-elections.

Politics

Political activities continue to revolve around the BSPP, the ruling organization dominated by an elite of military officers. In its effort to create a unified, stable, and prosperous nation, the BSPP is inspired by a mixture of Burmese nationalism and ideals deriving from both Buddhism and socialism. Political and other national priorities and programs are legitimized through the formality of party congresses held ordinarily every four years or extraordinary congresses when necessary.

The Burma Socialist Programme Party

The ruling party has undergone two distinct stages of growth since its inception in 1962 as an appendage of what was then called the Revolutionary Council—the top governing body formed by 17 military coup leaders under General Ne Win (see Military Rule under General Ne Win, ch. 1). The BSPP was formed as a transitional organization initially to function as "a cadre party," meaning a party which performs such basic functions as recruiting nucleus personnel called cadres, and training and testing them." Popular participation was not an immediate objective of the coup leaders who, in insisting on quality over quantity, placed a premium on centralized control, political tutelage, and national solidarity. The BSPP's preeminence has been ensured under a 1964 law abolishing all other political parties and by the State Party Protection Law enacted in 1974. The 1974 statute bans agitation, conspiracy, collaboration, or any organized or individual attempt to weaken or destroy the BSPP—offenses punishable by three to 14 years' imprisonment.

The BSPP began with 20 regular members, 17 of whom were concurrently on the Revolutionary Council. The council was defined as "the supreme authority of the party during the period of its construction." Within the party, the top organ was the Central Organizing Committee, whose members were drawn also from the Revolutionary Council. Membership application was opened to the public in March 1963 so that nearly 100,000 candidate members had been accepted by 1965. The number of regular members was, however, only 24 through the end of 1969. An effort to broaden the base of the BSPP was initiated in earnest in the closing days of 1969. By July 1970 party regulars had increased to 879 and to over 73,000 as of April 1971. Most of the regular members were based in the urban areas, and functionally nearly 60 percent of the 1971 figure were members of the armed forces. Structurally, both regular and candidate members were attached to the basic party cells, each consisting of three to 15 members. Three to nine cells constituted a section. Above the party sections were party units at the township and state and division levels. The party units were established on both geographical and functional bases. The armed forces, government ministries, and state enterprises were among these functional organizations.

The second stage of party growth began in June–July 1971, when the BSPP convened its long-awaited First Congress. This event marked the end of a nine-year period of military-directed tutelage and signaled the start of what the BSPP called "a mass party" based on democratic centralism and collective leadership. The congress, the highest organ of the ruling party, was attended by locally elected delegates representing both territorial and functional units. These deputies heard Party Chairman U Ne Win's report on organizational matters, adopted a new party constitution (replacing the 1962 version), and took part for the first time in public debates in the state of the economy. These debates seemed to reflect growing realization among top party leaders that a realistic reassessment and possibly also a shift in emphasis were in order if the country's stagnant economy was to be revitalized soon. At the congress, U Ne Win also expressed the need to draft a new state constitution so that "the envisaged constitution may be free from all defects of the previous constitution and that national solidarity be achieved."

After adopting the Twenty-Year Plan (FY 1974–93), the First Congress elected the Central Committee of the BSPP and reconfirmed U Ne Win as party chairman and his deputy, General San Yu, as general secretary or second in command of the Party. The third top party post, also elective, was called the joint general secretary. The Central Committee in turn endorsed the Central Executive Committee and the Central Inspection Committee and also appointed the Central Discipline Committee. The most influential of these party organs has been the 15-member Central Executive Committee, responsible for directing and coordinating the work of all party apparatuses, including the 14 party regional committees at the state and division level. The executive committee's functions were carried out through the permanent secretariat, several departments, and central affairs committees (see fig. 12).

In October 1973, when the Second Congress was held, membership—about 834,000 (137,000 regulars and 697,000 candidates)—showed an increase of 150 percent over the 1971 level. It was officially acknowledged, however, that the growth was not matched by quality as measured by dedication, political indoctrination, and organizational work.

In 1973 military preponderance as "the pillar of the Party" continued. More than two-thirds of top party officials were

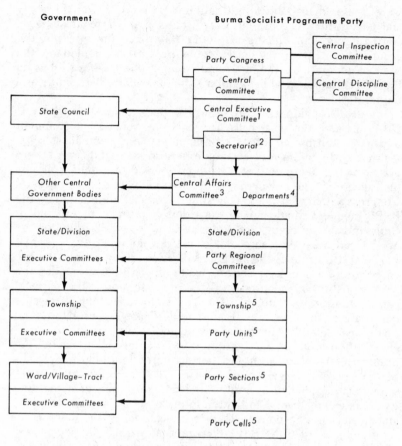

Government   Burma Socialist Programme Party

NOTE–Based on Fourth Congress, August 1981.

[1] The head of this committee is party chairman.

[2] Consists of general secretary, joint general secretary, and four secretaries.

[3] Its six functions are concerned with organization, management, education, publications, research, and Central Institute of Political Science.

[4] Responsible for 11 committee functions.

[5] Formed in village-tracts, wards, townships, mills, factories, state enterprises, government bodies, universities, armed forces, and other places, depending on size of membership.

→ Control

Figure 12. Organization of the Burma Socialist Programme Party, 1981

military, including the retired. They could be classified into two major categories: the "political" wing, composed of those who were assigned to political and administrative duties in the party and government organs; and the "professional" or "combat" wing consisting of line officers active in the party units within the armed forces. Both categories could be further divided on the basis of generation—the older and younger cliques—as well as on the basis of ideological inclination—the doctrinaire hard-liners and moderates.

It was also evident in 1973 that the party leadership under U Ne Win was not as doctrinaire as it once was about its commitment to the establishment of a self-reliant economy without foreign assistance. In the face of economic deterioration, however, there was growing sentiment at the top in favor of some economic liberalization. The downgrading of leftist ideologues at the Second Congress confirmed a gradual shift in official thinking that the BSPP ideology should not be regarded as permanent and that it could and should be modified somewhat if this was justified by the need to advance the cause of socialist development.

The BSPP's role as the vanguard of the working people and the backbone of a one-party state is made official not only under the party constitution adopted in 1971 but also under the national constitution promulgated in 1974. This is not surprising in that the basic law of the land was drafted under party sponsorship. The BSPP also acted as the mobilizer of public support for the draft constitution in its early stages and played a key role in having the draft formally endorsed in a national referendum held in December 1973. In the years after 1974 the BSPP became more conscious of the need to exemplify its leadership role, to strengthen its organizational work, to tighten internal discipline and cohesion, and to be more responsive to the expectations of the masses.

In October 1976 the BSPP convened an extraordinary congress to address the problem of political unrest and economic shortcomings that had become increasingly manifest by the early 1970s. In its report to the extraordinary session, General Secretary U San Yu admonished many party members who had become indolent, corrupt, and unworthy of their special status. In the following month alone, about 54,200 regular and candidate members were expelled from the BSPP; this was in addition to about 100,000 members who had been dismissed since the Second Congress in October 1973.

The Third Congress took place in February 1977, attended by some 1,300 delegates representing 885,000 party members— 182,000 full members and 703,000 candidate or probationary members. It elected a new 240-member Central Committee: at least half of the committee members were new, reflecting the leadership's resolve to improve the quality of party regulars. The policy objectives approved by the congress called for a more effective party leadership role, pursuit of an independent and active foreign policy, elimination of insurgency through active mass support, and improved economic performance. Significantly, the party leadership also publicly acknowledged the failure of past economic plans and formally approved new guidelines for seeking "foreign assistance."

In November 1977 an extraordinary congress was again called into session, this time "to purge the Central Committee of factionalists" and to restore unity to leadership. One immediate consequence was the election of a new 250-member Central Committee (no alternate members were chosen this time). Dropped from the new lineup were 113 members of the previous committee for "antiparty" and "antipeople" activities; they were also barred from attending the party congress sessions. Military presence in the new Central Committee was as conspicuous as ever. Evidently, the influence of moderates in party affairs also seemed to have become firmer at the expense of doctrinaire, leftist elements. This development was consistent with the BSPP's decision at the Third Congress in February 1977 to give renewed emphasis to economic development, which was to have been promoted with the infusion of foreign aid.

BSPP objectives enunciated in 1977 were essentially reaffirmed at the Fourth Congress, which convened in August 1981 to elect leading party organs and to adopt political and economic policies for the next four years. To no one's surprise, on August 7 the congress reelected U Ne Win to another four-year term (1981–85). On the following day, however, he surprised the party delegates and the nation by announcing his intention to step down from the presidency after parliamentary elections two months later. U Ne Win explained that this was to prepare for an orderly transition of power. Citing his age and ill health as additional reasons, he stated, "It is not proper to relinquish my duties only at death." He told the congress that he would have preferred to retire also from the party chairmanship, had he not been urged by his colleagues to "continue to guide and advise them" in the conduct of national affairs. U Ne Win chided them for not having more confidence in themselves but cautioned them at the same time not to "overrate" themselves.

The announcement had portentous implications, not the least of which concerned the future of national leadership after U Ne Win. For the moment, however, there was no question about U Ne Win's being the most powerful man. The consensus of informed observers was that U Ne Win was giving up only the presidency, not the real power that was based in the two interwoven organizations, the BSPP and the armed forces.

At the party congress the leadership structure was realigned, but the change did nothing to alter the political reality of Burma— the preeminent role of the armed forces and the BSPP. The delegates to the congress elected 260 members to the Central Committee, which in turn endorsed 15 members of the party high command—the Central Executive Committee under U Ne Win's chairmanship. Among the key members of the high command were U Thaung Kyi, an ex-colonel, who replaced U San Yu as the party's general secretary; Lieutenant General Aye Ko, the joint general secretary; General Thura Kyaw Htin, defense minister and concurrently deputy prime minister; Brigadier General Tin Oo, formerly U Ne Win's military assistant. Because of U Thaung Kyi's untimely death a month later, Aye Ko and Tin Oo moved up as the new general secretary and joint general secretary, respectively.

BSPP membership as of January 1981 was about 1.5 million, an increase of 41 percent over the 1977 level. The 1981 figure graphically illustrated the centrality of the military to the ruling party. Although the armed forces personnel accounted for only 9.6 percent of the total party strength, that percentage was equal to 80 percent of the total active-duty personnel. Three other groups— youths, workers, and peasants—were identified as the major components of the membership without disclosing, however, their respective share of the membership. Figures released by the BSPP showed that youths over the age of 18 as party members represented 6.2 percent of the total youth population in the country. Workers and peasants constituted 5.2 percent and 4.6 percent, respectively, of their national total. The BSPP's policy was "to increase the number of party members from those two basic classes [workers and peasants] so that the construction of a society of affluence could be carried out with might and main." By sex, female members accounted for a paltry 1.5 percent of the 1981 total.

The policy objectives, or "future tasks" as they are officially called, adopted by the Fourth Congress in August 1981 came under three categories: political, economic, and organizational. The seven political objectives were the establishment of an "effective socialist democratic machinery"; the unity of national races; the elimination of "insurgents and destructive elements"; the participation of the entire people in the defense and security of the nation; the pursuit of an independent and active foreign policy; the betterment of the educational system; and the expansion and improvement of health services.

There were eight economic objectives relating particularly to the implementation of the Fourth Four-Year Plan (FY 1982–85). These were to boost production in the agricultural, fishery, and livestock sectors; to set up meat and fish development facilities in cooperatives; to promote regional development by relying on local resources; to increase exports; to expand transportation; to ensure adequate supplies of raw materials; to develop an effective manpower plan; and to enhance the efficiency of state economic enterprises.

The organizational category was in reference to the BSPP. The six-point tasks for strengthening the party's "organizational prowess" were to improve "the calibre of party members"; to strive further for the realization of common ideological view, common political outlook, and common organizational methods and style of party members and party cadres; to expand organizational work among the youths; to strengthen "class organizations under party leadership"; to provide party leadership to mass organizations; and to gain popular trust in party leadership in all spheres of socialist endeavors.

Mass and Class Organizations

The BSPP's effort to deepen its roots in the society was being carried out in part through what it called "mass and class organizations." The English-language *Working People's Daily* (December 20, 1982), published in Rangoon, editorialized that these organizations were "agitating and organizing the people into appreciating and accepting the Party's policies and decisions and to induce wide mass participation in the national development projects." As of 1981 the mass organizations included the War Veterans' Organization, the Literary Workers' Organization, the Motion Picture Council, the Theatrical Council, and the Music Council Organizing Committee. The formation of other social and cultural groups was also under active consideration at that time.

The best known of these mass organizations was the Lanzin Youth Central Organizing Committee, formed in 1971 to train the youths as the "reserve forces" and future cadres of the BSPP. This committee was actively involved in efforts to organize three groups—Lanzin youths (for those 15 to 25 years of age), Shesung youths (10 to 15 years of age), and Teza youths (five to 10 years of age). In 1981 the three groups had a membership of over 1 million, nearly half a million, and over 3 million, respectively. More important than the other two, the Lanzin youth group was organized into committees in universities and colleges, in the armed forces and other functional units, and at the township level. Lanzin youths were given training courses in the party ideology, political programs, and organizational work. They were also reported to have been contributing "voluntary services" in the villages, at mills and factories, on construction sites, and to literacy campaigns. According to U Ne Win's report to the Fourth Congress, "continued efforts" were needed to "combat decadent culture and repulse the narcotic drug menace" in the BSPP's activities relating to youths.

The two basic class organizations were the Workers' Asiayone (Workers' Association) and the Peasants' Asiayone (Peasants' Association), which had central bodies at the national level. These organizations actually appeared in one form or another in the second half of the 1960s, but it was not until after the Third Congress in 1977 that systematic campaigns got under way to mobilize these two classes. Their assigned missions were to motivate the working people toward higher productivity, to improve their living standards, to heighten their political awareness, and to involve the working people in the BSPP's effort to build a genuine socialist state.

As of October 1982 there were 7.8 million members in the peasant organization, which had a three-tier structure—the state and division, township, and village-tract and ward levels. The workers' organization claimed a membership of 1.5 million as of December 1982. These workers were mobilized into primary units formed at all state-owned enterprises, but not all workers in these enterprises opted for membership for unspecified reasons. According to a report of the Workers' Asiayone Central Body in December 1982, the workers who had not been admitted to the association were "mostly casual workers and those belonging to private-owned enterprises." As a result, workers in the private sector were not enjoying "as much welfare as workers or state-owned enterprises."

Ideology

The basic principles of the party ideology were first laid down in April 1962 in a policy statement called "The Burmese Way to Socialism." Predicated on the conviction that the exploitation of man by man should be brought to an end in Burma, the statement called for the establishment of a socialist democratic state, the principal strength of which was to derive from the class alliance of workers and peasants. The purpose of a socialist economic system envisaged by then-General Ne Win's coup leadership was to give the "maximum satisfaction to the material, spiritual, and cultural needs of the whole nation, " eschewing the "narrow self-interest of a group, an organization, a class, or a party."

As envisaged by the U Ne Win leadership, Burmese socialism was to be achieved by avoiding "the evils of deviation towards right or left"; making full use of "the opportunities provided by progressive ideas, theories, and experiences at home or abroad"; and nationalizing the vital means of production, distribution, transportation, communication, and foreign trade. All able-bodied persons would work according to their ability and be compensated according to the quantity and quality of work performed. A new Burma would have no place for "fraudulent practices, profit motive easy living, parasitism, shirking and selfishness." It would have a new political and administrative structure more conducive to socialist development and to the "solidarity of all the indigenous racial groups"—such solidarity or national unity being an essential condition in building a socialist body politic. The pre-1962 version of "parliamentary democracy' was rejected because of its negative association with bourgeois class interests.

The ideology was too abstract or too vague for all but a small number of Marxist-inspired ideologues to understand. In January

1963 the BSPP sought to give a more comprehensive explanation by publishing a document called *The System of Correlation of Man and His Environment.*Essentially, the document, an embodiment of the party philosophy, stated that the BSPP valued man and spiritual factors over Marxist-Leninist materialism. It was heavily laden with an assortment of Marxist and Buddhist concepts. As the ruling party veered toward the ideological left after 1963, however, some members of the *sangha* became increasingly concerned and publicly criticized the BSPP ideology as procommunist and anti-Buddhist.

In predominantly Buddhist Burma, members of the *sangha* are popularly trusted and held in high esteem (see The Buddhism of Burma, ch. 2).In a rapidly depoliticized Burmese setting under military leadership, the *sangha* constituted the only social grouping potentially capable of articulating dissenting views outside the BSPP channel of political communication. Hence the party was sensitive to criticisms leveled against itself by some *sangha* members and in September 1964 took pains to deny any link with communism, pointing out significant differences between the BSPP and communist parties. For example, it was noted that, unlike the communists, the BSPP gave full freedom of conscience and religious worship to believers and nonbelievers alike. Another critical difference concerned the party's belief in the Buddhist concept of impermanence, holding no political, economic, or social doctrine to be infallible, universal, or unchanging. In stressing that the BSPP was beholden to no single foreign ideology, the party declared: "The Burmese Socialist Programme Party studies the texts and treatises of the Marxist-Leninists and of the non-Marxist-Leninists alike. In no area, political, economic, or otherwise, is the study restricted. What is good and useful for the human society in the Union of Burma will be extracted in its essence, adapted and applied." Eclecticism was thus tempered by Burmese nationalism.

In the early 1980s the BSPP's policies and programs were still based on the general principles of socialism enunciated in the early 1960s. Its ideology was extolled as containing "progressive ideas from the history of international socialism combined with Burmese experience, Burmese culture, and Burmese traditions to fit with the Burmese society." Evidently, it continued to provide the focus for what the party leadership hoped would be a common political outlook and national unity. It was difficult to ascertain the extent to which the ideology was appreciated or accepted by the masses, let alone by the politically more conscious members of the BSPP. The *Working People's Daily* editorially stressed on October 9, 1981, that every party cadre must strive to understand "the essence of this philosophy" and be able "to expound it to others who still do not grasp it."

Efforts to popularize the party ideology were undertaken through both educational and party channels. After 1977, for example, "moral education" geared specifically to the instilling of "socialist morals in youths" became compulsory from kindergarten up to and including high school. The Central Institute of Political Science in Mingaladon regularly offered a "basic political science course" and an "organizational refresher course" to those party personnel at the central, state and division, and township levels. In these courses, topics covered included ideology, party history, economic and political organizational affairs, mass and class organizations, and even agriculture and livestock-breeding work.

National Unity

In Burma the term "national unity" refers to harmony and solidarity among the country's numerous "national races" or ethnic groups, including the historically dominant majority, the Burmans. The overriding need for such unity, a top national goal since independence, is annually reaffirmed on February 12, which is celebrated as Union Day (see The Nationalities Issue and Insurgency, ch. 1). In 1983 national unity remained a vexing problem, being manifest in continuing insurgencies by communist and ethnic elements, which posed a threat to the security of border areas (see Insurgency in the Periphery, ch. 5).

Long before Burmese independence a multitude of ethnic groups in the border regions enjoyed varying degrees of autonomy in exchange for their acceptance of British paramountcy. Thus on the eve of independence, the Burman-dominated interim Burmese government found it necessary to assure the minorities that their traditional rights and customs would be protected in an independent, federated Burma. Some groups, notably the Shans and the Kayahs, were even granted the right of secession from the federal union after 10 years if they were not satisfied with the federal scheme. Nevertheless, the minorities as a whole continued to press for the fullest possible autonomy within the political system legitimized under the 1947 constitution. Within six months of independence, the Karens, the largest of the discontented minorities, were in armed rebellion, thus joining a band of communists who had already launched armed struggles against the central government. These insurrectionists were soon joined by other minority groups; rebel groups remained independent of one another, however, and were unable to pool their forces under a single antigovernment banner.

The military coup of March 1962 was defended in part as an effort to prevent the onset of political disintegration in the face of growing insurgencies. The new leadership moved swiftly to tighten control in the border regions by abolishing locally elected governing bodies and replacing them with a centralized, military-led bureaucracy. In an attempt to end the insurgencies through peaceful means, the government in April 1963 issued a general amnesty for all rebels, communist and ethnic, and in July it invited all groups in revolt to peace parleys. Negotiations that followed brought no solutions, and hostilities resumed in November 1963. The government intensified its suppression campaigns while doubling its efforts to win over the disaffected minorities by expanding developmental activities in the fields of education, health, agriculture, industry, and communications. Furthermore, the government sought to promote national integration by gradually instituting measures for administrative and judicial uniformity throughout the country. The official commitment to national unity was aptly described by General Ne Win in February 1964: "The national races must sink or swim together in order that the Union might contrive to exist and prosper."

A major instrument of government policies toward the minorities was the Academy for the Development of National Groups, established in October 1964 at Sagaing (later moved to Ywathitgyi). The four-year school was designed to train high-school-age minority students as organizers, teachers, and leaders for their respective areas of origin. Among the subjects taught at the academy were political science, basic military training, languages and literatures of the national groups (for the Kachin, Kayah, Karen, Chin, and Shan groups only), culture and traditions of national groups, basic health care, animal husbandry and veterinary science, agriculture, physical education, handicrafts, home economics, music and fine arts, and primary school level teacher training. As of March 1981 the academy had produced a total of 1,921 graduates representing 50 ethnic groups. Eighty percent of the total graduates were represented by seven political subdivisions, Shan State accounting for 24.5 percent of the total; Sagaing Division, 11.4 percent; Karen State, 9.9 percent; Chin State, 9.6 percent; Kachin State, 9.3 percent; Kayah State, 8.1 percent; and Tenasserim Division, 6.6 percent.

The concept of unity in diversity is central to the government's commitment to the goal of national unity. From all indications, however, diversity is considered to be significant only when it is compatible with the higher goal of national solidarity. The Constitution is explicit in granting all ethnic groups "the freedom to profess their religion, use and develop their language, literature and culture, and follow their cherished traditions and customs." In practice, this freedom must be exercised, however, prudently and within limits, so that the security, cohesion, and socialist development of the nation are not undermined, especially in view of the lingering separatist sentiments on the part of some disaffected minority elements. It is not surprising that the 1974 Constitution has not retained the provision dealing with "the right of secession" for some of the minorities as under the old constitution. Under the military-controlled, unity-conscious BSPP leadership, uniformity, not diversity, has become an article of faith in its attempt to establish unassailable authority in insurgent-affected border regions.

For years the government was convinced that a real test of national unity was the spontaneity of popular support for and participation in the appropriate levels of administrative and party hierarchies. This was believed especially to be the case in areas affected by insurgents but also inhabited by law-abiding ethnic minorities. Local participation, a major concern in the official effort to isolate rebels and to foster the spirit of unity, was ensured in part through the electoral process and in part by allowing some minorities to exercise the freedom, limited as it might be, to pursue their respective cultural activities and administer justice according to customary practices. People's councils at different levels of local administration provided a channel through which citizens could be represented. Evidently, candidates in local elections usually belonged to the ethnic group most numerous in a given constituency. Obviously, this measure helped the voters, especially in minority areas, overcome the traditional fear of intrusions by outsiders, meaning in this case the numerically and politically dominant Burmans.

Recent Political Developments

In the early 1980s Burmese politics showed little or no outward sign of turmoil. Except for the seemingly endless insurgent activities in the frontier areas, the political arena was marked by tranquillity. The military-dominated power structure showed no evidence of internal stress. If there was any low-key jockeying for advantages to prepare for eventual succession to U Ne Win, this was not readily apparent. Shortly before U Ne Win's retirement from the BSPP in 1985, politics could become heated, but at least for the moment continuity was the dominant theme of the ruling party in its earnest effort to match political independence with economic independence, to ensure internal and external security, and to maintain an independent and active foreign policy.

Among the noteworthy recent developments was U Ne Win's effort in 1980 to restore peace and harmony within the country. In May of that year a national convention of Buddhist monks—the First Congregation of the Sangha of All Orders for Purification, Perpetuation, and Propagation of the Sasana—was held to bring about unity and discipline within the *sangha* (see The Socialist Transformation, ch. 2; Public Order in Central Burma, ch. 5). The four-day convention, officially labeled "the first of its kind in Burma's contemporary history of religion," brought representatives from nine different Buddhist sects in the country and deliberated many issues facing the community of monks. Convened under strong government encouragement, the congregation adopted several resolutions, among other things formally recognizing the legitimacy of nine existing sects, creating a centralized national committee with self-policing powers, requiring the registration of monks and nuns, and reviving religious courts that had been suspended in 1962. Actually, the government effort to bring order and unity to the sect-ridden, loosely regulated, and sometimes politically intrusive *sangha* had begun in the mid-1960s—with little success (see Student and Sangha Reactions, ch. 1).

To celebrate the "successful conclusion" of the congregation in promoting "unity and peace," the government declared, on May 28, 1980, amnesty for "those engaged in insurrection against the State," provided that they reported to authorities within 90 days. Under the amnesty, which applied also to political offenders and some convicted criminals, about 21,000 insurgents and political opponents were reported to have returned "to the legal fold," and some 4,000 political prisoners and felons were released from prison.

The most prominent of the rehabilitated was U Nu who, after receiving a personal message from U Ne Win, returned from India where he was in exile after having led a short-lived anti-Ne Win movement based in Thailand. In that message, U Ne Win invited U Nu to return "in recognition of his past services to the country and to enable him to take part in the government's efforts to purify and propagate the Buddhist faith, both at home and abroad" (see the Socialist Republic of the Union of Burma, ch. 1). Among other important returnees were two of U Ne Win's World War II comrades-in-arms; a Shan rebel leader; a Karen resistance leader; a member of the Central Committee of the Burmese Communist Party (BCP); and a onetime Shan leader best known for his opium trafficking in the Golden Triangle.

In June 1980 the government announced the creation of an award to honor those patriots and distinguished public officials who had served the nation with selfless dedication from 1920 to 1974. The official recognition, transcending political ideologies or affiliation, carried cash awards under the Political Pension Law enacted in October 1980. Another purpose of this law was to provide retirement pensions to all public officials elected after 1974 to the People's Assembly and the people's councils at various levels. In announcing the plan for the law in July, U Ne Win stated: "The prospect of getting a pension will save these people from worrying about their life after retirement, and so enable them to give undivided attention to their work"—freeing them from the temptation of bribe-taking and corruption.

Widely publicized in the state-run media, these measures for national reconciliation and unity evidently evoked considerable popular goodwill toward the government. But national unity was still elusive because the gap separating the government and insurgents could not be narrowed. In May 1981 U Ne Win disclosed that after the 90-day deadline for amnesty expired, the BCP leader, Thakin Ba Thein Tin, had requested secret peace talks, but the negotiations in late 1980 had been terminated without success. It was revealed that the Communists initially demanded government recognition of the BCP, its armed forces, and its bases in border areas. In response, the government called on the BCP members to join the BSPP on an individual basis, the BCP soldiers to enlist in the government security and police forces, and the BCP to disband its border bases. According to political scientist Josef Silverstein, the counterproposal by the BCP called for "government recognition of the BCP in a multiparty system; inclusion of its armed forces as a military unit under the State Defense Council with at least one or two BCP representatives on that body; [and] recognition of its territory as an autonomous region under a single national government." In his report to the Central Committee of the BSPP on May 14, Ne Win stated that "in overall assessment of the discussions between the two sides, it was found that Thakin Ba Thein Tin's side was holding on to the three points they first proposed." He declared that because the three points "should not and could not be conceded to, it was decided to terminate the discussions."

Negotiations were held also with the Kachin Independence Organization (KIO), but they were broken off in July 1981. The government found it difficult to accept the Kachin rebels' demand for recognition of the KIO as a Kachin political party and for establishment of an autonomous Kachin state with constitutional protection of full rights and freedoms for the Kachins. Unlike the BCP and the KIO, however, the Karen and Shan rebel groups, factionally divided as all of them were, vowed to fight on until their goal of secession and full independence was achieved.

At the Fourth Congress the BSPP claimed that insurgency was "breaking up" and that it was confined only to "some border regions." Whatever the case, it seemed quite clear that armed rebels were unable to overthrow the constitutional government by force of arms partly because of their difficulty in forming an effective coalition and partly because the BCP could no longer obtain material support from its traditional patron, China, across the border (see Foreign Affairs, this ch.).

In October, two months after the party congress, more than 17.4 million voters went to the polls for the third time since 1974 to elect the BSPP-nominated candidates to the People's Assembly and local people's councils. Convened in November 1981, the People's Assembly elected the State Council, which in turn elected U San Yu as its chairman and U Aye Ko as the secretary. This meant that U San Yu—a former general, U Ne Win's longtime deputy, and until then the secretary of the State Council—succeeded U Ne Win as president and head of the state. The presidency under U San Yu, however, no longer symbolized the fusion of both formal and real power as had been under U Ne Win. It also meant that U Aye Ko's new post as secretary placed him second in rank after the president in the government, matching his second most senior position as general secretary in the

U Ne Win

party hierarchy. Also in November the State Council reelected U Maung Maung Kha, a former army colonel, to a second four-year term. In 1983 the leadership structure erected two years earlier remained intact under the supreme command of U Ne Win.

Foreign Affairs

In the early 1980s the socialist government of Burma had friendly relations with other nations according to the principles of nonalignment and noninterference. It was no longer as isolationist as it had been during much of the 1960s. The need to draw on foreign assistance for the country's economic development had been a major factor in Burma's decision in the early 1970s to broaden its contacts with the rest of the world.

Foreign Policy Environment

Generally, Burmese foreign relations are dictated by a combination of factors, such as national and internal security, political solidarity at home, distrust of foreign powers, and economic pragmatism. In both historical and contemporary terms, the Burmese perception of its foreign policy milieu has been strongly influenced by the fact that Burma shares borders with two giant neighbors—China and India. The perception of being hemmed in by these two powers seemed, on balance, to have predisposed Burma toward a policy of offending no foreign powers—a policy of noninvolvement and neutrality.

Independence and entry into the community of nations came at a time when the Cold War became intense but Burmese leaders showed little interest in ideological issues. Instead, in defining their policy priorities, they focused on three interrelated objectives. These were to preserve the nation's fragile territorial integrity through a policy of caution and accommodation in relation to China; to seek national unity by suppressing civil insurgencies and forging a common loyalty to the union government; and to diversify and modernize the economy, thus reducing the country's overwhelming dependence on rice exports for foreign exchange.

U Nu, who was deposed as prime minister in 1962 and who was a principal architect of Burma's nonaligned foreign policy, defined nonalignment as an impartial examination of every external issue on its merits; noninterference in the internal affairs of other nations; friendly relations with all nations; and acceptance of aid from all sources, provided that the aid carried no political preconditions. In practice, this policy meant nonparticipation in any military alliance. After 1962 General Ne Win added another dimension to the policy—an elimination of foreign influence, communist and noncommunist alike.

The achievement of the policy objectives hinged most of all on peaceful and neighborly relations with China, whose historic claims to several tracts on the Burmese side of the frontier had been a major source of concern to the newly independent Burma until the issue was settled in a 1960 border agreement. Burma's apprehensions have also been heightened by the fact that communist rebels and some ethnic minorities in the border regions have maintained armed insurrection with instigation and support from across the border.

Believing that Burma alone was not capable of coping with China's growing menace, Burma turned to the United Nations (UN) for possible support. After Burma joined the world organization, U Nu declared: "We were not prompted by considerations of . . . aid, education missions . . . and such other benefits likely to accrue from our membership. These things, however desirable, are immaterial. What was foremost in our minds was the expectation of United Nations assistance if our country should be subjected to aggression by a stronger power." Moreover, it was fear of China that influenced Burma's decision to be the first to recognize the new communist regime in China in December 1949. The Chinese seizure of Tibet and intervention in the Korean War in 1950 confirmed Burma's negative perception of China. Burma defended the UN police action in Korea but refrained from condemning China as the aggressor in order not to antagonize the latter.

The concept of peaceful coexistence naturally appealed to Burma, which joined India, China, and others in endorsing the five principles of coexistence as proclaimed by the Afro-Asian Conference held at Bandung, Indonesia, in April 1955, which is better known as the Bandung Conference. These principles called for mutual respect for each other's territorial integrity and sovereignty, mutual nonaggression, mutual noninterference in each other's internal affairs, equality and mutual benefits, and peaceful coexistence.

Predictably, Burma did not opt for membership in the now defunct Southeast Asia Treaty Organization (SEATO), which it believed was anticommunist and pro-Western. Nor did it join any of the regional associations in Southeast Asia, including the Association of Southeast Asian Nations (ASEAN), formed in 1967 by Indonesia, Malaysia, the Philippines, Singapore, and Thailand. For practical reasons, however, Burma became a member of what it regarded as strictly economic groupings, such as the Colombo Plan and the Asian Development Bank.

Nonalignment has become an article of faith for the Burmese leadership—popularly accepted as a desirable means of shielding the nation from harmful consequences of foreign ventures or entanglements. As early as 1969 the Burmese delegation to a consultative conference of nonaligned nations held in Belgrade expressed its concern that if a bloc or faction was created within the nonaligned movement, this bloc would not only become a pawn in a great-power conflict but would also cause disunity among nonaligned nations.

Burma withdrew from the Nonaligned Movement in September 1979, citing a series of violations of the original principles on which the movement was founded. Its delegation to the Sixth Nonaligned Summit Conference in Havana declared that the movement had deteriorated since 1964 because of disturbing developments involving nonaligned countries. These developments included intensification of disputes, a tendency on the part of some to form "active factions," the use of force by some members for settlement of disputes, and interference in the internal affairs of others. The Burmese delegation put forward a motion that the movement "as it stands torn and divided today" be dissolved and a committee be appointed to draft a charter so that the principles and working procedures of the movement could be defined and clarified. In short, the movement needed to be "purified" and returned to its "true original principles." Burma also let it be known that "should the Summit reach no decision and let things drift," it would have no choice but to withdraw from the conference and terminate its participation in the movement. In late September, shortly after the summit, Burma informed the

UN General Assembly that the Havana conference had "failed to take heed of [the] motion, and concluded without even a mention of it."

Relations with Selected Countries

Burma has attached special importance to the UN and other international and regional organizations for both bilateral and multilateral cooperation, especially since the early 1970s. Its most visible symbol of interest in the activities of the world organization was U Thant of Burma, who served as secretary general of the UN from 1962 to 1971.

In bilateral relations with other countries, China looms especially large. Until 1960 relations with Beijing were correct but less than warm because of a historic border dispute. The discord was resolved peacefully under a Sino-Burmese border agreement in 1960, when the two countries also concluded a treaty of friendship and mutual nonaggression. These were followed by an agreement on economic and technical cooperation in 1961. Cordiality after 1960 was not affected until 1967, when Burmese and Chinese students clashed violently in Rangoon over an issue related to the so-called Great Proletarian Cultural Revolution, then under way inside China. The result was that diplomatic relations became strained, China suspending its aid projects granted under the 1961 agreement. Burmese reaction was circumspect. By March 1971 the ambassadors of the two countries had returned to their respective posts, and General Ne Win's visit to China in August 1971 was followed by the resumption of Chinese aid programs two months later.

Relations with China improved steadily on a government-to-government level, as evidenced in the signing of a new economic and technical cooperation agreement in July 1979. Under this accord signed in Beijing, China agreed to extend a loan equivalent to US$63 million. Nevertheless, the Burmese leadership was uneasy about reports of Chinese aid to Burmese communist insurgents. During his numerous visits to China (11 times in the period 1960–80), U Ne Win reportedly sought to dissuade China from supplying weapons to the Burmese rebels. In February 1981, while visiting Thailand, Chinese Premier Zhao Ziyang was reported to have stated that Chinese relations with communist parties in Southeast Asia, including the BCP, were confined to a "political and spiritual level."

Relations with India were cordial in the early 1980s. For over a decade after the Burmese promulgation of an enterprise nationalization law in 1963, however, relations with India were strained. Although not directed against any specific foreign group, the nationalization had hit Burma's Indian Community the hardest— Indians having dominated the twentieth-century economic life of the country. By mid-1968 nearly 158,000 Indians had left Burma without compensation for assets left behind. The problem of compensation was finally settled in December 1973 when Burma announced a compensation schedule. About 150,000 persons of Indian origin were estimated to be eligible under the plan. Of that total, about 100,000 persons were believed to be still residing in Burma at the end of 1973. In April 1974 U Ne Win paid a goodwill visit to India. By early 1976 most of the 1,600-kilometer border between Burma and India had been demarcated, based on an agreement signed in 1967. In the early 1980s India had a modest aid program in Burma.

In mid-1983 relations with Bangladesh (formerly East Pakistan) were friendly. U Ne Win paid a state visit to Bangladesh in April 1974—two years after that country had gained independence from Pakistan. At that time Prime Minister Sheikh Mujibur Rahman thanked U Ne Win for having provided temporary shelter to thousands of Bengali Muslims fleeing the war between Pakistani troops and Bengali fighters for independence. Relations between the two countries became strained briefly in mid-1978, when nearly 200,000 Burmese Muslims in the northwestern areas of Rakhine State (formerly Arakan State) fled the country, crossing the border onto Bangladesh. The mass flight was triggered by rumors of arrest and religious persecution by Burmese officials who had entered the areas to look for illegal immigrants from Bangladesh. An aggravation of the relationship was averted through an accord signed in July 1978 providing for repatriation of most of these Muslims in stages. In May 1979 another accord was signed to demarcate their land boundary. This was followed by still another agreement in December 1980 concerning border arrangements and cooperation. The repatriation was completed by the end of 1979, and in the early 1980s there was no irritant in relations between the two countries. In February 1982, at the end of his state visit to Rangoon, the President of Bangladesh, Abdus Sattar, joined his Burmese counterpart, U San Yu, in expressing satisfaction with the state of relations between the two nations.

Thailand, with which Burma shares a 1,600-kilometer border as well as a history of friction dating back to the sixteenth century, remains an important factor in Burmese domestic and foreign affairs. This was owing to insurrections in Burma among minorities who straddle the border between the two countries. Relations between Rangoon and Bangkok were polite through much of the 1960s until they turned sour after 1969 when Thailand granted political asylum to U Nu—who had vowed to overthrow the U Ne Win government—even though the government of Thailand assured Burma that U Nu would not be permitted to engage in any anti-Burmese political activities while residing in Thailand. Coolness gave way to warmth, however, after May 1973 when the two countries agreed to restore cordiality and reestablish cooperation. Two months later Thailand expelled U Nu for having violated the terms of his asylum. Thereafter, the two countries gradually expanded their cooperation in trade and economic fields and in the control of smuggling and opium trafficking. Thailand also began evicting some Burmese rebels and opium smugglers operating from their hideouts inside Thailand. In July 1980 the two countries removed an obstacle by signing an agreement on the delineation of the maritime boundary in the Andaman Sea. This became necessary after 1977 when Burma declared a 200-mile exclusive economic zone and Thailand became concerned about the adverse effect this zone would have on its fishing industry.

In mid-1983 relations with other Southeast Asian countries were free of discord and were amicable. On the question of Kampuchea (formerly Cambodia), Burma maintains a deliberate ambiguity. After Vietnam invaded Kampuchea in early 1979 and installed a pro-Hanoi regime headed by Heng Samrin, the Burmese government denounced the Vietnamese action and refused to recognize the new Kampuchean regime; it continued to recognize the ousted Khmer Rouge regime, which was reportedly backed by China. Because Vietnam was widely believed to have been backed by the Soviet Union at that time, the Kampuchean question posed a delicate problem for the Burmese leadership. To condemn the invasion was consistent with the principle of noninterference that Burma subscribed to as a main guideline of the Nonaligned Movement, and in fact the Burmese delegation to the nonaligned summit in Havana made it clear that any attempt to legitimize the Heng Samrin regime would constitute a serious affront to the Nonaligned Movement.

Presumably, however, Burma was aware that its position, however highly principled it might be, would incur Vietnamese and Soviet displeasure. In October 1980 Burma abstained from voting in the UN General Assembly for a motion that would have approved the credentials of the Khmer Rouge delegation, which a number of pro-Soviet countries had rejected. Nevertheless, Burma continued to withhold its recognition of the Heng Samrin regime, thereby maintaining a correct neutralist posture palatable to both China and the Soviet Union.

In 1983 Burmese relations continued to be friendly with the Soviet Union, which maintained a low profile in Burma. After General Ne Win's seizure of power in 1962, the Soviet Union was slow in extending its recognition, but as Burmese relations with China deteriorated after 1967, it sought in earnest to befriend the U Ne Win government. In 1969, for example, Moscow commented favorably on the "non-capitalist road" that Burma was said to be taking in its efforts to establish a socialist state. In June 1971 the Soviet Union announced its readiness to extend military aid to Burma if the latter so desired and also to provide economic aid—especially in oil technology—in exchange for Burmese rice.

Over the years Moscow was not loath to play on Burmese fear of China; in June 1978, for example, the Soviet Union commented that despite the frequent Chinese expression of a good neighbor policy toward Burma, China was actually pursuing a policy that "cannot be assessed as anything but crude interference." It went on to declare: "Fanning up strife in Burma between ethnic groups, encouraging separatists, providing nationalistic opposition groupings with arms, the Maoists are seeking to impose their diktat upon Burma and make it carry out a foreign policy line which is to China's liking." Earlier in 1978 Burma was reported to have declined a Soviet offer to provide a loan. Evidently, the Soviet government also restated its offer in June 1979. In early 1983 there was no indication of any Soviet aid's being provided to Burma.

In October 1982 a Soviet source publicly expressed its concern about "revival of insurgent activities" in Burma and about the obstructionist effect it would have on Burma's earnest effort to solve its "socioeconomic problems" and to build "a socialist democratic state." Posing a rhetorical question, "How have the insurgents survived for so long?" it asserted that the answers to such a question "can be seen in the Burmese papers." In short, the insurgents received "support from abroad" and they posed "the danger of external threat"—a dark hint that China was the principal source of threat to Burma.

Meanwhile, the Soviet government reported in July 1982 the "Soviet-Burmese economic cooperation" had played an "important role" in Burma's economic progress in recent years, adding hopefully that such cooperation could be expanded since there was "the scope" for "further developing trade, economic, cultural, and scientific ties between the two countries."

The need for foreign economic assistance continues to be a top foreign policy priority. Accordingly, relations with Japan are especially important, Japan having maintained a special relationship dating back to the 1940s and being the single largest provider of concessional loans and direct grant aid (see The Japanese Occupation, ch. 1). Japan is also unique in having been allowed to maintain its aid program throughout the 1962–72 period during which Burma was, by design, one of Asia's most isolationist countries. In addition to the World Bank (see Glossary) and the Asian Development Bank, other major sources of assistance include the Federal Republic of Germany (West Germany), France, Britain, Australia, Canada, the United States, the Netherlands, Czechoslovakia, and China (see Foreign Economic Relations, ch. 3).

Relations with the United States were close and friendly. In the first two decades of Burmese independence, the United States actively supported Burma's efforts to develop its economy and to strengthen its internal security. Its aid program was discontinued, however, in the mid–1960s at Burma's request. Nevertheless, bilateral ties continued on a cordial basis, the main area of cooperation being in the cultural and educational fields. Burmese-American cooperation was broadened in June 1974, when the two countries signed an agreement under which the United States provided the country with helicopters, transport aircraft, and communications equipment; these were needed for a more effective Burmese campaign against the cultivation, refining, and trading of opium. This assistance was justified in the United States by the assertion that as much as 30 percent of the heroin reaching the United States was believed to be originating in the so-called Golden Triangle; most of the opium grown on the Burmese part of the triangle was in eastern frontier areas controlled by Burmese communist insurgents and Shan rebels. United States economic aid resumed on a modest scale under an agreement signed in August 1980, providing for a small amount of assistance for improving Burma's primary health care facilities in rural areas. A second agreement signed two months later was to help Burma develop oilseed crops and boost its cooking oil production.

* * *

The most useful sources on the current political developments of Burma are found in the February issues of the monthly *Asian Survey*, the yearbook *Southeast Asian Affairs*, and the Far Eastern Economic Review's *Asia Yearbook*. Official views and policies concerning politics and government are well reflected in the Rangoon-based English-language dailies, *Guardian* and *Working People's Daily*. For broader perspectives on the evolution and dynamics of Burmese politics and government, the following sources merit further consultation: F.K. Lehman's *Military Rule in Burma since 1962: A Kaleidoscope of Views*; Josef Silverstein's *Burma: Military Rule and the Politics of Stagnation*, and David I. Steinberg's "Burma under the Military: Towards a Chronology," in *Contemporary Southeast Asia*, December 1981. (For further information and complete citations, see Bibliography.)

Chapter 5.   National Security

Military units on parade

DEVELOPING NATIONAL UNITY and establishing internal order in the face of uninterrupted challenge from numerous armed insurgent groups continued to be Burma's primary security concern in early 1983. Since 1962, when General Ne Win led a successful military coup, the government has held firm control over central Burma—the territory encompassing the Irrawaddy and Sittang river systems. Antigovernment activity has been successfully confined to remote border areas and has been limited to ethnic minorities who did not seriously threaten the paramountcy of the national leadership, which was dominated by the ethnic majority—the Burmans. The government has never been in complete control of the entire national territory, however, and since independence from Britain in 1948, Burma's armed forces have repeatedly conducted counterinsurgency campaigns and occasionally engaged in fixed-position battles against rebel forces. This sustained level of combat has given the armed forces more experience in fighting in the field than that of most other Third World countries.

In the early 1980s various ethnic separatist movements, the outlawed Burmese Communist Party, and several warlords continued to maintain their own armies and exert control over peripheral sections of the country. Most operated in the hard-to-police forests, jungles, and mountains of northern and eastern Burma, near the borders with China, Laos, and Thailand. Armed insurgents, at most, represented less than 1 percent of the total population. Nonetheless, they were able to disrupt public order and internal security in as much as 30 percent of the national territory and thus presented a very serious national burden. The growing involvement by insurgent groups in smuggling and, increasingly, opium trafficking has further complicated the problem.

The government made progress, although slowly, against insurgent groups during the late 1970s and early 1980s, through both military action and other means, such as negotiating politically with its opponents and making diplomatic overtures to neighboring countries that have supported or harbored rebel groups. The government has also benefited from the general internal disorganization of most insurgent groups, their mutual hostilities and rivalries, and their inability to maintain effective long-term alliances. Given the ethnic diversity of the nation, the tradition of insurgency in some groups, the terrain of the regions most rebels inhabit, and the limited resources available to the government, however, establishing and maintaining order and security over the entire national territory would not be an easy task.

The opium trade has been of particular concern, not only as it related to supporting insurgent activity but also because of the growing number of heroin addicts in the nation. Burma has passed tough antinarcotics legislation and launched numerous antidrug publicity campaigns. In the mid-1970s, in cooperation with the United Nations and the United States, it initiated a multifaceted program designed to limit poppy cultivation, refining, and trafficking within its borders. These efforts have been of limited success, however, primarily because, as of early 1983, the major poppy-growing areas were under the insurgents' control.

Since the 1962 coup, military and ex-military officers have monopolized the dominant positions in government and politics, and the armed forces mission has been augmented to provide for both the defense of the nation and the construction of a socialist state. In keeping with this twofold role, units of all three military services have frequently participated in civic action programs— building roads, aiding in community development, and harvesting the nation's all-important rice crop. Personnel were regularly instructed in the doctrine of the state's single party, the Burma Socialist Programme Party (BSPP), and party committees have been set up at every level in the defense establishment.

Militarily, the armed forces have prosecuted the perennial counterinsurgency campaigns with very little modern equipment. The army, the largest and the predominant branch, was essentially a light infantry force that operated primarily in small units much like the guerrilla forces it opposed. The navy and air force mainly provided support for army operations.

The nation has not been faced with direct foreign aggression since independence and, given the scope of its internal problems, Burma has been careful not to provoke or be drawn into any external conflict. The nation continued to follow a foreign policy of independence and strict nonalignment. The experiences of Vietnam and the rest of Indochina in the last few decades were widely viewed as examples of the dangers of becoming involved in regional or superpower disputes. The nation has not entered into any defense alliances and has relied on diversified sources to meet its modest requirements for military aid and equipment. The policy of independence and nonalignment, however, has not precluded efforts by national authorities to secure the cooperation of neighboring states in limiting foreign support for domestic insurgents and in combating rebels and opium traffickers who operated across international borders.

Public Order in Central Burma

Since the 1962 coup, a major leadership priority has been to achieve national and political unity and end the communist and ethnic insurgencies that had bedeviled the country during its first decade of independence. The active-duty and retired military officers, who have occupied the highest decisionmaking and administrative posts in the government, had been particularly alarmed by real or potential dangers posed by political dissent and by the advocacy of specialized regional or ethnic interests at the expense of national interests. Having taken over the country to prevent national disintegration, they sought above all to bind the country together.

Discarding the federal style of government in 1962, the self-proclaimed socialist revolutionary government established a new centralized system of rule intended to mobilize the country's diverse population in a harmonious and conformist manner. Effort was made to expand minority participation in the government and to celebrate Burma's cultural and ethnic diversity as enriching the national character; ethnicity and regionalism were not permitted to develop political expression, however. Instead, reflecting the socialist revolutionary ideology with which both military and civilian leaders were imbued, citizens were grouped into mass organizations of workers, peasants, or youth, which cut across traditional patterns of political and social cleavage (see Mass and Class Organizations, ch. 4). All political expression was then channeled through the Burma Socialist Programme Party (BSPP), the single government-sanctioned party. Political expression outside that framework was not tolerated.

Little or no scope has been left available for public expression of nonofficial viewpoints in any case. All organizations, political or otherwise, had to meet government approval in order to exist and were required to promote the official ideology. The government owned and controlled all communications media, and journalists were issued strict guidelines regarding what could permissibly be published or broadcast. Efficient intelligence and internal security forces operated virtually free from legal restraints (see Intelligence agencies, this ch.). Using block and neighborhood wardens attached to local government "security committees," the security forces kept tabs on people in both rural and urban areas and did not hesitate to deal summarily with any persons or activities the leadership believed might pose a threat to the government, public order, or national security. Burmese and foreigners alike were subject to travel restrictions; Burmese were legally required to obtain permission to leave the townships where they resided, although in practice those with valid identity papers could travel without specific permission except in certain restricted areas where insurgency was prevalent. Foreign travel was very difficult, and international news publications were rarely available. Normally, foreign visitors were permitted to stay in Burma for only seven days.

Many groups in central Burma that have traditionally been politically active (hence were sources of potential opposition) had been successfully neutralized or co-opted throughout the 1962–early 1983 period. Student demonstrations in 1962 ceased quickly after the military dealt forcibly with campus unrest by demolishing the Rangoon University Student Union building. Protests did not recur until the 1974–76 period, when they were apparently motivated in part by dissatisfaction over national economic conditions. On those occasions, the government sent in military and police units, made arrests, and enacted laws forbidding any antistate activities (see Crime and the Criminal Justice System, this ch.). In the late 1970s the university system was completely decentralized, effectively dispersing the traditionally Rangoon-centered student population; as of early 1983, campus unrest had not resurfaced.

The government has long been worried that antigovernment elements were able to move freely about the country simply by shaving their heads and donning the saffron robes of members of the *sangha,* or Buddhist monkhood. The *sangha* successfully resisted official attempts to regulate its membership in 1965. In 1980, however, the government successfully imposed its authority over the *sangha,* convening the First Congregation of the Sangha of All Orders for Purification, Perpetuation, and Propagation of the Sasana, in which delegate monks established a central body to bring about unity and discipline within the *sangha* (see Recent Political Developments, ch. 4). The delegates also assented to the requirements that all monks and nuns carry identification cards that could be checked by the authorities, making it possible for the government to enforce residency and movement controls similar to those imposed over the general population.

Sensitive that resistance to the central government has been strongest among members of ethnic minorities who resented what they perceived as official attempts to extend the ethnic Burman culture over all groups, the government has worked assiduously to de-emphasize ethnic differences. In the interests of promoting national unity, it has mandated equal opportunities for all indigenous ethnic groups and has been careful not to interfere with minority cultural, social, and religious beliefs and practices that did not hinder the orderly functioning of the state. Since 1964 it has maintained the Academy for the Development of National Groups at Sagaing (and later moved to Ywathitgyi) to instruct minority students in the ideology and policy of the BSPP so that in turn they might transmit it to their local communities.

Communism, another long-standing source of antigovernment opposition and agitation, has also been effectively muted in central Burma. The government co-opted some communists into the BSPP during the early 1960s. Most of those who remained underground were either members of the Burmese Communist Party (BCP) White Flag faction, located in the highlands known as the Pegu Yoma, or associated with the Red Flag faction in Rakhine State (formerly Arakan State). Both groups suffered such heavy defeats in confrontations with the Burmese armed forces during the late 1960s and early 1970s that communist influence among ethnic Burmans and within central Burma was virtually eliminated. Since that time, Burma's socialist government has successfully arrogated those goals traditionally championed by communists and thus prevented a resurgence of ideological challenge from the far left. As of early 1983 communist opposition appeared to exist only among ethnic minorities in the border areas (see Revolutionary, Separatist, and Warlord Groups, this ch.).

The government continued to express its official distrust regarding the loyalty of those it termed "nonnationals" (see Chinese, Indians, and Other Minorities, ch. 2). These included primarily persons of South Asian and Chinese descent, of whom some were long-term residents or had been born in Burma, and some were recent illegal immigrants, mainly from Bangladesh or Yunnan Province in China. Since independence, restrictions, both formal and informal, have been placed on the freedom of movement and residency of these individuals as well as on their opportunities for employment and political participation. This has occurred in response both to pervasive popular sentiments against what was perceived as an unfair monopolization of wealth by nonindigenous Burmese and to official fears that these individuals might sympathize with or aid local insurgent groups, particularly the pro-Chinese BCP.

Under these conditions, many nonindigenous Burmese have emigrated. Land tenancy policies and the nationalization of the nonagricultural sectors of the economy in the early 1960s led to a mass exodus of foreigners, especially Indians, and anti-Chinese rioting in Rangoon in 1967 prompted the emigration of Chinese, mostly residents in urban ares.

Immigration authorities, concerned over the tens of thousands of Muslims from Bangladesh who had illegally entered the country, launched a campaign in the 1977–78 period to register aliens in the western half of Burma. They focused on Rakhine State, where some of the illegal immigrants were suspected of having tried to link up with local separatist groups. After rumors spread of violence against aliens by civilian and military officials conducting the operation, an estimated 200,000 persons—both Muslims from Bangladesh and many whose ancestors had lived in Burma for up to several centuries—fled across the border into Bangladesh. The Burmese had accepted back some 170,000 by 1980, but the problem of who should be guaranteed the rights and privileges of citizenship nonetheless remained an active issue.

A new citizenship law was enacted in October 1982 to deal with the matter. According to an editorial published in a government-run, English-language daily, the old citizenship provisions, which made it possible for non-Burmese to gain citizenship, were outdated, having been adopted in 1948 at a time when it was important to represent a united stand to press for independence. "Now we are building socialism in our country and loyalty to the

State is essential for safeguarding the sovereignty and national independence. It would be unfair to label all non-nationals as untrustworthy, but in certain cases their loyalty may be divided. Therefore it becomes necessary to gauge carefully how far we can trust them in our national affairs."

The new law, the Burma Citizenship Law, defines citizens as those nationals who are members of ethnic groups that had settled in Burma before 1824, the date that marked the beginning of the First Anglo-Burmese War and the beginning of the British colonial period, during which foreigners, especially Indians and Chinese, freely entered the country. Nonnationals, who were estimated to constitute as much as 10 percent of the population in the early 1980s, were eligible to be classified as "associate" or "naturalized" citizens, according to detailed procedures specified in the law. Many of these persons have a significant portion of Burmese, as well as nonnational, ancestry. The new law bars nonnationals from holding important state and party positions, serving in the armed forces and the police, and pursuing higher education in national institutions. These provisions have effectively withdrawn from certain individuals rights and privileges they had previously enjoyed.

Insurgency in the Periphery

Burma has suffered from endemic insurgencies since 1948 when, immediately after independence, forces loyal to the new government were besieged by various groups, including mutinying army units, demobilized veterans of the struggle for independence, and two communist party factions—the Red Flag and the White Flag. Armed separatist movements organized by the Karen and other ethnic groups and by Burmese Muslims living in the western border areas also took arms against the government (see Parliamentary Government, 1948–62, sh. 1). Although the situation rapidly become so serious that the government's control was limited primarily to Rangoon and its environs, the rebels were not unified and were slowly worn down. By late 1949 the Burmese armed forces had assumed the initiative and by late 1951 held relatively firm control over the central Irrawaddy Plain and most towns elsewhere—though often not the surrounding countryside.

The government's efforts to consolidate and extend its control were made more difficult, however, by the need to divert troops to remote areas near the border with China, where remnants of the Nationalist Chinese Army had fled after the victory of the communist forces. Settling in the eastern Shan State area near the border with China in the 1949–51 period, these remnants, called the Chinese Irregular Forces (CIF), began to live off the land and to assert their authority over the local territory, operating much like the warlords of China in the 1920s. They quickly began to support themselves by harnessing and expanding the cultivation of opium by ethnic minorities living in what became known a the Golden Triangle, where Burma, Laos, and Thailand converge. During the early 1950s the Burmese army launched limited military campaigns against CIF groups, many members of which were evacuated in 1953–54 in a United Nations-sponsored airlift to Taiwan. Several thousand remained behind, however, beyond the reach of Burmese forces.

During the mid-1950s Burmese armed forces continued to press against rebels in the nation's center, pushing the force of the outlawed Karen National Union eastward into the border areas with Thailand, virtually eliminating Muslim insurgent groups, and cutting the strength of communist and other groups to that of limited, guerrilla-type organizations. Despite these successes, insurgency threatened to increase in the late 1950s when members of the Shan, Kayah, and Kachin ethnic groups that had theretofore remained loyal began to complain that the government was encroaching on affairs they considered properly to belong to the states. Many in Shan State were also alienated by official anti-CIF campaigns, in which the Burmese armed forces had failed to distinguish between local ethnic minorities and the outlawed CIF groups.

In consequence, Shan and Kayah ethnic groups began to call for the implementation of provisions included in the 1947 constitution, which explicitly granted Shan and Kayah states the right to secede from the Union of Burma 10 years after independence. After the government discouraged these aspirations and in 1959 persuaded Shan *sawbwas* (chieftains) to relinquish their traditional powers and hereditary rights, ethnic insurgency erupted in Shan State among those who disapproved of the *sawbwa* decision. A second evacuation of CIF remnants in 1961–62 again depleted but did not exhaust their numbers, and the situation in northern and northeastern Burma worsened steadily. After the military suspended the 1947 constitution in 1962, insurgency in Shan, Kachin, and Kayah states grew still more ative.

Thereafter, the character of insurgent activity in Burma as a whole underwent a change. As the government consolidated its control over the central part of the country in the 1960s, the locus of antigovernment activity shifted to the eastern border areas— especially to Shan State—and increasingly, insurgency became a phenomenon restricted to ethnic minorities. This transformation became particularly apparent after the destruction of strongholds of the White Flag faction of the BCP in the Pegu Yoma in 1967–68 and the nearly simultaneous reorganization of a new BCP insurgency along the Chinese border in Shan State.

Established under Chinese guidance, the new BCP was composed overwhelmingly of Shan, Kachin, Wa, and other ethnic minorities, recruited from both sides of the Burma-China border (see The Nationalities Issue and Insurgency, ch. 1). By the early 1970s, with the aid of Chinese-supplied arms, training, and equipment, it was able to assemble an army some several thousand strong and to control a strip along the Chinese border in Shan State some 12 to 30 kilometers wide, stretching from near Namhkam in the north to near Keng Tung in the south. Although its forces sometimes clashed with other insurgents operating in the area, the BCP, by virtue of its capacity to supply arms to major Kachin and Shan separatist groups, was able to forge shifting alliances with them and with other small, armed rebel groups. By the early 1970s government forces rarely crossed into the area east of the Salween River in Shan State and then kept only to major roads and towns.

Armed opposition in Burma also increased in the early 1970s after the exiled former prime minister, U Nu, in 1969 formed a movement to restore parliamentary democracy in the nation. His group, based in Thailand, worked in a loose alliance with insurgent groups on the Thai border. U Nu resigned from the group in 1972, but remnants of the movement claimed responsibility for terrorist attacks on targets in central Burma and elsewhere during the early and mid-1970s. The U Ne Win regime was not seriously threatened, however, and the movement attracted few followers. Relatively inactive in the late 1970s, it apparently collapsed altogether after certain of its leaders surrendered during an amnesty declared in 1980.

Problems in Shan State and in other border areas were compounded in the 1970s by the growing black market and narcotics trade, which not only provided insurgent groups with lucrative sources of revenue but also encouraged the growth and proliferation of established independent armed groups, organized to protect illicit market and drug trafficking activities. These groups, including the Shan United Army and groups run by the CIF (remnants of which remained entrenched in Shan State), battled among themselves and with government forces for control of territory and trade routes, contributing significantly to the increasing disorder in eastern border areas.

In the mid-1970s the government began to make some headway, militarily, in containing rebel and outlaw groups in the northeastern part of the country and elsewhere. Most notable in this regard were government attacks against CIF remnants in 1975 that broke their hold on the opium trade and forced most members to retreat into Thailand. Additionally, from 1975 to 1978 Burmese armed forces turned back several major attempts by the BCP to expand its territory into southern Shan State.

In combating the complex mixture of insurgency and lawlessness in the late 1970s and the early 1980s, the government has continued to use a variety of tactics in addition to military action. It has sought to mobilize the population against the insurgents and to undercut support for them by organizing frequent anti-insurgency rallies and demonstrations and by publicly characterizing rebels as drug dealers, bandits, and perpetrators of heinous crimes against the rest of the population. Village defense units, known as the People's Militia, have been established throughout the country and were regularly enlisted in internal security campaigns. Armed forces units operating in border areas were repeatedly cautioned to respect the cultural traditions and customs of local residents so as not to drive them into the enemy camp.

The government has also tried to persuade insurgents to lay down their arms. In mid-1980 it declared a general amnesty for those charged with political offenses, offering many an added inducement to surrender by enacting new laws granting awards and pensions to veterans of the struggle for independence. Several communist and ethnic insurgents, as well as former prime minister U Nu and members of his group, responded. A few opposition politicians living in exile also returned to Burma.

In another attempt to combat insurgency using peaceful means, the government met separately with representatives of the BCP and the Kachin Independence Organization in 1980 and 1981 in an attempt to negotiate a political settlement with each. Both efforts were unsuccessful, however, because the government was firmly committed to the 1974 Constitution and to its provisions for a one-party state, while both insurgent groups demanded they be allowed to enter the government under a multiparty framework. Kachin demands for autonomy for Kachin State and BCP demands that it keep control over its "liberated" areas were also unacceptable to the government, as were the objectives of each group to maintain armed forces separate from those of the government.

The government has been sensitive to any international dimension to local insurgency. It worked hard to keep relations with Bangladesh cordial during the flight of refugees from Rakhine State in 1977–78, in part to preclude foreign support for any insurgent reaction. Discussions with Thailand have often centered on efforts to persuade that government to take a more active role against insurgents and drug dealers operating from sanctuaries in that country.

Since the early 1970s, when it became apparent that Chinese aid to the BCP and other groups in northern and northeastern Burma was fanning the flames of insurgency in those regions, the government has worked to develop close and cordial relations with China to forestall support for local rebels. Conciliatory gestures went so far as to include forbidding Burmese armed forces to operate within five kilometers of the border with China, lest stray bullets fall in that nation. These diplomatic overtures were rewarded in the late 1970s by China's apparent decision to pursue closer state-to-state relations with noncommunist nations in Asia and to downgrade party-to-party relations with fraternal communist parties, including the BCP.

In the face of the new Chinese priorities and the subsequent sharp drop-off in Chinese aid, the BCP, whose ideology has closely mirrored that of China since the 1960s, concluded that it must change its military strategy to take into account both the failures of its campaigns in the 1970s and the changed international situation. In 1979 the BCP indicated in broadcasts transmitted over its China-based radio station that it would discontinue large-scale military action against Burma and would focus instead on guerrilla warfare designed in large part to ensure the party's self-defense. Burma has benefited since then by the reduced aggressiveness and capability of the BCP; this strategy has also weakened other rebel groups that had relied on the BCP to supply them with arms and ammunition and contributed to disunity among antigovernment forces as alliances based on arms transfers fractured or failed.

Despite these developments, however, during the 1978–82 period the Burmese armed forces were estimated to have suffered 100 to 200 casualties monthly in counterinsurgency campaigns. These figures were much higher during large government operations east of the Salween River in the 1979–80 dry season when government forces—moving within five kilometers of the Chinese border for the first time—were generally unsuccessful in loosening the BCP's hold on that region. Casualties were also higher during operations in 1980 and 1981 against rebel strongholds in Karen State.

The Black Market and the Opium Trade

As of early 1983 it had become very difficult to distinguish the problems of insurgency from those of the black market network and the international narcotics trade because most antigovernment groups were heavily involved in one, if not both, pursuits. For the CIF, the Shan United Army, and a few other groups, this was not a new development; they had always been armed commercial enterprises. Most ethnic insurgents and the BCP, however, had organized for political purposes. Although they often had engaged in smuggling, permitted poppy cultivation in their areas, or allowed passage of opium caravans through territories they controlled, most clearly had not been oriented primarily toward illicit commercial activities.

The distinction between armed economic enterprises and others came to be less clear-cut in the mid-1970s. Official economic programs, which put controls on the import of consumer goods and increased public sector participation in the retail and distribution network, produced an unintended by-product—the black market quickly mushroomed as basic and luxury goods became increasingly difficult to obtain. Some of the subsequent rapid growth in smuggling of black market goods took place across the borders with Bangladesh and India to the west, but the large majority of smugglers went east to the borders with Thailand, where Shan and Karen insurgents, among others, controlled territory. These groups quickly developed large and lucrative businesses, taxing and transporting the outflow of such goods as jade, antiques, gems, minerals, and teak, as well as of returning cargos, which included everything from Japanese motorcycles and electronics to housewares, edibles, and weaponry. Other insurgent groups also profited by selling protection to smugglers who passed through territory under their control.

As of early 1983 the black market remained a ubiquitous feature of urban and village life throughout the nation—flourishing to a certain extent because the government lacked sufficient resources to control it and because the demand for goods unavailable elsewhere made for high profits to smugglers and to those who turned a blind eye to their activities. More important, however, was the fact that national authorities appeared to view the black market, or the underground economy, in a somewhat ambiguous manner, which was then reflected in the tactics used to control it. On the one hand, insofar as the black market provided critical support for insurgent groups, diverted sorely needed customs revenues, and encouraged among many a psychology of noncompliance with the law, it was viewed negatively. In this regard, law enforcement officials sought to combat what they characterized as "economic insurgency" with regular military campaigns against insurgent smuggling groups. They also set up checkpoints on road, river, and rail routes to Rangoon and other cities and offered reward to those who reported black marketeers and smugglers to the authorities. On the other hand, it was clear that the black market served the government positively insofar as it functioned as a safety valve to allay public discontent by satisfying consumer demands that could not otherwise be met under the prevailing economic conditions or the official development priorities. In consequence, although major offenders sometimes attracted official displeasure, local illegal dealers were rarely if ever shut down, and those who bought or possessed black market goods were not prosecuted. Lacking more thoroughgoing control measures or a substantial change in economic conditions, the black market promised to remain a persistent feature of life in the nation.

The government viewed one branch of the black market—opium smuggling—with uncompromising seriousness, however. Introduced into Burma by Portuguese traders in the early nineteenth century, opium poppies have since been grown by many hill peoples for medicinal and recreational purposes and because opium has been a valuable cash crop. Until 1948 cultivation was legal east of the Salween River, and laws forbidding its use and production elsewhere were not vigorously enforced. The situation changed only very slowly after independence, and it was not until the 1960s that strict antinarcotics legislation was passed, opium dens in Shan State and elsewhere were closed down, and limited crop substitution programs were initiated. Unfortunately, by that time both the scope of production and the international demand for illegal narcotics were too great for these measures to have much effect.

In the late 1960s, after international law enforcement officials shut down opium refineries in Europe and elsewhere, CIF groups and independent operators began to set up refineries on the Burma-Thailand border. Within a short time large amounts of heroin appeared on the streets of Rangoon and other cities, and heroin addiction, especially among the young, became a serious problem for the first time.

The government reacted strongly to this development. New, stiffer penalties for drug-related offenses were passed in 1974. During the same year, in order to upgrade the capabilities of the armed forces and the police to find and destroy poppy fields, opium caravans, and heroin refineries, the Burmese accepted several helicopters and light aircraft from the United States. In 1975 the armed forces ended CIF domination of the drug trade. Also in 1975 the government initiated a multifaceted antidrug program entailing crop eradication, law enforcement, income and crop substitution, opium transport interdiction, and addict rehabilitation. Buttressed by a 1981 law offering rewards to those who turned in offenders, the program was continuing as of early 1983.

These efforts have done little to reduce poppy cultivation and opium traficking, however. The Shan United Army took advantage of the disruptions caused by the government's initiatives and expanded its own operations, controlling some 70 to 80 percent of the trade by 1978. After its hold was broken in early 1982, several other groups, including the BCP, were poised to take over.

Crop substitution has had only a limited effect. Cultivators were generally very poor and lived in areas where there were no roads or developed resources; opium was therefore a specially valued cash crop because it was low in volume, easily transportable, and highly profitable. Even though thousands of hectares of poppies were destroyed by hand each year (herbicides being considered too dangerous to use), a far larger amount evaded discovery by the armed forces and the police. Moreover, opium smuggling routes were generally narrow, tree-lined mountain paths that were almost impossible to spot by air and difficult to reach by ground, and refineries were usually small, portable, and easily camouflaged.

As of early 1983 Burma remained the largest producer of opium in the Golden Triangle, from which an estimated one-third of the world's supply of illegal narcotics originated. Poppies were cultivated in regions over 900 meters above sea level throughout much of the Shan Plateau area, stretching from eastern Kachin State near the Chinese border south nearly 1,000 kilometers into Kayah State. Prime growing areas were located east of the Salween River and north of Keng Tung. From 1976 to 1978 an estimated 300 to 400 tons of opium was produced in the nation annually, approximately one-half of which was then sold on the world market. In 1979 and 1980 production was affected by a severe drought, but in 1981 and 1982 crops may have run as high as 500 tons annually.

Raw opium gathered from the poppy was usually first refined—close to where it was grown—into a morphine base, using a simple process that reduced its volume by a factor of 10. Trafficking organizations then transported the base by human porters or mule caravans to refineries located several hundred kilometers distant. Most of the refineries were situated in Burma a few hundred meters from the Thai border, where they could be readily moved out of reach of Burmese authorities as the need arose. Unconfirmed press reports in 1982 stated that the BCP had also established refineries at its headquarters at Pang Hsang near the border with China. Chemicals necessary for converting the morphine base into heroin for smoking or for intravenous use were usually supplied illegally from industrial sources in Thailand or Malaysia. Most heroin reached world markets through northern Thailand, but other routes included transit through central Burma to the Andaman Sea or down the coast of Tenasserim Division to Malaysia.

Revolutionary, Separatist, and Warlord Groups

One observer of the Burmese scene has noted that although in practice the distinctions between national insurgent groups were often blurred, all could be classified as one of three kinds according to their organizational goals. The first, revolutionary movements, were established to overthrow the existing central government and create a new structure in its place. As of early 1983, U Nu's movement being defunct, only the BCP was representative of this kind. Ethnically rooted insurgencies, however, were legion. In fact, it has been said that in Burma, if a group was ethnically distinct from the Burmans or other ethnic groups, then it would be represented by at least one insurgent movement—the only exceptions as of early 1983 appearing to be persons defined as nonnationals under the new citizenship law. Unlike the revolutionaries, ethnic insurgents were interested only in ruling their own people and territory and sought either greater autonomy from the central government or outright independence. A third group belonged to what were characterized as warlord associations, organized feudally around one or more leaders in order to conduct illicit market activities and control trade routes. The last kind were essentially armed economic enterprises and included, among others, the CIF groups and the Shan United Army.

Despite these differences in basic goals, the day-to-day operations of most groups were often indistinguishable because all had to devote significant resources and attention to supporting themselves. The raison d'être of warlord groups was precisely that, of course, and they were not troubled by the need to balance any other considerations. As became clear in the late 1970s and early 1980s, however, other groups often found that administering commercial interests could work to the detriment of maintaining group cohesiveness. Even incidental participation in commerce appeared to carry temptations for deeper involvement, leading to the development of rivalries between individual entrepreneurs. Political ideals were also undermined as some group members became more interested in securing profits than in working to achieve political goals. Moreover, the complexity of black market and opium trade operations created attractive opportunities for individuals to set up their own specialized operations, either as a sideline activity or as an independent splinter organization.

Geography, ethnic diversity, and commercial considerations worked to keep groups small and mutually competitive. At the same time, however, a countervailing factor encouraged the formation of alliances that were temporary and limited in scope: groups were not powerful enough to defend themselves independently against all their opponents or to control single-handedly all aspects of the black market and narcotics trade. Instead, they often found it efficacious to cooperate toward certain limited goals or to rally opponents against a common enemy, whether it be the Burmese government or a commercial or political rival.

One example of formal cooperation among ethnic insurgents for the sake of enhanced strength was the National Democratic Front (NDF), founded in 1975. The five groups within the NDF were geographically isolated from each other, however, and the organization met for the second time only in 1982, when three other groups joined its ranks. As of early 1983 the NDF had served as little more than a forum for discussion.

Many insurgent groups have been successful in securing support from external sources, the BCP's ties with China being only the most obvious example. Some noncommunist insurgent groups that operated in eastern Burma have maintained sanctuaries in Thailand, where they were officially viewed both as security forces against the insurgent Communist Party of Thailand and as buffers between Thailand and its historical enemy, Burma. Most notable in this regard were the CIF groups, members of which established legal residence in Chiang Rai Province, Thailand, in 1971. Until 1982 the Shan United Army also worked out of strongholds in Thailand and reportedly maintained close ties with senior government officials of that country. Bases in Thailand were subsequently destroyed, however.

Some insurgent groups have been successful in attracting support from the Burmese government itself in return for fighting other insurgents and drug traffickers. For instance, about 50 small private armies obtained patents from the Burmese government in 1966–67 allowing them to continue their smuggling activities in return for carrying out anticommunist operations in Shan State. Many of these groups, which were designated Ka Kwe Yei (KKY), or official militias, used their status to enhance their own interests or to move deeper into the drug trade, however, and only contributed to the growing lawlessness and disorder in the area. All KKY were declared illegal in the 1971–73 period.

In 1980 the Burmese government commissioned a group formed by Lo Hsing-han as an anti-BCP militia. Lo was an ex-KKY leader, who from 1967 until his arrest in 1973 for drug dealing was referred to as the King of the Golden Triangle. He was released from a Burmese prison during the 1980 amnesty, and his new militia included members of his old organization who had returned from Thailand under the same amnesty provisions. Should the Burmese government's support prove insufficient, Lo's group, the Shan State Volunteer Force, possessed the expertise to become a very effective drug trafficking organization.

Insurgent groups have also sought, and sometimes received, support from other external sources. From the 1950s until the early 1960s, the United States reportedly supplied aid to CIF groups, considering them a possible tool for use against China. Taiwan has also provided assistance to CIF groups as well as others, including the Shan United Army. Attempts by Shan State insurgents and warlord groups to strike deals with the United States have been firmly rejected, however. From 1972 to 1982 these groups made annual offers, often in letters to the president of the United States, to "solve the drug problem" by making preemptive sales of their drug stocks in return for financial and political support.

The North and the Northeast

Approximately 19 groups were believed to operate in Kachin and Shan states as of the early 1980s (see table A; fig. 13). These included the nation's largest insurgent group (the BCP), major Kachin and Shan ethnic separatist organizations, and several other ethnically based groups, as well as drug trafficking operations, such as the Shan United Army and the CIF groups. Insurgent groups, factions, and alliances have been subject to frequent change over the years, however, making it difficult to compile a final and inclusive account of their numbers, size, goals, or activities. Moreover, what little information that was available was not always reliable.

As of early 1983 the BCP was less a unified political movement than a loose confederation of ethnic minorities that were drawn together by organizing convenience. Many of these small groups have at various times left and then returned to the BCP fold. As of

Table A.   *Insurgent Groups, 1983[1]*

Location	Group Name (Leader)	Estimated Armed Strength	Supplementary Information
North and north-eastern Burma	Burmese Communist Party (Chairman Thakin Ba Thein Tin)	8,000–15,000	Includes Northeastern Command, Northwestern Command, 815th Military Region, Rakhine and Tenasserim structures. Personnel primarily drawn from Shan, Kachin, Wa, Lahu, Akha, Lisu, and other ethnic minority groups.
	Kachin Independence Organization (leader unknown)	4,500–8,000	Ally of Burmese Communist Party (BCP). Personnel primarily ethnic Kachins.
	Shan State Army[2] (Sao Hso Lane)	2,000–4,000	Member of National Democratic Front (NDF).[3] Personnel primarily ethnic Shans.
	Shan United Revolutionary Army (Mo Heng AKA Mo Hein)[4]	2,000–3,000	Ally of Third Chinese Irregular Forces. Personnel primarily ethnic Shans.
	Shan United Army (Khun Sa AKA Chang Chi-fu AKA Sao Mong Khawn)	1,400–8,000	Warlord organization. Personnel include ethnic Chinese, Shans, other minorities.
	Third Chinese Irregular Forces (General Li Wen-huan)	1,500–2,000	Remnant of 93d Nationalist Chinese Army.
	Fifth Chinese Irregular Forces (General Lei Yu-tien)	300–500	Remnant of 93d Nationalist Chinese Army.
	Shan State Volunteer Force (Lo Hsing-han)	500–700	Commissioned by Burmese government as an anti-insurgent militia in 1980.
	Wa National Army—Ma Ha San Faction (Ma Ha San)	approx. 300	Ally of Ai Hsiao-shih Group.
	Wa National Army (leader unknown)	approx. 150	Affiliation uncertain.
	Ai Hsiao-shih Group (Ai's wife, Li I-Ming)	approx. 150	Ally of Wa National Army—Ma Ha San Faction.
	A Bi Group (A Bi AKA A Pi)	approx. 200	Splinter of Lahu State Army and ally of BCP.
	Lahu State Army (Chau Ehr AKA Paya Ja Veh AKA Cha Eu Paya)	approx. 100	Member of NDF.
	United Pa-O Organization (leader unknown)	approx. 100	Ally of BCP. May be identical with Pa-O Shan State Independence Party or Pa-O Liberation Army.

Table A.—*Continued*

Location	Group Name (Leader)	Estimated Armed Strength	Supplementary Information
	Shan State Nationalities Liberation Organization (Tha Kalei)	n.a.	Ally of BCP.
	Pa-O National Organization (leader unknown)	n.a.	Member of NDF.
	Tai National Army (leader unknown)	50–75	n.a.
	Palaung State Liberation Organization (leader unknown)	approx. 50	Member of NDF.
	Yang Hwe-kang Group (Yang Hwe-kang)	50–100	Former element of Fifth Chinese Irregular Forces.
South-eastern Burma	Karen National Union (General Bo Mya)	approx. 5,000–8,000	Member of NDF: military arm is Karen National Liberation Army.
	Karenni National Progress Party (leader unknown)	approx. 500	Member of NDF: military arm is Karenni Liberation Army.
	Kayah New Land Revolution Council (leader unknown)	approx. 50	Ally of BCP.
	Karenni People's United Liberation Front (Than Nyunt)	approx. 70	Ally of BCP.
	New Mon State Party (Schwe Kyan)	approx. 100	Member of NDF.
Western Burma	Rohingya Patriotic Front (Mohammad Jafar Habib)	approx. 150	Possibly identical with Arakan Liberation Party.
	Arakan Liberation Party	n.a.	Member of NDF.
	Naga Group (exact name and leader unknown)	approx. 150	Possibly some links to Kachin Independence Organization.
	Chin Group (exact name and leader unknown)	approx. 50	Probably operating in southern Chin State.

n.a.—not available.

[1]Information cannot be regarded as authoritative or final. Groups, factions, and alliances are continually changing, and what little information is available may not be completely reliable.

[2]Military arm of Shan State Progress Party.

[3]National Democratic Front (NDF), created in 1975 to coordinate military operations and form a united antigovernment force. Established as a democratic alternative to the government and the Burmese Communist Party, the NDF met for a second time in mid-1982.

[4]AKA—also known as.

Source: Based on information from Charles B. Smith, Jr. (comp.), "Burmese Insurgent and Warlord Groups," February 6, 1983.

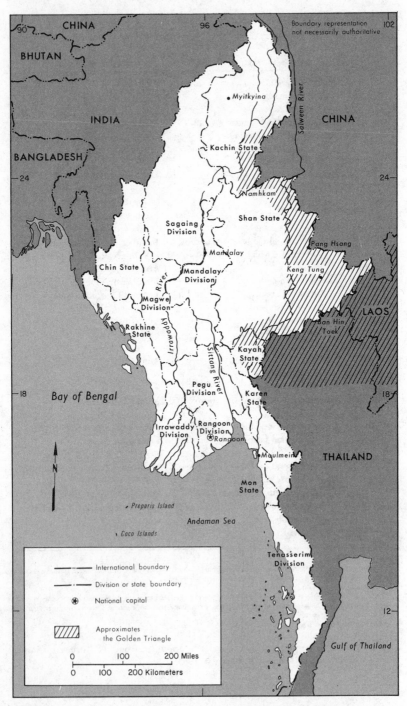

Figure 13. *Geographic Distribution of Insurgents, 1983*

Shan and Kachin states

Burmese Communist Party
Kachin Independence Organization
Shan State Army
Shan United Revolutionary Army
Shan United Army
Third Chinese Irregular Forces
Fifth Chinese Irregular Forces
Shan State Volunteer Force
Wa National Army—Ma Ha San Faction
Wa National Army
Ai Hsiao-shih Group
A Bi Group
Lahu State Army
United Pa-O Organization
Shan State Nationalities Liberation Organization
Pa-O National Organization
Tai National Army
Palaung State Liberation Organization
Yang Hwe-kang Group

Rakhine and Chin states and Sagaing Division

Rohingya Patriotic Front
Arakan Liberation Party
Naga Group
Chin Group

Karen and Kayah states

Karen National Union
Karenni National Progress Party
Kayah New Land Revolution Council
Karenni People's United Liberation Front
New Mon State Party

Figure 13. Continued.

early 1983 the BCP's major base area was located in Shan State east of the Salween River along the entire length of the Chinese border. Smaller enclaves were reportedly maintained along he Chinese border in Kachin State and in other parts of Shan State, particularly west of the Salween near Lashio. The BCP claimed to have additional very small units operating in Rakhine State and in Tenasserim and Magwe divisions.

In justifying its insurgency, the BCP has worked hard to differentiate itself from the avowedly socialist Burmese government by attacking the latter's economic, land reform, and ethnic relations policies. It has repeatedly accused the "Ne Win-San Yu military regime" of representing the forces of "imperialism, feudal landlordism, and bureaucratic capitalism" and has vowed to construct a united front, led by the BCP and the working class, in order to establish a new "people's democratic republic." The BCP has also promised to pursue an agrarian revolution under the slogan "Those who work the land must own the land," in recognition of the critical role that the nation's rural population would have to play in any successful revolution. The BCP has indicated that it would welcome the participation of all ethnic minorities, the petite bourgeoisie, and national capitalists in forming the people's democratic republic but noted that once that was accomplished, a second stage of revolution aimed at building socialism would commence, and struggle would ensue on a class basis.

Despite these efforts to attract the broad support needed to overthrow the Burmese government, as of early 1983 the BCP appeared to have virtually no following in central Burma. Its membership, claimed in party documents to be some 3,000 in 1979, was drawn primarily from minority ethnic groups in Kachin and Shan states. That made it very difficult for the Burman ethnic majority to view the BCP as a serious alternative to the present government rather than just another minority ethnic insurgency. At the same time, the BCP's ability to attract increased support was sometimes frustrated among minority ethnic groups as well; the BCP leadership in Beijing consisted largely of ethnic Burmans, and the group's aspirations to form a new central government were antithetical to the separatists' own desires for independence or increased autonomy.

The BCP's organizational structure was headed by the Politburo and the larger Central Committee. It extended downward through communist-designated district and township committees and in some locations also included small "people's administrative bodies" in villages. The BCP maintained mass organizations, such as peasants' and women's unions and youth associations. It also ran schools and hospitals in most areas under its control. In 1980 a party training school was opened near the party headquarters at Pang Hsang to strengthen the grasp of BCP doctrine by party and military leaders, the latter of whom reportedly were very weak in this area.

Since the cutoff of Chinese aid in the late 1970s forced the BCP to become more self-sufficient, it has relied increasingly on profits derived from the opium trade to supplement revenues raised from taxing agricultural production in its area. The BCP's Shan State territory encompassed the Golden Triangle's most productive poppy-growing regions, some 40 to 70 percent of the total opium crop being estimated to grow there. When the BCP first became active in the region in the late 1960s, it made attempts to reduce the reliance of the resident hill tribes on poppy cultivation and in the mid-1970s officially imposed a ban on cultivation and trading. Enforcement was never complete, however, because the BCP was not able to control some of its own military commanders, who continued to maintain and develop the drug trade in their locales.

In the 1978–79 period the BCP abruptly changed its policies and began to boost poppy cultivation in its territory. It also attempted to make use of the experienced drug traders in its ranks and to establish its own trading routes to the border with Thailand. How much success the BCP has had with the latter was unclear as of early 1983. It clashed with other groups in 1979 and 1980 during efforts to move south and east of Keng Tung into areas near the Burma-Thailand border. It reportedly met with greater success in 1981 and 1982 in attempts to establish trading routes to the west of the Salween River and south through Kayah State, where it maintained alliances with two very small ethnic separatist movements.

The military arm of the BCP, the People's Army, was estimated to number some 8,000 to 15,000 in the early 1980s. Essentially a guerrilla force, it was a loose organization of units—some as large as battalion size—which operated primarily east of the Salween River. The People's Army was led by a central military committee, and party political cadres were assigned to all units. The command structure was reportedly too weak to enforce rigid discipline; many commanders and soldiers had only a vague understanding of the BCP's political stance, having joined the group less from ideological motivation than because it was the major antigovernment organization in the area.

Since the BCP abandoned its strategy of conducting multibattalion military campaigns against the Burmese government in the late 1970s, military operations have come to be characterized by the use of antipersonnel mines and by ambushes and raids on small government outposts. The People's Army has continued to rely on its Chinese-made arms, but ammunition was reported to be in short supply during the early 1980s.

The Kachin Independence Organization (KIO), at least some elements of which have been allied with the BCP, has dominated vast, but by and large economically unimportant areas of mountains, forests, and jungles in Kachin State since the 1960s. It was generally regarded as a collection of partly rightist and partly leftist elements that had originally joined together in the late 1950s to press for an independent Kachin State. The KIO reportedly controlled gem deposits of uncertain size in Kachin State from which gold, jade, and precious stones were mined and then sold on the black market. Its territory encompassed poppy-growing areas, enabling the KIO to derive revenues from opium sales.

The KIO was estimated to have an army some 4,500 to 8,000 strong in the early 1980s. As an ally of the BCP, it enjoyed access to Chinese-made arms until the late 1970s. Shortages after that time forced the KIO to limit its military operations mainly to attacks on government buildings and, in 1981, on a Myitkyina theater, in which a bomb killed some 60 civilians.

Cooperation between the KIO and the BCP was initiated in the early 1970s on the basis of the two organizations' shared short-term goals of challenging government control in the area. According to reports broadcast by the BCP, the alliance became closer in 1980—despite the arms cutoff—when the KIO agreed to forswear its goal of independence for Kachin State and joined hands with the BCP in a united front effort to topple the Burmese government. Subsequent KIO demands for a separate political party, expressed during its negotiations with the Burmese government during the 1980–81 period, provided supporting evidence that at least some elements of the KIO had decided to pursue greater regional autonomy instead of total independence. Reports appeared in the international press in 1982 that the KIO has actually split along Christian rightist and pro-BCP lines, but as of early 1983 these could not be confirmed.

Another sometime ally of the BCP was the Shan State Army (SSA), the political arm of which, the Shan State Progress Party, was formed from a 1963 union of Shan separatist movements. Although styling itself a legitimate separatist group, the SSA also has a history of involvement in the drug trade. From 1963 until 1967 when the CIF preempted its role, the SSA supported itself almost entirely through opium trafficking. After 1971 it again entered the drug trade, first in alliance with Lo Hsing-han and then independently. Dissension over the propriety of such activities provoked a split in the SSA's ranks in 1976, one brigade allying itself with the BCP in the area near Pang Hsang. In 1979 the breakaway faction, angered by the BCP's interference with Buddhist religious practices, returned to the SSA. Fighting was reported between SSA and BCP forces in 1980, and all ties were thought to have been broken off. Battle reports in 1982, however, indicated that at least some units were still cooperating with the BCP.

As of early 1983 the SSA's main base area was located in southern Shan State near the Burma-Thailand border. It also claimed to have units operating in northern and central Shan State. Its strength was estimated to include some 2,000 to 4,000 men armed mainly with BCP-supplied Chinese weapons.

The Shan United Revolutionary Army (SURA) was another group that had originally been formed as a separatist organization but was heavily involved in the narcotics trade in the early 1980s. Formerly the Tangyan KKY, it was the SSA's major rival separatist group in Shan State and since 1972 has skirmished constantly with that group. Conflict occurred mainly on trade corridors through which opium and jade caravans travel. The SURA claimed to have 2,000 to 3,000 armed fighter in five permanent camps. They were reportedly armed with United States-made weapons obtained through Laos during the Vietnam Conflict or bought on the black market in Thailand. The SURA maintained a press that published educational and political texts in the Shan language. Its constitution provided for a federal organization of tribal groups under a parliamentary democratic framework that would ensure the preservation of tribal and ethnic heritages.

In an interview in 1982, the leader of the SURA, Mo Heng, stated that the group was an anticommunist ethnic separatist movement that disapproved of the opium trade but allowed those living within its territory to cultivate poppies because local residents were too poor to survive otherwise. The SURA maintained close ties with a very experienced CIF drug-trafficking organization, in addition to Wa and Lahu groups that were also active in the drug trade. It derived significant revenues from taxing poppy cultivation and setting levies on the traffic of black market goods moving in and out of Thailand.

A number of other ethnic insurgent groups also operated in Shan State. These included Wa, Lahu, Palaung, and Pa-O groups, most of which were very small and basically sought to rule themselves according to their own traditions and to prevent outside interference in their activities. Relatively unsophisticated politically, some have been allied at one time or another with the BCP while others have been identified as members of the noncommunist NDF. Most members of these groups were primitive tribesmen: in 1973 scores of members of one Lahu group were killed by government forces after their 80-year-old patriarch assured them they would be invulnerable to bullets if they fought from a standing position. The Wa National Army and the Lahu State Army in particular have been heavily involved in poppy cultivation and opium trafficking.

Approximately five major warlord organizations, in addition to various small syndicates and consortia, maintained private armies in northern and northeastern Burma. As of early 1983 these included the Shan United Army (SUA), two CIF groups, a CIF breakaway faction, and Lo Hsing-han's government-sponsored militia.

The SUA has had a colorful history, its fortunes and those of its leader, a half-Chinese, half-Shan known as Khun Sa or Chang Chi-fu, rising and falling again and again in a manner typifying the complex and unstable milieu insurgent groups inhabit. After breaking with the CIF in the early 1960s, Khun Sa was deputized by the Burmese government to form a village defense force at his birthplace, Loi-maw. By 1964, when he broke with the government, he had developed a small drug-running organization that had its own refineries and a safe haven in Thailand. In 1966 the government again deputized the group as the Loi-maw KKY, Khun Sa once more using the opportunity to continue building up his forces. Shortly thereafter, the CIF placed an embargo on the SUA's drug shipments, and in reaction Khun Sa's group fought a running battle with the CIF across Shan State in what came to be called the Opium War of 1967. The opium caravan in dispute was chased into Laos, where it was confiscated by the Laotian armed forces, and Khun Sa was arrested by the Burmese government.

The SUA's fortunes declined for the next few years until the group, under the command of Khun Sa's brother, kidnapped two Soviet doctors in 1973 from a hospital being built by the Soviet Union. The doctors were then exchanged for Khun Sa's release from prison to home confinement. In 1975 Khun Sa bribed his guards, escaped, and returned to take command of the SUA. When government forces broke the CIF control of the drug trade in 1975, Khan Sa and the SUA moved in and by 1978 had assumed the dominant role in Golden Triangle drug trafficking.

In the late 1970s and early 1980s, the SUA bought opium from fields controlled by the BCP and others, maintained mobile refineries, protected jade and opium caravans crossing Shan State, and sold opium to the ethnic Chinese syndicates in Thailand that controlled access to world markets. Estimates of SUA strength ranged from 1,400 to 8,000, the larger figure probably including a great number of part-time caravan guards and unarmed porters. Most forces were based along the Burma-Thailand border, with some remaining in the Loi-maw area and some near Ban Hin Taek, Thailand. Despite its name, Shan State residents did not generally regard the SUA as an ethnic separatist movement but referred to the group as the "Chinese from Loi-maw." Conscripts often had to be forcibly recruited.

Although the SUA has maintained a stronghold in Thailand for many years—suffering only occasional light harassment from that country's armed forces—in mid-1981 Thailand issued a warrant for Khun Sa's arrest and sent a small unit to Ban Hin Taek to capture him. Angered that additional armed forces then had to be sent to rescue the original unit, in early 1982 Thailand launched a full-scale attack on the stronghold, driving the SUA from its positions and destroying refineries and large quantities of drug stocks. Similar attacks followed in late 1982, and as of early 1983 the SUA was reported to be in complete disarray and its hold on the drug trade up for grabs.

The Southeast

The oldest of the ethnically rooted insurgencies was that mounted by the Karen National Union (KNU), the single most important antigovernment group in southeastern Burma. According to a 1981 statement by its leader, General Bo Mya, the KNU was a pro-Western, anticommunist organization seeking to establish a democratic Karen republic that would guarantee individual rights, freedom from corruption, and freedom of religion. The KNU was reported to have set up its own radio transmitter in late 1982 over which it hoped to broadcast its policies and attract greater support.

The KNU viewed its insurgency in a historic context. Karens and Burmans have battled each other for centuries; fighting during World War II between pro-British Karens and pro-Japanese or nationalist Burmans provokes particularly bitter memories. When it became clear that Britain intended to grant Burma its independence, Karen leaders formed the KNU to press for a separately administered territory. Although some Karens supported the formation of the Union of Burma, the KNU set up a military arm to press for separate status. During the immediate postindependence period, KNU troops, augmented by Karen and other units that had mutinied against the regular Burmese army, launched a military campaign designed to topple the new government. Although coming very close to succeeding, the KNU was eventually defeated by government forces and declared an illegal organization. By the mid-1950s it had been pushed back into the hills of Kawthule State (now Karen State) and into the western reaches of Thailand where it continued to maintain strongholds, control territory, and battle government forces in early 1983.

The KNU has supported itself by imposing levies on paddy and timber production and tin, wolfram, and antimony mining in the area under its control. It has also earned considerable revenues by assessing a 5-percent tax on the sizable volume of black market trade between Burma and Thailand, the largest portion of which traversed KNU-controlled territory. Although the KNU maintained alliance with groups in the narcotics trade, however, poppies were not cultivated in Karen State, and as of early 1983 the group did not engage in opium trafficking and has publicly expressed its intentions never to do so.

Most sources estimated that the military arm of the KNU, the Karen National Liberation Army (KNLA), numbered some 5,000 to 8,000 armed fighters. KNU leaders claimed that the number would be far higher were weapons and ammunition not in such short supply. The KNLA was armed with weapons captured from government forces, including mortars, machine guns, and rifles. It also bought arms on the black market, usually United States-made items, such as M-16 rifles and M-79 grenade launchers recovered from the Vietnam Conflict. Organized into six brigades, when not engaged in combat with government forces the KNLA aided in the administration of KNU territory, assessed and collected taxes, and patrolled for or escorted smugglers.

Since the late 1970s the government has mounted regular campaigns against the KNU, putting the group on the defensive—able to beat back its attackers and hold onto the area under its control but not often moving beyond it. In September 1982, however, five heavily armed KNU members attacked a police station and the headquarters of the Burma Broadcasting Service in Rangoon. Government forces killed two and captured the other three, after two policemen were killed and 17 people, including eight civilians, were wounded. According to reports in the *Far Eastern Economic Review*, analysts in Rangoon suggested that the attack was designed to bolster unity in the KNU, whose forces were reportedly divided between those closely tied to the revolutionary cause and those more interested in the economic rewards of the smuggling trade.

The KNU was sometimes joined in its operations by soldiers of the small New Mon State Party based to its south near the Three Pagoda Pass area. That group sought to establish an independent Mon state, with its capital at Moulmein. In the early 1980s its leaders and many of its members lived across the border in Thailand as did many members of the KNU.

The KNU also sometimes cooperated with Karenni (Kayah) groups based in the remote jungles of Kayah State. The largest of these was the Karenni National Progress Party (KNPP), a noncommunist movement that based its claims for an independent Karenni nation on an 1875 treaty between the Burmese kings and Britain. According to the KNPP, that treaty, which stated that the Karenni states (Kayah State) would remain a separate and independent territory, made the original inclusion of Kayah State into the Union of Burma illegal. The KNPP exercised political and administrative control over affairs in its territory, running schools and hospitals and appointing village chiefs. Like the Mon and Karen groups, the KNPP financed its activities with revenues from local mines and by assessing customs duties on smuggled goods. Unlike the former, however, the KNPP permitted the cultivation of opium poppies in its territory and reportedly also engaged in narcotics trafficking.

The military arm of the KNPP, the Karenni Liberation Army, was estimated to be some 500 strong in the early 1980s. Its soldiers, who were often trained by the Karens, have clashed with BCP forces to the north as well as with two other very small procommunist Karenni groups, the Kayah New Land

Revolution Council and the Karenni People's United Liberation Front.

The West

Insurgency in the western border areas occurred on a far smaller scale than in other outlying areas in Burma. Aside from a very small communist movement in Rakhine State that was aligned with the BCP, most antigovernment groups were ethnically based.

In Rakhine State most of these were Muslim groups, formed either by groups with links to Bangladesh—as was the case with the Rohingya Patriotic Front—or by residents of ethnic Indian enclaves. Groups of the latter kind were often differentiated by their members' affiliations with particular Indian subnationalities and were less armed insurgencies than secret brotherhoods organized to promote and protect member's interests and cultural heritages.

A small ethnic Chin group, name unknown, appeared to be operating in southern Chin State during the early 1980s. In Sagaing Division, ethnic Nagas living along the India-Burma border were seeking autonomy from both India and Burma and have claimed responsibility for antigovernment acts in the early 1980s.

Armed Forces

Although the nation took pride in its precolonial military traditions, the roots of the modern defense establishment lay in two very different military organizations, the British colonial Burmans during the colonial period, the Burma Army was thorpendence Army (BIA) and its successors. The former, organized to serve British colonial interests, was manned primarily by Indians and by Burmese ethnic minorities. Widely resented by ethnic Burmans during the colonial period, the Burma Arm was thoroughly discredited in the eyes of most Burmese by its hasty retreat before advancing Japanese forces in 1942.

The BIA, however, was an ethnic Burman organization that, although formed in late 1941 under Japanese guidance, had as its core elements a group of Burman nationalists known as the Thirty Comrades. These men, convinced that independence could be achieved only through armed struggle, had left British-controlled Burma in 1940 to seek military aid and training from the Japanese. Forming the cadre of the BIA, they accompanied the Japanese army in its invasion of Burma, mobilizing Burman nationalist sentiments. Under Japanese rule, the BIA was forcibly demobilized, but a smaller Burmese military organization was retained, first under the name Burma Defense Army and then, after the Japanese granted Burma "independence" in 1943, as the Burma National Army. Trained by the Japanese, both forces were under the nominal leadership of General Aung San, the leader of the Thirty Comrades, and his comrade-in-arms, Brigadier Ne Win.

Disenchanted with Japanese overlordship, which quickly proved even more repressive than British rule, nationalist military and civilian leaders formed an underground antifascist organization in 1944, and on March 25, 1945, General Aung San led the Burmese forces in an uprising against the Japanese. In recognition of the army's switch to the Allied side, it was rechristened the Patriotic Burmese Forces (PBF). As the military arm of the newly formed Burmese political party, the Anti-Fascist People's Freedom League (AFPFL), and the first independent Burmese army since the nineteenth century, the PBF emerged from World War II with the identity of a legitimate nationalist political and military force. It became a symbol of a time when all Burmese had been unified against a common enemy.

When the British attempted to reestablish colonial rule in 1945, a new Burma Army was formed from a merger of the old colonial forces and the PBF. Under the terms of an agreement between General Aung San and the British, the PBF was disbanded, some of its members entering the new army as part of five battalions of the Burma Rifles. Only an estimated 200 PBF officers were incorporated into the new structure, the top leadership of which remained in British hands. In theory, the Burman units differed only in name from Shan, Chin, Kachin, and Karen battalions that had been established at the same time in recognition of wartime contributions to the British cause. In practice, however, the four minority ethnic battalions and the five Burman ones, including the Fourth Burma Rifles led by Brigadier Ne Win, were clearly separated by ethnic cleavages and by differing military traditions and experiences.

The underlying defects in both the merger solution and the structure of the army itself quickly became apparent. The surplus of PBF members entered a private army, called the People's Volunteer Organization (PVO), which was allied with AFPFL. PVO branches were soon established in most districts and townships and came to represent a parallel and sometimes competing authority within the state. These problems were compounded by political disagreements among nationalist leaders who, though unified under the AFPFL rubric, represented a wide spectrum of ideologies and beliefs.Their differences were transmitted to PVO units and to the component battalions of the Burma Army, where many leaders served or maintained close contacts.

After General Aung San's assassination in July 1947, no nationalist leader had the requisite authority and prestige to stem the growing political chaos or to compel unity in the military. Immediately after independence, civil war erupted, and the new national army, which contained small naval and air elements, was wracked by mutinies in the ranks of some minority ethnic battalions and by widespread defections to the communist underground in the Burman ones.

The army emerged from these crises shorn of most of its ideological extremes, its leadership united in experience and firmly committed to establishing a unified and orderly socialist nation and to developing defense forces better able to perform those tasks. During the early and mid-1950s, the military continued to press against rebel forces and consolidate its own organization. Under the direction of the army commander, General Ne Win, the number of ground force battalions was greatly expanded. More importantly, all units were ethnically integrated, eliminating what had been a serious source of internal friction in the defense services. The army and navy were also confirmed as separate branches.

The government's firm commitment to a nonaligned foreign policy and its persistent refusal after the early 1950s to accept anything it construed as foreign military aid, however, meant that qualitative equipment upgrading for the nascent forces had to be financed almost exclusively from the nation's own scarce national resources. This placed severe constraints on the armed forces development, for although the nearly constant anti-insurgency campaigns caused defense expenditures to account for over 30 percent of the total government budget in the 1950s and the 1960s, almost all defense outlays were taken up by current expenditures, leaving very little with which to make major, and sometimes even minor, equipment purchases.

Under these straitened circumstances, the armed forces were required to become very self-reliant, able to operate with little logistical support and under very spartan conditions. The ground forces, equipped mainly with light arms, developed into a small-unit, light infantry force, well suited to counterinsurgency campaigns. The navy and air force, by virtue of their small equipment inventories, functioned essentially as support elements for the army.

There was occasional relief from the stringent financial constraints that allowed for modest equipment upgrading, though not for a substantial improvement in overall capability. After the government reached agreement with a West German manufacturer in the late 1950s to establish a licensed production facility in Burma, scarce foreign currency no longer had to be spent on light arms and ammunition, and these items were less frequently in short supply. In the same period, military hardware was purchased from Yugoslavia, Israel, and the United States, the last with foreign military sales credits.

Although capable of exerting great influence in national politics during the 1948–62 period, the military leadership by and large had accepted civilian rule and kept the armed forces' role in the national life limited primarily to that of a conventional defense force. After Ne Win led a military coup in 1962, however, the armed forces' leadership took over the running of the country. Thereafter, the military was assigned the dual mission of defending the national security and developing a socialist state. In consequence, a large portion of the armed forces began to perform what were essentially nonmilitary tasks (see Political and Administrative Roles, this ch.)

In keeping with the new national direction, General Ne Win declared in 1968 that the military had to draw closer to the people and contribute more directly to socialist construction. He renamed the armed forces the People's Armed Forces and gave them a new motto: "Fight while producing, produce while fighting." He also announced a new military doctrine of waging a "people's war." After that time military units were called upon to aid in such projects as road and irrigation canal construction, bridge building, and rice harvesting. Village militias were formed, and national organizations throughout the nation began to be given regular military training.

Despite the armed forces' leading role in the nation after 1962, however, conditions in the services continued to be straitened. They were eased only slightly by the nation's improved economic performance in the 1970s, which allowed for small increases to be allotted to defense, particularly for aircraft purchases. The air force also benefited from the government's 1974 bilateral cooperation agreement with the United States, under which helicopters and light transport planes were delivered to the Burmese government for use in narcotics control activities. Notwithstanding these limited improvements, the armed forces were still badly undercapitalized as of early 1983, and any change in that situation would probably necessitate a substantive shift in the government's attitude toward accepting foreign military assistance.

Political and Administrative Roles

The tradition of maintaining a separation between military and civilian spheres has not taken root in Burma. From its inception, the BIA was essentially a political movement in military garb, and both before and after independence military officers kept in close contact with civilian politicians and filled posts in the national administration, particularly at local levels in areas where the government's structure was weak or nonexistent. Starting in 1951 a few officers gained experience in running economic enterprises through their involvement in the Defense Services Institute, which began as a modest organization responsible for obtaining food and uniforms for personnel. By the time it was nationlized in 1962, however, it controlled about 50 companies dealing in diverse pursuits such as domestic commerce, housing, international shipping, and book publishing. The performance of such nonmilitary roles was widely accepted as a legitimate extension of the armed forces' mission to maintain national security.

Moreover, within the military leadership and the civilian government as well, it was generally understood that the armed forces were entitled to share in national decisionmaking by virtue of having played the leading role in the struggle for independence. During the nation's first years the military was tied down with counterinsurgency campaigns and eschewed direct involvement in national politics. By the late 1950s, however, the rebel threat was at least temporarily within control, and the military was able to devote more attention to the state of the civilian government, which it soon concluded to be in considerable disarray. In 1958 after U Nu, with the support of the military, invited Ne Win to form a "caretaker" government, the armed forces took over the running of the country while the civilian government tried to reorganize itself to resume rule. Although some officers reportedly were reluctant, the military then peaceably returned power to U Nu in 1960.

As U Nu's new government took shape, however, a number of officers strongly disapproved of the nonsocialist orientation of the faction of AFPFL that U Nu headed, as well as certain policies his government was pursuing. In mid-1961 Ne Win reassigned two of the most prominent critics to posts overseas, but discontent with the civilian government continued to grow. The military leadership was particularly alarmed by U Nu's promotion of Buddhism as a state religion and his apparent intentions to grant more autonomy to some minorities; most officers feared both moves would seriously endanger the national unity that the armed forces had fought so long to preserve.

Convinced that the armed forces not only had a duty to protect the nation but also had been proved capable of governing efficiently, on March 2, 1962, Ne Win, with the support of all army regional commanders, staged a coup. The military leadership, calling itself the Revolutionary Council, then suspended the constitution, announced it would launch a socialist revolution in the nation, and took over the running of the country. All political activity was confined within the framework of the newly created Burma Socialist Programme Party (BSPP), the membership of which over the 1962–72 period was predominantly military.

The Revolutionary Council relied primarily on military officers to fill key administrative posts in the central and local government organs and the newly nationalized economic enterprises. Throughout the nation, military officers, schooled intensively in BSPP doctrine, took control of state- and division-level administration. At the township level, commanders served as chairmen of security and administrative committees—the basic unit of local government—as well as chairmen of area party and mass organizations.

The dominance of the military in the BSPP and the national administration, combined with hierarchical command structures in both, effectively excluded civilian participation in either structure.

In the late 1960s dissatisfaction over the nation's poor economic performance and concern that popular support for the military's revolution had not been forthcoming prompted the military government to reassess the system, and in the early 1970s a number of changes were instituted. In 1971–72 the BSPP began to be converted into a mass rather than a cadre party, causing the ratio of military participation to the total membership to fall. In 1972 an estimated 150 to 200 top military leaders in the government, including Ne Win, retired from the military to continue filling the same positions in mufti. Finally, a new constitution was enacted in 1974, establishing a socialist government in which the BSPP was mandated to take over the leadership of the nation.

Although these changes had the effect of lowering the visibility of the military, they did not substantially affect its influence in the government; the armed forces had launched the revolution in 1962 and as of early 1983 remained its central pillar. Although the 1974 Constitution had replaced the Revolutionary Council with the State Council, 26 of the latter's 29 members were active-duty or retired military officers, including its chairman, U San Yu, who also served as the nation's president after November 1981. Some 80 percent of the delegates to the national legislature, the People's Assembly, were also military or ex-military. U Ne Win continued to serve as chairman of the BSPP, and 14 of 15 members of the BSPP's top decisionmaking body, the Central Executive Committee, were active-duty or retired members of the armed forces. At the state and division levels, 12 of 14 chairmen of party committees were military: only at the township level and below had civilians come to dominate party leadership. Within the defense establishment itself, party organizing committees were maintained at every level of command from the Ministry of Defense to the platoon level. Some 80 percent of all armed forces personnel were BSPP members as of mid-1982.

Manpower and Personnel

Overall strength of the armed forces was approximately 179,000 as of early 1983—a relatively small number when compared with the total available manpower, which was estimated at 7.5 million. Under these circumstances military service did not affect the economy adversely by creating manpower shortages. On the contrary, in light of the limited employment opportunities in the nation, the armed forces probably provided jobs for many who might otherwise be unemployed.

According to articles 170 and 171 of the 1974 Constitution, every citizen has the duties to "protect and safeguard the independence, sovereignty, and territorial integrity" of the nation and to "undergo military training and undertake military service for the defense of the State." Although these provisions, in addition to the National Defense Law of 1959, established a legal basis for conscription, as of early 1983, except in the cases of a few needed doctors, engineers, and technicians, enlistments have been more than adequate to meet required military force levels, and the armed forces have been maintained entirely on a volunteer basis. Enlistment was generally for a two-year period.

Articles 170 and 171 were also frequently cited as providing a basis for mobilizing the population into a consolidated defense force, in accordance with the national defense strategy of "people's war." As of early 1983 an estimated 35,000 men and women served in units of the People's Militia, which was maintained by the Ministry of Defense and organized on a local basis to provide for village defense. Thousands of students, members of mass organizations, and government and factory workers had also been given rudimentary training in self-defense, the use of small arms, and military discipline. As far as could be determined, however, no detailed mobilization plan had been developed; and unless equipment, facilities, and training instructors were augmented considerably, it would be very difficult for these forces to contribute significantly to the nation's military defense capability. Even members of the People's Militia units were sometimes armed only with swords or bamboo stakes.

Very little information was made public concerning armed forces personnel because such matters were considered to relate to the national security. Specific data regarding ethnic and regional background were especially sensitive in view of the government's commitment to build national unity and to downplay ethnic differences. It appeared, however, that the armed forces were ethnically integrated at all levels and that a military career provided a very successful channel of upward mobility for members of ethnic minorities. Female personnel in the armed forces numbered under 500, representing less than 1 percent of the total. They were primarily assigned medical and clerical duties, but a few worked in supply, signals, or engineering units. None were in combat fields. The officer corps was kept fairly small in relation to other ranks. This was especially true at the topmost levels, where there were only some 20 officers of general rank.

Although detailed surveys of attitudes within the officer corps have not been conducted, one observer of Burma has posited that there were two lines of cleavage among officers. The first and most important, in his opinion, was a functional division between officers who have been assigned to conventional military tasks, such as commanders of field units, and those who have filled positions in the government, the national administration, and the BSPP. Before the 1962 coup the officer corps was unified by its common experience and enjoyed great solidarity within its ranks.

After the coup, however, hundreds of officers were needed to fill nonmilitary assignments. When instructed to select personnel for these duties, commanders often took the opportunity to weed out those considered incompetent or troublemakers. By the late 1960s it had become apparent that officer corps solidarity had been undermined by the opening of this second, very different career path, in which those assigned to nonmilitary tasks exercised more influence in the national leadership and lived in far more comfortable surroundings than did officers in the field.

Competition between the two wings of the armed forces has since been apparent, one side or the other gaining ascendancy according to which stood in better favor with U Ne Win at the time. The political-administrative wing seems to have been stronger in 1971 during the first Congress of the BSPP, but line officers displaced them two years later at the Second Congress. The political faction attempted to stage a resurgence in 1977 at the Third Congress in February, but after some members reportedly sought to replace U Ne Win as party chairman, the BSPP convened an extraordinary congress in November in order to bolster U Ne Win's position. The wing of the armed forces representing line officers continued to exercise greater influence at the Fourth Congress in 1981.

As of early 1983 it was difficult to evaluate the depth of the division between the two groups. Certain senior officers appeared to have the support of both. Brigadier General Tin Oo, for instance, the joint general secretary of the BSPP since 1981, rose to his position through assignments in the intelligence services and as chief military assistant to U Ne Win. He also maintained close and friendly contacts with several influential line officers

A second, generational line of cleavage was believed to separate officers identified with the struggle for independence from those who entered the military after that time and made a career fighting insurgents or, after 1962, serving in political or administrative positions. Although many of the older generation have retired, they maintained control over decisionmaking positions in both the armed forces and the government, sometimes to the frustration of ambitious younger officers. The older group has drawn upon the struggle for independence, the Thirty Comrades, and Aung San himself to provide national inspiration and to form the basis for the country's military traditions. Younger officers have reportedly found such symbolism to be outside their own experience and to overwhelm their own role in preserving the national unity and in launching and carrying out a socialist revolution.

Defense Spending and Industry

The cost of maintaining internal order in the face of endemic insurgencies has been very high, both in terms of the portion of the total central government expenditures that had to be devoted to national defense and in terms of national resources diverted from government control or left unexploited altogether. Certainly in human terms the expense of physical injury or loss of life and the psychological damage that fear and uncertainty have inflicted have been incalculable, producing especially heavy burdens for those living or fighting in disputed areas.

Although perennial insurgencies have kept the military in the forefront of the national life since independence, the defense establishment has grown only slowly, and equipment has remained in very short supply—even after active-duty and retired military officers assumed the dominant role in national decisionmaking. Defense expenditures accounted for over 30 percent of the total national budget from the mid-1950s until the early 1970s, and military spending grew steadily, but Burma was a very poor nation. Even so high a portion was generally sufficient to fund only current expenditures—if they were kept low—and very little was left over for equipment replacement or spares, not to mention modernization.

The situation changed little after the national budget began to expand significantly during the mid-1970s. Military expenditures continued to grow steadily in absolute terms—nearly doubling in size from K722 million (for value of the Kyat—see Glossary) in fiscal year (FY—see Glossary) 1974 to over K1.4 billion in FY 1981. When inflation was factored in, however, defense spending actually decreased in real terms in FY 1975 and FY 1976, then grew at a very uneven rate thereafter. Total government expenditures, on the other hand, increased at a much faster rate over the same period, causing the ratio of military spending to the total to fall from 27 percent in FY 1974 to 19.5 percent in FY 1981. While even the latter figure was a significant one, representing a sizable diversion of sorely needed resources from national development projects, it did not translate into significant sums compared with other nations of the world. According to one researcher, Burma ranked 114 out of 141 world nations in terms of public expenditures per capita devoted to the military, and 129 out of 141 in terms of public expenditures per soldier.

The armed forces budget was divided into two categories: current expenditures for routine matters, such as pay and allowances, maintenance, and travel; and capital expenditures, generally used to purchase new equipment. Over the FY 1974–81 period, current expenditures accounted for between 85 and 92 percent of the total. Of the small amount left over, most was used to acquire spare parts for imported equipment.

The nation's defense industry was very small, in general supplying only uniforms, light arms, and ammunition. The government dockyards at Rangoon possessed limited shipbuilding capability. Most of the rest of military hardware was imported from various nations. In the late 1970s and early 1980s major suppliers included Denmark, the Federal Republic of Germany (West Germany), Australia, and the United States.

Military Structure and Training

The command of the armed forces was channeled downward from the State Council, whose chairman was the nation's president, through the Council of Ministers to the Ministry of Defense, which functioned in the dual capacity of a government ministry and a joint integrated military headquarters. The ministry was headed by the nation's highest ranking military officer, who served concurrently as minister of defense and as chief of staff of the defense services. As such, he exercised supreme operational command over all three military services, and his office in the ministry served as a general headquarters for the establishment as a whole. The chief of staff was assisted by three vice chiefs of staff—one each for the army, navy, and air force—who were commanders of their respective services as well as deputy ministers of defense.

The combined defense services staff had three major components: the general staff, the adjutant generals' department, and the quartermaster general's department. There were also special staffs for the directorates of Procurement, Comptroller of Military Accounts, Inspector General, Defense Services Intelligence, and People's Militia and Social Relations. Additional directorates corresponded to functional corps, such as medical services, judge advocate general, and ordnance.

The top BSPP organization within the ministry was the Defense Services Organizing Committee, which oversaw party activities in all three services. It exercised jurisdiction over a network of party organizing committees paralleling the armed forces structure from the level of the separate service headquarters down to the platoon level. At the ministry level, the organizing committee was headed by a permanently assigned chairman, who was assisted by a small staff. Selected top officers assigned to the ministry served simultaneously as committee members. Lower level committees were usually chaired by commanders of their respective units.

Operational command in the field was unified under the control of the ministry in a framework of nine regional commands. They were Northwestern (headquarters Mandalay), Western (Sittwe [Akyab]), Central (Toungoo), Southwestern (Bassein), Northern (Myitkyina), Northeastern (Lashio), Eastern (Taunggyi), Southeastern (Moulmein), and Rangoon. Each regional command has at its disposal from three to 12 infantry battalions. Six army infantry divisions, in addition to all naval and air units, remained at the disposal of the minister of defense, to be dispatched as necessary to the regional commands.

Logistics matters for all three services were handled by the quartermaster general's staff, except for major purchases, which were handled by the director of procurement. Supply was often complicated by lack of funds, long supply lines, and the time lag in deliveries from abroad. Distribution was hampered by insufficient transportation capacity and by the nation's sparse road network. Supplies for day-to-day operations were decentralized down to battalion level. Storage depots for other items were scattered throughout the country, but reserve matériel and equipment were limited. Units in the field often operated without lines of supply, purchasing food and requisitioning shelter, transportation, and labor from local sources.

Two principal training facilities turned out officers for all three services, cadets receiving the same fundamental instruction before being assigned to their respective branches. The Defense Services Academy, established in 1955 at Maymyo, offered a four-year degree course. Candidates applied at age 16 after having passed national matriculation exams. Competition for entry was keen: approximately 3,000 applied yearly for the estimated 150 to 200 slots available. Curriculum included, as at all training institutions, instruction in BSPP doctrine. Graduating cadets were assigned to the army, navy, or air force based on manpower requirements. The Officer Training School conducted a four-month training course for university graduates and an 18-month course for selected enlisted men. Graduates of both the academy and the training school were sent to specialized courses run by the service they entered.

Each service maintained its own stations for receiving recruits and for conducting their basic training, which usually lasted between three and nine months. Advance administrative training was available in schools near Maymyo. The National Defense College, located in Rangoon, provided advanced professional training for senior offices of all three services under the direction of the ministry.

Army

Essentially a light infantry force, the army—totaling 163,000 in early 1983—was the largest and by far the dominant branch of the nation's armed forces. By virtue of their relative numbers, army officers filled most positions in the integrated ministry staffs and held most national political and administrative assignments.

The battalion was the basic maneuver formation, although divisional structures were present, mainly as command organizations. Battalions were organized into four rifle companies with supporting mortar, machine gun, recoilless rifle, and administrative units. Artillery and armored units were deployed separately as necessary. Battalion strength was officially set at 750 officers and other ranks, but in practice most had a strength of some 500 or less.

The army has retained something of a regimental system under which battalions were grouped primarily for morale and for administrative purposes. These included the Burma Regiment having some 90 battalions, the Light Infantry Regiment having about 10 battalions, plus the Burma Rifles, the Kachin Rifles, the Chin Rifles, the Shan Rifles, and the Kayah Rifles, all having between one and six battalions. Despite their names, regiments were ethnically integrated as of early 1983. Operationally, the army was organized into six light infantry divisions of 10 battalions each, two armored battalions, some 85 independent infantry battalions, four artillery battalions, one combination antitank and artillery battalion, and one antiaircraft battery (see table 15, Appendix).

Officially the army's equipment inventory in early 1983 included Comet medium battle tanks, Humber armored cars, Ferret scout cars, 25-pounder field guns, 76mm and 105mm howitzers, 81mm and 120mm mortars, 6- and 17-pounder antitank guns, and 40mm and 3.7-inch antiaircraft guns. Many of these systems, particularly the tanks, armored cars, and field guns, would be considered obsolete or even antiquated by most of the world's armed forces and hence presented special maintenance and performance problems. That many were kept in functioning order was a testament to the skill and inventiveness of the army's maintenance personnel, who have long had the task of making do with what little was available. For light arms, the army mainly relied on West German- and Italian-designed rifles and machine guns made in Burma.

The army ran a variety of training schools for its personnel. Most basic training was given at unit depots located throughout the nation. Several specialized and advanced training schools were located at the Bahtoo training facility near Taunggyi. These included the Combat Forces' School, the Noncommissioned Officers' School, and the Artillery and Armor School. Also at Bahtoo were the Animal Transport Training School for those charged with caring for the mules and horses used to transport goods and the Command and General Staff College for middle-grade officers. Various corps, such as signals, engineers, supply, and ordnance, maintained training schools elsewhere in the nation.

Air Force

Founded in the early 1950s with British assistance, the air force's primary mission was to support the army in counterinsurgency operations and to provide internal reconnaissance of insurgent activity as well as of poppy cultivation, opium trafficking, and refinery positions. The air force's capabilities have always been limited by budget allocations that have restricted the modernization of its inventory, however. As of the early 1980s comparatively obsolete equipment, much of which was poorly maintained and plagued by shortages of spare parts, formed the bulk of the force.

Combat aircraft were organized into two attack squadrons in the early 1980s. These were equipped with a combination of Lockheed AT-33s supplied by the United States in the 1960s and Pilatus PC-7s, which operated in a dual strike-trainer role. Some two dozen light aircraft provided liaison and transport capabilities. There were also two training squadrons that primarily relied on Siai Marchetti SF-260MBs. Helicopters numbered approximately 43, some 14 of which had been supplied in 1975 by the United States for antinarcotics patrols. As of the early 1983 they had been integrated into the air force for a variety of military roles.

The air force was responsible for its own administration and training, but operations were conducted with the army on a unified basis. The principal air force supply and maintenance base was at Mingaladon Airport near Rangoon, where storage, repair, and overhaul activities were centered. The Flight Training School was at Meiktila. Other airfields were located at Bhamo, Hmawbi, Keng Tung, Lashio, Magwe, Mandalay, Mergui, Moulmein, Myitkyina, Sittwe, and Tavoy. The airforce's strength was some 9,000 as of early 1983.

Navy

Functioning primarily as a fisheries protection and coastal and riverine patrol fleet in the early 1980s, the navy has also been a victim of tight budget constraints. Major craft comprised one ex-British frigate of World War II vintage and four corvettes—two of which were ex-United States craft commissioned in the 1940s and two, products of the nation's own boatyards in 1960. Light forces included some 41 river and coastal patrol craft and approximately 36 gunboats, ranging in displacement from 49 to 381 tons. The navy operated an additional 12 coastal patrol craft for the People's Pearl and Fishery Corporation for use against piracy, smuggling, and illegal fishing.

The navy's strength was some 7,000 as of early 1983. The main naval dockyard was located at Rangoon, where facilities could handle most ship repair and where virtually all naval supplies were stored and issued. The Naval Training Center was at Syriam near Rangoon. The fleet was assigned on a regional basis out of commands at Sittwe, Bassein, Rangoon, and Moulmein.

Conditions of Service

Military service has received widely varying degrees of acceptance, but by and large the military has been considered a desirable and respected career. Pay was generally commensurate with or higher than that received for comparable civilian employment, and perquisites raised the standard of living above that enjoyed by most civilians. Military posts were usually of tropical construction as benefitted the services' needs. Families often resided in these installations along with their service sponsor.

Living conditions differed sharply between those assigned to combat units and those serving in the national administration and the BSPP. For the former, daily routine was exacting and dangerous. The constant state of hostilities and shortages of logistics support forced many units to spend much of their time in the field living off the land under very harsh conditions. Casualties and deaths were a constant threat. In contrast, those filling nonmilitary positions lived in the comparative comfort of Rangoon or other cities, where more amenities were available and life was far less dangerous.

All personnel and their families received free medical attention, rations, transportation during assignment transfers, and accommodations. Housing varied according to rank, but ration allotments were standard for all ranks. Personnel assigned to outlying regions, where it was difficult to procure supplies for their families, could at the discretion of area commanders receive extra ration allotments to provide for their dependents. Leave policies were liberal, all personnel accruing 30 days of leave each year. Retirement could be for disability, length of service, or age and could be statutorily mandated according to rank upon request. Retirement pay varied, reaching a maximum of 75 percent of the active-duty rate.

Uniforms, Ranks, and Insignia

The rank and grade structure of the three services designated personnel as officers and "other ranks." Officers' ranks parallel these of the United States forces. An honorific title, *bogyoke*, loosely translated as "supreme general," has been reserved for Aung San and for U Ne Win. Navy personnel were divided among seven noncommissioned officer and enlisted ranks; those in the air force and the army were divided into eight. Officers' insignia were displayed on shoulder boards; those of the other ranks were on the upper sleeve (see fig. 14).

The uniforms of all three services were patterned after those of the British. The navy used dark blue trousers and light blue shirts; the air force used all khaki. Army service uniforms were a fawn khaki, and field uniforms were dark green. Officers wore a standard visored hat. Generals' hats had two laurel bands on the peaks, those of colonels and lieutenant colonels had one, and majors and below had none. Lieutenant colonels and above had gold chin straps; majors and below had black. Enlisted men wore a cloth cap or a wide-brimmed jungle hat for field duty.

ARMY, AIR FORCE, and NAVY									
ARMY and AIR FORCE	Second Lieutenant	First Lieutenant	Captain	Major	Lieutenant Colonel	Colonel	Brigadier General	Major General	Lieutenant General	General
UNITED STATES EQUIVALENT	Second Lieutenant	First Lieutenant	Captain	Major	Lieutenant Colonel	Colonel	Brigadier General	Major General	Lieutenant General	General
NAVY	Sub-Lieutenant	Lieutenant Junior Grade	Lieutenant	Lieutenant Commander	Commander	Captain	Commodore	Rear Admiral	Vice Admiral	Admiral
UNITED STATES EQUIVALENT	Ensign	Lieutenant Junior Grade	Lieutenant	Lieutenant Commander	Commander	Captain	Commodore	Rear Admiral	Vice Admiral	Admiral

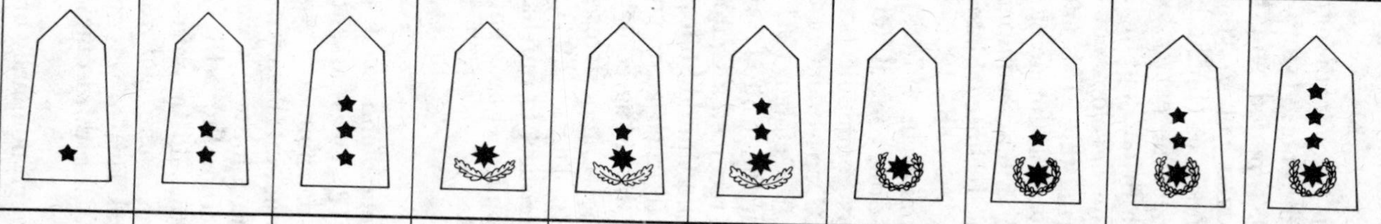

NOTE.—The color of the uniform on which these insignia are worn varies with the branch of service.

Figure 14. Officers' Ranks and Insignia for People's Armed Forces, 1983

257

Foreign Military Relations

In light of its strong commitment to maintaining a nonaligned foreign policy, the nation had not entered into any defense treaties during the 1948-early 1983 period and had accepted miliary aid only when it was judged not to compromise the country's jealously guarded independence. Having little domestic defense industry, however, it has been necessary to obtain much military hardware from abroad. Both Britain and the United States made significant contributions to the development of the armed forces in their early years, but during the 1970s and early 1980s West Germany, which provided favorable financing terms but no grant aid, was the major source for military equipment.

The Burmese government allowed United States military aid programs initiated in 1958 to lapse over the 1966–80 period but did accept antinarcotics aid beginning in 1974. Totaling some US$47 million through late 1983, drug control aid has included helicopters, transport aircraft, and communications equipment furnished under the United States Department of State International Narcotics Control Program. In October 1981 the Burmese government signed an accord with the United States to renew military aid and in December 1981 received a United States naval delegation, headed by the chief of the United States Naval Operations in the Pacific, the first visit by such an important military delegation in over 30 years. Under the aid agreement, six military officers were sent for training in the United States in 1981, 20 in 1982, and a proposed 44 in 1983. During 1983 the Burmese government was also expected to request to purchase spare parts and ammunition for previously supplied equipment using United States Foreign Military Sales credits.

Intelligence Agencies

The nation's principal intelligence and security organ, the National Intelligence Board (NIB), was essentially a small policymaking body that was responsible for coordinating the activities of the country's various intelligence and security agencies. Responsible to the prime minister, it was headed by a director who received guidance from the NIB Control Board, which comprised the prime minister and the ministers of foreign affairs, planning and finance, and home and religious affairs. As of early 1983 Brigadier General Tin Oo was the secretary of the NIB Control Board, as well as the third-ranking member of the BSPP.

Four intelligence agencies, although nominally organized under separate ministries, reported through the NIB. The largest, the Directorate of Defense Services Intelligence (DDSI), was the intelligence arm of the Ministry of Defense. The DDSI and its Military Intelligence Service detachments throughout the nation focused mainly on military intelligence, particularly as related to insurgents. They also provided an information network devoted to such matters as taxes, customs duties, and criminal investigation.

The Criminal Investigation Department and the Special Investigation Department (SID) of the People's Police Force were also under the jurisdiction of the NIB. The former, as its name implied, was responsible mainly for investigating matters of a purely criminal nature. The SID, however, was a political police charged with investigating subversion, treason, or antigovernment activities. The SID has also played a role in coordinating narcotics control operations.

A fourth agency under the NIB was the Bureau of Special Investigation (BSI), which was technically under the control of the Ministry of Home and Religious Affairs. The BSI was first organized by U Nu as the People's Property Protection Police, and as of early 1983 it remained principally responsible for investigating matters relating to economic crimes and corruption.

The People's Police Force

Responsibility for law enforcement was vested in the People's Police Force, which was attached to the Ministry of Home and Religious Affairs. Since 1964 the police have been a unified national force organizationally independent from the military establishment. Previous to that time, relations between the military and the police were often strained by jurisdictional disputes and complaints by the police of low supply priorities relative to the armed forces. By the late 1960s, however, tensions had eased, and military and police units cooperated closely in maintaining internal order and engaging in civic action projects. Another reorganization of the police was instituted in 1972 to accommodate the newly created system of people's councils established at state and division, township, and ward and village-tract levels.

In the early 1980s the police force's mission included maintaining law and order, preserving the peace, defending the socialist economic system, protecting life and property, preventing and detecting crime, and apprehending offenders. Police officers were charged with preparing cases for criminal trial and shared with the military the responsibility for safeguarding national security and controlling subversion. During the 1970s the police's role in antinarcotics operations increased significantly, the force taking charge of efforts to locate and destroy poppy fields, track down and apprehend drug traffickers, and bring drug offenders to justice. The police have received support in performing these tasks from a United Nations antinarcotics aid program under which vehicles, radios, laboratory equipment, and technical training were supplied in the mid-1970s.

As was the case with the armed forces, matters relating to the People's Police Force were considered to affect the national security, and detailed information regarding its affairs was not made public. As far as could be determined in early 1983, however, the force was headed by a director general who was the nation's highest ranking police officer. Police headquarters, located in Rangoon, handled supply, finance, administration, and training for the entire force. It also maintained the Criminal Investigation Department and the Special Investigation Department, both of which reported to the prime minister through the National Intelligence Board. The Police Officers' Academy in Mandalay was also under headquarters control. As in the armed forces, personnel were instructed in BSPP ideology, and a system of party organizing committees existed at most levels.

Below the headquarters level, the remainder of the police force performed regular law enforcement tasks throughout the nation. They were stationed in 14 units, the jurisdictions of which corresponded to the seven states and the seven divisions. Each of these was subdivided further into township and ward and village-tract forces. In areas where railroads were located, state and division-level forces maintained units of Railroad Police, whose members were assigned to keep order on trains and to regulate the transport of goods by rail.

Facilities in the regionally assigned forces included stations, substations and, in outlying areas, outposts. In rural areas these were usually compounds in which families of police also resided. In lightly populated areas of the country, outposts were mainly bases of operations for area surveillance, but in areas of insurgent activity they were often fortified defense posts.

In late 1982 the strength of the police force was raised by some 7,000 to near 58,000 to enable the police to assume responsibility for law and order in areas that previously had been under the control of the armed forces. Information regarding the composition of police personnel was not made public, but observers have noted that members of ethnic minorities were often stationed in areas near their homes in order to capitalize on their understanding of local cultures. The overwhelming majority of police officers were male, only a few women being present in the Rangoon People's Police Force, where they functioned primarily as traffic police.

Crime and the Criminal Justice System

Statistics on the incidence of crime in the late 1970s and early 1980s were incomplete, and those available were seriously flawed by the uneven quality of reporting throughout the nation. According to the government, however, crime rates declined steadily during 1978–80, and raw data released during 1980–82 suggested that the trend was continuing. Within the central sections of the nation, crimes associated with drug abuse were a cause for official concern as were economic crimes associated with smuggling and with low-level corruption, such as misappropriation of state property and embezzlement of cooperative funds. Crimes of violence, including murder and extortion, were prevalent in border areas where conditions of insurgency promoted lawlessness.

The major source for the nation's criminal law was the Penal Code, which listed categories of offenses and kinds and limits of punishments. Two general levels of offenses—felonies and misdemeanors—were recognized. Major categories of crime distinguished between offenses against the state; against public tranquility; against persons or property; and against public health, safety, and morality. Other broad areas, such as crimes against public servants, marriage, and religion, were also included. The code provided for the death penalty, exile to a penal colony, fine, or imprisonment, which could involve hard labor. Its interpretation of criminal responsibility took into account extenuating and mitigating circumstances, including self-defense and impairment of mental faculties. Juveniles under the age of 12 years received special treatment. One section of the Penal Code was concerned with offenses germane to the armed forces and served as the basis for military justice.

Drug-related offenses were covered by the 1974 Narcotics Drug Law, which prohibited the cultivation of opium poppies and drug trafficking. It also required all addicts to register with the authorities and undergo rehabilitative treatment. Severe penalties were assessed for failure to comply with any provisions of the law. An order published by the Council of Ministers in 1981 provided procedures for granting rewards to those who aided in the seizure of controlled substances and the apprehension of drug suspects. As of early 1983 registered addicts numbered some 38,000 across the nation, but authorities conceded that many more were unregistered. Most of those registered were either male university and college students or young male adults associated with commercial and black market enterprises.

Three laws enacted in the mid-1970s established criminal penalties for opposition—political or otherwise—to the BSPP or the state. The first two, the State Party Protection Law and the violation of Party Discipline Law, made it an offense punishable by three to 14 years imprisonment, fine, or both for any citizen to agitate against the BSPP or attempt to steal party secrets. Party members were also forbidden to organize or publish opposition to party principles. In early 1975 the Protection of the State from Subversive Elements Law, which was passed in the wake of serious student rioting, gave the State Council broad powers to deal with any perceived threat to the national security, including the right to detain persons without trial, to restrict their constitutional rights, and to declare a state of emergency over the whole of the country or any part of it for up to 60 days. This last law has since provided a legal basis for the unrestrained use of police powers by security, military, and police officials in countering antistate activities and any other behavior officially construed as affecting national security.

Other laws mandating criminal liability included the 1964 Socialist Economy Protection Law and the 1970 Cooperative Societies Law, both of which specified offenses against publicly owned and cooperative enterprises. According to reports in the Burmese press, crimes under these laws comprised some 30 percent of all criminal cases brought to trial in the early 1980s.

The administration of criminal justice was completely overhauled in 1972, changing from a system based on that in use during the British colonial period to what was officially titled the People's Justice System. According to the government, the change was necessary because the former judicial system, which was relatively independent from executive and legislative control, was a remnant of colonial times and irrelevant to Burmese cultural traditions. It was criticized for giving too much power to individual judges and magistrates, for benefiting the rich and powerful at the expense of the poor, and indulging in legal sophistry. The new People's Justice System was intended to overcome these shortcomings by mandating civilian participation in the administration of justice and explicitly allowing for expression of local customs and traditional law so long as they did not hinder the orderly functioning of the state.

The new framework has permitted government and party officials, as well as the general population, to exercise considerable influence in the functioning of the judicial system. Under the new framework, courts—usually referred to by the government as people's courts—have been established at the national level and in state and division, township, and ward and village-tract jurisdictions throughout the nation (see Central Government, ch. 4). As of early 1983 these had been formed in all but a few rural village-tracts and in six townships in Shan State where conditions of insurgency prevented the establishment of government administration. Courts were presided over by panels of lay judges, members of which were selected by judges' committees formed at corresponding levels of government administration. Committee members were elected by local people's councils from a slate of candidates chosen by the BSPP; they were assisted by regionally assigned legal professionals attached to the courts, which were under the control of the State Council. Most judges were also members of judges' committees; the majority were BSPP members, and many were retired or active-duty military personnel.

Little information could be located regarding the way in which the new legal system actually functioned. The law did not provide for habeas corpus protection, and in common criminal cases a suspect could be held for up to 24 hours before police obtained a detention order from local judges' committees. These orders were renewable, and suspects could be held until the time of trial, although bail was possible for certain offenses. There was no limit on how long a suspect could be held for political or security offenses.

When police or security officials concluded that available evidence warranted bringing an accused to trial, lay judges heard the case, conducted the proceedings, rendered judgment, and affixed a sentence. Judges were advised on court procedures and intricate matters of law by the trained judges and lawyers attached to the judges' committees. In some minor criminal cases police officials presented the state's case, but in most instances, law officers organized under the Council of People's Attorneys, responsible to the People's Assembly, performed this function. The prosecution had the burden of proof. Defendants were entitled to secure assistance in their behalf either from privately or publicly employed trained legal professionals or, as was more often the case, from laymen whose knowledge or position in the community they respected. In the event a defendant was charged with a capital crime, the appropriate judges' committee was required to provide him with qualified legal representation. Both the government and the defendant could appeal findings and sentences imposed by lower courts.

The 1974 Constitution provides for public trial except for offenses where it is legally prohibited; in practice, most common criminal cases were held in open court. In cases relating to security or political offenses, however, special judicial committees and special courts have at times been created by the State Council, and trials have been closed to the public. Military personnel could be tried either in civilian courts or at courts-martial, but civilians could only be tried in civilian courts. Courts-martial decisions could also be appealed to higher courts.

The prison system was administered by the Department of Prisons of the Ministry of Home and Religious Affairs. According to statistics compiled in the mid-1970s, the nation had some 40 permanent jails in addition to several other detention camps and police lock-ups. Convicts were also assigned to work camps to engage in manual labor, including roadbuilding and quarry work. Prisons were subject to inspection by local judicial committees, which during the early 1980s have regularly expressed concern over the need to improve existing conditions. Their efforts have been hampered by insufficient funds, however, and conditions in all facilities remained generally poor. Overcrowding was common, and diet and medical services were usually limited.

* * *

As of early 1983 no definitive studies that deal comprehensively with national security matters in contemporary Burma had been published. Yearly issues of the *Country Reports on Human Rights Practices*, prepared by the United States Department of State for Congress, provide some insight on conditions of order in Burma, especially in the central sections of the nation. Articles on insurgent activity appear regularly in issues of the *Far Eastern Economic Review*. Two documents published by the United States Congress, *Proposal to Control Opium from the Golden Triangle and Terminate the Shan Opium Trade* (1975) and *Southeast Asian Drug Trade* (1982), also treat the insurgent problems particularly as it relates to opium trafficking. Annual summaries on activities by the Burmese Communist Party are available in the *Yearbook on International Communist Affairs*. Information on the armed forces can be found in *World Armies*, edited by John Keegan, in the annual *Jane's Fighting Ships*, and in yearly issues of *The Military Balance*, published by the International Institute for Strategic Studies. (For further information and complete citations, see Bibliography.)

Appendix

Table 1. Metric Conversion Coefficients

When you know	Multiply by	To Find
Millimeters..............................	0.04	inches
Centimeters.............................	0.39	inches
Meters....................................	3.3	feet
Kilometers...............................	0.62	miles
Hectares (10,000 m^2)..................	2.47	acres
Square kilometers	0.39	square miles
Cubic meters	35.3	cubic feet
Liters.....................................	0.26	gallons
Kilograms................................	2.2	pounds
Metric tons..............................	0.98	long tons
....	1.1	short tons
....	2,204	pounds
Degrees Celsius........................	9	degrees Fahrenheit
(Centigrade)	divide by 5 and add 32	

*Table 2.   Growth of the Gross Domestic Product (GDP),
Selected Periods, FY 1962–81[1]*
(average percentage change per year)

	FY 1962–70 Actual	FY 1971–74[2] Actual	Second Four-Year Plan FY 1974–77[3] Actual	Second Four-Year Plan FY 1974–77[3] Planned	Third Four-Year Plan FY 1978–81 Actual	Third Four-Year Plan FY 1978–81 Planned
GDP	3.1	2.0	4.7	4.5	6.6	6.8
Adjusted GDP[4]	2.6	3.2	4.3	n.a.	6.2	6.5
Investment	4.6	–9.5	16.6	n.a.	17.1	14.6
Imports[5]	–4.6	–22.1	14.5	n.a.	24.2	23.2
Exports	–10.3	–0.9	1.7	n.a.	8.5	17.8
Sector						
Crop farming	3.7	2.7	3.6	4.0	8.7	8.0
Livestock and fishing	6.8	2.2	2.9	3.4	5.0	5.1
Forestry	1.6	–2.2	5.6	3.1	7.9	7.7
Mining	0.7	2.0	6.9	2.4	8.2	13.2
Processing and manufacturing	3.4	–0.4	7.1	7.6	6.0	6.6
Power	7.0	9.8	10.3	9.2	13.0	11.7
Construction	4.3	–3.0	6.0	1.0	18.7	18.8
Transportation	3.4	–1.3	3.1	3.7	7.4	6.9
Communications	3.4	3.5	8.3	4.5	9.8	6.0
Finance	3.0	13.2	15.3	4.8	13.9	12.9
Social and administrative services	4.5	6.2	7.7	4.0	5.4	5.6
Rentals and other services	3.4	2.4	2.2	3.5	3.0	2.8
Wholesale and retail trade	1.2	1.4	4.0	4.9	3.6	3.7

n.a.—not available.

[1]Calculated at constant FY 1970 prices using year before the first year of the period given as a base and the last year of the period as the end point. Considerable fluctuations during the FY 1962–70 period are therefore not apparent in the average growth rate. Target growth rates differ from published government documents because the government utilizes a simple arithmetic average of annual rates.

[2]FY 1974 refers to the fiscal year (see Glossary) ending September 30, 1974.

[3]FY 1974 refers to the fiscal year beginning April 1, 1974.

[4]Gross domestic product (see Glossary) is adjusted to fit the standard definition, including the value of exports minus imports.

[5]Imports and exports are expressed at free on board (f.o.b.) values.

Source: Based on information from Burma, Ministry of Planning and Finance, *Report to the Pyithu Hluttaw on the Financial, Economic, and Social Conditions of the Socialist Republic of the Union of Burma for 1978–79*, Rangoon, 1978, 26–27; and *Report to the Pyithu Hluttaw on the Financial, Economic, and Social Conditions of the Socialist Republic of the Union of Burma for 1982–83*, Rangoon, 1982, 28–33.

Table 3. Shares of the Gross Domestic Product by Sector,
FY 1962 and FY 1981
(value in millions of kyat)[1]

Sector	FY 1962		FY 1981[2]	
	Value	Percentage	Value	Percentage
Crop farming	1,685.8	25.3	16,565.8	38.5
Livestock and fishing	351.1	5.3	3,030.6	7.0
Forestry	224.1	3.4	681.6	1.6
Mining	54.7	0.8	514.0	1.2
Processing and manufacturing	616.0	9.3	4,109.8	9.5
Power	35.6	0.5	168.7	0.4
Construction	151.1	2.3	717.8	1.7
Transportation	409.8	6.2	1,475.8	3.4
Communications	25.8	0.4	100.0	0.2
Finance	88.3	1.3	725.1	1.7
Social and administrative services	574.9	8.6	2,079.9	4.8
Rentals and other services	575.2	8.6	1,873.3	4.4
Wholesale and retail trade	1,865.8	28.0	11,015.3	25.6
TOTAL[3]	6,658.2	100.0	43,057.7	100.0

—not applicable.

[1]For value of the kyat—see Glossary
[2]Data for FY 1981 are preliminary estimates that probably overestimate the value of industrial production.
[3]Imports are excluded from this accounting of gross domestic product (see Glossary).

Source: Based on information from Burma, Ministry of Planning and Finance, *Report to the Pyithu Hluttaw on the Financial, Economic, and Social Conditions of the Socialist Republic of the Union of Burma for 1982–83*, Rangoon, 1982, 29.

Table 4. Shares of the Gross Domestic Product by Ownership, FY 1962 and FY 1981[1] (in percentage)

Sector	FY 1962				FY 1981			
	State Enterprise	Cooperative Enterprise	Private Enterprise	Total[2]	State Enterprise	Cooperative Enterprise	Private Enterprise	Total
Crop farming	...	...	100.0	100.0	0.3	1.9	97.8	100.0
Livestock and fishing	0.1	0.1	99.8	100.0	2.0	1.7	96.3	100.0
Forestry	17.8	0.1	82.1	100.0	40.0	3.5	56.5	100.0
Mining	1.5	...	98.5	100.0	86.5	2.9	10.6	100.0
Processing and manufacturing	28.6	0.8	70.7	100.0	58.9	3.6	37.5	100.0
Power	100.0	...	...	100.0	99.9	0.1	...	100.0
Construction	51.5	...	48.5	100.0	79.9	0.5	19.6	100.0
Transportation	31.4	...	68.6	100.0	37.1	6.5	56.4	100.0
Communications	100.0	...	...	100.0	100.0	...	...	100.0
Finance	43.5	...	56.5	100.0	98.7	1.3	...	100.0
Social and administrative services	100.0	...	...	100.0	100.0	...	...	100.0
Rentals and other services	0.5	0.3	99.2	100.0	12.8	4.5	82.7	100.0
Wholesale and retail trade	33.4	1.9	64.7	100.0	45.4	9.2	45.4	100.0
Gross domestic product[3]	24.8	0.7	74.5	100.0	38.2	3.8	58.0	100.0

... means negligible or zero.

[1]FY 1981 data are preliminary estimates. All percentages are based on constant FY 1970 prices. FY 1962 was the first year of the military takeover.

[2]Figures may not add to totals because of rounding

[3]Imports are excluded from this accounting of gross domestic product (see Glossary).

Source: Based on information from Burma, Ministry of Planning and Finance, *Report to the Pyithu Hluttaw on the Financial, Economic, and Social Conditions of the Union of Burma for 1977–78*, Rangoon, 1977, 22; and *Report to the Pyithu Hluttaw on the Financial, Economic, and Social Conditions of the Socialist Republic of the Union of Burma for 1982–83*, Rangoon, 1982, 30–31.

Table 5. *Public Investment by Sector, Selected Periods, FY 1964–85*[1]
(in percentage of total public investment)

Sector	FY 1964–73 Actual	Second Four-Year Plan (FY 1974–77)		Third Four-Year Plan (FY 1978–81)		Fourth Four-Year Plan (FY 1982–85)
	Actual	Actual	Target	Actual	Target	Target
Crop farming	8.8	10.7	10.4	9.2	13.6	14.0
Livestock and fishing	n.a.	3.3	3.8	7.2	8.7	6.0
Forestry	2.0	4.9	5.4	3.8	5.0	4.0
Mining......................	5.4	11.2	12.3	12.4	6.6	14.0
Processing and manufacturing						
Agriculture support	n.a.	n.a.	n.a.	4.9	10.3	n.a.
Agriculture based...	n.a.	n.a.	n.a.	7.0	4.2	n.a.
Other.................	n.a.	n.a.	n.a.	24.9	21.6	n.a.
Total................	29.3	25.5	27.8	36.8	36.1	27.0
Power	3.9	6.2	6.1	4.9	5.1	5.0
Construction...............	8.3	3.1	2.4	2.9	2.2	3.0
Transportation and communications........	14.8	17.4	16.6	12.7	13.2	13.0
Trade........................	27.5[2]	2.6	2.1	1.7	1.0	14.0[2]
Social Services	n.a.	3.3	2.5	2.4	1.7	n.a.
Administration	n.a.	8.0	7.8	4.7	5.5	n.a.
Town and city development............	n.a.	2.7	2.7	1.3	1.1	n.a.
Finance	n.a.	0.1	0.1	0.1	0.2	n.a.
TOTAL[3]	100.0	100.0	100.0	100.0	100.0	100.0
(in billions of kyat)[4]...	(7.0)	(5.5)	(7.1)	(23.4)	(15.6)	n.a.

n.a.—not available.
[1]Data for FY 1980 are provisional; those for FY 1981 are preliminary estimates.
[2]Incorporates data from Trade and all sectors below.
[3]Figures may not add to totals because of rounding.
[4]For value of the kyat—see Glossary.

Table 6. Consolidated Public Sector Budget, FY 1975–81[1]
(in percentage of total expenditure)

	FY 1975	FY 1976	FY 1977	FY 1978	FY 1979	FY 1980	FY 1981
Revenues							
Income and profits tax	17.1	3.2	3.7	2.9	1.9	1.5	1.6
Commodities and services tax	0.0	37.0	33.6	25.1	23.4	20.5	21.2
Taxes on international trade	13.7	9.8	9.6	8.9	9.3	6.8	6.4
Other taxes	19.9	2.2	1.7	1.4	1.1	0.8	1.0
Contributions from public enterprises	...	9.7	10.5	12.6	14.4	11.1	8.7
Other nontax revenues	8.3	8.8	9.3	8.5	7.3	7.3	5.6
Local government revenues	2.6	2.4	2.2	1.8	1.5	1.4	1.5
Public enterprise's operating surplus[2]	21.3	31.5	14.2	-0.7	6.6	11.2	11.2
Total revenues	82.9	104.6	84.8	60.5	65.5	60.6	57.2
Expenditures							
Current Expenditures							
Administration	14.6	13.7	11.1	9.2	7.5	7.3	9.9
Defense	22.6	19.7	16.3	12.6	10.8	10.2	9.9
Economic services	10.6	10.0	8.0	7.1	6.3	6.0	6.2
Education	11.1	9.4	7.3	6.1	5.1	4.8	4.7
Health	5.3	4.5	3.3	3.1	2.6	2.6	2.4
Other social welfare	4.2	4.3	3.9	3.4	3.0	2.9	2.9
Interest payments	5.1	4.6	4.0	5.9	7.1	7.4	9.2
Other central government	0.6	0.4	0.3	0.6	0.3	1.7	1.6
Local government	2.2	2.0	1.5	1.2	1.1	1.1	1.1

Table 6—Continued.

	FY 1975	FY 1976	FY 1977	FY 1978	FY 1979	FY 1980	FY 1981
Capital expenditures							
Defense	2.0	2.1	1.5	1.4	1.5	1.8	1.4
Economic services	3.8	3.6	5.5	5.0	6.1	7.5	6.8
Education	0.5	0.4	0.2	0.4	0.2	0.6	0.4
Health	0.3	0.6	0.6	1.0	0.8	0.5	0.4
Other central government[3]	2.1	2.2	2.0	1.1	0.9	1.0	2.5
Local government	0.6	0.6	1.2	0.9	0.5	0.7	0.7
State enterprises	14.4	22.0	33.2	40.3	46.2	43.9	42.3
Total expenditures[4]	100.0	100.0	100.0	100.0	100.0	100.0	100.0
(in billions of kyat)[5]	(3.5)	(4.5)	(5.1)	(7.9)	(9.8)	(11.5)	(12.6)
Overall deficit or surplus	-17.1	4.6	-15.2	-39.6	-34.4	-39.4	-42.8
Deficit financing							
Foreign grants	4.8	4.0	2.5	5.1	4.4	5.5	2.7
Foreign loans	2.0	5.0	17.2	13.5	18.4	12.7	14.0
Domestic financing	10.3	-13.6	-4.5	20.9	11.6	21.2	26.1
Total deficit financing	17.1	-4.6	15.2	39.5	34.4	39.4	42.8

. . . means negligible or zero.
[1] Data for FY 1980 are provisional; data for FY 1981 are based on the draft budget.
[2] Current revenues minus current expenditures.
[3] Including net lending.
[4] Figures may not add to totals because of rounding; revenues include the operating surplus of the public enterprises.
[5] For value of the kyat—see Glossary.

Table 7. Size and Distribution of Landholdings, FY 1962 and FY 1981

Size of Landholding	FY 1962		FY 1981*	
	Number of Households	Area in Hectares	Number of Households	Area in Hectares
Under 2.02 hectares............	} 2,337,965	3,393,157	{ 2,621,785	2,459,234
2.02 to 4.04 hectares			1,053,768	3,039,206
4.04 to 8.10 hectares	353,509	1,893, 453	498,153	2,870,806
8.10 to 20.24 hectares.........	88.878	96,034	109,127	1,220,645
20.24 to 40.49 hectares	4,706	116,768	1,929	51,795
Above 40.49 hectares..........	557	42.228	610	166,067
TOTAL......................	2,785,615	5,541,640	4,285,372	9,807,753

*Preliminary estimates.

Source: Based on information from Burma, Ministry of Planning and Finance, *Report to the Pyithu Hluttaw on the Financial, Economic, and Social Conditions of the Socialist Republic of the Union of Burma for 1977–78*, Rangoon, 1977, 30; and *Report to the Pyithu Hluttaw on the Financial, Economic, and Social Conditions of the Socialist Republic of the Union of Burma for 1982–83*, Rangoon, 1982, 50.

Table 8. Indicators of Agricultural Development, Selected Years, FY 1940–81[1]

Indicator	Units	FY 1940	FY 1962	FY 1972	FY 1975	FY 1980	FY 1981
Cultivated area............	thousands of hectares	7,109.3	7,165.2	7,965.2	8,132.8	8,320.6	8,457.1
Irrigated area............	-do-	632.4	536.0	890.3	984.6	1,073.3	1,051.0
Multiple-cropped irrigated area......	-do-	n.a.	33.5	121.4	143.3	121.6	143.3
Flood-protected area	-do-	n.a.	n.a.	n.a.	1,095.1[2]	1,105.9	1,122.6
High-yield paddy area......	-do-	...	...	147.7	250.8	2,308.9	2,603.6
Chemical fertilizer utilized......	thousands of tons	...	26.7	100.8	122.2	251.3	239.4
Chemical insecticides utilized	-do-	...	0.3	0.2	1.0	0.6	1.0
Draft cattle............	thousands	2,469.9[3]	3,227.9	4,200.8	5,087.0	5,877.0	5,960.0
Farm tractors at stations[4]	number	...	1,391	n.a.	2,779	3,625	3,770
Farm tractors at cooperatives[5]	-do-	...	...	n.a.	3,307	3,754	3,853
Power tillers at cooperatives	-do-	...	n.a.	n.a.	111	371	394
Village managers	-do-	n.a.	1,737	3,882	5,592	6,308	6,693
Agricultural loans......	millions of FY 1970 kyat[6]	n.a.	294.1[7]	139.0	17.8	246.6	288.3
State rural development expenditures..........	-do-	n.a.	6.9[8]	9.1	3.2	2.4	2.4

n.a.—not available.

... means negligible or zero.

[1] Data for FY 1980 are provisional; those for FY 1981 are preliminary estimates.

[2] FY 1977.

[3] FY 1946.

[4] Only tractors in use on farms and in working condition.

[5] Includes tractors not in working condition.

[6] For value of the kyat—see Glossary.

[7] FY 1967, the first year of the program.

[8] FY 1965, the first year of the program.

Table 9.   *Cultivated Area and Production of Major Crops,*
Selected Periods, FY 1974–81[1]
(area in thousands of hectares; production in thousands of tons)

Crop	FY 1974–76 Average		FY 1980		FY 1981	
	Area	Production	Area	Production	Area	Production
Paddy (unmilled)	5,154.9	9,036.3	5,128.7	13,316.7	5,105.3	14,145.8
Wheat..................	93.4	65.7	123.9	116.8	103.6	117.9
Maize	83.3	61.3	151.4	166.6	191.9	231.6
Pulses[2]..................	721.1	288.2	807.7	408.4	887.0	508.0
Groundnuts............	657.1	433.2	514.6	437.9	616.2	566.9
Sesame..................	1,039.5	107.4	1,308.1	157.5	1,396.0	169.7
Sunflower	5.9	1.7	57.9	21.3	106.9	45.7
Cotton	196.8	37.3	221.1	74.2	236.8	108.7
Jute......................	60.9	34.9	101.2	98.6	49.4	32.5
Rubber..................	83.9	14.9	81.0	16.3	80.6	16.3
Sugarcane	95.7	1,486.7	100.4	2,135.0	110.9	2,610.1
Burmese tobacco	51.7	46.3	49.8	48.8	49.0	46.7
Virginia tobacco.......	5.4	17.6	8.9	28.4	11.3	40.6
Other crops[3]...........	1,224.6	204.9	1,387.9	303.0	1,376.5	317.4

[1]Data for FY 1980 are provisional; those for FY 1981 are preliminary estimates.
[2]Including soybeans.
[3]Area of all other crops; production of dried chilies, onions, garlic, and potatoes in gross weight.

Source: Based on information from Burma, Ministry of Planning and Finance, *Report to the Pyithu Hluttaw on the Financial, Economic, and Social Conditions of the Socialist Republic of the Union of Burma for 1978–79*, Rangoon, 1978, 63–65; and *Report to the Pyithu Hluttaw on the Financial, Economic, and Social Conditions of the Socialist Republic of the Union of Burma for 1982–83*, Rangoon, 1982, 81–82.

Table 10. State Procurement and Net Export of Major Crops, Selected Periods, FY 1974–81*
(in thousands of tons)

Crops	FY 1974–76 Average		FY 1980		FY 1981	
	Procurement	Net Exports	Procurement	Net Exports	Procurement	Net Exports
Paddy	2,959.3	350.2	4,211.6	641.3	4,296.3	898.1
Wheat	...	–8.8	...	–6.2	23.5	–6.8
Maize seed	6.8	5.0	22.5	9.7	28.1	20.0
Pulses	41.0	30.1	83.1	72.6	84.7	105.0
Sugarcane	376.9	...	614.3	...	552.2	...
Cotton	21.6	–5.8	34.4	–5.1	34.9	–3.4
Jute	22.8	21.4	67.9	66.2	43.3	40.6
Virginia tobacco	14.6	...	26.0	0.2	27.8	...
Rubber	7.8	6.2	13.7	10.2	14.0	10.2

... means negligible or zero.
*Data for FY 1980 are provisional; those for FY 1981 are preliminary estimates.

Source: Based on information from Burma, Ministry of Planning and Finance, *Report to the Pyithu Hluttaw on the Financial, Economic, and Social Conditions of the Socialist Republic of the Union of Burma for 1978–79*, Rangoon, 1978, 63–65; and *Report to the Pyithu Hluttaw on the Financial, Economic, and Social Conditions of the Socialist Republic of the Union of Burma for 1982–83*, Rangoon, 1982, 89, 207.

Table 11. *Livestock, Fishing, and Forestry Production,
Selected Periods, FY 1974–81*[1]

	Units	FY 1974–76 Average	FY 1979	FY 1980	FY 1981
Cattle	thousands	7,410	8,307	8,531	8,661
Water buffalo	-do-	1,710	1,817	1,901	1,957
Sheep and goats	-do-	725	805	846	870
Pigs	-do-	1,597	1,961	2,196	2,304
Poultry	-do-	19,202	23,915	26,577	27,933
Fresh milk	tousands of tons	258.7	316.1	325.8	343.9
Beef	-do-	28.1	31.7	32.5	31.9
Pork	-do-	26.7	33.1	37.1	37.3
Other meat	-do-	32.3	64.8	71.7	80.6
Eggs	millions	570.1	708.9	787.7	810.7
Agriculture					
State-owned	thousands of tons	0.3	0.5	0.5	0.5
Private and cooperative	-do-	2.0	2.2	2.4	2.7
Total	-do-	2.3	2.7	2.9	3.2
Freshwater fisheries					
State-owned	-do-	2.6	3.3	3.5	3.9
Private and cooperative	-do-	129.2	145.0	145.4	136.0
Total	-do-	131.8	148.3	148.9	139.9
Marine fisheries					
State-owned	-do-	7.3	21.2	18.0	39.6
Private and cooperative	-do-	359.4	406.8	426.3	431.5
Total	-do-	366.7	428.0	444.3	471.1
Mother of pearl	tons	32.9	34.5	38.6	50.8
Pearls	kilograms	2.4	3.0	3.4	3.0
Teak	millions of cubic meters	0.5	0.7	0.7	0.9
Hardwood timber[2]	-do-	1.5	2.0	2.1	2.2
Hardwood for fuel	-do-	n.a.	0.4	0.3	0.2

n.a.—not available.
[1]Data for FY 1980 are provisional; those for FY 1981 are preliminary estimates.
[2]Whole and sawn logs; includes production for firewood and charcoal in FY 1974–76 period.

Source: Based on information from Burma, Ministry of Planning and Finance, *Report to
the Pyithu Hluttaw on the Financial, Economic, and Social Conditions of the
Socialist Republic of the Union of Burma for 1982–83*, Rangoon, 1982, 99–101;
and Food and Agriculture Organization, *Forest Resources of Tropical Asia*,
Rome, 1981, 159.

Table 12. Mining Production, Selected Periods, FY 1974–81[1]
(in tons unless otherwise specified)

	FY 1974–76 Average	FY 1978	FY 1979	FY 1980	FY 1981
Tin concentrates					
Production............	513	738	1,155	1,016	3,340
Export.................	582	832	1,053	441	n.a.
Tungsten concentrates					
Production............	478	713	812	902	1,401
Export.................	581	765	573	621	n.a.
Refined lead					
Production............	3,416	5,547	5,957	6,542	7,620
Export.................	4,454	5,852	3,353	5,509	n.a.
Zinc concentrates					
Production............	4,724	5,339	6,370	7,104	9,144
Export.................	6,467	6,820	3,081	8,128	n.a.
Copper matte					
Production............	69	121	131	240	173
Export.................	117	. . .	370	. . .	n.a.
Nickel speiss					
Production............	56	49	65	130	80
Export.................	115	. . .	. . .	. . .	n.a.
Refined silver					
Production............	6.0	9.8	9.4	10.0	13.4
Export.................	7.4	10.5	6.3	11.7	n.a.
Antimonial lead					
Production............	132	203	343	279	254
Export.................	219	. . .	. . .	. . .	n.a.
Jade......................	14.2	9.0	51.2	46.3	8.9
Coal......................	16,060	12,184	13,818	11,213	28,100
Pig iron..................	. . .	. . .	. . .	. . .	2.8
Crude petroleum (in millions of barrels)					
Production.........	7.5	10.0	11.0	10.1	9.8–12.0[3]
Export.............	−1.1	0.8	1.0	. . .	n.a.
Natural gas (in millions of cubic meters)	202.6	277.0	336.8	415.4	657.1

n.a.—not available.
. . . means negligible or zero.
[1]Data for FY 1980 are provisional; those for FY 1981 are preliminary estimates and probably overstated.
[2]Minus sign indicates imports.
[3]Lower estimate is from United States embassy in Rangoon; upper estimate is from Burma government.

Source: Based on information from Burma, Ministry of Planning and Finance, *Report to the Pyithu Hluttaw on the Financial, Economic, and Social Conditions of the Socialist Republic of the Union of Burma for 1982–83*, Rangoon, 1982, 134–35; and United States Department of State, Embassy in Rangoon, *Foreign Economic Trends and Their Implications for the United States: Burma*, Washington, June 1982, 7.

Table 13. *Manufacture of Major Industrial Products,*
Selected Periods, FY 1974–81[1]

	Units	FY 1974–76 Average	FY 1979	FY 1980	FY 1981
Cigarettes..................	millions	1,959	2,272	2,737	2,811
Longyi[2]					
Men's	-do-	8.5	11.8	11.2	17.2
Women's	-do-	1.0	0.8	0.2	0.7
Children's..............	-do-	1.0	0.5	0.4	0.6
Gunny sacks..............	-do-	15.5	20.0	28.8	33.1
Paper......................	thousands of tons	8.7	14.1	13.6	23.0
Candles....................	-do-	3.4	10.8	11.8	10.9
Cement....................	-do-	218.7	388.0	377.0	372.0
Fertilizer..................	-do-	121.9	132.3	132.6	131.8
Sheet glass................	-do-	. . .	4.8	9.8	7.0
Aluminum ware	-do-	0.8	0.8	0.7	1.7
Gasoline....................	millions of liters	223.0	276.5	275.3	273.1
Kerosine...................	-do-	191.7	91.7	66.7	78.4
Other oils	-do-	135.0	546.2	543.2	581.4
Radios......................	thousands	28.0	7.0	2.0	2.0
Dry-cell batteries	-do-	15,519.0	19,442.0	16,965.0	23,274.0
Motor vehicles............	-do-	1.0	1.5	1.5	2.2
Tractors...................	-do-	0.6	0.8	1.1	0.6
Bicycles....................	-do-	10.8	9.4	9.6	14.8
Electricity[3]					
Produced...............	millions of kilowatt-hours	760.7	1,081.0	1,227.0	1,405.0
Consumed	-do-	564.0	762.0	850.0	1,012.0

. . . means negligible or zero.
[1]Data for FY 1980 are provisional; those for FY 1981 are preliminary estimates and probably too high.
[2]See Glossary.
[3]Electric Power Corporation only; the difference between electricity produced and that consumed is that lost in generation and distribution.

Source: Based on information from Burma, Ministry of Planning and Finance, *Report to the Pyithu Hluttaw on the Financial, Economic, and Social Conditions of the Socialist Republic of the Union of Burma for 1982–83*, Rangoon, 1982, 148–49.

Table 14.   *Balance of Payments, FY 1977–81*[1]
(in millions of United States dollars)

	FY 1977	FY 1978	FY 1979	FY 1980	FY 1981
Exports					
Goods					
Rice and rice products.	119.3	41.1	178.9	202.1	n.a.
Teak	54.2	117.5	73.6	120.7	n.a.
Hardwood	1.0	15.7	10.2		
Base metals	11.9	24.4	29.0	70.7	n.a.
Precious stones.........................	16.5	17.8	40.1		
Pulses and beans........................	10.2	8.7	18.8	23.8	n.a.
Jute	3.0	8.4	6.1	15.0	n.a.
Rubber......................................	5.8	9.1	11.1	12.4	n.a.
Fish and prawns[2]	5.3	7.3	10.1	12.3	n.a.
Animal feed...............................	9.3	8.0	9.9	9.6	n.a.
Other agricultural items	2.1	3.4	4.5	5.6	n.a.
Subtotal[3]..................................	240.3	237.8	396.1	481.2	514.0
Services..............	23.4	19.6	41.0	50.9	36.9
Total exports......................	263.7	257.4	437.1	532.1	550.9
Imports					
Goods					
Capital goods	126.4	254.5	365.5	293.1	n.a.
Raw materials and fuel.................	81.2	101.8	115.5	180.1	n.a.
Tools and spare parts	29.0	40.9	65.4	100.0	n.a.
Consumer goods.........................	27.7	27.6	25.8	39.3	n.a.
Subtotal[3].................................	378.2	505.2	583.7	633.1	793.4
Services....................................	30.1	40.2	52.1	60.3	64.2
Total imports........................	408.3	545.4	635.8	693.4	857.6
Net factor income[4]......................	−8.4	−13.5	−21.7	−24.1	−35.4
Net transfers[5]......................	. . .	12.4	15.2	16.5	13.7
CURRENT ACOUNT BALANCE...................................	−153.0	−289.1	−205.2	−168.9	−328.4
Capital Movements[6]					
Official grants................................	21.7	58.9	64.7	96.8	71.2
Long-term loans	145.1	262.7	292.2	155.2	329.3
Other[7]...	15.1	9.4	−8.9	19.6	n.a.
OVERALL BALANCE.........................	28.9	41.9	142.8	102.7	72.1

n.a.—not available.
. . . means negligible or zero.
[1]Data for FY 1980 are provisional; those for FY 1981 are preliminary estimates.
[2]Including insignificant amounts of animal products.
[3]Totals are derived from official balance of payments statistics, which differ from customs records on commodity trade, and do not add. The difference includes unspecified trade and accounting differences. Imports are converted to free on board (f.o.b.) value, using a coefficient. Exports are f.o.b. value as reported.
[4]Receipts and payment of interest.
[5]Private remittances and some foreign aid.
[6]Net of payments.
[7]Short-term loans, transactions with the International Monetary Fund, and errors and omissions.

Table 15.   Order of Battle for People's Armed Forces, 1983

	Number	Comment
Army		
Total strength—163,000		
Organization		
Light infantry divisions	6	
Armored battalions	2	
Independent infantry battalions ..	85	
Artillery battalions	4	
Antitank/artillery battalion	1	
Antiaircraft battery...................	1	
Equipment		
Comet medium battle tanks	25	Ex-British, World War II vintage
Humber armored cars...............	40	-do-
Ferret scout cars	45	Made in Britain
25-pounder field guns...............	50	Ex-British, World War II vintage
5.5-inch guns.........................	n.a.	-do-
76mm howitzers......................	120	Made in Yugoslavia
105mm M-101 howitzers	80	Made in the United States
120mm mortars.......................	n.a.	Made in Israel
81mm mortars	n.a.	-do-
6- and 17-pounder antitank guns.	50	Ex-British, World War II vintage
3.7-inch antiaircraft guns...........	n.a.	-do-
40mm Bofors antiaircraft guns.....	10	Made in Britain
Air Force		
Total strength—9,000		
Organization and equipment		
2 attack squadrons with:		
AT-33s..................................	5	Made in the United States
Pilatus PC-7 turbo-trainers	20	Made in Switzerland
4 transport squadrons with:		
Fokker F27 Mk100 twin turboprop	1	Made in the Netherlands
FH-227 transports	4	Made in the United States
Pilatus PC-6/6As.....................	7	Made in Switzerland
Cessna 180 Skywagons..............	6	Made in the United States
DHC-6 Twin Otters.................	6	Made in Canada
2 training squadrons with:		
SF-260MB light aircraft.............	20	Made in Italy
T-37C trainers	10	Made in the United States
Helicopters:		
KB-47G trainers.....................	10	Made in Japan
KV-107s	2	-do-
HH-43Bs...............................	7	Made in the United States
Alouette IIIs...........................	10	Made in France
UH-1s..................................	14	Made in the United States

Table 15.—Continued

	Number	Comment
Navy		
Total strength—7,000		
Equipment		
Algerine frigate	1	Ex-British
Corvettes..............................	4	2 ex-United States, 2 made in Burma
River and coastal patrol craft	41	10 made in Burma, 25 made in Yugoslavia, 6 origin unknown
Gunboats.............................	36	Range in displacement between 49 and 381 tons
Transports	9	Ex-United States landing craft
Fishery protection vessels..........	12	3 made in Denmark, 6 made in Australia, 3 made in the United States
Survey vessels	2	1 made in Yugoslavia, 1 made in the Netherlands
Support ship.........................	1	Made in Japan

Bibliography

Chapter 1

Adas, Michael. *The Burma Delta: Economic Development and Social Change on an Asian Rice Frontier, 1852–1941.* Madison: University of Wisconsin Press, 1974.

———. "Imperialist Rhetoric and Modern Historiography: The Case of Lower Burma Before and After Conquest," *Journal of Southeast Asian Studies* [Singapore], 3, No. 2, 1972, 175–92.

———. "'Moral Economy' or 'Contest State'? Elite Demands and the Origins of Peasant Protest in Southeast Asia," *Journal of Social History*, 13, No. 4, Summer 1980, 521–46.

Aung Thwin, Michael. "Jambudipa: Classical Burma's Camelot." Pages 38–61 in John P. Ferguson (ed.), *Essays on Burma.* Leiden: Brill, 1981.

———. "Kingship, the Sangha, and Society in Pagan." Pages 205–56 in Kenneth R. Hall and John K. Whitmore (eds.), *Explorations in Early Southeast Asian History: The Origins of Southeast Asian Statecraft.* Ann Arbor: Michigan Papers on South and Southeast Asia, University of Michigan Center for South and Southeast Asian Studies, 1976.

Badgley, John, and Jon A. Wiant. "The Ne Win-BSPP Style of Bama-Lo: A Strange Revolution." Pages 43–64 in Josef Silverstein (ed.), *The Future of Burma in Perspective: A Symposium.* (Papers in International Studies, Southeast Asia series, No. 35.) Athens: Center for International Studies, Ohio University, 1974.

Ba Maw. *Breakthrough in Burma: Memories of a Revolution, 1939–1946.* New Haven: Yale University Press, 1968.

de Bary, William Theodore (ed.). *Sources of Indian Tradition.* 2 vols. New York: Columbia University Press, 1958.

Asia 1976 Yearbook. (Ed., Rodney Tasker.) Hong Kong: Far Eastern Economic Review, 1976.

Asia 1977 Yearbook. (Ed., Donald Wise.) Hong Kong: Far Eastern Economic Review, 1977.

Asia 1978 Yearbook. (Ed., Donald Wise.) Hong Kong: Far Eastern Economic Review, 1978.

Asia 1979 Yearbook. (Ed., Donald Wise.) Hong Kong: Far Eastern Economic Review, 1979.

Asia 1980 Yearbook. (Ed., Donald Wise.) Hong Kong: Far Eastern Economic Review, 1980.

Asia 1981 Yearbook. (Ed., Donald Wise.) Hong Kong: Far Eastern Economic Review, 1981.

Asia 1982 Yearbook. (Ed., Donald Wise.) Hong Kong: Far Eastern Economic Review, 1982.

Aung Kin. "Burma in 1979: Socialism with Foreign Aid and Strict Neutrality." Pages 93–117 in *Southeast Asian Affairs, 1980.*

Singapore: Institute of Southeast Asian Studies, Heinemann Asia, 1980.

_____. "Burma in 1980: Pouring Balm on Sore Spots." Pages 103–25 in *Southeast Asian Affairs, 1981*. Singapore: Institute of Southeast Asian Studies, Heinemann Asia, 1981.

Bekker, Sarah M. "The Concept of *Anade*: Personal, Social, and Political Implications." Pages 19–37 in John P. Ferguson (ed.), *Essays on Burma*. Leiden: Brill, 1981.

Bennett, Paul J. "Conference under the Tamarind Tree: Burmese Politics and the Accession of King Thibaw, 1878–1882." Pages 57–102 in Paul J. Bennett (ed.), *Conference under the Tamarind Tree: Three Essays in Burmese History*. New Haven: Southeast Asia Studies, Yale University, 1971.

_____. "Two Southeast Asian Ministers and Reactions to European Conquest: the Kinwun Mingyi and Phan-Thanh-Gian." Pages 103–44 in Paul J. Bennett (ed.), *Conference under the Tamarind Tree: Three Essays in Burmese History*. New Haven: Southeast Asia Studies, Yale University, 1971.

"Biruma." Pages 9/1–9/31 in *Tōnan Ajia Yōran 1981*. Tokyo: Tōnan Ajia Chōsakai, 1981.

Blaustein, Albert P., and Gisbert H. Flanz. "Socialist Republic of the Union of Burma." In Albert P. Blaustein and Gisbert H. Flanz (eds.), *Constitutions of the Countries of the World*. Dobbs Ferry, New York: Oceana, 1982.

Brailey, N.J. "A Re-Investigation of the Gwe of Eighteenth-Century Burma," *Journal of Southeast Asian Studies* [Singapore], 1, No. 2, September 1970, 33–47.

Bunge, Frederica M., et al. *Thailand: A Country Study*. (DA Pam 550–53.) Washington: GPO for Foreign Area Studies, The American University, 1981.

Burma Socialist Programme Party. *The System of Correlation of Man and His Environment: The Philosophy of the Burma Socialist Programme Party*. Rangoon: Sarpay Beikman Press, 1973.

Bussagli, Mario. *Oriental Architecture*. New York: Abrams, 1973.

Butwell, Richard. *U Nu of Burma*. Stanford: Stanford University Press, 1963.

Cady, John F. *A History of Modern Burma*. Ithaca: Cornell University Press, 1958.

_____. "Our Burma Experience of 1935–1938." Pages 131–65 in John P. Ferguson (ed.), *Essays on Burma*. Leiden: Brill, 1981.

_____. *The United States and Burma*. Cambridge: Harvard University Press, 1976.

Chakravarti, Nalini Ranjan. *The Indian Minority in Burma: The Rise and Decline of an Immigrant Community*. London: Oxford University Press for the Institute of Race Relations, 1971.

Chew, Ernest C.T. "The Fall of the Burmese Kingdom in 1885: Review and Reconsiderations," *Journal of Southeast Asian Studies* [Singapore], 10, No. 2, September 1979, 372–80.

Coedès, G. *The Indianized States of Southeast Asia.* Honolulu: East-West Center Press, 1968.

———. *The Making of South East Asia.* Berkeley and Los Angeles: University of California Press, 1967.

Collis, Maurice. *The Land of the Great Image.* New York: New Directions, 1958.

———. *Trials in Burma.* London: Faber and Faber, 1945.

Davis, Tony. "Regional Insurgency: Peking's New Tune," *Asiaweek* [Hong Kong], August 7, 1981, 34–36.

Daw Mya Sein. "The Historical Background of the New Constitution." Pages 1–9 in Josef Silverstein (ed.), *The Future of Burma in Perspective: A Symposium.* (Papers in International Studies, Southeast Asia series, No. 35.) Athens: Center for International Studies, Ohio University, 1974.

Dupuy, Trevor N. "Burma and Its Army: A Contrast in Motivations and Characteristics," *Antioch Review*, 20, No. 4, Winter 1960–61, 428–40.

Fairbank, John K., et al. *East Asia: The Modern Transformation.* (A History of East Asian Civilization, 2.) Boston: Houghton Mifflin, 1965.

Ferguson, John P. "The Quest for Legitimation by Burmese Monks and Kings: The Case of the Shwegyin Sect (19th–20th Centuries)." Pages 66–86 in Bardwell L. Smith (ed.), *Religion and Legitimation of Power in Thailand, Laos, and Burma.* Chambersburg, Pennsylvania: Conococheaque Associates, Anima Books, 1978.

Furnivall, John Sydenham. *Colonial Policy and Practice: A Comparative Study of Burma and Netherlands India.* New York: New York University Press, 1956.

Guyot, James F. "The National Identity Problem in Burma and Malaysia," *Bucknell Review*, 19, No. 2, Fall 1971, 67–84.

———. "Political Involution in Burma," *Journal of Comparative Administration*, 2, No. 3, November 1970, 299–322.

Hall, D.G.E. *Henry Burney: A Political Biography.* New York: Oxford University Press, 1974.

———. *A History of South-East Asia.* London: Macmillan, 1964.

Harriman, James. "The Knives Are Out for Ne Win," *Far Eastern Economic Review* [Hong Kong], July 30, 1976, 13–14.

Harvey, G.E. *British Rule in Burma, 1824–1942.* London: Faber and Faber, 1946.

Hoefer, Hans Johannes, et al. *Burma.* Hong Kong: Apa, 1981.

Kamm, Henry. "Burma's Chief to Give Up Job, but Not Power," *New York Times*, September 27, 1981, 12.

———. "Ousted Burmese Chief Forgives His Usurper," *New York Times*, October 11, 1981, 25.

_____. "Proposed Law to Create Two Kinds of Burmese Citizenship Worries Millions," *New York Times*, August 13, 1980, A14.

Keeton, Charles Lee. *King Thebaw and the Ecological Rape of Burma*. New Delhi: Manohar Book Service, 1974.

Keyes, Charles F. "Some Reflections on Contemporary Burma." Pages 82–84 in F.K. Lehman (ed.), *Military Rule in Burma since 1962: A Kaleidoscope of Views*. Singapore: Maruzen Asia, 1981.

Khin Maung Kyi, U, and Daw Tin Tin. *Administrative Patterns in Historical Burma*. (Southeast Asian Perspectives, No. 1.) Singapore: Institute of Southeast Asian Studies, 1973.

Kitzan, Laurence. "Lord Amherst and Pegu: The Annexation Issue, 1824–1826," *Journal of Southeast Asian Studies* [Singapore], 8, 1977, 176–94.

Law-Yone, Edward M. "Dr. Ba Maw of Burma." Pages 1–19 in John P. Ferguson (ed.), *Essays on Burma*. Leiden: Brill, 1981.

Lebar, Frank M., et al. *Ethnic Groups of Mainland Southeast Asia*. New Haven: Human Relations Area Files Press, 1964.

Lehman, F.K. "On the Vocabulary and Semantics of 'Field' in Theravada Buddhist Society." Pages 101–11 in John P. Ferguson (ed.), *Essays on Burma*. Leiden: Brill, 1981.

Lieberman, Victor B. "Ethnic Politics in Eighteenth-Century Burma," *Modern Asian Studies* [Cambridge], 12, No. 3, July 1978, 455–82.

Ling, Trevor. *Buddhism, Imperialism and War: Burma and Thailand in Modern History*. London: Allen and Unwin, 1979.

_____. "Burmese Philosophy Today." Pages 1–46 in Dale Riepe (ed.), *Asian Philosophy Today*. New York: Gordon and Breach, 1981.

Lissak, Moshe. "The Class Structure of Burma: Continuity and Change," *Journal of Southeast Asian Studies* [Singapore], 1, No. 1, March 1970, 60–73.

Mahadevan, Raman. "Immigrant Entrepreneurs in Colonial Burma: An Exploratory Study of the Role of Nattukottai Chettiars of Tamil Nadu, 1880–1930," *Indian Economic and Social History Review* [New Delhi], 15, No. 3, July–September 1978, 329–58.

Maring, Joel M., and Ester G. Maring. *Historical and Cultural Dictionary of Burma*. (Historical and Cultural Dictionaries of Asia, No. 4.) Metuchen, New Jersey: Scarecrow Press, 1973.

Martin, Edwin W. "Burma in 1975: New Dimensions to Non-Alignment," *Asian Survey*, 16, No. 2, February 1976, 173–77.

_____. "Burma in 1976: The Beginnings of Change?" *Asian Survey*, 17, No. 2, February 1977, 155–59.

_____. "Comments on the Recent Situation in Burma." Pages 79–81 in F.K. Lehman (ed.), *Military Rule in Burma since*

1962: A Kaleidoscope of Views. Singapore: Maruzen Asia, 1981.

————. "The Socialist Republic of the Union of Burma: How Much Change?" *Asian Survey*, 15, No. 2, February 1975, 129–35.

Maung Htin Aung. *Burmese Law Tales: The Legal Element in Burmese Folk-Lore*. London: Oxford University Press, 1962.

————. *A History of Burma*. New York: Columbia University Press, 1967.

————. *The Stricken Peacock: Anglo-Burmese Relations, 1752–1948*. The Hague: Nijhoff, 1965.

Maung Maung. *Aung San of Burma*. The Hague: Nijhoff, 1962.

————. *Burma in the Family of Nations*. Amsterdam: Djambatan, 1957.

————. *From Sangha to Laity: Nationalist Movements of Burma, 1920–1940*. (Australian National University Monographs on South Asia, No. 4.) New Delhi: Manohar, 1980.

————. *A Trial in Burma: The Assassination of Aung San*. The Hague: Nijhoff, 1962.

Maung Maung Gyi. "The Crucial Third Dialectic of Burma's Neutralism under U Ne Win." Pages 24–42 in Josef Silverstein (ed.), *The Future of Burma in Perspective: A Symposium*. (Papers in International Studies, Southeast Asia series, No.35.) Athens: Center for International Studies, Ohio University, 1974.

————. "Foreign Policy of Burma since 1962: Negative Neutralism for Group Survival." Pages 9–28 in F.K. Lehman (ed.), *Military Rule in Burma since 1962: A Kaleidoscope of Views*. Singapore: Maruzen Asia, 1981.

Mya Maung. "Military Management of the Burmese Economy: Problems and Prospects." Pages 10–23 in Josef Silverstein (ed.), *The Future of Burma in Perspective: A Symposium*. (Papers in International Studies, Southeast Asia series, No. 35.) Athens: Center for International Studies, Ohio University, 1974.

Myint Aung. "A Gold Coin from Vesali," *Working People's Daily* [Rangoon], November 24, 1980, 5.

Nai Pan Hla. "The Ancient Pyu of Burma," (Pt. 1.) *Working People's Daily* [Rangoon], December 21, 1981, 5.

————. "The Ancient Pyu of Burma," (Pt. 2.), *Working People's Daily* [Rangoon], December 22, 1981, 5.

————. "Origins of the Mons and Their Literature," *Working People's Daily* [Rangoon], March 19, 1980, 5.

Nu, U. "Political Ideology Defined at AFPFL Congress," *Nation* [Rangoon], January 30, 1958, 5–12.

————. *U Nu: Saturday's Son*. (Trans., U Law Yone; Ed., Kyaw Win.) New Haven: Yale University Press, 1975.

"Perspective of Burma: An Atlantic Supplement," *Atlantic Monthly*, 201, No. 2, February 1958, 102–70.

Phayre, Arthur P. *History of Burma.* New York: Kelley, 1969.

"The Philosophy of the 'Burmese Way to Socialism'," *Yuva Newsletter* [London], 3, No. 6, November 1964, 5–14.

Pollak, Oliver B. "Crisis of Kingship: Dynasticism and Revolt in Burma, 1837–1852," *Journal of Southeast Asian Studies* [Singapore], 7, 1976, 187–96.

_____. *Empires in Collision: Anglo-Burmese Relations in the Mid-Nineteenth Century.* (Contributions in Comparative Colonial Studies, No. 1.) Westport, Connecticut: Greenwood Press, 1979.

Raja, Segaran Arumugam. "Burma: A Political and Economic Background." Pages 41–48 in *Southeast Asian Affairs, 1975.* Singapore: Institute for Southeast Asian Studies, Heinemann Asia, 1975.

Ross, Nancy Wilson. "Our Far-Flung Correspondents: Full Moon in Burma," *New Yorker,* June 26, 1954, 33–54.

Rudner, Martin. "Traditionalism and Socialism in Burma's Political Development." Pages 105–39 in S.N. Eisenstadt and Yael Azmon (eds.), *Socialism and Tradition.* Jerusalem: Van Leer Jerusalem Foundation, 1975.

Sarkisyanz, E. *Buddhist Backgrounds of the Burmese Revolution.* The Hague: Nijhoff, 1965.

_____. *Peacocks, Pagodas, and Professor Hall: A Critique of the Persisting Use of Historiography as an Apology for British Empire-Building in Burma.* (Papers in International Studies, Southeast Asia series, No. 24.) Athens: Center for International Studies, Ohio University, 1972.

Scully, William L., and Frank N. Trager. "Burma 1978: The Thirtieth Year of Independence," *Asian Survey,* 19, No. 2, February 1979, 147–56.

_____. "Burma 1979: Reversing the Trend," *Asian Survey,* 20, No. 2, February 1980, 168–75.

Seekins, Donald M. "The Socialist Republic of the Union of Burma." In George Delury (ed.), *The World Encyclopedia of Political Systems and Parties.* New York: Facts on File, 1983

Shaplen, Robert. "Letter from Burma," *New Yorker,* August 27, 1973, 61–70.

Silverstein, Josef. "Burma in 1980: An Uncertain Balance Sheet," *Asian Survey,* 21, No. 2, February 1981, 212–22.

_____. "Burma in 1981: The Changing of the Guardians Begins," *Asian Survey,* 22, No. 2, February 1982, 180–190.

_____. *Burma: Military Rule and the Politics of Stagnation.* Ithaca: Cornell University Press, 1977.

_____. "Burmese and Malaysian Student Politics: A Preliminary Comparative Inquiry," *Journal of Southeast Asian Studies* [Singapore], 1, No. 1, March 1970, 3–22.

_____. *Burmese Politics: The Dilemma of National Unity.* New Brunswick: Rutgers University Press, 1980.

————. "From Soldiers to Civilians: The New Constitution of Burma in Action." Pages 80–92 in Josef Silverstein (ed.), *The Future of Burma in Perspective: A Symposium.* (Papers in International Studies, Southeast Asia series, No. 35.) Athens: Center for International Studies, Ohio University, 1974.

————. "Minority Problems in Burma since 1962." Pages 51–58 in F.K. Lehman (ed.), *Military Rule in Burma since 1962: A Kaleidoscope of Views.* Singapore: Maruzen Asia, 1981.

————. *The Political Legacy of Aung San.* (Data Paper, No. 86.) Ithaca: Southeast Asia Program, Department of Asian Studies, Cornell University, 1972.

Singhal, D.P. *The Annexation of Upper Burma.* Singapore: Eastern Universities Press, 1960.

Smith, Bardwell L. "The Pagan Period (1044–1287): A Bibliographic Note." Pages 112–30 in John P. Ferguson (ed.), *Essays on Burma.* Leiden: Brill, 1981.

Smith, Charles B., Jr. "Armed Communism in Southeast Asia: The Burmese Communist Party." (Research paper presented at Institute of Southeast Asian Studies, Singapore, November 1982.) Washington: 1982.

Smith, Donald Eugene. *Religion and Politics in Burma.* Princeton: Princeton University Press, 1965.

Smith, Dun. *Memoirs of the Four-Foot Colonel.* (Data paper, No. 113.) Ithaca: Southeast Asia Program, Department of Asian Studies, Cornell University, 1972.

Spiro, Melford E. *Buddhism and Society: A Great Tradition and Its Burmese Vicissitudes.* (2d ed.) Berkeley and Los Angeles: University of California Press, 1982.

Steinberg, David I. *Burma's Road Toward Development: Growth and Ideology under Military Rule.* Boulder: Westview Press, 1981.

————. "Burma under the Military: Towards a Chronology," *Contemporary Southeast Asia* [Singapore], 3, No. 3, December 1981, 244–85.

————. "Burmese Economics: The Conflict of Ideology and Pragmatism." Pages 29-50 in F.K. Lehman (ed.), *Military Rule in Burma since 1962: A Kaleidoscope of Views.* Singapore: Maruzer Asia, 1981.

————. "Economic Growth with Equity? The Burmese Experience," *Contemporary Southeast Asia* [Singapore], 4, No. 2, September 1982, 124–52.

Sterba, James P. "Burma, Long Isolationist, Is Looking Abroad for Aid," *New York Times,* June 14, 1979, A3.

Tinker, Hugh. *The Union of Burma: A Study of the First Years of Independence.* (3d ed.) London: Oxford University Press, 1961.

Trager, Frank N. "Democratic and Authoritarian Rule in a not so Newly Independent Country." Pages 65–79 in Josef

Silverstein (ed.), *The Future of Burma in Perspective: A Symposium.* (Papers in International Studies, Southeast Asia series, No. 35.) Athens: Center for International Studies, Ohio University, 1974.

Trager, Frank N., and William J. Koenig. *Burmese Sit-Tans, 1764–1826: Records of Rural Life and Administration.* (Association for Asian Studies, Monograph No. 36.) Tucson: University of Arizona Press, 1979.

Trager, Frank N., and William L. Scully. "The Third Congress of the Burma Socialist Programme Party: 'The Need to Create Continuity and Dynamism of Leadership'," *Asian Survey,* 17, No. 9, September 1977, 830–38.

Tun, M.C. "No Short Cuts to Nirvana," *Far Eastern Economic Review* [Hong Kong], February 5, 1982, 38.

United States. Central Intelligence Agency. Directorate of Intelligence. "Peking and the Burmese Communists: The Perils and the Profits of Insurgency." (Intelligence Report RSS 0052/71.) Washington: July 1971.

Wiant, Jon A. "Lanzin: Ideology and Organization in Revolutionary Burma." (Unpublished Ph.D. dissertation.) Ithaca: Cornell University, June 1982.

_____. "Terry and the Pirates Revisited: The Political Economy of the Golden Triangle." (Paper presented at annual meeting of the International Studies Association, Cincinnati, March 1982.) Cincinnati: March 1982.

_____. "Tradition in the Service of Revolution: The Political Symbolism of Taw-hlan-ye-khit." Pages 59–72 in F.K. Lehman (ed.), *Military Rule in Burma since 1962: A Kaleidoscope of Views.* Singapore: Maruzen Asia, 1981.

Yoon, Won Z. *Japan's Scheme for the Liberation of Burma; The Role of the Minami Kikan and the "Thirty Comrades."* (Papers in International Studies, Southeast Asia series, No. 27.) Athens: Center for International Studies, Ohio University, 1973.

_____. "Military Expediency: A Determining Factor in the Japanese Policy Regarding Burmese Independence," *Journal of Southeast Asian Studies* [Singapore], 9, No. 2, September 1978, 248–67.

Zaw Win. "Burmese Dismiss U Nu's Return as Having Little Political Significance," *Asia Record,* 1, No. 9, September 1980, 5.

_____. "Ne Win Steps Down, Reshuffles Key Posts to Ensure Continuity," *Asia Record,* 2, No. 9, December 1981, 12.

Chapter 2

Allott, Anna J. "Prose Writing and Publishing in Burma: Government Policy and Popular Practice." Pages 1–35 in Tham

Seong Chee (ed.), *Essays in Literature and Society in Southeast Asia*. Singapore: Singapore University Press, 1981.

Aung Thaw. *Excavations at Beikthano*. Rangoon: Ministry of Union Culture, 1968.

———. *Historical Sites in Burma*. Rangoon: Ministry of Union Culture, 1972.

Bagshawe, L.E. "Moral and Intellectual Improvement of the People, 1868–1882." (Paper presented at Burma Studies Colloquium, Elmira, New York, October 1982.) Elmira, New York: 1982.

Bekker, Sarah M. "The Concept of *Anade*: Personal, Social, and Political Implications." Pages 19–37 in John P. Ferguson (ed.), *Essays on Burma*. Leiden: Brill, 1981.

Bigandet, P. *The Life or Legend of Gaudama, the Buddha of the Burmese, with Annotations: The Ways to Neibban and Notice on the Phongyies or Burmese Monks*. 2 vols. London: Trubner, 1880.

Burling, Robbins. *Hill Farms and Padi Fields*. Englewood Cliffs: Prentice-Hall, 1965.

Burma. *Burma and the Insurrections*. Rangoon: 1949.

Cady, John F. *A History of Modern Burma*. Ithaca: Cornell University Press, 1958.

Chakravarti, Nalini Ranjan. *The Indian Minority in Burma: The Rise and Decline of an Immigrant Community*. London: Oxford University Press for the Institute of Race Relations, 1971.

Denyer, C.H. *Dawn on the Kachin Hills*. London: Bible Churchmen's Missionary Society, 1927.

Enriquez, C.M. *A Burmese Arcady*. London: Seeley, Service, 1923.

Ferguson, John P. "The Great Goddess Today in Burma and Thailand: An Exploration of the Symbolic Relevance to Monastic and Female Roles." Pages 283–303 in James J. Preston (ed.), *Mother Worship: Theme and Variations*. Chapel Hill: University of North Carolina Press, 1982.

———. "The Quest for Legitimation by Burmese Monks and Kings: The Case of the Shwegyin Sect (19th–20th Centuries)." Pages 66–86 in Bardwell L. Smith (ed.), *Religion and Legitimation of Power in Thailand, Laos, and Burma*. Chambersburg, Pennsylvania: Conococheaque Associates, Anima Books, 1978.

———. *The Symbolic Dimensions of the Burmese Sangha*. (Ph.D. dissertation.) Ithaca: Cornell University, 1975.

Ferguson, John P. (ed.). *Essays on Burma*, 16. Leiden: Brill, 1981.

Fytche, Albert. *Burma, Past and Present: With Personal Reminiscences of the Country*. 2 vols. London: Kegan Paul, 1878.

Hall, H. Fielding. *The Soul of a People*. London: Macmillan, 1905.

Hanson, O. *A Dictionary of the Kachin Language* (rev. ed.) Rangoon: Baptist Board of Publication, 1954.

_____. *The Kachins: Their Customs and Traditions*. Rangoon: American Baptist Mission Press, 1913.

Harvey, G.E. *History of Burma*. London: Cass, 1925.

Head, W.R. *Haka Chin Customs*. Rangoon: Superintendent, Union Government Printing and Stationery, 1955 (reprint.).

Hoefer, Hans Johannes, et al. *Burma*. Hong Kong: Apa, 1981.

Judson, Adoniram. *Judson's Burmese-English Dictionary*. Rangoon: Baptist Board of Publications, 1953.

The Karens: Or Memoir of Ko Thah-Byu, the First Karen Convert. Tavoy: Karen Mission Press, 1841.

Keyes, Charles F. *The Golden Peninsula*. New York: Macmillan, 1977.

Keyes, Charles F. (ed.). *Ethnic Adaptation and Identity: The Karen on the Thai Frontier with Burma*. Philadelphia: Institute for the Study of Human Issues, 1979.

Kunstadter, Peter (ed.). *Southeast Asian Tribes, Minorities, and Nations*. 2 vols. Princeton: Princeton University Press, 1967.

La Raw, Maran. "Towards a Basis for Understanding the Minorities in Burma: the Kachin Example." Pages 125–46 in Peter Kunstadter (ed.), *Southeast Asian Tribes, Minorities, and Nations*, 1. Princeton: Princeton University Press, 1967.

Law-Yone, Edward M. "Dr. Ba Maw of Burma." Pages 1–19 in John P. Ferguson (ed.), *Essays on Burma*. Leiden: Brill, 1981.

Leach, Edmund R. *Political Systems of Highland Burma*. Boston: Beacon Press, 1954.

Lebar, Frank M., et al. *Ethnic Groups of Mainland Southeast Asia*. New Haven: Human Relations Area Files Press, 1964.

Lehman, F.K. "Burma: Kayah Society as a Function of the Shan-Burma-Karen Context." Pages 1–104 in Julian H. Steward (ed.), *Contemporary Change in Traditional Societies*, 2. Urbana: University of Illinois Press, 1967.

_____. "Ethnic Categories in Burma and the Theory of Social Systems." pages 93–104 in Peter Kunstadter (ed.) *Southeast Asian Tribes, Minorities, and Nations*, 1. Princeton: Princeton University Press, 1967.

_____. *The Structure of Chin Society*. Urbana: University of Illinois Press, 1963.

Lehman, F.K. (ed.). *Military Rule in Burma since 1962: A Kaleidoscope of Views*. Singapore: Maruzen Asia, 1981.

Lowry, John. *Burmese Art*. London: Victoria and Albert Museum, 1974.

Luce, Gordon H. "The Ancient Pyu," *Journal of the Burma Research Society* [Rangoon], 27, 1937, 239–53.

_____. "Mons of the Pagan Dynasty," *Journal of the Burma Research Society* [Rangoon], 36, No. 1, 1953, 1–19.

————. *Old Burma-Early Pagan*, 1. Locust Valley, New York: Augustin, 1969.

————. *Old Burma-Early Pagan*, 2. Locust Valley, New York: Augustin, 1970.

Mangrai, Sao Saimong. *The Padaeng Chronicle and the Jengtung State Chronicle Translated*, 19. Ann Arbor: Center for South and Southeast Asian Studies, University of Michigan, 1981.

Marshall, Harry I. *The Karen People of Burma*. (Bulletin series, 26, No. 13.) Columbus: Ohio State University, 1922.

————. *The Karens of Burma*. (Burma Pamphlets, No. 8.) London: Longmans, Green, 1945.

Mason, Ellen B. *Tounghoo Women*. New York: Randolph, 1860.

Mendelson, E. Michael. "Buddhism and Politics in Burma," *New Society* [London], 1, No. 38, June 20, 1963, 8–10.

————. "Buddhism and the Burmese Establishment," *Archives de sociologie des religions* [Paris], 17, 1964, 85–95.

————. "Initiation and the Paradox of Power: A Sociological Approach." Pages 214–21 in C.J. Bleeker (ed.), *Initiation*. Leiden: Brill, 1965.

————. "The King of the Weaving Mountain," *Royal Central Asian Journal* [London], 48, 1961, 229–37.

————. "A Messianic Buddhist Association in Upper Burma," *Bulletin of the School of Oriental and African Studies* [London], 24, 1961, 560–80.

————. "Observations on a Tour in the Region of Mount Popa, Central Burma," *France-Asie* [Saigon], 179, May–June 1963, 786–807.

————. "Religion and Authority in Modern Burma," *World Today* [London], 16, 1960, 110–18.

————. *Sanga and State in Burma: A Study of Monastic Sectarianism and Leadership*. (Ed., John P. Ferguson.) Ithaca: Cornell University Press, 1975.

————. "The Uses of Religious Skepticism in Burma," *Diogenes* [Florence], 41, 1963, 94–116.

Milne, Leslie. *The Home of an Eastern Clan*. Oxford: Clarendon Press, 1924.

Milne, Leslie, and Wilbur W. Cochrane. *Shans at Home*. London: Murray, 1910.

Mi Mi Khaing. *Burmese Family*. Bloomington: Indiana University Press, 1945.

Nash, Manning. *The Golden Road to Modernity*. New York: Wiley, 1965.

Nu, U. *U Nu: Saturday's Son*. (Trans., U Law Yone: Ed., Kyaw Win.) New Haven: Yale University Press, 1975.

Pfanner, David E. "The Buddhist Monk in Rural Burmese Society." Pages 77–96 in Manning Nash (ed.), *Anthropological Studies in Theravada Buddhism*. Hartford: Southeast Asia Studies, Yale University, 1966.

———. "Rice and Religion in a Burmese Village." (Ph.D. dissertation.) Ithaca: Cornell University, 1962.

Pfanner, David E., and Jasper Ingersoll, Jr. "Theravada Buddhism and Village Economic Behavior," *Journal of Asian Studies*, 21, No. 3, 1962, 341–61.

Sao Saimong Mangrai. *The Shan States and the British Annexation.* (Data paper, No. 57.) Ithaca: Southeast Asia Program, Department of Asian Studies, Cornell University, 1965.

Scott, James George. *The Burman: His Life and Notions.* New York: Norton, 1882.

Scott, James George, and J.P. Hardiman. *Gazetteer of Upper Burma and the Shan States.* 2 vols. Rangoon: Superintendent, Govenment Printing, 1900.

Sein, Kenneth, and J.A. Withey. *The Great Po Sein: A Chronicle of the Burmese Theater.* Bloomington: Indiana University Press, 1965.

Shorto, H.L. "The Gavampati Tradition in Burma." Pages 15–30 in Himansu B. Sarkar (ed.), *R.C. Majumdar Felicitation Volume.* Calcutta: Mukhopadyay, 1970.

Silverstein, Josef. *Burma: Military Rule and the Politics of Stagnation.* Ithaca: Cornell University Press, 1977.

———. "Minority Problems in Burma since 1962." Pages 51–58 in F.K. Lehman (ed.), *Military Rule in Burma since 1962: A Kaleidoscope of Views.* Singapore: Maruzen Asia, 1981.

Singh, Uma Shankar. *Burma and India (1948–1962).* New Delhi: Oxford and IBH, 1979.

Spiro, Melford E. *Buddhism and Society: A Great Tradition and Its Burmese Vicissitudes.* New York: Harper and Row, 1970.

———. *Burmese Supernaturalism.* Englewood Cliffs: Prentice-Hall, 1967.

———. *Kinship and Marriage in Burma.* Berkeley and Los Angeles: University of California Press, 1977.

Steinberg, David I. *Burma: A Socialist Nation of Southeast Asia.* Boulder: Westview Press, 1982.

———. "Burmese Economics: The Conflict of Ideology and Pragmatism." Pages 29–50 in F.K. Lehman (ed.), *Military Rule in Burma since 1962: A Kaleidoscope of Views.* Singapore: Maruzen Asia, 1981.

Stern, Theodore. "*Ariya* and the Golden Book: A Millenarian Buddhist Sect among the Karen," *Journal of Asian Studies*, No. 27, 1968, 297–328.

Stevenson, H.N.C. *The Economics of the Central Chin Tribes.* Bombay: Times of India Press, 1943.

———. *The Hill Peoples of Burma.* (Burma Pamphlets, No. 6.) London: Longmans, Green, 1944.

———. "Some Social Effects of the Religion and Sacrifices of the Zahan Chins," (Pt. 3.) *Journal of the Burma Research Society*

[Rangoon], 28, 1938, 177–92.

Steward, Julian H. *Contemporary Change in Traditional Societies*, 2. Urbana: University of Illinois Press, 1967.

Symes, Michael. *An Account of an Embassy to the Kingdom of Ava*. London: Bulmer, 1800.

Thaung, U. "Contemporary Burmese Literature." Pages 81–100 in John P. Ferguson (ed.), *Essays on Burma*. Leiden: Brill, 1981.

Varady, Robert G. "Environmental Profile of Burma." (Research paper for the Arid Lands Information Center, Office of Arid Lands Studies, University of Arizona.) Tucson: 1982.

Wheeler, Anthony Ian. *Burma: A Travel Survival Kit*. Victoria: Lonely Planet, 1979.

Wiant, Jon A. "Lanzin: Ideology and Organization in Revolutionary Burma." (Unpublished Ph.D. dissertation.) Ithaca: Cornell University, June 1982.

Williamson, Muriel C. "Aspects of Traditional Style Maintained in Burma's First 13 Kyo Songs," *Selected Reports in Ethnomusicology*, 2, No. 2, 1975, 117–64.

Working People's Daily [Rangoon], May 1981.

Yegar, Moshe. *The Muslims of Burma*. Wiesbaden: Harrassowitz, 1972.

Zagorski, Ulrich. *Burma: Unknown Paradise*. Tokyo: Kodansha International, 1972.

Chapter 3

Asia 1975 Yearbook. (Ed., Christopher Lewis.) Hong Kong: Far Eastern Economic Review, 1975.

Asia 1976 Yearbook. (Ed., Rodney Tasker.) Hong Kong: Far Eastern Economic Review, 1976.

Asia 1977 Yearbook. (Ed., Donald Wise.) Hong Kong: Far Eastern Economic Review, 1977.

Asia 1978 Yearbook. (Ed., Donald Wise.) Hong Kong: Far Eastern Economic Review, 1978.

Asia 1979 Yearbook. (Ed., Donald Wise.) Hong Kong: Far Eastern Economic Review, 1979.

Asia 1980 Yearbook. (Ed., Donald Wise.) Hong Kong: Far Eastern Economic Review, 1980.

Asia 1981 Yearbook. (Ed., Donald Wise.) Hong Kong: Far Eastern Economic Review, 1981.

"Black Market is Burma's Hidden Economic System," *Journal of Commerce*, April 30, 1982, E8.

Blake, Bill. "Letter from Rangoon," *Far Eastern Economic Review* [Hong Kong], July 17, 1981, 66.

Borsuk, Richard. "Burma's Growth Declines Greatly from Past Years." *Asian Wall Street Journal* [Hong Kong], March 3, 1983, 1.

———. "There's Speculation in Rangoon of Bad News about Oil Imports," *Asian Wall Street Journal* [Hong Kong], March 3, 1983, 14.

Burma. *Report to the People by the Government of the Union of Burma on the Financial, Economic, and Social Conditions for 1971–72*. Rangoon: Central Press, 1972.

Burma. Ministry of Information. Department of Information and Broadcasting. *The Socialist Republic of the Union of Burma*. Rangoon: 1981.

Burma. Ministry of Planning and Finance. *Five-Year Development Programme, 1980–81 to 1984–85*. Rangoon: 1979.

———. *Report to the Pyithu Hluttaw on the Financial, Economic, and Social Conditions of the Socialist Republic of the Union of Burma for 1977–78*. Rangoon: 1977.

———. *Report to the Pyithu Hluttaw on the Financial, Economic, and Social Conditions of the Socialist Republic of the Union of Burma for 1978–79*. Rangoon: 1978.

———. *Report to the Pyithu Hluttaw on the Financial, Economic, and Social Conditions of the Socialist Republic of the Union of Burma for 1980–81*. Rangoon: 1980.

———. *Report to the Pyithu Hluttaw on the Financial, Economic and Social Conditions of the Socialist Republic of the Union of Burma for 1982–83*. Rangoon: 1982.

Burma Socialist Programme Party. *The System of Correlation of Man and His Environment: The Philosophy of the Burma Socialist Programme Party*. Rangoon: Sarpay Beikman Press, 1973.

"Burma: Happily Going Backwards," *Economist* [London], October 31, 1981, 50–55.

"Burma's Rocky Road to Socialism," *Business in Thailand* [Bangkok], 14, No. 1, January 1982, 80–82.

Chadwick, John R. "Burma—High Level of Unrealized Mineral Potential," *World Mining*, 5, No. 5, May 1982, 51–53.

Fawthrop, Tom. "Smuggled Goods Large Part of Burma's Economy," *Business in Thailand* [Bangkok], 13, No. 8, August 1981, 20–26.

Fenichel, Allen, and Azfar Khan. "The Burmese Way to 'Socialism'". *World Development* [Oxford], 9, Nos. 9–10, September–October 1981, 813–24.

Food and Agriculture Organization. *Forest Resources of Tropical Asia*. (UN Document No. 32/6.1303-78-04, Technical Report No. 3.) Rome: 1981.

"Fourth Four-Year Plan Objectives Explained," *Working People's Daily* [Rangoon], March 16, 1982 (supplement.).

Government Finance Statistics Yearbook, 1982. Washington: International Monetary Fund, 1982.

Harriman, James. "Burma's Bid to Stop the Rot," *Far Eastern Economic Review* [Hong Kong], April 14, 1976, 42–46.

————. "Burma's First Steps to Capitalism," *Far Eastern Economic Review* [Hong Kong], December 24, 1976, 100–102.

————. "Party Grasps an Economic Lifeline," *Far Eastern Economic Review* [Hong Kong], March 11, 1977, 12–13.

Ho Kwon Ping. "The Cautious Search for Success," *Far Eastern Economic Review* [Hong Kong], January 18, 1980, 36–42.

————. "Reforms Can Be Profitable," *Far Eastern Economic Review* [Hong Kong], January 18, 1980, 38–39.

Hough, G. Vernon. "New Finds Point to Brighter Future," *Petroleum Economist*, No. 49, April 1982, 129–30.

Länderkurzbericht Birma, 1979. Stuttgart: Statistisches Bundesamt Wiesbaden, 1979.

"Letter from Rangoon," *Far Eastern Economic Review* [Hong Kong], August 27, 1982, 70.

McBeth, John. "The Green Revolution Means a Classic Dilemma for Burma," *Far Eastern Economic Review* [Hong Kong], October 9, 1981, 62–63.

————. "Paranoia of Progress," *Far Eastern Economic Review* [Hong Kong], October 16, 1981, 89–91.

————. "The Party Aids the Paddy," *Far Eastern Economic Review* [Hong Kong], October 16, 1981, 91–92.

————. "The Search Offshore Is on Again," *Far Eastern Economic Review* [Hong Kong], October 9, 1981, 63–64.

Maring, Joel M., and Ester G. Maring. *Historical and Cultural Dictionary of Burma.* (Historical and Cultural Dictionaries of Asia, No. 4.) Metuchen, New Jersey: Scarecrow Press, 1973.

Martin, Edwin W. "Burma in 1976: The Beginnings of Change?" *Asian Survey*, 17, No. 2, February 1977, 155–59.

Odling-Smee, John. "Adjustment with Financial Assistance from the Fund," *Finance and Development*, 19, No. 4, December 1982, 26–30.

O'Sullivan, J. "Umbrella Factor," *Policy Review*, 17, Summer 1981, 117–18.

"Reply to Discussions on Economic Plan Targets," *Working People's Daily* [Rangoon], March 19, 1982, 1.

Richardson, Dennis. "Letter from Mandalay," *Far Eastern Economic Review* [Hong Kong], June 19, 1981, 94.

Scully, William L., and Frank N. Trager. "Burma 1978: The Thirtieth Year of Independence," *Asian Survey*, 19, No. 2, February 1979, 147–56.

————. "Burma 1979: Reversing the Trend," *Asian Survey*, 20, No. 2, February 1980, 168–75.

Silverstein, Josef. "Burma in 1980: An Uncertain Balance Sheet," *Asian Survey*, 21, No. 2, February 1981, 212–22.

————. "Burma in 1981: The Changing of the Guardians Begins," *Asian Survey*, 22, No. 2, February 1982, 180–90.

————. *Burma: Military Rule and the Politics of Stagnation.* Ithaca: Cornell University Press, 1977.

Sricharatchanya, Paisal. "The Prize of Isolation," *Far Eastern Economic Review* [Hong Kong], October 8, 1982, 73–80.

Statistical Yearbook for Asia and the Far East, 1972. Bangkok: United Nations Economic and Social Commission for Asia and the Far East, 1973.

Statistical Yearbook for Asia and the Pacific, 1980. Bangkok: United Nations Economic and Social Commission for Asia and the Pacific, 1981.

Statistical Yearbook, 1975. Rangoon: Central Statistical Organization, 1976.

Steinberg, David I. *Burma: A Socialist Nation of Southeast Asia.* Boulder: Westview Press, 1982.

————. *Burma's Road Toward Development: Growth and Ideology under Military Rule.* Boulder: Westview Press, 1981.

————. "Burma under the Military: Towards a Chronology," *Contemporary Southeast Asia* [Singapore], 3, No. 3, December 1981, 244–85.

————. "Economic Growth with Equity? The Burmese Experience," *Contemporary Southeast Asia* [Singapore], 4, No. 2, September 1982, 124–52.

————. *"In Medias Res*—Burma's Third Four-Year Plan: Half Way to Socialism and Industrialization?" (Paper presented at the Burma Studies Colloquium, Elmira, New York, October 1982.) Elmira, New York: 1982.

Trager, Frank N., and William L. Scully. "Burma in 1977: Cautious Changes and a Careful Watch," *Asian Survey,* 18, No. 2, February 1978, 142–52.

Tun, M.C. "Even Nationalised Banks Can Be Profitable," *Far Eastern Economic Review* [Hong Kong], April 4, 1980, 98–101.

————. "Huge Doses of Foreign Capital Have Worked," *Far Eastern Economic Review* [Hong Kong], March 26, 1982, 96.

————. "Old Style Techniques Facilitate Frauds," *Far Eastern Economic Review* [Hong Kong], March 27, 1981, 104.

"Union Day Special Supplement," *Guardian* [Rangoon], February 12, 1981, (supplement.).

United States. Department of State. Embassy in Rangoon. *Foreign Economic Trends and Their Implications for the United States: Burma.* (International Marketing Information Series, FET 82-043.) Washington: Department of Commerce, International Trade Administration, June 1982.

————. "Petroleum Outlook Report—Burma." Rangoon: April 6, 1981.

Wiant, Jon A. "The Ne Win Legacy." (Paper presented at New York State Conference on Asian Affairs, Oneonta, New York, October 1981.) Oneonta, New York: October 1981.

World Development Report, 1982. New York: Oxford University Press for the World Bank, 1982.

(Various issues of the following publications were also used in the preparation of this chapter: *Asian Wall Street Journal* [Hong Kong], January 1982–February 1983; *Economist* [London], January 1979–February 1983; *Far Eastern Economic Review* [Hong Kong], January 1973–February 1983; *Guardian* [Rangoon], January 1978–December 1982; Joint Publications Research Service, *South and East Asia Report*, January 1979–December 1982; and *Working People's Daily* [Rangoon], January 1978–December 1982.)

Chapter 4

Asia and Pacific, 1981. (Ed., Graham Hancock.) Essex, England: World of Information, 1981.

Asia 1983 Yearbook. (Ed., Donald Wise.) Hong Kong: Far Eastern Economic Review, 1983.

Aung Kin. "Burma in 1979: Socialism with Foreign Aid and Strict Neutrality." Pages 93–117 in *Southeast Asian Affairs, 1980.* Singapore: Institute of Southeast Asian Studies, Heinemann Asia, 1980.

_____. "Burma in 1980: Pouring Balm on Sore Spots." Pages 103–25 in *Southeast Asian Affairs, 1981.* Singapore: Institute of Southeast Asian Studies, Heinemann Asia, 1981.

Aye Ko, U. "Report of the Council of State Submitted," *Guardian* [Rangoon], October 12, 1982, 1-2.

_____. "Speech Delivered by Council of State Secretary U Aye Ko as Chairman at Union Day Discussions," *Guardian* [Rangoon], February 12, 1982, 1.

Badgley, John. "Burma: The Army Vows Legitimacy," *Asian Survey*, 12, No. 2, February 1972, 177–81.

_____. "The Union of Burma: Age Twenty-Two, *"Asian Survey,"* 11. No. 2, February 1971, 149–58.

"The Basic Working Style of the Lanzin Party," *Working People's Daily* [Rangoon], October 10, 1982, 4.

"Bill on Amendment to Constitution Submitted," *Guardian* [Rangoon], March 17, 1981, 5.

Blaustein, Albert P., and Gisbert H. Flanz. "Socialist Republic of the Union of Burma." In Albert P. Blaustein and Gisbert H. Flanz (eds.), *Constitutions of the Countries of the World.* Dobbs Ferry, New York: Oceana, 1982.

"BSPP Congress Ends, Ne Win Announces Retirement," Foreign Broadcast Information Service, *Daily Report: Asia and Pacific*, 4, No. 153 (FBIS-APA-81-153), August 10, 1981, G1-G5.

Burma. *The Constitution of the Socialist Republic of the Union of Burma.* Rangoon: Printing and Publishing, 1974.

"Burma: Political Situation Post-Ne Win Is Murky," *Asia Record*, 3, No. 10, January 1983, 12.

Burson. "People's Judicial System," *Forward* [Rangoon], 12, No.

4, January 1, 1974, 16–19.

Butwell, Richard. "The Burmese Way of Change," *Current History*, 71, No. 422, December 1976, 205–08.

———. *U Nu of Burma*. Stanford: Stanford University Press, 1963.

Chen, David H. "Modern Burma: National Development, Problems, and Perspectives," *Asian Profile*, 7, No. 1, February 1979, 37–48.

Chit Hlaing, U. "Minister U Chit Hlaing Addresses 37th Session of United Nations General Assembly," *Working People's Daily* [Rangoon], October 7, 1982, 1.

Davis, Tony. "Regional Insurgency: Peking's New Tune," *Asiaweek* [Hong Kong], August 7, 1981, 34–36.

Eisenstadt, S.N., and Yael Azmon (eds.). *Socialism and Tradition*. Jerusalem: Van Leer Jerusalem Foundation, 1975.

"English Comes Back to Burma," *Asiaweek* [Hong Kong], August 7, 1981, 40–41.

The Far East and Australasia 1980–81: A Survey and Directory of Asia and the Pacific. London: Europa, 1980.

Fathers, Michael. "Burma's Economy Quickens as Leader Warms to Outside World," *Asia Record*, 2, No. 8, November 1981, 1.

———. "Government Moves to Clean Up Buddhist Clergy, Win Support," *Asia Record*, 2, No. 8, November 1981, 4.

———. "San Yu Likely to Become New President as Ne Win Steps Down," *Asia Record*, 2, No. 8, November 1981, 4.

Joint Publications Research Service—JPRS (Washington). *Translations on South and East Asia Report*. "President Ne Win an Invisible Dictator," *Business Times*, Kuala Lumpur, July 13, 1979. (JPRS 74019, No. 836, August 16, 1979.).

Kamm, Henry. "Burma's Chief to Give Up Job, but Not Power," *New York Times*, September 27, 1981, 12.

———. "Burmese About to Sign Aid Accord with U.S.," *New York Times*, October 25, 1981, 13.

———. "Ousted Burmese Chief Forgives His Usurper," *New York Times*, October 11, 1981, 25.

———. "Proposed Law to Create Two Kinds of Burmese Citizenship Worries Millions," *New York Times*, August 13, 1980, A14.

Kerns, Hikaru. "Burma: A State of Strife," *Far Eastern Economic Review* [Hong Kong], November 26, 1982, 36–39.

"Lanzin Youths in Socialist Democratic Structure," *Working People's Daily* [Rangoon], April 16, 1981, 4.

Lehman, F.K. (ed.). *Military Rule in Burma since 1962: A Kaleidoscope of Views*. Singapore: Maruzen Asia, 1981.

Martin, Edwin W. "Burma in 1975: New Dimensions to Non-Alignment," *Asian Survey*, 16, No. 2, February 1976, 173–77.

———. "Burma in 1976: The Beginnings of Change?" *Asian Survey*, 17, No. 2, February 1977, 155–59.

"Mass Organization under Party Leadership," *Guardian* [Rangoon], May 16, 1982, 4.

Maung Maung Gyi. "Foreign Policy of Burma since 1962: Negative Neutralism for Group Survival." Pages 9–28 in F.K. Lehman (ed.), *Military Rule in Burma since 1962: A Kaleidoscope of Views*. Singapore: Maruzen Asia, 1981.

Maung Maung Kha, U. "Council of Ministers' Report," *Guardian* [Rangoon], October 12, 1982, 1.

Misra, K.P. "Burma's Farewell to the Nonaligned Movement," (Pt. 1.), *Asian Affairs* [London], 12 (Old Series, 68), February 1981, 49–56.

"Moral Development of Youths," *Guardian* [Rangoon], June 27, 1982, 4.

Myint Maung, U. "Report of the Council of People's Attorneys," *Guardian* [Rangoon], October 12, 1982, 2.

Ne Dun. "For Development of National Groups," *Guardian* [Rangoon], April 2, 1981, 4.

————. "National Day Political Objectives," *Guardian* [Rangoon], December 7, 1982, 4.

"Ne Win Still Calls the Shots in Burma," *Straits Times* [Singapore], November 20, 1982, 4.

Ohn Kyaw, U. "Workers Asiayone Central Body Chairman's Address," *Guardian* [Rangoon], December 8, 1982, 1.

"Party Chairman's Address" *Guardian* [Rangoon], May 15, 1981, 4.

"Party General Secretary Presents Political Report of the Central Committee," *Guardian Supplement* [Rangoon], August 4, 1981, 1–5.

"Peasants Asiayone Organization," *Guardian* [Rangoon], October 14, 1981, 4.

"People Welcome Constitution Amendment,"*Guardian* [Rangoon], March 24, 1981, 4.

"President San Yu: A Profile," *Asia Record*, 2, No. 9, December 1981, 12.

Raja, Segaran Arumugam. "Burma: A Political and Economic Background." Pages 41–48 in *Southeast Asian Affairs, 1975*. Singapore: Institute of Southeast Asian Studies, Heinemann Asia, 1975.

"The Role of Rural Youths," *Working People's Daily [Rangoon]*, August 17, 1982, 4.

San Maung, U. "Report of the Council of People's Inspectors," *Guardian* [Rangoon], October 12, 1982, 3.

San Yu, U. "Party General Secretary Presents Political Report of the Central Committee," *Working People's Daily* [Rangoon], August 3, 1981, 1.

————. "Presentation of the Council of State in Connection with Burma's Action at the Sixth Non-Aligned Summit Conference," *Guardian* [Rangoon], October 9, 1979, A–D.

Scully, William L., and Frank N. Trager. "Burma 1978: The Thirtieth Year of Independence," *Asian Survey*, 19, No. 2, February 1979, 147–56.

_____. "Burma 1979: Reversing the Trend," *Asian Survey*, 20, No. 2, February 1980, 168–75.

Silverstein, Josef. "Burma in 1980: An Uncertain Balance Sheet," *Asian Survey*, 21, No. 2, February 1981, 212–22.

_____. "Burma in 1981: The Changing of the Guardians Begins," *Asian Survey*, 22, No. 2, February 1982, 180–90.

_____. *Burma: Military Rule and the Politics of Stagnation.* Ithaca: Cornell University Press, 1977.

_____. "The Military and Foreign Policy in Burma and Indonesia," *Asian Survey*, 22, No. 3, March 1982, 278–91.

_____. "Minority Problems in Burma since 1962." Pages 51–58 in F.K. Lehman (ed.), *Military Rule in Burma since 1962: A Kaleidoscope of Views.* Singapore: Maruzen Asia, 1981.

Smith, Bardwell L. (ed.). *Religion and Legitimation of Power in Thailand, Laos, and Burma.* Chambersburg, Pennsylvania: Conococheague Associates, Anima Books, 1978.

Steinberg, David I. *Burma's Road Toward Development: Growth and Ideology under Military Rule.* Boulder: Westview Press, 1981.

_____. "Burma under the Military: Towards a Chronology," *Contemporary Southeast Asia* [Singapore], 3, No.3, December 1981, 244–85.

Tin Sung Hein, U. "Report of the Council of People's Justices," *Guardian* [Rangoon], October 12, 1982, 3.

Tōnan Ajia Yōran 1981. Tokyo: Tōnon Ajia Chōsakai, 1981.

Trager, Frank N., and William L. Scully. "Burma in 1977: Cautious Changes and a Careful Watch," *Asian Survey*, 18, No. 2, February 1978, 142–52.

_____. "The Third Congress of the Burma Socialist Programme Party: The Need to Create Continuity and Dynamism of Leadership'," *Asian Survey*, 17, No. 9, September 1977, 830–38.

Tun, M.C. "Dads and Mums," *Far Eastern Economic Review* [Hong Kong], August 19, 1972, 20.

United States. Congress. 98th, 1st Session. Senate. Committee on Foreign Relations. House of Representatives. Committee on Foreign Affairs. *Country Reports on Human Rights Practices for 1982.* (Report submitted by the Department of State.) Washington: GPO, February 1983.

Wiant, Jon A. "Burma: Loosening Up on the Tiger's Tail," *Asian Survey*, 13, No. 2, February 1973, 179–86.

_____. "Burma 1973: New Turns in the Burmese Way to Socialism," *Asian Survey*, 14, No. 2, February 1974, 175–82.

_____. "Tradition in the Service of Revolution: The Political

Symbolism of Taw-hlan-ye-khit." Pages 59–72 in F.K. Lehman (ed.), *Military Rule in Burma since 1962: A Kaleidoscope of Views*. Singapore: Maruzen Asia, 1981.

Wiant, Jon A., and Charles B. Smith. "Burma." Pages 169–74 in *Yearbook on International Communist Affairs 1982*. (Ed., Richard F. Staar.) Stanford: Hoover Institution Press, 1982.

Ye Goung, U. "Peasants Asiayone Central Body Chairman's Address," *Guardian* [Rangoon], November 26, 1982, 1.

"Youth Organization and Training," *Guardian* [Rangoon], December 15, 1982, 4.

The World Factbook, 1982. Washington: GPO, 1982.

Zau Tawng, N.D., U. "Report of the Elections Commission," *Guardian* [Rangoon], October 12, 1982, 4.

Zaw Win. "Ne Win and BSPP Riding High on Popularity of Reconciliation Policy," *Asia Record*, 2, No. 6, September 1981, 12.

―――――. "Ne Win Steps Down, Reshuffles Key Posts to Ensure Continuity," *Asia Record*, 2, No. 9, December 1981, 12.

(Various issues of the following publications were also used in the preparation of this chapter: *Asian Recorder* [New Delhi], April 1971–December 1979; *Christian Science Monitor*, January 1976–February 1983; *Far Eastern Economic Review* [Hong Kong], May 1971–December 1982; Foreign Broadcast Information Service, *Daily Report: Asia and Pacific*, January 1979–February 1983; *Guardian* [Rangoon], January 1977– December 1982; *Keesing's Contemporary Archives* [London], May 1971–December 1982; *New York Times*, May 1971–February 1983; *Washington Post*, May 1971–February 1983; and *Working People's Daily* [Rangoon], January 1981–December 1982.)

Chapter 5

Amnesty International Report, 1981. London: Amnesty International, 1981.

Asia 1974 Yearbook. (Ed., Derek Davies.) Hong Kong: Far Eastern Economic Review, 1974.

Asia 1978 Yearbook. (Ed., Donald Wise.) Hong Kong: Far Eastern Economic Review, 1978.

Asia 1979 Yearbook. (Ed., Donald Wise.) Hong Kong: Far Eastern Economic Review, 1979.

Asia 1980 Yearbook. (Ed., Donald Wise.) Hong Kong: Far Eastern Economic Review, 1980.

Asia 1981 Yearbook. (Ed., Donald Wise.) Hong Kong: Far Eastern Economic Review, 1981.

Asia 1982 Yearbook. (Ed., Donald Wise.) Hong Kong: Far Eastern Economic Review, 1982.

Asia 1983 Yearbook. (Ed., Donald Wise.) Hong Kong: Far Eastern Economic Review, 1983.

Burma. *The Constitution of the Socialist Republic of the Union of Burma.* Rangoon: Printing and Publishing, 1974.

Burma. *Report to the People by the Government of the Union of Burma on the Financial, Economic, and Social Conditions for 1971–72.* Rangoon: Central Press, 1972.

Burma. Ministry of Planning and Finance. *Report to the Pyithu Hluttaw on the Financial, Economic, and Social Conditions of the Socialist Republic of the Union of Burma for 1982–83.* Rangoon: 1982.

"Burma: Anti-State Activities Law," *Asian Recorder* [New Delhi], 21, No. 6, February 5–11, 1975, 12424.

"Burma: Party Protection Bill," *Asian Recorder* [New Delhi], 20, No. 42, October 15–24, 1974, 12243.

"Burmese Citizenship Law," *Guardian* [Rangoon], April 25, 1982, 4.

"The Burmese Impasse," *Far Eastern Economic Review* [Hong Kong], June 27, 1975, 24–26.

Burson. "People's Judicial System," *Forward* [Rangoon], 12, No. 4, January 1, 1974, 16–19.

"Constitution of the Burmese Communist Party: 13 September 1979," Foreign Broadcast Information Service, *Daily Report: Asia and Pacific,* 4, No. 033 (FBIS-APA-80-033), February 15, 1980, G1–G6.

"Constitution of the Burmese Communist Party: 13 September 1979," Foreign Broadcast Information Service, *Daily Report: Asia and Pacific,* 4, No. 037 (FBIS-APA-80-037). February 22, 1980, G1-G7.

"Constitution of the Union Burma." Pages 68–115 in Amos Peaslee (ed.), *Constitutions of Nations, Volume II: Asia, Australia, and Oceania.* The Hague: Nijhoff, 1966.

Copley, Gregory R. (ed.). *Defense and Foreign Affairs Handbook.* Washington: Copley, 1981.

DMS Market Intelligence Report: South America/Australasia. Greenwich, Connecticut: DMS, 1982.

Economic Survey of Asia and the Far East, 1961. Bangkok: United Nations Economic Commission for Asia and the Far East, 1962.

"Eliminate Dangers of Narcotic Drugs," *Working People's Daily* [Rangoon], November 9, 1982, 4.

"The Entire Party: Unite and March to Achieve Victory," Foreign Broadcast Information Service, *Daily Report: Asia and Pacific,* 4, No. 242 (FBIS-APA-79-242), December 14, 1979, G1–G5.

"The Entire Party: Unite and March to Achieve Victory," Foreign Broadcast Information Service, *Daily Report: Asia and Pacific,* 4, No. 242 (FBIS-APA-79-242), December 14, 1979, G1–G5.

"The Entire Party: Unite and March to Achieve Victory," Foreign Broadcast Information Service, *Daily Report: Asia and Pacific,* 4, No. 246 (FBIS-APA-79-246), December 20, 1979, G1–G4.

"The Entire Party: Unite and March to Achieve Victory," Foreign Broadcast Information Service, *Daily Report: Asia and Pacific*, 4, No. 251 (FBIS-APA-79-251), December 28, 1979, G1–G5.

"The Entire Party: Unite and March to Achieve Victory," Foreign Broadcast Information Service, *Daily Report: Asia and Pacific*, 4, No. 003 (FBIS-APA-80-003), January 4, 1980, G1–G6.

"The Entire Party: Unite and March to Achieve Victory," Foreign Broadcast Information Service, *Daily Report: Asia and Pacific*, 4, No. 008 (FBIS-APA-80-008), January 11, 1980, G1–G5.

"The Entire Party: Unite and March to Achieve Victory," Foreign Broadcast Information Service, *Daily Report: Asia and Pacific*, 4, No. 011 (FBIS-APA-80-011), January 16, 1980, G1–G5.

"The Entire Party: Unite and March to Achieve Victory," Foreign Broadcast Information Service, *Daily Report: Asia and Pacific*, 4, No. 017 (FBIS-APA-80-017), January 24, 1980, G1–G6.

"The Entire Party: Unite and March to Achieve Victory," Foreign Broadcast Information Service, *Daily Report: Asia and Pacific*, 4, No. 028 (FBIS-APA-80-028), February 8, 1980, G1–G6.

Fawthrop, Tom. "Smuggled Goods Large Part of Burma's Economy," *Business in Thailand* [Bangkok], 13, No. 8, August 1981, 20–26.

Fenichel, Allen, and Azfar Khan. "The Burmese Way to 'Socialism'," *World Development* [Oxford], 9, No. 9/10, September/October 1981, 813–24.

"General Program of the Burma Communist Party, 13 September 1979," Foreign Broadcast Information Service, *Daily Report: Asia and Pacific*, 4, No. 028 (FBIS-APA-80-028), February 8, 1980, G6–G11.

Government Finance Statistics Yearbook, 1982. Washington: International Monetary Fund, 1982.

Gunston, Bill (ed.). *Encyclopedia of World Air Power*. New York: Crescent Books, 1980.

Hail, John. "A Blow to the Heartland," *Far Eastern Economic Review* [Hong Kong], May 9, 1980, 38–39.

Hewish, Mark, et al. *Air Forces of the World*. New York: Simon and Schuster, 1979.

Hla Aung. "The Burmese Concept of Law," *Journal of the Burma Research Society* [Rangoon], 52, December 1969, 27–41.

"How the Secret Armies Operate," *Far Eastern Economic Review* [Hong Kong], April 25, 1980, 21–22.

Husain Haqqani. "The Roots of Rebellion," *Far Eastern Economic Review* [Hong Kong], November 5, 1982, 26–28.

Jane's All the World's Aircraft, 1980–81. (Ed., John W.R. Taylor.) London: Jane's, 1980.

Jane's Fighting Ships, 1980–81. (Ed., John E. Moore.) London: Jane's, 1980.

Jane's Weapons Systems, 1980–81. (Ed., Ronald T. Pretty.) London: Jane's 1980.

Joint Publications Research Service—JPRS (Washington). *Translations on South and East Asia Report:* "Convict Labor Used for Development Projects," *Business Times*, Kuala Lumpur, October 20, 1982. (JPRS 1230, No. 82504, December 20, 1982, 7.).

"The Kachins Go Back to War," *Asiaweek* [Hong Kong], April 16, 1982, 27.

Kamm, Henry. "Proposed Law to Create Two Kinds of Burmese Citizenship Worries Millions," *New York Times*, August 13, 1980, A14.

"The Karenni Connection," *Far Eastern Economic Review* [Hong Kong], June 18, 1982, 26–28.

Keegan, John (ed.). *World Armies*. New York: Facts on File, 1979.

Kerns, Hikaru. "A State of Strife," *Far Eastern Economic Review* [Hong Kong], November 26, 1982, 36–39.

Kurian, George Thomas (ed.). *Encyclopedia of the Third World*. New York: Facts on File, 1982.

Lehman, F.K. (ed.). *Military Rule in Burma since 1962: A Kaleidoscope of Views*. Singapore: Maruzen Asia, 1981.

Liu, Melinda. "The Jungle Road to Fortune," *Far Eastern Economic Review* [Hong Kong], January 4, 1980, 12–13.

_____. "Warlords, Rebels, and Smugglers," *Far Eastern Economic Review* [Hong Kong], August 31, 1979, 10–12.

McBeth, John. "Drugs: The New Connections," *Far Eastern Economic Review* [Hong Kong], August 14, 1979, 37–40.

_____. "Rebels Widen the Net," *Far Eastern Economic Review* [Hong Kong], January 4, 1980, 13.

_____. "Who's Who in the Opium Trade," *Far Eastern Economic Review* [Hong Kong], April 25, 1980, 20–21.

The Military Balance, 1982–83. London: International Institute for Strategic Studies, 1982.

"The Military Line, Dated 13 September 1979" Foreign Broadcast Information Service, *Daily Report: Asia and Pacific*, 4, No. 066 (FBIS-APA-80-066), April 3, 1980, G2–G9.

"More Police Take Over from Military Security," *Asia Record*, 3, No. 8, November 1982, 7.

Mullin, Chris. "An Enduring Struggle for Independence," *Far Eastern Economic Review* [Hong Kong], April 1, 1974, 22–23.

"National Campaign Against Dangerous Drugs," *Working People's Daily* [Rangoon], June 4, 1982, 4.

"People's Police Force Commanded," *Working People's Daily* [Rangoon], June 4, 1982, 4.

Robinson, Anthony (ed.). *Air Power*. New York: Ziff-Davis, 1980.

Silverstein, Josef. "Burma in 1980: An Uncertain Balance Sheet," *Asian Survey*, 21, No. 2, February 1981, 212–22.

_____. "Burma in 1981: The Changing of the Guardians Begins," *Asian Survey*, 22, No. 2, February 1982, 180–90.

_____. *Burma: Military Rule and the Politics of Stagnation.*
Ithaca; Cornell University Press, 1977.
Smith, Charles B., Jr. "Armed Communism in Southeast Asia:
The Burmese Communist Party." (Paper presented at Institute
of Southeast Asian Studies, Singapore, November 1982.)
Washington: Department of State, 1982.
_____. "Golden Triangle Narcotics and the Burmese Insurgen-
cies." (Lecture for the Foreign Service Institute Southeast Asia
Area Studies Program.) Washington: April 28, 1982.
Sricharatchanya, Paisal. "Few Friends in the Jungle," *Far Eastern
Economic Review* [Hong Kong], October 8, 1982, 16–18.
_____. "Some Are More Equal" *Far Eastern Economic Review*
[Hong Kong], October 8, 1982, 27–28.
Statistical Yearbook for Asia and the Far East, 1972. Bangkok:
United Nations Economic Commission for Asia and the Far
East, 1973.
Statistical Yearbook, 1975. Rangoon: Central Statistical Organiza-
tion, 1976.
Steinberg, David I. *Burma's Road Toward Development: Growth
and Ideology under Military Rule.* Boulder: Westview Press,
1981.
Tinker, Hugh. *The Union of Burma: A Study of the First Years of
Independence.* (3d ed.) London: Oxford University Press,
1961.
Tōnan Ajia Yōran 1980. Tokyo: Tōran Ajia Chōsakai, 1980.
Trager, Frank N. *Burma: From Kingdom to Republic.* New York:
Praeger, 1966.
Tun, M.C. "Back to School—With a Warning," *Far Eastern
Economic Review* [Hong Kong], October 8, 1976, 22.
_____. "Burma: The Futility of Confrontation," *Far Eastern Eco-
nomic Review* [Hong Kong], April 15, 1974, 24–27.
_____. "Dads and Mums," *Far Eastern Economic Review* [Hong
Kong], August 19, 1972, 20.
_____. "Tackling the Poppy," *Far Eastern Economic Review*
[Hong Kong], March 18, 1974, 13–14.
United States. Central Intelligence Agency. Directorate of
Intelligence. "Peking and the Burmese Communists: The Per-
ils and the Profits of Insurgency." (Intelligence Report RSS
0052/71.) Washington: July 1971.
United States. Congress. 94th, 1st Session. House of Representa-
tives. Committee on International Relations.Subcommittee on
Future Foreign Policy Research and Development. *Proposal
to Control Opium from the Golden Triangle and Terminate the
Shan Opium Trade.* Washington: GPO, 1975.
United States. Congress. 97th, 2d Session. Senate. Committee on
Foreign Relations. Subcommittee on East Asian and Pacific
Affairs. *Southeast Asian Drug Trade.* Washington: GPO, 1982.
United States. Congress. 97th, 2d Session. Senate. Committee on

Foreign Relations. House of Representatives. Committee on Foreign Affairs. *Country Reports on Human Rights Practices for 1982.* (Report Submitted by the Department of State.) Washington: GPO, February 1983.

United States. Congress. 98th, 1st Session. Senate. Committee on Foreign Relations. House of Representatives. Committee on Foreign Affairs. *Country Reports on Human Rights Practices for 1981.* (Report submitted by the Department of State.) Washington: GPO, February 1982.

United States. Department of Defense. Security Assistance Agency. *Congressional Presentation: Security Assistance Programs FY 1983.* Washington: 1982.

————. *Foreign Military Sales, Foreign Military Construction Sales, and Military Assistance Facts.* Washington: 1981.

Wiant, Jon A. "Lanzin: Ideology and Organization in Revolutionary Burma." (Unpublished Ph.D. dissertation.) Ithaca: Cornell University, June 1982.

————. "The Ne Win Legacy." (Paper presented at New York State Conference on Asian Affairs, Oneonta, New York, October 1981.) Oneonta, New York: October 1981.

————. "Terry and the Pirates Revisited: A Political Economy of the Golden Triangle." (Paper presented at annual meeting of the International Studies Association, Cincinnati, March 1982.) Cincinnati: March 1982.

————. "The Vanguard Army: The Tatmadaw and Politics in Revolutionary Burma." (Paper presented at Conference on Role of Armed Forces in Contemporary Asian Societies, Naval Postgraduate School, August 1982.) Monterey, California: August 1982.

Yearbook on International Communist Affairs, 1978. (Ed., Richard F. Staar.) Stanford: Hoover Institution Press, 1978.

Yearbook on International Communist Affairs, 1979. (Ed., Richard F. Staar.) Stanford: Hoover Institution Press, 1979.

Yearbook on International Communist Affairs, 1980. (Ed., Richard F. Staar.) Stanford: Hoover Institution Press, 1980.

Yearbook on International Communist Affairs, 1981. (Ed., Richard F. Staar.) Stanford: Hoover Institution Press, 1981.

Yearbook on International Communist Affairs, 1982. (Ed., Richard F. Staar.) Stanford: Hoover Institution Press, 1982.

Yoon, Won Z. *Japan's Scheme for the Liberation of Burma: The Role of the Minami Kikan and the "Thirty Comrades."* (Papers in International Studies, Southeast Asia Series, No. 27.) Athens: Center for International Studies, Ohio University, 1973.

Zealey, Philip. "United Nations/Burma Programme for Drug Abuse Control: the First Phase, 1976 to 1981," *Bulletin on Narcotics*, 33, No. 3, 1981, 1–21.

(Various issues of the following publications were also used in the preparation of this chapter: *Asian Survey*, January 1972–

December 1982; *Far Eastern Economic Review* [Hong Kong], January 1972–March 1983; Foreign Broadcast Information Service, *Daily Report: Asia and Pacific,* January 1978–March 1983; *Forward* [Rangoon], January 1969–December 1982; *Guardian* [Rangoon], January 1972–March 1983; Joint Publications Research Service, *South and East Asia Report,* January 1979–December 1982, and *Southeast Asia Report,* January 1983–March 1983; *New York Times,* January 1981–March 1983; *Washington Post,* January 1979–March 1983; and *Working People's Daily* [Rangoon], January 1972–March 1983.)

Glossary

AFPFL—Anti-Fascist People's Freedom League. The political organization, consisting of a coalition of parties and individuals, that led the independence movement and dominated politics until 1958.

BSPP—Burma Socialist Programme Party, the ruling party led by Chairman U Ne Win; known by the Burmese word *lanzin* (*q.v.*), meaning program on policy.

Burman(s)—Member(s) of, or descriptive of, the dominant ethnic group. A narrower term than Burmese, which is used to refer to all the peoples in Burma and to the national language.

Burma Proper—Term used during the British colonial period to describe the central region of the country, roughly approximating the seven divisions of the Socialist Republic of the Union of Burma, which was ruled directly by the central government, while the Frontier Areas, including the Shan Plateau, retained a measure of autonomy ostensibly to protect the interests of the minority peoples. The 1947 Panglong Agreement retained the distinction, for minorities were promised limited autonomy, but the 1974 Constitution does not recognize the concept of Burma Proper because all areas are under the direct control of the central government.

fiscal year (FY)—From October 1 of previous calendar year to September 30 of specified year for FY 1946 to FY 1974; from April 1 of specified year to March 31 of following year for all other years. Because of the change in fiscal dating, FY 1974 can refer to either the year from October 1, 1973, to September 30, 1974, or the year from April 1, 1974 to March 31, 1975. Unless specifically stated in the text, FY 1974 refers to the latter period. In most statistical series, therefore, a gap occurs for the period from October 1, 1973, to March 31, 1974.

gross domestic product (GDP)—The total value of all final goods and services produced by an economy in a given period, usually a year. Burmese statistics on production in specific economic sectors are based on a unique notion of "net output" and therefore do not sum exactly to the GDP. Likewise, the Burmese government values imports by their cost, insurance, and freight (c.i.f.) charges, and imports should be adjusted to fit the standard definition of GDP. In the text, GDP refers to this adjusted value.

gross national product (GNP)—The value at market prices of all final goods and services produced during a given year.

Hinayana—*See* Theravada.

International Monetary Fund (IMF)—Established along with the World Bank (*q.v.*) in 1945, the IMF is a specialized agency affiliated with the United Nations and is responsible for

313

stabilizing international exchange rates and payments. The main business of the IMF is the provision of loans to its members (including industrialized and developing countries) when they experience balance of payments difficulties. These loans frequently carry conditions that require substantial internal economic adjustments by the recipients, most of which are developing countries. In late 1982 the IMF had 146 members.

Karenni(s), or Red Karen(s)—Alternate name for Kayahs (*q.v.*), the ethnic group that predominates in Kayah State (once the Karenni states).

Kayah(s)—A Karen ethnic group, also known as the Red Karen, or Karenni (*q.v.*) Found mainly in Kayah State.

KNDO—Karen National Defense Organization. An armed insurgent group.

kyat—Burmese currency, divided into 100 pya. The government controls the foreign exchange value, fixing the exchange rate to the special drawing right (SDR), reserve currency of the IMF (*q.v.*). From the previous devaluation in May 1977 through February 1983, one SDR was equivalent to K8.51. The average exchange rate per United States dollar was K6.77 in 1976, K7.14 in 1977, K6.87 in 1978, K6.65 in 1979, K6.61 in 1980, K7.31 in 1981, K7.81 in 1982, and K7.87 in February 1983. The exchange rate on the black market was often four or five times the official rate.

Lanzin—Burmese term for Burma Socialist Programme Party (BSPP—*q.v.*). *Lanzin* is Burmese word meaning program or policy.

longyi—Traditional item of clothing for men, women, and children. A wraparound garment folded and tucked in at the waist.

Lower Burma—Term in use since British colonial period. Refers to the area annexed by British in 1853. The area, which includes the deltas of the Irrawaddy and Sittang rivers, is in the southern portion of the country.

Mahayana—Literal meaning, Great Vehicle. One of the two schools of Buddhism that established itself in China, Japan, Korea, Nepal, Tibet, and Vietnam but also was practiced in Burma around the time of the establishment of the Pagan Dynasty (1044–1287). Its eclipse is linked to the Pagan kings' patronage of the Theravada (*q.v.*) school.

mandala—(Sanskrit: circle). In some forms of Buddhism, the mandala is a focus for meditation; a "mandala of power" is a model of the distribution of political power in which power is concentrated in the center and radiates out from there.

Pali—Language of the sacred scriptures of Theravada (*q.v.*) Buddhism.

PL-480 grants—United States foreign assistance granted under the Food for Peace Program, legislated in 1954 as Public Law (PL)-480.

sangha—Pali *(q.v.)* term meaning assembly or order of Buddhist monks. Includes ordained monks and novices. Members of the *sangha* reside separately from the laity, usually in a *kyaung* (monastery).

shifting cultivation—Farming characterized by the rotation of fields rather than crops, the use of short cropping periods and long fallow periods, and the maintenance of fertility by the regeneration of natural vegetation on fallow land. Clearing of newly or previously cropped land is often accomplished by burning. Also called slash-and-burn, swidden, or land rotation agriculture.

Tai—Member of ethnic group or descriptive of speakers of the Tai language. Includes the indigenous Tai of Burma, usually called Shans, and the Tai of Thailand, Laos, Vietnam, and southern China.

Thakin—Literal meaning, master. Term used as a prefix to a man's name. In colonial period, usually reserved for Europeans, equivalent to Indian word *sahib*. Adopted as a gesture of defiance by members of nationalist group in 1930s.

Theravada—One of the two major schools of Buddhism; the principal religion of Burma and several other Southeast Asian countries. Sometimes known as the Hinayana *(q.v.)*, or Small Vehicle, school in contradistinction of Mahayana *(q.v.)* Buddhism.

Upper Burma—Term in use since British colonial period designating the area annexed by British in 1886; corresponds approximately to northern half of the country. Includes all of the country except Lower Burma *(q.v.)*, Arakan (present-day Rakhine State) and Tenasserim (both annexed in 1826), the Shan Plateau, and the territory now included in Kayah State.

World Bank—Informal name used to designate a group of three affiliated international institutions: the International Bank for Reconstruction and Development (IBRD), the International Development Association (IDA), and the International Finance Corporation (IFC). The IBRD, established in 1945, has the primary purpose of providing loans to developing countries for productive projects. The IDA, a legally separate loan fund but administered by the staff of the IBRD, was set up in 1960 to furnish credits to the poorest developing countries on much easier terms than those of conventional IBRD loans. The IFC, founded in 1956, supplements the activities of the IBRD through loans and assistance designed specifically to encourage the growth of productive private enterprises in the less developed countries. The president and certain senior officers of the IBRD hold the same positions in the IFC. The three institutions are owned by the governments of the countries that subscribe their capital. In 1982 the IBRD had over 140 members, the IDA had 130, and the IFC over 120. To participate in the World Bank group, member states must first belong to the International Monetary Fund (IMF—*q.v.*).

Index

317

PUBLISHED COUNTRY STUDIES

(Area Handbook Series)

550-65	Afghanistan		550-151	Honduras
550-98	Albania		550-165	Hungary
550-44	Algeria		550-21	India
550-59	Angola		550-154	Indian Ocean
550-73	Argentina		550-39	Indonesia
550-169	Australia		550-68	Iran
550-176	Austria		550-31	Iraq
550-175	Bangladesh		550-25	Israel
550-170	Belgium		550-182	Italy
550-66	Bolivia		550-69	Ivory Coast
550-20	Brazil		550-177	Jamaica
550-168	Bulgaria		550-30	Japan
550-61	Burma		550-34	Jordan
550-83	Burundi		550-56	Kenya
550-50	Cambodia		550-81	Korea, North
550-166	Cameroon		550-41	Korea, South
550-159	Chad		550-58	Laos
550-77	Chile		550-24	Lebanon
550-60	China		550-38	Liberia
550-63	China, Republic of		550-85	Libya
550-26	Colombia		550-172	Malawi
550-91	Congo		550-45	Malaysia
550-90	Costa Rica		550-161	Mauritania
550-152	Cuba		550-79	Mexico
550-22	Cyprus		550-76	Mongolia
550-158	Czechoslovakia		550-49	Morocco
550-54	Dominican Republic		550-64	Mozambique
550-52	Ecuador		550-35	Nepal, Bhutan and Sikkim
550-43	Egypt		550-88	Nicaragua
550-150	El Salvador		550-157	Nigeria
550-28	Ethiopia		550-94	Oceania
550-167	Finland		550-48	Pakistan
550-155	Germany, East		550-46	Panama
550-173	Germany, Federal Republic of		550-156	Paraguay
550-153	Ghana		550-185	Persian Gulf States
550-87	Greece		550-42	Peru
550-78	Guatemala		550-72	Philippines
550-174	Guinea		550-162	Poland
550-82	Guyana		550-181	Portugal
550-164	Haiti		550-160	Romania

550-160	Romania	550-53	Thailand
550-84	Rwanda	550-178	Trinidad and Tobago
550-51	Saudi Arabia	550-89	Tunisia
550-70	Senegal	550-80	Turkey
550-180	Sierra Leone	550-74	Uganda
550-184	Singapore	550-97	Uruguay
550-86	Somalia	550-71	Venezuela
550-93	South Africa	550-57	Vietnam, North
550-171	Southern Rhodesia	550-55	Vietnam, South
550-95	Soviet Union	550-183	Yemens, The
550-179	Spain	550-99	Yugoslavia
550-96	Sri Lanka (Ceylon)	550-67	Zaire
550-27	Sudan	550-75	Zambia
550-47	Syria		
550-62	Tanzania		

☆ U.S. GOVERNMENT PRINTING OFFICE: 1984 -0- 421 658 (124)